DINING WITH
William Shakespeare

Wedding scene detail from the painting of the
LIFE OF SIR HENRY UNTON (1557-1596). *Artist unknown.*
Courtesy of the National Portrait Gallery, London.

DINING WITH
William Shakespeare

MADGE LORWIN

"But my five wits nor my five senses can
Dissuade one foolish heart from serving thee."

SONNET 141

ATHENEUM

NEW YORK

1976

Jacket photo, frontispiece and illustrations on pages 189, 268, 270 and 374 reproduced by permission of the National Portrait Gallery, London.

Illustrations on pages 50, 86, 88, 92, 122, 181, 183, 191, 222, 244 reproduced by permission of the Royal Ontario Museum, Canada.

Illustrations on pages 57, 186, 293 reproduced by permission of the Lee of Fareham Collection, Massey Foundation, Canada.

Illustrations on page 117, 118, 412 reproduced by permission of English Life Publications, Ltd.

Library of Congress Cataloging in Publication Data

Lorwin, Madge.
　　Dining with William Shakespeare.

　　Bibliography: p.
　　Includes indexes.
　　1. Dinners and dining.　2. Cookery, English.
3. Shakespeare, William, 1564–1616.—Quotations.
I. Title.
TX731.L57　　　614.5′942　　　76–11856
ISBN 0–689–10731–5

Preface

The Eugene (Oregon) Shakespeare Club, as American literary clubs go, is venerable. It was started in 1908 by a small group of women interested in reading and studying the works of Shakespeare. By 1912 the group was thriving and decided to organize formally as a club. In the fall of 1966, the club members included their husbands in a theatre party to see *Twelfth Night,* which the University of Oregon drama department was producing.

On an impulse I invited the whole group to our home for an after-theatre Shakespearean collation. I had only one cookbook of Elizabethan England to assist me, a reprint of Sir Hugh Plat's *Delightes for Ladies.* With this and what little I could glean from social histories of Elizabethan and Jacobean England, I managed somehow to cook up a respectable collation.

When our guests arrived they were offered scented water to wash their hands before sitting down to eat. Only those table utensils that had been available to Shakespeare's contemporaries were provided—knives and spoons. Fingers did the work of forks—without problems and with much amusement for our guests. Linen cloths covered the tables and linen napkins were provided, as they would have been in any well-to-do-home in Shakespeare's day. The electric lamps had been hidden away, and we ate by candlelight.

Our meal, for lack of servants and space, was served buffet style. Each dish was introduced by a quotation from one of Shakespeare's plays. As our guests departed we gave to each a copy of the quotation menu and a sprig of rosemary, explaining, as Ophelia did, "There's rosemary, that's for remembrance" (*Hamlet,* Act IV, Scene 5).

"How far that little candle throws his beams!" (*The Merchant of Venice,* Act V, Scene 1). Shortly after our collation, the Friends of the University of Oregon Museum asked me to serve as consultant for an Elizabethan feast they wished to prepare for their annual dinner meeting. I happily prepared a Shakespeare quotation menu and provided the recipes and instructions for setting the tables. Close to four hundred people feasted Elizabethan style that evening and—judging from the response—enjoyed themselves immensely.

In 1973 the Renaissance Institute of Ashland, Oregon, decided to celebrate the four hundredth anniversary of Ben Jonson's birth with an Elizabethan feast and asked me to serve as consultant. This time, having finished testing the recipes for this book, I had a far greater range of dishes to choose from. As the guests began to move toward the dining room, groups of students in Elizabethan costumes offered them scented water and towels. During the dinner musicians from the Shakespeare Festival company played for the guests, as musicians would have done for feasts in Elizabethan days.

So many of the nearly two hundred people who attended suggested that it should become an annual affair that the Renaissance Institute repeated the feast in 1974. In its 1975 annual report, the Institute noted that the Elizabethan feast had become "an instant tradition" at the Shakespeare Festival.

Although I have taught "gourmet" cooking, writing a cookbook had never interested me, and I wasn't receptive at first to the idea of doing a Shakespearean cookbook, as many of our guests had urged after our collation. My husband, Val Lorwin, intrigued by the idea, offered to be my research assistant. Having a professor of European social history as an assistant proved irresistible, and I agreed to give it a try.

He was as good as his word. Not only did he help search the university and other libraries for books on the social customs of sixteenth- and seventeenth-century England, but on a research trip of his own, he took time off to have xeroxed for me all of the cookbooks of that period available in the British Museum in London. He also had xeroxed many of the dietaries, as the health books were called in Shakespeare's day. In addition he was my ever-willing taster—and a critical one, with high gastronomic standards. When the manuscript was finally written, his editing was very helpful, as was his checking of historical facts. His typing is abominable, so I was unable to get from him that classic service that is so often rendered by the spouses of male authors.

The text of Shakespeare from which I have quoted is the Oxford edition, edited by W. J. Craig. (There are many small, occasionally significant, differences of wording among the various editions.) Spelling, punctuation, and capitalization were all far from standardized in Shakespeare's time, and the best of writers might spell the same word several different ways on the same page or even in the same sentence. For example, the mixture of grains, especially wheat and rye, that we now call "maslin" was then also spelled "meslin," "masseldine," "messledine," and "messleden." Many words were used then in meanings different from those of today, and words that were current then have disappeared from the language. Wherever the understanding of a word or a phrase in a writing of the period requires explanation, I have inserted the modern equivalent in brackets, thus: "put it into a clean Kimnel [mixing trough]."

Weights and measures were not yet standardized either. But it is generally possible to find modern equivalents of the old amounts, and this I have done where it is necessary for a recipe, or interesting for a discussion of food or drink.

For sums in money of the period I have not given any current equivalents. The translation of prices or wages across four centuries would be wildly unreal and misleading.

The book, as it has evolved, is a Shakespearean menu cookbook with a background of related social history and literary allusions and comments. I have described cooking facilities, foods, food preparation, menu preparation, serving traditions, and table manners, and given brief biographies of some of the professional cooks who wrote the cookbooks of that period, as well as of literary men who published cookbooks. In other words, I have tried to give a human dimension to the recipes in the book.

An introductory chapter offers evidence from Englishmen and foreign visitors on the place of food and drink and dining in English life of the sixteenth and early seventeenth centuries. The book as a whole does not attempt a structured history of food and dining customs in Elizabethan and Jacobean England; but it is for people interested in the food and cookery, and more specifically, English cookery, of a bygone age. It will also interest those who would enjoy catching glimpses of William Shakespeare and other writers of his day as they related to, and used, food and dining customs in their writings.

I have tried to select the best and most representative recipes from the various cookbooks I worked from. Here let me add that the recipes are typical of dishes prepared in the homes of well-to-do families and the upper classes. If cookbooks for the lower classes existed at this period, they have not survived. From time to time I have referred to the diets of the poor, but the book does not attempt to give recipes for dishes that might have been eaten by them.

All chapters are built around Shakespeare quotation menus. Each dish in each menu is accompanied by a brief quotation from Shakespeare, keyed to the main ingredient of the recipe and identified by play, act and scene, and speaker, or by title and lines when from a poem. The recipes follow in the order in which they appear on the menu, first in the original version, word for word, then in a modernized working version.

All the recipes are authentic. The working versions modernize them only to the extent that quantities and measurements have been given in precise modern amounts and the often picturesque directions put into understandable present-day terms. "Take a bushel of meal" began the first of the bread recipes I worked out. Where I thought it helpful, I have simplified procedures for the preparation of the dishes.

Cookbooks often left decisions about seasoning and flavoring to the individual cook, who was expected to know the proper amounts needed to suit his master's or mistress's tastes, as well as to adjust a particular recipe to the herbs, spices, or other ingredients available to him or her at the time. "Flavor as you list" or "use good store of" a particular ingredient might be all the direction given. "All kind of good herbs" was as often called for as were specific herbs. "And then with Sugar, season it according to the taste of the master of the house," says Gervase Markham in *The English Hus-wife*.

I have necessarily used my own culinary judgment and repeated testing of each recipe to arrive at the working versions of the original. Some recipes call for ingredients in very small amounts —spices, for example, in amounts as small as ⅛ teaspoon. These amounts can be difficult to meaure, but fortunately at least one manufacturer (Foley) makes a set of measuring spoons that includes ⅛ teaspoon.

I have stayed within the bounds of ingredients available and in use during the sixteenth and seventeenth centuries. If you note the absence of vanilla or chocolate in the recipes, it is because neither of these was in culinary use in England, although they were used for medicinal purposes. Nor will you find tomatoes in any form. Only one cookbook of the period mentions them and then only to note with surprise that they were eaten in Italy.

How did the cookery of sixteenth- and seventeenth-century England differ from today's? Mainly in the seasonings and flavorings used and the form in which meat and fish dishes were presented at the table. The combinations of herbs with spices in seasoning meat and fish dishes and the use of perfumes such as ambergris, musk, and distilled flower essences for desserts and other sweetmeats were often imaginative, sometimes exotic, occasionally confused, at times excessive. But often these combinations produced interesting taste sensations.

Refrigeration was lacking, so many meats and fishes were salted, smoked, or pickled. As in today's kitchens, foods were boiled, stewed, fried, broiled, and baked. However, in Shakespeare's day, "roasting" meat meant broiling on spits in front of an open fire. The closest equivalents to our roast meats were the double-crust meat pies made with solid pieces of meat. Most meat pies, however, were made with minced meat. Currants and raisins were sometimes added, but the kinds of meat and vegetable pies we serve today were not made in Shakespeare's England. Fish, poultry, rabbits, game and game birds, as well as beef, veal, mutton, lamb, pork, and kid, were made into pies, as were cheese, eggs, and many vegetables. Game and wild fowl were a more important part of the diet, and many wild fowl, especially water fowl, that were eaten have long since disappeared from English tables.

Cereal puddings made of whole grains were important parts of everyone's diet. Often they served the purpose that potatoes do today. Baking powder was unknown; all leavening was done with liquid yeast. Breads were coarser but better flavored than most of the bread eaten today—in the United States at least. Wheat, rye, oats, and barley were all used for bread-making, sometimes in combinations and sometimes alone. Apple pie was as popular in Shakespeare's day as it is today.

I chose for the book only recipes for which ingredients are obtainable in the United States. Whenever unusual ingredients are called for, I have given addresses where they can be purchased. However, most ingredients are available in local markets.

The recipes are meant to serve four people, but some will serve six, depending on the number of dishes in your menu and the appetites of your family and your guests. The menus are all what Elizabethans would have called feasts. They include more dishes than would have appeared on the table of even well-to-do families when only the family or one or two guests were present. You can, of course, choose from among the dishes as large or small a menu as you wish. If you plan to try a large menu, include dishes that can be prepared ahead of time. Stews, for example, can be cooked, except for the final thickening, a day or two ahead and refrigerated. Pickled (soused) meats and fishes will keep under refrigeration for a week to ten days. Baked breads and unbaked pies, except custard pies, freeze well. Many of the desserts can be made a day or two ahead.

When we entertain with Shakespeare feasts, we offer quotation menus similar to those given in the book. You can choose from among the menus in the book or work up your own sets of quotations. Our guests have always enjoyed reading the quotations.

The facts of social history that follow many of the recipes are an effort to answer questions that have been asked of me. Whenever possible I have quoted the words of contemporary writers so as to re-create the spirit and flavor of Shakespeare's times. I have retained the original spelling, punctuation, and capitalization in these quotations except where I have quoted from a publication that has modernized spelling and so forth.

An index of recipes as well as a general subject index are included at the back of the book. For those interested in reading more on the subject, I have provided a bibliography of some of the books, articles, and documents I used.

I wish to thank Judith T. Kern of Atheneum Publishers for her careful reading and sympatheic editing of the manuscript.

And now, in Sebastian's words (*The Tempest,* Act III, Scene 3), "Will't please you to taste of what is here?"

CONTENTS

ILLUSTRATIONS

DINING WITH
William Shakespeare

Introduction

"Does not our life consist of the four elements?" [fire, water, earth, and air], Sir Toby Belch, Lady Olivia's wine-soaked uncle, asks Sir Andrew Aguecheek in *Twelfth Night* (Act II, Scene 3).

"Faith, so they say," his drinking companion answers, "but, I think, it rather consists of eating and drinking."

Sir Toby, drunkenly grave, responds, "Thou art a scholar; let us therefore eat and drink."

Shakespeare and his contemporaries did their best to enjoy life, and eating and drinking played an important part in that enjoyment. They were only following a long English tradition and one that rarely failed to elicit wonderment and comments from foreign travelers to England. About 1500 the secretary of the Venetian ambassador to the court of Henry VII prepared a report for his ambassador on English life in which he said, "They take great pleasure in having a quantity of excellent victuals, and also in remaining a long time at table." In fact "they think that no greater honor can be conferred or received than to invite others to eat with them, or to be invited themselves." But, he added sourly, "they would sooner give five or six ducats to provide entertainment for a person, than a groat [fourpence] to assist him in distress." The Englishman's pride in the good things England had to offer amused him. "When they partake of any delicacy with a foreigner, they ask him 'whether such a thing is made in *their* country?'"

Stephen Perlin, a French traveler who visited England a few years before Shakespeare was born, later published his impressions. They were generally not friendly, but, he admits, "The

English are merry with one another . . . they make great cheer, and like much to banquet. . . . And in a tavern they make good cheer oftener than once a day with rabbits, hares, and every sort of food." They were also great drinkers, he said, and, gracious for once, added, "They will say to you usually at the table, *goud chere.*"

A little later a Dutch merchant, a diplomat as well as an historian, who lived in England during the entire reign of Queen Elizabeth, described the English in more friendly terms. In his *History of the Netherlands,* Emanuel Van Meteren wrote, "They are eloquent and very hospitable." But, he added, "as the Germans pass the bounds of sobriety in drinking, these do the same in eating."

Levinus Lemnius, another Dutchman, a physician and ecclesiastic who traveled in England in 1581, was much taken with the English. There was, he said, an "incredible curtesie and frendliness in speache and affability used in this famous realme." The gluttony that others denounced he did not find: "At their tables althoughe they be very sumptuous, and love to have good fare, yet nether use they to overcharge themselves with excesse of drincke, neyther thereto greatly provoke and urge others, but suffer every man to drincke in such measure as best pleaseth hymself."

The English who were aware of critical Continental opinions of them were mostly inclined to shrug them off as signs of envy. Fynes Moryson, an English world traveler, also did a good bit of traveling inside England, and he tried to put English habits and manners in a good light. In his *Itinerary, 1605–1617,* Moryson wrote, "It is true that the English prepare largely for ordinarie dyet for themselves and their friends cumming by chance, and at feastes for invited friends are so excessive in the number of dishes, as the table is not thought well furnished, except they stand one upon another." And at a feast they "will drinke two or three healths in remembrance of special friends, or respected honourable persons." He recognized that excesses did occur and that other nations called them "gluttons and devourers of flesh," but, he explained, "the English tables are not furnished with many dishes, all for one mans diet, but severally for many mens appetite, and not only prepared for the family, but for strangers and relief of the poor."

In Shakespeare's day moderation was, in fact, a valued trait.

Physicians and dietary writers counseled moderation in eating and drinking for health's sake; preachers did so for the sake of men's souls. Essayists, dramatists, even poets, spoke out in favor of moderation—in more moderate tones, however, than the Puritan pamphleteers who fulminated against the evils of gluttony and intemperance in sulfuric language. From their writings one would have to think that all England wallowed in roast venison and beef and swam in strong drink.

Shakespeare, who wrote with such gusto about the pleasures of eating and drinking with friends, also counseled moderation. *Timon of Athens* is an example of the end to which lack of moderation can lead—although Timon's problem was a basic lack of judgment. When the lavish feasts and rich gifts he showers on his friends empty his coffers, he finds his "friends" vanishing, one by one, as he asks for their help.

John Harington, Queen Elizabeth's talented and witty godson, also disapproved of lavish meals and excessive drinking. In his poem "Against Feasting," he criticizes his host's extravagant menu:

Kind Marcus, me to supper lately had,
And to declare how well to us he wishes,
The roome was strow'd with Roses, not with Rushes,
And all the cheere was got, that could be had.
Now in the midst of all our dainty dishes,
Methinke, said he to me, you looke but sadd.
Alas (said I) 'tis to see thee so made,
To spoile [despoil] the skies of Fowles, the seas of fishes,
The land of beasts, and be at so much cost,
For that which in one hour will all be lost.

Philip Stubbes, one of the most violent of the Puritan pamphleteers of the late sixteenth century, in his *Anatomie of Abuses,* published in 1583, denounces the "Gluttonie and Drunkennesse" of the people of a mythical island that he calls Ailgna (Anglia spelled backwards). His commentator, Philoponus, reports, "I have seen that which greeveth me to report. The people there are marveilously given to daintie fare, gluttony, bellicheer, and many also to drunkennesse and gourmandice."

Hospitality, says Philoponus, "is good and godly, but when it is practised to excess is not tolerable . . . for now adaies, if the table be not covered from one end to the other as thick as one

dish can stand by another, with delicat meats of sundry sorts
. . . and to every dish a severall sawce appropriate to his kind,
it is thought there unworthye the name of a dinner. . . . And
to these dainties all kinds of wynes are not wanting, you may be
sure. . . . What vanitie, excesse ryot and superfluitie is heare!"

Philoponus predicts not only damnation in the next world for
those guilty of gluttony and drunkenness, but poor health and an
early death in this world. "Doo we not see the poor man that
eateth brown bread (whereof some is made of rye, barlie, peason,
beans, oates, and such other grosse grains) and drinketh small
drink, yea, sometimes water, feedeth upon milk, butter, and
cheese; (isay) doo wee not see such a one helthfuller, stronger,
and longer living than the other that fare daintily every day?"

Excess makes better copy than does moderation, and reformers
sometimes shut their eyes to the fact that most people practiced
moderation most of the time. The poor had no other choice.
Not even the rich feasted all the time; their purses, if not their
good sense, counselled moderation. Many who might entertain
lavishly ate simply when they dined alone.

William Harrison, who earned his living as a clergyman, gives
a reasoned picture of the English at table in his *Description of
England*—published in 1577—the best single source of social
history for the Tudor period. He is most critical of the nobility
and the wealthy merchants. "In number of dishes and change of
meat," he wrote, "the nobility of England (whose cooks are for
the most part musical-headed Frenchmen and strangers [for-
eigners]) do most exceed, sith there is no day in manner that
passeth over their heads wherein they have not only beef, mutton,
veal, lamb, kid, pork, cony [rabbit], pig, or so many of these
as the season yieldeth, but also some portion of the red or fallow
deer, besides a great variety of fish and wild fowl, and thereto
sundry other delicates [delicacies]."

Gentlemen and ordinary merchants, he says, dine more mod-
estly. "Each of them contenteth himself with four, five or six
dishes, when they have but small resort [few guests], or per-
adventure with one, two or three at the most, when they have
no strangers to their tables. As for the poorest sort," he adds,
"they generally dine and sup when they may."

Wealthy farmers ate well, although often of simple dishes,
And although the average yeoman farmer's family dined mod-
estly most of the time, on holidays they expected to eat well and
to provide the servants and hired workers, if any, with generous

holiday dinners. Thomas Tusser, in *Five Hundred Points of Good Husbandry,* offered advice to farmers and their wives on household as well as farm matters. Tusser was a kindly, sociable man who enjoyed having guests, especially on holidays, but he disapproved of extravagance. When no guests are being entertained, he tells his readers:

> Good husband and huswife will sometimes alone
> Make shift with a morsell, and pick of a bone.

And for guests, except for festival days:

> Three dishes well dressed, and welcome with all,
> Both pleaseth thy friend, and becometh thine hall.

Tusser had been trained as a boy to be a musician and had had a post at court, but he disliked the life there and took up farming instead. He acquired considerable knowledge of farming principles and methods, although he was not successful as a farmer. His books for farmers were written in a sort of doggerel, perhaps in the hope that the rhymes would help his readers remember his counsels. He had a sound appreciation of the role of the farmer's wife in running the farm as well as her house. In his preface he says:

> Take huswife from husband, and what is he than?
> . . . .
> Though husbandry seemeth, to bring in the gains,
> Yet huswifery labours, seem equal in pains.
> Some respite to husbands the weather may send,
> But huswive's affairs have never an end.

The greater part of England's folk rarely tasted a piece of roast beef or drank anything better than small (weak) beer. Nicholas Breton, in *Fantastickes,* describes the English workers' usual diet: "Butter, milke, and cheese, are the Labourers dyet, and a pot of good Beere quickens his spirit." In *Pasquil's Madcappe* he speaks of "the peasant newly from the cart, That lives by puddings, beans, and pease. . . . Who thicks her pottage but with brown-bread crumbs."

These were the fortunate poor. Thousands of English men, women, and children went hungry. Many of them were also homeless, and some formed bands of what were known as "sturdy beggars," who roamed the countryside looking for work. They

A laborer at his humble dinner (16th-century print)

begged for food when work was not to be found, and when
begging was fruitless they sometimes stole. When they came
within the clutches of the law, they were harshly punished.

In *Coriolanus* (Act I, Scene 1), Shakespeare gives us a picture
of the feelings of hopelessness and anger among the poor. Caius
Marcius, the most hated of the Roman senators, is describing a
band of famished and mutinous citizens:

> They said they were an-hungry; sigh'd forth proverbs;
> That hunger broke stone walls; that dogs must eat;
> That meat was made for mouths; that the gods sent not
> Corn [grain] for the rich men only.

The English were not generally a healthy people, any more
than any of the Continental peoples of the time. Frequent
bouts with disease counseled moderation in eating and drinking.
Both the rich and the poor suffered from stomach ailments. Part
of the reason, it was clear, was that the rich ate too much and the
poor ate too little. But lack of proper refrigeration for food and
poor sanitation may well have been the greater villains. Few
houses, even in London, had water piped into them in Shake-

Portrait of Dr. Andrewe Boorde (16th-century woodcut by Wynkyn de Worde)

speare's day; sanitation was still primitive. John Harington had invented a "water closet" not unlike modern ones, but, although his royal godmother had one installed in Richmond Castle, the idea did not catch on—even among the wealthy—for nearly a century.

The popularity of health books or "dietaries" attested to people's concern about personal health, as did the sections on home remedies for the sick to be found in many cookbooks. The dietaries were comprised largely of advice on diet as related to health. Every edible thing was analyzed with relation to its effect on health. Those with a "melancholicke" nature were advised to eat certain foods and avoid others; those of "cholericke" temperament were warned against foods that might increase their choler. Some foods were dangerous because they caused "bad blood"; still others could fill the body and head with "evil vapours." And some foods could "increase man's seed," a desirable thing, it may have seemed to many, since so many children died young.

There was also an enormous interest in foods considered aphrodisiacs, a subject to which Shakespeare, like other writers, frequently alluded. "Let the sky rain potatoes . . . hail kissing-comfits and snow eringoes [the candied roots of the shrub eringo]," says Falstaff, embracing Mistress Ford in *The Merry Wives of Windsor* (Act V, Scene 5). All three sweetmeats were considered aphrodisiacs.

Most of the dietaries said more or less the same things, and all counseled temperance in eating and drinking, as well as in love-making. Although some were written by physicians, other dietaries were compilations by nonmedical men from medical books going back as far as ancient Greek times; they all recommended healthful ways of preparing certain foods but were not meant to compete with the cookbooks.

One of the popular dietaries was Andrewe Boorde's *A Compendyous Regyment or a Dyetary of healthe*. Boorde was a practicing physician who had been educated at Oxford University for both the Church and medicine. A bishop and a doctor, Boorde counseled that happiness was good for both body and soul; that food which was enjoyed did the eater more good than food which was not; that dining should be a pleasant occasion, but that one should be moderate in eating and drinking. "At dyner and supper use not," he advised, "to drynke sundry drynkes, and eate not of dyvers meates; but feed of ii or iii dysshes at the most . . . and drink not moch after dyner. At your supper, use lyght meates of dygestyon and refrayne from grose meates: go not to bed with a full nor an empty stomacke," and, he added, "go to bed with myrth [happy]."

He worried about the English habit of spending long hours at table. "Englande," he said, "hathe an evyll use in syttynge longe at dyner and at supper. . . . It is nat good to syt longe at dyner and supper. An houre is suffycyent to syt at dyner, and nat so longe at supper."

The worthy doctor enjoyed eating well and knew the value of a good cook. "A good coke," he wrote, "is halfe a phicicion. For the chiefe phisicke (the councell of a phisicion except) dothe come from the kytchen, wherefore the phisicion and the coke for sicke men must consult togyther for the preparacion of meate [food] for sicke men. For yf the phisicion without the cooke prepare any meate except he be very expert, he will make a merysshe dyshe of meate [unsuitable concoction] the which the sycke can nat take." He noted that good cooks were hard to find and quoted the old English proverb: "God may send a man good meate but the devyl may send evyl cokes to dystrue [spoil] it."

Thomas Muffett's *Health's Improvement* was another dietary that remained popular until the middle of the eighteenth century. Dr. Muffett chided his compatriots for their love of eating and drinking and he, too, counseled moderation. "The Spaniard eats, the German drinks," he wrote, but "the Englishman exceeds in both."

Some English cookbooks offered Continental as well as English recipes. Robert May included a sizable number of Italian as well as French recipes in his *The Accomplisht Cook, or the Art and Mystery of Cookery*. English cookbook authors generally identified recipes of non-English (or allegedly non-English) origin as prepared "in the French way," or in the Italian, Dutch, Spanish, or Portuguese manner. The identification was intended to give a kind of cachet to their books and to heighten the reputation of the authors by showing that they had traveled on the Continent and had picked up the best of foreign dishes there. Nor were their claims always merely efforts to sell more copies of their books. Some cookbook authors, John Murrell, Robert May, and William Rabisha, among others, had actually acquired some of their experience and training as cooks on the Continent, usually while serving English employers abroad.

Fine French cooking goes back only to the middle of the

sixteenth century, after Catherine de Médicis came to France—
in 1533—to marry its future king, Henry II, and brought with
her a large staff of cooks from her native Florence. But by the
latter part of the sixteenth century, French cooks had already
become fashionable in certain English circles, to the great distress
of native English professional cooks. Cookbooks with the word
"French" in their titles began to appear and compete with books
of English cookery, but most Englishmen still preferred good old
English cooking.

Most cookbooks were addressed to professional cooks as an
aid in expanding their repertoires. Although a few were written
for housewives responsible for feeding their families and servants, cookbooks with "Ladies and Gentlewomen" in the titles
were usually collections of recipes for desserts, sweetmeats, preserving, and distilling of flower and herb waters.

The wives and daughters of professional men, great merchants,
and wealthy farmers, as well as ladies of gentle and noble
families, purchased the cookbooks and treasured them. Most of
their copies have disappeared with the centuries, but now and
then a sixteenth- or seventeenth-century cookbook turns up with
the name of its first owner on the flyleaf. Mary Prinne must have
been proud of her copy of John Partridge's *Treasurie of commodious Conceits, & hidden Secrets,* or else charmed with the
sight of her name, for her signature (which is approximately
contemporary with the date of the book's publication in 1573)
appears in three places on the title page. Doubtless men with
lively amateurs' interests in cooking also purchased cookbooks.
Many cookbooks went through numerous editions, but the editions were rather small as the government of Shakespeare's time
set a limit of 1,250 copies per edition on the average book.

Ladies and gentlewomen were expected to, and did, have other
cooking skills than preserving, distilling sweet waters, and making sweetmeats. William Harrison was full of admiration for the
skills of the queen's ladies-in-waiting. He praises their abilities
at playing musical instruments, their singing, their skill at fine
needlework, lace-making, and silk-spinning, as well as their
knowledge of distilling flower waters and medicinal herb drinks.
And "As each of them are cunning in something whereby they
keep themselves occupied in the court, so there is in manner
none of them but when they be at home can help to supply the
ordinary want of the kitchen with a number of delicate dishes
of their devising."

Shakespeare makes frequent and effective use of cooks and cooking, eating and drinking. In fact, there is not a play in which he has not woven some scene around food or drink, or based some simile or metaphor upon them. He uses these to create an atmosphere, set a mood, bring out the lineaments of character.

The homely, everyday activities relating to food Shakespeare turns into scenes of poignance, tragedy, or comedy. They fill us with sorrow or horror, charm or amuse, terrify or anger us, and give us characters who move or delight us still.

In a mere three lines, he paints a picture of civic disaster in *Pericles* (Act I, Scene 4), as Cleon comments on the condition into which the citizens of his city have fallen:

> Those palates who, not yet two summers younger,
> Must have inventions to delight the taste,
> Would now be glad of bread, and beg for it.

How moving is Lord Capulet's grief as he gazes on Juliet, cold and seeming dead:

> All things that we ordained festival,
> Turn from their office to black funeral;
> Our instruments to melancholy bells,
> Our wedding cheer to a sad burial feast.
> *Romeo and Juliet*, Act IV, Scene 5

Hamlet's bitterness and brooding on his father's death and his mother's hasty remarriage (Act I, Scene 2) are revealed in his words to Horatio:

> Thrift, thrift, Horatio! the funeral bak'd meats
> Did coldly furnish forth the marriage tables.

In the comic vein Falstaff's appetite for food and drink is the source of much broad humor. And in the *Comedy of Errors*, there is the delightfully wry response which Dromio of Ephesus (Act I, Scene 2) makes to the twin brother of his own master, who mistakes Dromio for his own servant, and asks how it is that Dromio has returned so soon from an errand he had just left to perform:

> Return'd so soon! rather approach'd too late:
> The capon burns, the pig falls from the spit,
> The clock hath strucken twelve upon the bell;
> My mistress made it one upon my cheek:

She is so hot because the meat is cold;
The meat is cold because you come not home;
You come not home because you have no stomach
    [are not hungry];
You have no stomach, having broke your fast;
But we, that know what 'tis to fast and pray,
Are penitent for your default to-day.

Then there is Queen Titania's charming order to her fairies in
A Midsummer-Night's Dream (Act III, Scene 1) to make
Bottom—in his ass's head—happy:

Be kind and courteous to this gentleman;
Hop in his walks, and gambol in his eyes;
Feed him with apricocks and dewberries,
With purple grapes, green figs, and mulberries.

In a scene of rural hospitality, the Shepherd in *The Winter's
Tale* (Act IV, Scene 3) urges his adopted foundling daughter,
Perdita, to put aside her shyness and welcome the invited guests
as well as several strangers who have come to their sheep-
shearing feast:

Fie, daughter! when my old wife liv'd, upon
This day she was both pantler, butler, cook;
Both dame and servant; welcom'd all, serv'd all,
Would sing her song and dance her turn; now here,
At upper end o' the table, now i' the middle;
On his shoulder, and his; her face o' fire
With labour and the thing she took to quench it,
She would to each one sip. You are retir'd,

. . . .
. . . pray you, bid
These unknown friends to's welcome; for it is
A way to make us better friends, more known.
Come, quench your blushes and present yourself
That which you are, mistress o' the feast.

A Bill of Fare to Celebrate Shakespeare's Birthday April 23, 1564

At thy birth, dear boy,
Nature and Fortune join'd to make thee great.
King John, Act III, Scene I (*Constance*)

SACK (Sherry)

*I drink to you in a cup of sack: and fear
not, neighbor, you shall do well enough.*
Henry VI, Part II, Act II, Scene 3 (*First Neighbour*)

PICKLED MUSHROOMS

*Stew'd in brine,
Smarting in lingering pickle.*
Antony and Cleopatra, Act II, Scene 5 (*Cleopatra*)

A DISH OF CAVIAR

*The play, I remember, pleased not the
million; 'twas caviare to the general.*
Hamlet, Act II, Scene 2 (*Hamlet*)

OYSTERS IN CLARET SAUCE

*With humble and familiar courtesy . . .
Off goes his bonnet to an oyster-wench.*
Richard II, Act I, Scene 4 (*Richard*)

ROAST KID WITH A DRESSING (PUDDING) IN IT

Exchange me for a goat
When I shall turn the business of my soul
To such exsufflicate and blown surmises.
> Othello, Act III, Scene 3 (*Othello*)

A SALAD OF BOILED LEEKS

His eyes were green as leeks.
> A Midsummer-Night's Dream,
> Act V, Scene 1 (*Thisbe*)

A VENISON ROAST

He that strikes
The venison first shall be the lord o' the feast.
> Cymbeline, Act III, Scene 3 (*Belarius*)

A TURKISH DISH OF MEAT

This is the English, not the Turkish court;
Not Amurath an Amurath succeeds,
But Harry Harry.
> Henry IV, Part II, Act V, Scene 2 (*Henry V*)

A TURKEY PIE

Here he comes, swelling like a turkey-cock.
> Henry V, Act V, Scene 1 (*Gower*)

RABBIT IN RED WINE SAUCE

They will out of their burrows, like conies
after rain, and revel all with him.
> Coriolanus, Act IV, Scene 5 (*Second Servingman*)

ARTICHOKES STEWED IN CREAM

There Thou prick'st her with a thistle.
> Much Ado About Nothing, Act III, Scene 4 (*Hero*)

MANCHET BREAD

I live with bread like you, feel want,
Taste grief, need friends.
> Richard II, Act III, Scene 2 (*Richard*)

A RED WINE

The red wine first must rise
In their fair cheeks, my lord; then, we shall have 'em
Talk us to silence.

Henry VIII, Act I, Scene 4 (*Lord Sands*)

A RHINE WINE

Set a deep glass of Rhenish wine on the contrary
casket, for, if the devil be within and that temptation
without, I know he will choose it.

The Merchant of Venice, Act I, Scene 2 (*Portia*)

JOSEPH COOPER'S SWEET POTATO PIE

Let the sky rain potatoes; let it thunder
to the tune of 'Green Sleeves.'

The Merry Wives of Windsor, Act V, Scene 5 (*Falstaff*)

METHEGLIN

Given to . . . sack and wine and metheglins.

The Merry Wives of Windsor, Act V, Scene 5 (*Evans*)

A DYSCHEFULL OF SNOW (CREAM)

Chaste as the icicle
That's curdied by the frost from purest snow.

Coriolanus, Act V, Scene 3 (*Coriolanus*)

A PARMESAN SAVORY

Our stomachs will make what's homely savoury.

Cymbeline, Act III, Scene 6 (*Belarius*)

RED IPOCRAS

He shall taste of my bottle: if he have never drunk
wine afore it will go near to remove his fit.

The Tempest, Act II, Scene 2 (*Stephano*)

O! who can . . . cloy the hungry edge of appetite
By bare imagination of a feast?

Richard II, Act I, Scene 3 (*Bolingbroke*)

HOW TO PICKLE MUSHROOMS

Take a bushell of Mushrooms, blanch them over the crown, barm them beneath; if they are new, they look red as a Cherry; if old, black; this being done, throw them into a pan of boyling water, then take them forth and let them drain; when they are cold, put them up into your Pot or Glass, put thereto Cloves, Mace, Ginger, Nutmeggs, whole Pepper; Then take white wine, a little Vinegar, with a little quantity of salt, so pour the Liquor into your Mushrooms, and stop them close for your use all the year.

William Rabisha, *The whole Body of Cookery Dissected*

THE WORKING VERSION:

½ pound fresh young mushrooms, about 1 inch in diameter	2 cloves
	1 large piece of whole mace
2 cups water	1 thin slice fresh ginger
1 teaspoon salt	½ nutmeg, broken up
1 teaspoon peppercorns	¾ cup white wine
	1 tablespoon vinegar

Wash the mushrooms under cool running water. Slice off the stems to within ½ inch of the caps. Put the water, ½ teaspoon of salt, and the mushrooms into a saucepan and bring to a rapid boil. Drain the mushrooms immediately and put them into a half-pint, screw-top jar with the spices and the rest of the salt. Pour the wine and the vinegar over them—if there is not enough liquid to cover the mushrooms, add more wine vinegar.

Cover the jar with a piece of plastic before screwing on the top—otherwise the vinegar will corrode the metal. Turn the jar upside down several times to distribute the seasonings. Store in a cool place (but do not refrigerate) for three or four days before using.

Pickled mushrooms were used as "salad" appetizers both when mushrooms were in season and during the cold months to add some zest to usually heavy meals.

Sir Kenelme Digbie (also spelled Digby), whose collection of recipes was published after his death as *The Closet of the Eminently Learned Sir Kenelme Digbie, Kt., Opened*, begins his recipe for pickled mushrooms in the fields where they grow. "Champignons [the French word for mushrooms] are best that grow upon gravelly dry rising Grounds," he said. "Gather them of the last nights growth; and to preserve them white, it is well to cast them into a pitcher of fair [clean] water, as you gather them: But that is not absolutely necessary, if you will go about dressing them as soon as you come home."

TO PICKLE CAVEAR

Wash it with Vinegar, season it with salt, then press it two or three dayes, so that all the liquor or excrements may run away from it, then take it again forth, and mix it together with a quantity of Pepper beaten small to dust, and salt as before, then put it into your press again; let it stand two or three dayes, then taste if it be seasoned high enough; if not, you must do so the third time; then take it and put it into an earthen Pot, and strow salt on the top of it; when you make any use to serve up any of it, take out a quantity thereof, and wash it with Vinegar, and with your knife separate your Caveer from the strings, and bring it into small certain parcells, as big as a sprat; dish it up in your dish round about, and in the middle put slices of Lemmon between, pour on oyl and Vinegar; and garnish it with Lemons and Barberries.

William Rabisha, *The whole Body of Cookery Dissected*

THE WORKING VERSION:

4 ounces black caviar	⅛ teaspoon black pepper
1 tablespoon olive oil	1 lemon, sliced thin
1 tablespoon red wine vinegar	1 tablespoon barberries or huckleberries, optional

Arrange the caviar in small mounds on a cold serving plate. Mix the oil, vinegar, and pepper until blended.

Spoon the dressing over the mounds of caviar as evenly as you can and garnish the dish with the slices of lemon and, if you wish, the berries. Serve with thin slices of buttered manchet bread (see page 38 for manchet recipe).

The barberries would probably have been pickled in vinegar. If you have barberry shrubs in your garden, the berries can be pickled by washing them, putting them into a jar, and covering them with wine vinegar. They will be ready in a few days.

Caviar was difficult to obtain and costly, but for those with gastronomic interests, it added elegance to dinner and supper parties. Like other unusual foods, it was likely to be distrusted or scorned by those with simple tastes. As Hamlet points out (Act II, Scene 2), caviar was too exotic for the general taste.

William Rabisha is the only cookbook writer who includes it in his bills of fare. Caviar appears in four of the five menus he offers, each time as a "second course" dish. Ordinarily, caviar was purchased in small barrels, imported probably from Russia. Since sturgeon was available at most times of the year, sturgeon roe, of which caviar is made, must also have been available. But few cooks, apparently, were willing to bother making the roe into caviar.

If caviar was served to Queen Elizabeth, it was not recorded in any of the meticulously detailed household accounts that have been published. Caviar does, however, appear in a manuscript of 1605 entitled "A Breviate touching the order and government of a Nobleman's House." The anonymous author, who is thought to have been the steward in a noble family's house, includes "caviare" in his "Generall Table of necessarie provisions for the whole year" and in two sample supper menus or "Diatrees," as he calls them.

The Court and Country, Nicholas Breton's amusing dialogue on the respective merits of life in the country and at court, pictures the countryman's attitudes toward new and unusual foods. He has just described his father's and mother's disgust at their first taste of a porpoise pie sent them as a gift from "a Lord," and continues, "Another gift of food of a great Lady sent him . . . was a little Barrell of Caviary, which was no sooner opened and tasted, but quickly made up again and sent back with this message, 'Commend me to my good Lady, and thanke her honour, and tell her we have black sope [soap] enoughe already; but if it be any better thing, I beseech her Ladyship to bestow it

The Court and Country,

OR

A briefe Difcourfe Dialogue-wife fet downe
betweene a Courtier and a Country-man.

Contayning the manner and condition of their liues with many
Delectable and Pithy Sayings worthy obferuation.

Alfo, neceffary Notes for a COVRTIER.

Written by *N. B.* Gent.

The Country-man.　　　　　　　　*The Courtier.*

Printed at *London* by G. ELD for *Iohn Wright*, and are to be fold at his fhop
at the Signe of the Bible without *Newgate*, 1618.

z

Title page to Nicholas Breton's The Court and Country *(1618)*

upon a better friend, that can better tell how to use it.' Now if such be your fine dishes, I pray you let me alone with my Country Fare."

TO STEW OYSTERS

Take a pottle [two quarts] of large oysters, parboil them in their own liquor, then wash them in warm water, wipe them dry, and pull away the fins, flour them and fry them in clarified butter fine and white, then take them up and put them in a large dish with some white or claret wine, a little vinegar, a quarter of a pound of sweet butter, some grated nutmeg, large mace, salt and two or three slices of an orange, stew them two or three walms [moments], then serve them in a large scoured [clean] dish, pour the sauce on them, and run them over with beaten butter, slic't lemon or orange, and sippets around the dish.

Robert May, *The Accomplisht Cook*

THE WORKING VERSION:

8 large or 12 medium oysters in their shells	¼ teaspoon salt
	½ teaspoon grated fresh orange rind
3 tablespoons flour	
¾ cup claret	1 tablespoon orange juice
1 tablespoon vinegar	½ lemon sliced thin and seeded
5 tablespoons butter	
⅛ teaspoon nutmeg	4 slices hot buttered toast cut into triangles
⅛ teaspoon ground mace	

Scrub the oysters under cold water before opening them. Drain the oyster juice into a saucer and set aside. Sprinkle the flour over a plate and dip each oyster lightly in it, coating both sides.

Bring the claret, vinegar, reserved oyster juice, one tablespoon of the butter, the nutmeg, mace, salt, orange rind, and orange juice to a boil in a small saucepan. Lower the heat to simmer and cook for ten minutes, stirring occasionally.

Melt the rest of the butter in a skillet, and when it bubbles put the floured oysters in the skillet side by side. Sauté them only

until they turn white, turning them once. Add the sauce and
gently stir the oysters around in it for two or three minutes.

Transfer the oysters with the sauce to a heated serving dish
and garnish with alternating slices of lemon and toast.

This recipe is one of thirty-two ways Robert May offers for
preparing oysters. He has half a dozen ways of stewing them;
he broils them and roasts them, fries them, pickles them, makes
them into pottage and pies, and stuffs them into meat roasts.

Oysters, however, were most often eaten raw with vinegar,
onions, and dark bread. They were cheap enough so that even the
poor could enjoy them now and then, either at home or in the
street, directly from the oysterman's cart. The streets bore
witness to this custom. "In January," wrote Nicholas Breton,
"the gaping Oister leaves his shell in the streets."

TO ROAST A . . . KID

*Truss your . . . Kid pricking the head backwards over the
shoulder, tying it down; set it, and lard it with Bacon, and draw
it with Time, and a little Lemmon-pill; . . . and when it is
enough [done] serve it up with Venison sauce.*

William Rabisha, *The whole Body of Cookery Dissected*

OTHER FORCING OF LIVERS
OF POULTRY OR KID

*Take the Liver raw, and cut it into little bits like dice, and as
much interlarded bacon cut in the same form, some sweet herbs
chopped small amongst; also some raw yolks of eggs, and some
beaten cloves and mace, pepper and salt, a few prunes and raisins,
or no fruit, but grapes or gooseberries, a little grated parmeson,
a clove or two of garlick; and fill your . . . Kid.*

Robert May, *The Accomplisht Cook*

THE WORKING VERSION:

1 hindquarter of a young kid, boned	2 tablespoons minced chives
¼ pound chicken livers or kid liver	2 tablespoons minced parsley
¼ pound lean bacon	½ teaspoon salt
¼ cup grated Parmesan cheese	⅛ teaspoon mace
1 egg yolk	⅛ teaspoon pepper
1 small bud of garlic, puréed	1 pinch of ground cloves
1 dried prune, seeded and minced	FOR BASTING
1 teaspoon raisins, minced	2 tablespoons melted butter
	1 teaspoon salt
	1 teaspoon ground nutmeg

Flatten the boned kid meat and remove any tendons. Mince the livers and bacon together or put them through a grinder. Add all the rest of the ingredients to the minced bacon and livers and mix until thoroughly blended.

Spread this dressing over the center of the flattened meat and bring the two sides together, overlapping them. Tie the roast crosswise and lengthwise with heavy white thread or cord. Melt the butter for basting and add the salt and the nutmeg. Brush the roast with this mixture and roast uncovered at 350° for one hour, basting every fifteen minutes.

Slice the roast before you remove the strings. Arrange the slices on a heated serving platter and spoon the pan gravy over them.

Very young kids were usually roasted whole. Since there is not a great deal of meat on them, they were sometimes roasted with a "pudding" (dressing) in the belly, which made the meat go further. Occasionally, a suckling pig was substituted for a kid, in which case the skin would be removed and the pig would be trussed like a kid for roasting.

Pasties (pies) were also made from kid. The Petre larder at Ingatestone contained three kid pasties the Friday and Saturday that the bishop of Norwich, an old friend of Sir William Petre's, came for a visit. But he was not permitted to taste them; the punishment for violating statutory fish days was so severe that the cook was afraid to serve them. Friday was a fish day on religious grounds, but Saturday was a statutory fish day, that is, a day on which meat-eating was forbidden by an act of parliament.

To be eaten at its best, kid should not be more than three months old. It may be difficult to find in some areas of the United States. But in towns and cities with sizable foreign populations, or in areas where goats are raised for their milk, it should be available. The best time to try is just before Easter in an Italian neighborhood, as it is an Easter meat in many Italian homes. If you are unable to find kid, try a leg of spring lamb weighing no more than 3½ pounds. It is not as delicately flavored as kid but is the nearest available substitute. "Yonge kydde is beste between Christmas and lente and good from Easter to Witsontyde but Kyd is ever good," *A Proper newe Booke of Cokerye* advises its readers, and adds that the proper sauce for it is "Sauce Orengers," that is, the juice of oranges.

A SALLET OF BOYLED LEEKS

Parboyle leekes and chop them fine with the edges of two hard Trenchers upon a board, or the backs of two Chopping-knives: then set them on a Chafingdish of coales with Butter and Vinegar. Season it with Sinamon, Ginger, Sugar, and a few parboyled Currans. Then cut hard Egges into quarters to garnish it withall, and serve it upon Sippets. Egges are necessary, or at least very good for all boyled Sallets.

John Murrell, *A New Booke of Cookerie*

THE WORKING VERSION:

8 leeks, about 1 inch in diameter at the white end	½ teaspoon brown sugar
	⅛ teaspoon cinnamon
1 quart water	⅛ teaspoon ginger
4 tablespoons butter	2 hard-boiled eggs
4 tablespoons vinegar	2 slices buttered toast, quartered
1 tablespoon currants, parboiled	

Cut off the roots and green part of the leeks and discard them. Wash the white sections in several cool waters until they are free of sand. Then drop them into boiling water for five minutes.

Drain and cool until the leeks are comfortable to handle, then mince or slice them very thin.

Melt the butter in a small saucepan and add the vinegar, minced leeks, currants, brown sugar, cinnamon, and ginger. Cook over very low heat until the leeks are tender, stirring them occasionally. Peel and quarter the eggs.

Arrange the toast quarters in a heated serving dish. Spoon the leeks over them and garnish with the quartered eggs.

"Divers other sallets," the recipe adds, can be made the same way, such as "Burrage [borage], Buglosse, Endisse [endive], Suckory [chicory], Coleflowers [cauliflower], Sorrel, Marigold [calendula] Leaves, Water cresses, onions and Sparragus."

The word "vegetable" had not come into common use in Shakespeare's day. He uses the term "vegetives," in the sense of growing things, in *Pericles* (Act III, Scene 2), where Cerimon speaks of "the blest infusions that dwell in vegetives." But cooked vegetables were generally called boiled salads, although other terms for them were also used.

English writers, including Shakespeare, enjoyed poking fun at leek-eaters, especially at the Welsh, for whom the leek had become a national emblem after a great military victory had been won in a field of leeks. The Welsh still wear leeks in their hats on the day of their patron saint, St. David. In *Henry V* (Act V, Scene 1), Shakespeare builds a comic scene out of the pugnacious pride of Fluellen, one of the king's Welsh officers, in leeks. "If you can mock a leek," he threatens Pistol, "you can eat a leek," and forces the ignoble Pistol to eat one.

Thomas Tusser thought leeks well worth growing. In the "farmers' calendar" of his *Five Hundred Points of Good Husbandry,* he says:

> Now leeks are in season, for pottage full good,
> and spareth the milch-cow, and purgeth the blood:
> These having with peason, for pottage in Lent,
> Thou sparest both oatmeal and bread to be spent [used].

The dietaries were of two minds about leeks. Sir Thomas Elyot, in *The Castle of Health,* wrote that leeks "bee of ill juyce, and doe make troublous dreams" but "they do extenuate and cleanse the body." Andrewe Boorde said, "Lekes dothe open the breste . . . but they doth make and increase evyll blode [blood]."

TO ROAST VENISON

If you will Roast any Venison, after you have washt it and clensed all the blood from it, you shall stick it with Cloves all over the outside; and if it be lean, you shall either lard it with Mutton lard, or Pork lard, but mutton is best: then spit it and roast it by a soaking [moderate] fire, then take vinegar, bread crums, and some of the gravy which comes from the venison, and boyl them well in a dish: then season it with Sugar, cinamon, ginger, and salt, and serve the Venison forth upon the sawce when it is roasted enough.

Gervase Markham, *The English Hus-wife*

SAUCE FOR ROAST VENISON

As [it] roasts put a dish under [it] with Claret wine [to catch the gravy] . . . take your dish and set it on the coals, put grated bread, beaten Cinamon, Vinegar and Sugar to your wine, with a ladleful of drawn Butter, so dish up your Venison and pour on this Lear [sauce], being not to thick, all over it.

William Rabisha, *The whole Body of Cookery Dissected*

THE WORKING VERSION:

6 slices bacon
5 pounds haunch or shoulder of venison
1 tablespoon whole cloves
⅓ cup claret
⅓ cup red wine vinegar

1½ teaspoons salt
1 teaspoon brown sugar
¼ teaspoon cinnamon
2 tablespoons butter
2 teaspoons grated bread crumbs

Wrap the slices of bacon around the roast, attaching them with the cloves. If you have a rotisserie, broil the meat; otherwise roast the venison in an open pan at 375° for two hours.

Mix the claret, vinegar, salt, sugar, and cinnamon together and baste the roast with this every fifteen minutes. About fifteen minutes before the roast is done, pour off the gravy into a soup plate and set it on a tray of ice to harden the fat. When the fat has hardened, skim it off and pour the gravy into a small saucepan.

Add the butter to the gravy and bring it to a boil. Lower the heat to simmer, add the bread crumbs, and cook five minutes, stirring constantly as the sauce thickens. Taste the sauce and add more salt if needed. Serve the roast whole and pass the gravy separately, or slice it and pour the gravy over the slices.

Most health writers warned against eating venison. They quoted the ancient Greek and Roman physicians as authorities for the belief that venison could cause melancholy and "coloryke humors." Andrewe Boorde explained the medical argument without sharing it. "Englishmen have a passion for venison," he said. "I have gone rounde about crystendome & a thousande or two and more miles out of crystendome, yet there is nat so muche pleasure for harte & hynde, buck and doo; and roo buck and doo, as in Englande."

Boorde accepted the contemporary legal and social prejudices that held that venison was not for ordinary people: "I am sure it is a lordes dysshe," he wrote, "and I am sure it is good for an Englysheman, for it doth anymate him to be as he is: which is strong and hardy, but I do advertyse every man for all my wordes nat to kyll and so eate of it, except it be legull, for it is meate for greate men. And greate men do not set so moch by the meate as they do by the pastyme of kyllinge of it." Wistfully he adds, "although the flesshe be dispraised in physycke, I pray god to send me part of the flesshye to eate natwithstandynge."

A TURKISH DISH OF MEATE

Take an interlarded piece of beef, cut it into thin slices, and put it into a pot that hath a close cover, or stewing pan; then put into it a good quantity of clean picked rice, skim it very well, and put

*into it a quantity of whole pepper, two or three whole onions,
and let this boil very well, then take out the onions, and dish it on
sippets, the thicker it is the better.*

Robert May, *The Accomplisht Cook*

THE WORKING VERSION:

1 pound boned lean chuck	½ cup long-grain rice
16 tiny white onions	⅔ cup beef broth
3 tablespoons butter	2 slices buttered toast,
1 teaspoon peppercorns	quartered
1 teaspoon salt	

Remove any gristle and fat from the meat and slice it very thin.
You will need a sharp knife for this, and it will be easier to slice
if you put the meat into the freezer just long enough to stiffen
it. Peel the onions.

Melt the butter in a small heavy casserole with a tight-fitting
lid. Add the meat, peppercorns, and salt and stir just until the
meat changes color, then stir in the rice and the onions. Heat
the broth to boiling and pour it over the meat and rice.

Cover the casserole and lower the heat to simmer—on an
electric stove to warm—and cook until the rice has absorbed
most of the liquid. Arrange the toast in a heated serving dish and
spoon the beef and rice over it. Serve immediately.

Warn your guests to look out for the peppercorns. Or you can
substitute a scant ½ teaspoon of ground pepper for the peppercorns, but the flavor is not quite as good.

Things Turkish were popular in Shakespeare's day. Turkish
fruits, oil, pepper, and sweet wines graced the wealthier English
kitchens and tables. "Turkey" cushions and "Turkey" carpets—
used as table coverings rather than as floor coverings—were
much esteemed. In *The Comedy of Errors* (Act IV, Scene 1),
when Antipholus of Ephesus sends his servant Dromio home to
obtain the money for his bail, he tells him to tell his wife, Adriana,
that the money is "in the desk that's cover'd o'er with Turkish
tapestry." The domesticated fowl we call turkey did not come
from that part of the world; its name is an example of some
of the mistaken notions of Tudor England about the origins of
foreign livestock.

TO BAKE A TURKEY

Take a turkey, bone it, and lard it with pretty big lard, a pound and a half will serve, then season it with an ounce of pepper, an ounce of nutmegs, and two ounces of salt, lay some butter in the bottom of the pye, then lay on the fowl, and put in six or eight whole cloves, then put on all the seasoning with good store of butter, close it up, and baste it over with eggs, bake it, and being baked fill it up with clarified butter. . . . To be eaten hot, [give] but half the seasoning, and liquor it with gravy and juyce of orange.

Bake this pye in fine paste, for more variety you make a stuffing for it as followeth; mince some beef-suet and a little veal very fine, some sweet herbs, grated nutmeg, pepper, salt, two or three raw yolks of eggs; some boiled skirrets or pieces of artichokes, grapes, or gooseberries, etc.

Robert May, *The Accomplisht Cook*

THE WORKING VERSION:

One 5- to 6-pound dressed
 turkey
 2 tablespoons salt
 ½ teaspoon pepper
 1 teaspoon nutmeg
 ⅛ teaspoon cloves
 4 tablespoons butter

THE STUFFING
 ½ pound lean veal, ground
  or minced fine
 ¼ pound beef suet, ground
 2 egg yolks
 1 artichoke bottom, cooked
  and diced
 ¼ cup minced parsley
 2 tablespoons minced chives
 ¼ teaspoon salt
 ¼ teaspoon nutmeg

THE PASTRY
 2 cups sifted unbleached
  flour
 1 teaspoon salt
 ¾ cup cold butter
 ½ cup cold, clear chicken
  broth, approximately
 1 egg, separated

THE SAUCE
 1¼ cups clear chicken broth
 6 tablespoons fresh orange
  juice
 ½ teaspoon salt
 ¼ teaspoon nutmeg
 ⅛ teaspoon pepper
 2 egg yolks

Remove the giblets from the turkey, rinse the turkey under cold running water and wipe it dry with a clean white cloth. Put a large clean piece of white cloth on your work surface and bone the turkey on the cloth—it helps to keep the bird from slipping while you work. Place the turkey breast side down on the cloth and, with a sharp boning knife or long-bladed paring knife, cut through the skin down along the backbone from the neck to the tail. Cut off the tips and the first sections of the wings.

With the knife at a slight angle and against the neck end of the bone, slowly but firmly cut and push the meat away from the frame in the direction of the wings and the legs. When you reach the joints attached to the body of the bird, use scissors to cut the tendons and loosen the joints so that they are free from the frame of the body.

Continue cutting downward along the ribs, first on one side of the breast, then on the other, to the end of the breastbone. Cut slowly and carefully around the cartilage end of the breastbone so as not to tear the skin, and lift out the bony frame of the turkey.

Mix all the ingredients for the stuffing lightly but thoroughly. Flatten the boned turkey, skin side down, and spread the stuffing over the center of the bird, piling it up lightly. Bring the two cut sides up over the dressing so that one side overlaps the other by about an inch.

Bring the wings and legs close to the body and fold the cloth up over the stuffed turkey. Just before you put the bird into the pastry, remove the cloth. Mix together the salt, pepper, nutmeg, and cloves and spread them over the entire skin of the bird.

To make the pastry, sift the flour and salt together into a large mixing bowl. Add ½ cup of the butter and crumble it into the flour until it is like fine meal. Dice the rest of the butter into ¼-inch cubes and stir them into the flour mixture.

Add enough of the cold chicken broth to the egg yolk to make ½ cup of liquid, and stir until well blended. Pour the mixture over the flour-butter mix and stir quickly until a ball of dough can be formed with the hands—if more liquid is needed, add additional broth, one tablespoonful at a time.

Sprinkle your work surface with flour and turn the ball of dough out onto the flour. Toss the ball lightly between your hands until it has taken on only enough flour to make it easy to handle. Divide the dough into two pieces, ⅔ of it for the lower crust and ⅓ for the top crust.

Pat the larger piece into rectangular shape and roll it out to fit a seven-by-eleven-inch oven-to-table ceramic baking dish. Loosen the sheet of pastry from the work surface and fit it into the baking dish. Then roll out the pastry for the top crust and loosen it from your work surface.

Place the prepared turkey in the center of the baking dish, breast side up, bringing the wings and legs close to the body. Cut the butter into thin slices and spread them over the top of the bird. Cover with the top sheet of pastry and seal the edges with the tines of a fork dipped in cold water.

Cut off the surplus pastry, and if there is enough to roll out, cut out small pastry turkeys, either freehand or with a cookie cutter. Brush the pie with the egg white and arrange the cutouts over the top of the pie. Then brush the tops of the cutouts with egg white.

Bake at 450° for twenty minutes, then lower the heat to 325° and continue baking for 1½ hours—if the pie seems to be browning too quickly, cover it with a piece of brown wrapping paper or kitchen parchment.

While the turkey is baking, put all the ingredients for the sauce, except the egg yolks, into a small saucepan and simmer for fifteen minutes. Cover the pan and set it aside until needed. Just before you are ready to serve the pie, beat two tablespoons of the sauce into the egg yolks. Heat the remaining sauce to boiling, lower the heat to simmer, and stir in the beaten egg yolks, stirring constantly until the sauce begins to thicken. Remove the saucepan immediately from the heat and keep the sauce warm over hot water.

To serve, cut open the top of the pie and divide the crust into serving-size portions. Carve the turkey and give each person a portion of crust with the meat. Pass the sauce separately or spoon a little of it directly over each serving.

If you prefer the turkey completely boned, cut and push the meat away from the bones in the wings and the legs as you did from the frame of the bird. Use scissors to cut the tendons free when you reach the leg joint and pull out the bone, which has been freed before starting on the lower part of the leg. Use scissors also to cut the skin free from the ends of the wings and the legs. Then push some of the dressing into the cavities left when the bones were removed.

You can bone, stuff, and season the bird the day before you plan to make the pie. Or, if you plan to serve the pie cold, bake it early in the day you plan to use it and set it aside to cool. Do not refrigerate it, as refrigerated pastry crusts are usually soggy. When I served this pie cold, I used a sauce of prepared mustard thinned down with heavy cream.

Clarified butter, which was poured into meat pies that were to be served over a period of time, helped to prevent spoilage and kept the meat from drying out. Pies meant to be eaten hot were made with tender crusts; the top crust was broken up and pieces of it were served with the meat. When the meat from a large cold pie was wanted, an opening was cut in the side of the pie, the desired amount of meat was scooped out, and the section of crust that had been cut away was then fitted back onto the pie.

Although several cookbooks offer recipes using boned turkey, none gives instructions on how to bone one. Perhaps only professional cooks tried boning poultry, and the skill was one they learned, or should have learned, as apprentices.

Turkeys first arrived in England in the 1530's, via Spain, whose explorers had brought them from Mexico, where the Aztec Indians had already domesticated them, in about 1519. The descendants of some of the turkeys brought into England were brought back to the North American continent by the early colonists to help build up their stocks of poultry. The colonists, however, depended to a large extent on the native wild turkeys for food.

Few of the dietaries mention turkeys. William Vaughan, in *Directions for Health,* suggests that "Turkies . . . if they be hanged by the necks five or sixe daies with waights at their feet, and afterwards eaten with a good sauce, doe greatly nourish and profit them with hot bellies."

William Harrison noted that turkeys were being gelded to improve the quality and quantity of the meat. This was a technique, he said, that was introduced into England by the Romans, who used it to turn cocks into capons. The new practice of gelding turkeys, he said, "was not used amiss, sith the rankness of that bird is much abated thereby and the strong taste of the flesh in sundry wise amended."

Turkeys were included in a number of suggested menus in

various cookbooks. They were boiled as well as roasted and made into pies. A roast turkey was served at Christmas-day dinner in 1572, but only for the "master of the house," in the home of the wealthy Fairfax family, and a cold turkey pie was served as a second-course dish. These were probably the two turkeys that were noted in the household accounts as having been received as "presentes" the previous week. Claudius Hollyband and Pierre Erondell thought turkey sufficiently well known in London to include the word in their French conversation manuals for their English readers.

TO BOYLE A RABBET WITH CLARET WINE

Trusse your Rabbet whole, and boyle it with strong broth, untill it bee ready. Then take a pinte of Claret-wine, slice Onyons, and a Carrot-root, a few Currins, and a Fagot of Hearbes, minst Parsley, Barberries pickt, large Mace, Nutmeg, and Ginger: throw them all into the Pipkin. Boyle it with halfe a pound of butter.

John Murrell, *A New Booke of Cookerie*

THE WORKING VERSION:

One 3-pound frying rabbit, dressed	2 teaspoons salt
¼ pound butter	1 large piece of whole mace
½ cup minced onions	½ teaspoon nutmeg
2 small carrots, scraped and sliced thin	½ tablespoon grated fresh ginger
¼ cup minced parsley	1 cup clear chicken broth
2 tablespoons currants	1 cup claret
½ teaspoon thyme	¼ cup barberries or huckleberries, optional
1 bay leaf	3 egg yolks, optional

Cut the rabbit into frying-size pieces, or ask your butcher to do so. Melt half the butter in an ovenware casserole with a close-fitting lid. Add the onions, carrots, parsley, currants, and the seasonings and sauté over low heat for five minutes, stirring occasionally. Add the rabbit and cook until the meat changes color.

Add the chicken broth, ½ cup of the claret, and the berries—if neither barberries nor huckleberries are available, their omission from the recipe will not affect the flavor enough for you to notice it. Cover the pot and bake in a 350° oven for one hour, or simmer over very low heat until tender. Remove the casserole from the oven and stir in the rest of the butter until blended with the sauce. If you prefer a thicker sauce, beat the egg yolks with the remaining claret and stir it into the sauce, over low heat, until it begins to thicken. If you do not use the egg yolks, just add the claret and simmer for ten minutes. Serve the rabbit hot, as John Murrell constantly advises his readers. Since the kitchens were often a long way from the dining rooms, serving food hot could be a problem.

Murrell begins this recipe with "use it as before shewed." Since he thickens the sauce in the previous recipe with egg yolks, I have also suggested using egg yolks. I suggested cutting up the rabbit because many kitchens may not have available pots large enough to hold a whole rabbit.

Wines had been used in English cooking since medieval days, and cooks in well-to-do homes were accustomed to using wines in their cooking.

TO STEWE HARTECHOCKES IN CREAM

Take the thickest bottomes of the thickest Hartechockes being very tender boyled, and stew them in a little butter and vinegar, whole Mace and Sugar, then take halfe a pinte of sweete Cream boyled with whole Mace, straine [mix] it with the yolkes of two-new-laide egges, and brewe them together with halfe a ladlefull of the best thicke butter and vinegar, a little Sugar, so dish up the bottomes of the Hartechockes, & lay it with sippets of a slickt Lemon round about, then poure your sauce on the toppe of the Hartechockes, and sticke them full of fryde tosts upright scrape on a little Sugar and serve it to the table hot.

John Murrell, *A Booke of Cookerie*

THE WORKING VERSION:

6 medium-large artichokes

2 quarts water

1 tablespoon salt

2 tablespoons vinegar

FOR THE SAUCE

1 cup light cream

3 tablespoons butter

1 large piece of whole mace

2 egg yolks

3 tablespoons white wine vinegar

¼ teaspoon brown sugar

1 lemon, sliced thin and seeded

2 slices buttered toast, cut into triangles

Wash the artichokes in cool water and cut off all but ½ inch of the stalks. Add the salt and vinegar to the water in a large pan and bring it to a boil. Place the artichokes in the boiling water, stem side down, and cook over moderate heat until tender —from thirty to forty-five minutes; when a leaf can be easily pulled out, the artichoke is cooked. Drain the artichokes stem side up, and when cool enough to handle, pull off the leaves.

With the side of a teaspoon scoop out the entire choke (the thistle section). Slice off the remaining stems and cut the artichoke bases into quarters. Scrape off the tender part at the base of the leaves and add to the artichoke bases.

Bring the cream, butter, and mace to a boil in a small saucepan, lower the heat to simmer, and cook five minutes. Remove the mace and add the artichoke bases and the meat scraped from the leaves, and simmer five minutes more. Beat the egg yolks with the wine vinegar and sugar, add them to the sauce, and cook, stirring gently so as not to break the artichokes, until the sauce begins to thicken.

Pour the artichokes and the sauce into a heated serving dish, and garnish with the slices of lemon and the toast. Serve immediately.

"Straine" could mean either strain or mix; in this recipe it means to mix with. The raw artichokes can be cooked in two batches if you have no pot large enough to hold six; they should be covered with at least one inch of water and cooked with one tablespoon of salt in each pot.

Only the solid bases of the artichokes were eaten in Shakespeare's day, although the leaves were sometimes used for garnishing. Artichokes were fried as well as stewed, and they were popular for pies. Seventeenth-century recipes for artichoke pies were richer than sixteenth-century recipes, and often included dates. All artichoke recipes contained sugar. Only two cookbooks give recipes for pickling them. Sir Hugh Plat, in *Delightes for Ladies,* puts artichokes up in a "strong decoction" made from the chopped-up stalks of the artichokes and water boiled together. Joseph Cooper, in *The Art of Cookery Refin'd and Augmented,* suggests that, pickled in salt-water brine, they can be used to make artichoke pies at Christmas or stews.

Artichokes were grown in Henry VIII's garden at Newhall, in 1530. Others soon followed his example, and artichokes were planted in the gardens of many nobles, gentry, and wealthy yeoman farmers. The Dutch, highly esteemed as gardeners by the English, had introduced artichokes into England. They were grown for market in the fields in and near London and other cities. "Buy my artichokes, mistress," was a familiar cry in London streets when they were in season.

Thomas Tusser listed artichokes as herbs to be grown for salads. Gervase Markham told English housewives to make a place for them in their gardens, and to plant them in March, when the moon was "at the wain."

Still, they were a delicacy and rather expensive. Like sweet potatoes, they were considered aphrodisiacs. "When they be almost rype," said Andrewe Boorde, "they must be soden [boiled] tender in the broth of befe, and after eate them at dyner, they both increase nature, and doth provoke a man to veneryous actes."

William Vaughan recommended that they be served like cucumbers with "oyle, vinegar, and pepper" to "further digestion." He also recommended them as a "restorative unto old age, a toothsome foode for greatbellied [pregnant] women, and an excellent nourishment for such as are weakened in their natural powers." But he added that they were unwholesome "for them which fear the approach of any watry or windy sickness."

TO MAKE MANCHET

Your best and principal bread is Manchet, which you shall bake in this manner: First your meal being ground upon the black stones, if it be possible, which makes the whitest flower, and boulted through the finest boulting cloth, you shall put it into a clean Kimnel [mixing trough], and opening the flower hollow in the midst, put into it of the best ale-barme, the quantity of three pints to a bushell of meale and some salt to season it with; then put in your liquor reasonable warme, and kneade it very well together, with both your hands, and through the brake, or for want thereof, fould it in a cloth, and with your feete treade it a good space together, then letting it lie an houre or thereabouts to swel, take it foorth and mould it into Manchets, round, and flat, scorcht them about the wast to give it leave to rise, and prick it with your knife in the top, and so put into the oven, and bake with a gentle heat.

Gervase Markham, *The English Hus-wife*

THE WORKING VERSION:

- 2 cups lukewarm water
- 2 cakes of fresh yeast or 2 tablespoons dry yeast
- 1 tablespoon salt
- 6 cups sifted unbleached flour

Pour the water into a large mixing bowl and crumble or sprinkle the yeast into it. When the yeast has softened and expanded, add the salt and stir in five cups of the flour, one cupful at a time.

Sprinkle the remaining cup of flour on your work surface and turn the dough out onto the flour. Knead it until it feels elastic —about five minutes—then put the dough into a clean mixing bowl. Cover the bowl with a clean towel or a plastic bowl cover and set the dough to rise in a warm place or an unheated oven.

When the dough has doubled in bulk—in 1 to 1½ hours—turn it out onto the floured work surface and knead into a smooth ball. Divide the ball into twelve more or less equal parts, and knead each one into a ball. Flatten each one with the palm of your hand to a thickness of ½ inch, and, with a sharp knife, cut around the circumference of the rolls ⅛ inch deep halfway between top and bottom.

Place the rolls an inch apart on a floured tin. Punch fork holes in the tops and set them to rise—forty-five minutes to one hour—until they have doubled in size. Bake at 400° for twenty minutes, or until golden brown. Cool on a wire grille.

Manchets freeze well. To use if frozen, remove the freezer wrappings and put the manchets into a preheated 350° oven for fifteen minutes.

These are about half the size they would have been in Shakespeare's day but are more suited to present-day habits of bread-eating. If you prefer the more authentic size, divide the rolls into six rather than twelve pieces.

A brake was a device for working the dough. The dough was placed on a flat surface and pushed from left to right with the left hand while the right hand banged a knifelike length of metal up and down on the dough. There is a good illustration of a brake in Dorothy Hartley's *Food in England*.

Of bread, William Harrison said, "We have sundry sorts brought to the table, whereof the first and most excellent is manchet, which we commonly call white bread . . . and our good workmen deliver commonly such proportion that of the flour of one bushel with another they make forty cast [a cast of bread usually meant a batch of bread; here it apparently means a dozen loaves] of manchet of which every loaf weigheth . . . six ounces each."

In the royal household only royalty and the highest-ranking officers and courtiers were served manchet. The rest of those entitled to eat at the palace—at royal expense—were expected to take their meals at common tables set up especially for them, and at which only the coarser white bread called fine cheate and a still-coarser bread called cheate were served.

Courtiers who did not fancy this ordinary fare, or eating at the common tables, sometimes managed not only to have their meals prepared by their own servants in their suites but also to obtain manchet for themselves from the royal bakehouse. It was an open secret that manchet and other delicacies were filched from the royal larders for courtiers with fastidious appetites.

In well-off homes, when manchet was served, it was only to members of the family and to important guests. Less-honored guests and the upper rank of servants usually ate cheate or coarser breads. The lowest ranks of servants ate breads made from mixtures of wheat and rye, wheat and barley, and sometimes rye and barley or oats mixed with other grains. In Archbishop Parker's household, however, according to household records, manchet was sometimes served to his gentlemen retainers, as servants born of gentle or noble families were called.

TO MAKE A POTATO PIE

Boyle your Potatoes tender and blanch them; slice them but not very thin, and mix them with some apple pared and sliced: season them with Cynamon, Ginger, Sugar & Salt. Your Pie being made, put in these meats with a good store of marrow on the top, being cut into lumps as big as a wallnut: pour a little verjuyce on the Pye and close it; being baked put to it verjuyce, sugar, butter, cynamon, and ginger, beat up thick together, cut up the lid, and fill it with leare [this sauce], raising it up with the knife to let in the liquor. You must put in Butter when you close up the Pie to bake it, otherwise it will burn in the oven, they being of very dry substance. Less than two houres will bake it. Scrape Sugar on it, and serve it up hot.

Joseph Cooper, *The Art of Cookery Refin'd and Augmented*

THE WORKING VERSION:

THE FILLING	½ ounce beef marrow, diced
1 pound sweet potatoes	
1 pound tart cooking apples	THE PASTRY
⅓ cup brown sugar	2 cups sifted unbleached flour
¼ teaspoon salt	1 teaspoon salt
½ teaspoon cinnamon	¾ cup cold butter
½ teaspoon ginger	½ cup cold water, approxi-
4 tablespoons butter, diced	mately
¼ cup white wine vinegar	1 egg, separated

Bake the potatoes at 400° for forty minutes. Peel off the skins immediately, and slice the potatoes into ½-inch slices. Cover and set aside.

Quarter, core, peel, and slice the apples ¼ inch thick, and

set them aside, covered. Make the piecrust following the method given on page 31, using water instead of the chicken broth.

Divide the pastry dough into two parts, ⅔ of it for the bottom crust and ⅓ for the top crust.

Roll out the larger piece to fit an eight-inch pie dish. Fit it into the dish and roll out the top crust.

Sift the sugar, salt, cinnamon, and ginger together. Stir the diced butter gently around in the mixture, and sprinkle the vinegar over the potatoes. Alternate layers of apples and potatoes in the pie dish, sprinkling each layer with some of the butter-sugar-spice mixture. Dot with the diced beef marrow and fit the top crust over it.

Seal the edges of the pie with the wet tines of a fork, and slice off the surplus pastry. Brush the pie with the egg white. Bake at 450° for twenty minutes, then lower the heat to 350° and bake twenty-five minutes longer. Serve warm.

If beef marrow is not available, dot the top layer of the pie with two tablespoons of butter, diced.

All recipes calling for potatoes were for sweet, or Spanish potatoes. The white, or Virginia, potato, so-called because Sir Walter Raleigh brought it back to England from Virginia, or so it was thought, was barely known during Shakespeare's lifetime.

Spanish potatoes, introduced by the Spaniards, who found them in South America, were known in England around the middle of the sixteenth century. William Harrison mentions them in the 1577 edition of *The Description of England,* but recipes for them do not appear in English cookbooks until the 1580's, when Thomas Dawson offered the recipe, much quoted by social historians of Tudor England, on how "to make a tart that is a courage to a man or woman." The recipe combines potatoes with the brains of cock robins, among other ingredients, making it clear to Elizabethans that it was a dish with aphrodisiac possibilities. The aphrodisiac reputation of cock robins' brains and sweet potatoes was accepted by educated people as well as by the medical profession. Sir Thomas Elyot in his *Castle of Health,* does not mention robins, but notes that "sparrowes be hard to digest, and are very hot, and stirreth up Venus, and especially the brains of them." Shakespeare mentions potatoes twice, both times with lecherous connotations.

METHEGLIN

Take all sorts of herbs that are good and wholesome, as balm, mint, rosemary, fennil, angelica, wilde time, hysop, burnet, agrimony, and such other field herbs, half a handful of each, boil and strain them and let the liquor stand till the next day, being settled take two gallons and a half of honey, let it boil an hour, and in the boiling scum it very clean, set it a cooling as you do beer, and when it is cold take very good barm and put it into the bottom of the tub, by a little and a little as to beer, keeping back the thick settling that lyeth in the bottom of the vessel that it is cooled in; when it is all put together cover it with a cloth and let it work very near three days, then when you mean to put it up, skim off all the barm clean, and put it up into a vessel, but you must not stop the vessel very close in three or four days, but let it have some vent to work; when it is close stopped you must look often to it, and have a peg on the top to give it vent when you hear it make a noise as it will do, or else it will break the vessel.

Sometimes make a bag and put in good store of slic't ginger, some cloves and cinamon boild or not.

Robert May, *The Accomplisht Cook*

THE WORKING VERSION:

4 quarts filtered water
2 large sprigs of rosemary
2 large sprigs of thyme
2 large sprigs of any mint
2 large sprigs of fennel or tarragon
1 quart liquid honey
One 2-inch stick of cinnamon
One 2-inch slice of fresh (green) ginger
16 cloves
½ tablespoon mead yeast

EQUIPMENT NEEDED

One 2-gallon crock, washed with boiling water
1 clean white cloth large enough to cover the top of the crock
2 glass gallon jugs (empty wine jugs with screw caps will do), washed thoroughly with boiling water
1 plastic fermentation lock
One 18-inch length of ½-inch rubber tubing

Add all the herbs to the filtered water and bring to a boil. Lower the heat to moderate and continue cooking for half an hour. Strain the herb water through a clean white cloth into the crock and let the liquid stand until it is lukewarm. Add the honey and stir until it melts. Then add the cinnamon, ginger, and cloves. Sprinkle the yeast over the top and cover the crock with a clean cloth.

Set the crock in a cool place until the yeast stops working—from ten to fourteen days—stirring it every other day. Then strain the metheglin through a clean white cloth and pour the strained liquor into one of the glass jugs.

Remove the cap from the fermentation lock and screw the lock onto the jug of metheglin. Fill the locks with water to the marked water lines. Put the jug in a cool place until bubbles no longer appear in the water in the fermentation lock. Then screw the jug cap on and set the jug in a cool, dark place to settle and mature for two months. Unscrew the cap once a week for the first month to permit any residual gas to escape.

To separate the clear metheglin from the sediment that accumulates during the maturing period, first wash the rubber tubing by pouring hot water through it. Carefully transfer the jug of metheglin to a work surface that is of comfortable height, being careful not to disturb the sediment. Place the other gallon jug on a stool or chair that is about a foot lower than your work surface.

Insert one end of the tubing into the jug of metheglin to about one inch above the top of the sediment, keeping the tube steady with one hand so that it does not slide down into the sediment. (If the sediment is disturbed and the metheglin clouds up, it will have to be set back on the shelf until it has again cleared.)

Place the other end of the tube between your lips and suck until some metheglin rises to your lips. At this point quickly remove the tubing, turn the opening downward, and set it into the lower jug—this process can be tricky and may take several tries, but I found it easier than using a bulb-siphoning tube.

Screw the cap on the jug of cleared metheglin and set it back on the shelf to mature for at least a month before using—two months is even better; metheglin improves with aging. If more sediment accumulates, siphon off the clear metheglin as you did previously.

Mead yeast, plastic fermentation locks, and siphoning tubes can be obtained at shops that carry wine-making equipment. Because of the alcoholic content, you must obtain a permit from the Internal Revenue Service to make metheglin in the United States. The permit, however, is available free.

TO MAKE A DYSCHEFULL OF SNOWE

Take a pottell of swete thycke creame and the whytes of eyghte egges, and beate them altogether wyth a spone, then putte them in youre creame and a saucerfull of Rosewater, and a dyshe full of Suger wyth all, then take a stycke and make it cleane, and than cutte it in the end foure square, and therwith beate all the aforesayde thynges together and ever as it ryseth take it of and put it in a Collaunder, this done take one apple and set it in the myddes of it, and a thick bushe of Rosemary, and set it in the myddes of the platter, then cast your Snowe uppon the Rosemarye and fyll your platter therwith. And yf you have wafers caste some in wyth all and thus serve them forthe.

Anonymous, *A Proper newe Booke of Cokerye*

THE WORKING VERSION :

1 medium-size apple	1 tablespoon sugar
One 8-inch sprig of fresh	1 cup whipping cream, chilled
rosemary	1 tablespoon rose water
1 egg white	8 small butter cookies

Wash and dry the apple, pull off the stem, and slice a piece off the base of it so that it will stand firmly. Remove the lower leaves of the rosemary to a height that will firmly anchor it in the center of the apple. Rinse the rosemary in cold water and shake off all the moisture.

Chill a flat serving dish, place the apple in the center of it, and insert the sprig of rosemary down to the base of the apple.

Beat the egg white until it starts to froth, add the sugar, and continue beating until the white is firm and glossy. Whip the chilled cream until it is stiff and fold it into the egg white. Stir in the rose water, a teaspoonful at a time.

Shake several spoonfuls of the whipped mixture over the

sprig of rosemary, then pile the rest lightly over and around the apple and the lower section of the rosemary. Set the cookies upright into the cream around the edge of the dish and serve immediately. To serve, spoon the cream into individual serving saucers and garnish with the cookies. The apple serves only to hold the rosemary firmly.

The lack of wire whisks or mechanical eggbeaters made desserts like this difficult to prepare, and not all cookbooks offer recipes for them. Robert May suggests using a spoon to beat the egg whites and the cream; Rabisha suggests a bunch of feathers, Kenelme Digbie "a bundle of white hard rushes such as they make whisks to brush cloaks, tyed together," and Dawson and Cooper let the cook worry about the problem.

Robert May, with a nice appreciation of the delicacy of the dessert, says that it should be served on "a fine silver dish," and instead of an apple he uses a "penny manchet, the bottom and upper crust being taken away and made fast with paste to the bottom of the dish." He also suggests that musk and ambergris be added for flavoring and the whole thing flecked with gold leaf. Joseph Cooper, as befits the former master cook to a king, elaborates his recipe to include almonds, "beaten fine," white wine, orange peel, and nutmeg.

A MADE DISH OF PARMYSANT

Take a Grater and grate half a pound of Parmyzant, then grate as much manchet, and mince some Tarragon together with Horse-Raddish; season this with almost a handful of Carraway Comfits; put to it a little brisk Claret-wine to moisten it over, then dish it in a small dish, from the middle to the brim, in parcels as broad as your knife; garnish it with carraway Comfits, Horse-Raddish and Tarragon; send it up as the last dish of your mess or messes, with Mustard and Sugar.

William Rabisha, *The whole Body of Cookery Dissected*

THE WORKING VERSION:

8 tablespoons grated Parmesan cheese
8 tablespoons grated bread crumbs
1 teaspoon caraway seeds
½ teaspoon light-brown sugar
2 tablespoons claret
1 teaspoon grated horseradish
½ teaspoon minced fresh tarragon, or ⅛ teaspoon dried tarragon

THE GARNISH

½ teaspoon minced fresh tarragon, or ⅛ teaspoon dried tarragon
½ teaspoon grated horseradish
½ teaspoon caraway seeds
½ teaspoon light-brown sugar

THE SAUCE

2 tablespoons prepared mustard
1 teaspoon light-brown sugar

Mix the cheese, bread crumbs, caraway seeds, and sugar together. Add the claret, horseradish, and tarragon and blend thoroughly.

Mix together all the ingredients for the garnish, and blend the mustard and sugar for the sauce. Arrange the cheese mixture in inch-wide bands, like the spokes of a wheel, on a small serving plate. Sprinkle the garnish lightly in the center and around the spokes. Serve the sauce on a separate dish.

Caraway comfits were sugar-coated caraway seeds. Since they are no longer available in shops and are very difficult to make, I have substituted caraway seeds and sugar.

It was apparently not considered proper to serve a solid block of cheese at a feast. "At a Feast it is not common to send up a whole Cheese," William Rabisha noted.

Cheese savories were also made of grated cheese seasoned with sage and sugar. These were offered to the dinner guests of the noble lady in Pierre Erondell's French-English conversation manual.

Shakespeare uses cheese in situations ranging from comic to charming. In *The Merry Wives of Windsor* (Act V, Scene 5), Falstaff, trying to protect himself from the pinches of his tormentors, who were dressed as fairies, exclaims, "Heavens defend me from that Welsh fairy, lest he transform me to a piece of cheese."

Hotspur, irritated by Glendower's constant preaching, tells Glendower's son, in *Henry IV, Part I* (Act III, Scene 1),

O! he's as tedious
As . . . a railing wife;
. . . I had rather live
With cheese and garlick in a windmill, far,
Than feed on cates [delicacies] and have him talk to me
In any summer-house in Christendom.

And there is Camillo's charming description of Perdita blushing,

He tells her something
That makes her blood look out.
Good sooth, she is
The queen of curds and cream.
The Winter's Tale, Act IV, Scene 3

TO MAKE IPOCRAS WITH RED WINE

Take a gallon of wine, three ounces of cinamon, two ounces of slic't ginger, a quarter of an ounce of cloves, an ounce of mace, twenty corns of pepper, an ounce of nutmegs, three pound of sugar, and two quarts of cream.

Robert May, *The Accomplisht Cook*

THE WORKING VERSION:

1 fifth (⅘ quart) of claret	1 large piece of whole mace
1 cup sugar	½ nutmeg, cut up
5 cloves	½ stick of cinnamon
5 peppercorns, lightly bruised	1 cup light cream

Pour the wine into a pitcher. Add the sugar, stir until dissolved, and add the spices. Pour the mixture into a quart jar, cover the jar with a piece of plastic, and screw the lid on.

Set the bottle in a cool place, but do not refrigerate, for twenty-four hours or longer. Half an hour before serving, strain the ipocras through a clean white cloth into a pitcher, stir in the cream and serve.

The spices used for ipocras varied very little; some recipes also included a sprig of rosemary, and William Rabisha used rose water in one of his recipes for red-wine ipocras. Most recipes omitted the cream.

"Here's that which is too weak to be a sinner, Honest water, which ne'er left man i' the mire," says Apemantus, in *Timon of Athens* (Act I, Scene 2). Water may have been honest, but in most places—except for clear spring water—it was not safe to drink. Only the poorest drank it, and not by choice. "When the butt [of the beer keg] is out, we will drink water; not a drop before," says Stephano, in *The Tempest* (Act III, Scene 2). Othello is harsher: "She was false as water," he replies to Emilia, who is defending Desdemona's honor against his accusations (*Othello*, Act V, Scene 2).

Dietaries all warned against drinking water, although they recognized its need in brewing and cooking. Cold water, said William Vaughan, in *Directions for Health*, "has no nourishment in it, yet being accommodated with other things, it serves to comfort Nature, eyther for brothes, suppings, Beere, Ale, or Ptisans [tisanes or infusions of herbs]." It was most healthful in summer, he said, "yet notwithstanding, seldome to be drunke: But if at any time you be compelled to drinke it see first that you seethe [boil] your water gently, for by seething, the grosse substance of it is taken away. Some use to try [test] water by putting a cleane Napkin in it, and if any spot appeare upon the same, then they suspect the goodness of the water."

Rain water was sometimes used for preserving fruits. *The Treasurie of commodious Conceits, & hidden Secrets,* compiled by John Partridge, recommends rain water in its recipe for "Plummes condict [preserved] in Syrarope [syrup]."

Most country houses had wells, and a few of the wealthier families had well water piped into their houses. The wealthy in some sections of London also had water piped into their homes from the public water conduits. But most families had to fetch their water from the public conduits, or have their servants fetch it, or buy it from street vendors.

ON WINES

Ale and beer were the usual drinks in Shakespeare's England, as they still are, and I shall speak of them in the next chapter. But first let us look at wine, to which Shakespeare's most flamboyant drinker beckons us: "If I had a thousand sons, the first human principle I would teach them should be, to forswear thin potations and to addict themselves to sack" (Falstaff in *Henry IV, Part II*, Act IV, Scene 3).

Almost all wine was imported, and expensive enough to be out of the range of the average Englishman's purse. But in wealthy homes and in inns and taverns a good deal of wine was consumed, and in increasing amounts as the sixteenth century went on. Upper-class homes usually had well-stocked wine cellars. Some people went to a nearby inn or tavern after dinner to drink wine, or sent there for wine to serve at home. "Gentlemen and citizens [well-to-do people not of the nobility] or the gentry garrawse [carouse] only in wine," said Fynes Moryson, in his *Itinerary*, the interesting account of his travels in England and on the Continent early in the seventeenth century.

Wealthy families often bought a year's supply of wines at one time, and filled in with more if they did some extraordinary entertaining. In the Earl of Rutland's home, for example, a year's supply was normally 6½ to 7 tuns of wine—a tun was 252 gallons. The great houses of Shakespeare's England needed large reserves of wine for the kind of entertaining they did. The most lavish entertaining, of course, came when a country house received Elizabeth or James I on one of their "progresses" through the realm. When Queen Elizabeth visited Lord North at Kirtlinge in 1577, six hogsheads—a hogshead was 54 gallons—of claret, one hogshead of white wine, and 20 gallons of sack were drunk.

The members of the Court of the Star Chamber were provided with their dinners, at royal expense, when the court was in session, and considerable amounts of wine were purchased to assuage their thirsts. For example, for the fifteen dinners served them during the Michaelmas term of 1590, fifty-five gallons of sack, ten gallons of muscadine, ten gallons of malmsey, twenty gallons

Earthenware wine bottle and drinking cup (*16th century*)

of old Rhenish, and ten gallons of new Rhenish, all of the best quality, were purchased. Although the sweet, dessert-type wines were usually purchased by the gallon, the wine cellar for the court's use was kept stocked with claret and the more ordinary white wines, which were bought by the barrel.

Even in the Tower of London, when Henry Percy, earl of Northumberland, was living there as James I's prisoner—in surprising comfort, although at his own expense—that powerful magnate had considerable supplies of wine. For one week in 1607, the clerk of his kitchen listed the purchase of thirteen gallons of claret and two gallons of Canary wine.

Not all wealthy families were wine-drinkers, however, and no expenditures for wine appear in the (published) accounts of Sir William Fairfax's household in Yorkshire. The Shuttleworths, an old landed gentry family in Lancashire, purchased very modest amounts of wine. In 1610, when the family was preparing for a wedding, they did buy claret, sack, Malaga, and white wines, but in 1619 the accounts listed purchases of only eight gallons of claret, three quarts of white wine, five pints of Canary, and three quarts of sherry—modest amounts indeed, especially considering that some of the wines purchased were for use by the cook.

Wine as well as ale had been used in cooking at least since medieval days. All the cookbooks of the Elizabethan and Jacobean periods contained many recipes for dishes made with wine or ale. The household accounts of William More of Losely note purchases of "wine to make a gallantine [sauce] for the red deer," a pottle [two quarts] of white wine, and a quart of claret for the cooks. The Shuttleworth accounts include a payment for "white wine to boil a capon." Wine jellies were fancied in the duchess of Suffolk's household, where the 1561 accounts include payment of twenty pence for "5 quarts of claret wine to make jelly." The Star Chamber Court kitchen accounts include expenditures for "Malmesey and White wine . . . for boiling of salads, tarts, and broths."

English soil and climate were not considered suitable for wine-grape growing, and little wine was produced in England in Shakespeare's day. William Harrison insisted, however, that the problem was not the soil but the unwillingness of the farmers to care for vineyards. Some wines had been produced in medieval days, but, as a chancellor to Henry II put it, they had to be drunk "with closed eyes and tense jaws." The wines that were produced in England continued to be of poor quality.

Writing in 1577, Harrison estimated that England imported between 20,000 and 30,000 tuns of wine a year—between 5 and 7½ million gallons. His estimates have been supported by later researchers. There were, however, great problems with imported wine. Little was known about how wines should be handled in shipping, and they frequently were spoiled or spoiling when they arrived. Most wines did not keep beyond the year in which they were produced. Nor was wine yet identified by vineyard or even wine-growing village, but only by region. The most popular wine of the time, that from the Bordeaux region of France, was generally called Gascon, or wine of Gascony. The day of vintage wines was still centuries away.

Harrison gives an indication of the large variety of wines that the English imported. There were what he called "small weak wines," such as "claret, white, red, French, etc., which amount to fifty-six sorts," and "thirty kinds of Italian, Grecian, Spanish, Canarian, etc., whereof vernage, cute, piment, raspis, muscatel, rumney, bastard, tyre, osey, caprike, clary, and malmsey are not least of all accounted because of their strength and valure [value]." Cute was new wine boiled down, piment was wine mixed with honey and spices, and clary was similar to piment. Bastard was a Spanish, or in some cases a Portuguese, wine that had been sweetened, but the term might be applied to any wine that had been sweetened. Bastards were called that, said Gervase Markham, because "they are oftentimes adulterated and fortified with honey." Rumney, or romney, was originally wine from Rumania. The rest were sweet dessert-type wines, of which malmsey, the best known, had become popular in England in the fourteenth century. Raspis was raspberry wine. The English liked fruit wines and some made them in their own households.

Sugar was frequently added to wine when it was found too sour to the taste. This custom, Fynes Moryson noted, "I never observed in any other place or Kingdome. . . . Because the taste of the English is thus delighted with sweetnesse, the Wines in Tavernes (for I speake not of Merchants or Gentlemens Cellars) are commonly the same." Had he been able to see the household accounts of merchants and gentlemen, he would have found that they too liked their wines sweet. "Sugar for wine" was a common item in their household accounts. Falstaff spoke for many of the English, at least those who could afford sack (sherry), when he told Prince Hal (*Henry IV, Part I,* Act II, Scene 4), "If sack and sugar be a fault, God help the wicked."

If sugar was thought necessary to bring out the best in wine, it also had the approval of the dietaries. William Vaughan, like most of the dietary writers, discussed wine in a good deal of detail. Of sack he said, "being drunke before Supper with store of Sugar, it provoketh appetite, comforteth the spirits marvellously. . . . White-wine drunk in the morning fasting with sugar cleanseth the lungs."

The first book in English devoted entirely to wines was William Turner's *A new Boke of the natures and properties of all Wines that are commonlye used here in England,* published in 1568. Turner wrote from a physician's point of view. His intent, he declares, is to inform his readers which wines are best for particular purposes. The outcome, however, is largely an advocacy of white wines. He speaks poorly of red wines and takes issue with those physicians who recommend such "heavy wines as Sacke, Malmesey, Muscadell, Clared [claret], French and Gascone wine." Though these are among the kinds preferred in England, he says, "red wines breed the stone [gallstones or kidney stones] more than whyte Rhennish and whyte French Wines doe." He quotes Galen, the renowned Greek doctor of the second century A.D., as authority that only very light wines should be drunk by those who are subject to headaches.

Wine which is neither very old nor very new is best, Turner advises, "For the olde doe heate to much, and the new Wines . . . heat nothing at all, so farre are they from helping of men to digest their meates [food], that they are very hardly digested themselves, and of times they hang and abide still in a mans stomacke, even as water." Old wines taste better and are sweeter, he admits, but "they hurt the sinews, and other instruments of the senses." Still, he adds, if a man is in good health and dilutes these wines with a little water, they too may be taken without harm.

Claret, which Harrison put in the category of "small or weak wines," had been drunk in England since the days—four centuries before Shakespeare's birth—when Henry II's marriage to Eleanor of Aquitaine added that vast rich region of southwestern France, which included Gascony and Bordeaux, to the realm of the English kings. They owned vineyards in the region and favored the import of wines made from their grapes. As a result, not only did the area have the greatest wine trade of the Middle Ages, but its vintners had a near-monopoly on the English wine trade until Henry VI, in the middle of the fifteenth century, lost all his French possessions except the city of Calais. During those centuries the English acquired a taste for the light red and white wines of the area. Prices rose after the loss of Bordeaux, and the character of the wine trade changed with the expulsion of the English, but they continued to prefer Bordeaux wines.

On a few great occasions, claret actually flowed instead of water from one of the London conduits. When the young Henry VI returned from his ill-fated coronation as king of France in Paris in 1431, the pageantry of rejoicing in London included three maidens, representing Mercy, Grace, and Pity, who drew claret from the conduit in Cheapside free for all comers. When James I's coronation, in Shakespeare's own lifetime, was celebrated in 1604, a London water conduit ran all day with claret. James had ascended the throne the year before, on Elizabeth's death, but the festivities had been curtailed then because the plague was again ravaging London.

Claret has come to mean red wines of the Bordeaux region, but at one time it referred to all Bordeaux wines, white and red, in England. The experts disagree about exactly which wines were designated claret in the Middle Ages, and there are conflicting usages in Shakespeare's day. Sometimes it seems to be a mixture of red with white wine, which produced a light red wine. Household accounts list purchases of claret and of red wines as separate items. William Turner discusses two kinds of red: a red wine that is "commonly called Claret wyne" in England, and a "blacke" that is "called commonlye . . . red wine." The latter was heavier-bodied and stronger than claret, probably close to what we know today as red Burgundy.

Dietaries were cautious in their discussions of claret. "Claret-wine being moderately drunke," said William Vaughan, "forceth the soule to partake with the body, so that both of them together, being full of animal spirits, might joyne in one pleasing sound, for the glorifying of their Soveraigne Benefactor. . . . Being moderately drunke, I meane a draught thereof now and then at meales, in colde weather doth fortifie the spirits. . . . But in Summer time, especially towards the evening, it must be spared of hot stomackes, and of such as be subject to the Gout." In December it was best to eat more and drink less, "but now and then drinke off a cup of good Claret-wine with a roasted apple in it. For the body hath need to be refreshed and cherished with such comfortable allurements." Englishmen who could afford to drink wine may or may not have read Vaughan's advice, but a good deal of claret refreshed English stomachs; perhaps three-quarters of the wine England imported in the latter half of the sixteenth century was called claret.

Sack, or sherry, was first imported into England during Henry VIII's reign, and it was the most fashionable wine drunk during Elizabeth's and James I's reigns. Sherry was a strong white wine, blended with the grapes used for sweet wines in order to meet English tastes. The most prized came from the Jerez district of Andalusia in southern Spain and from the Spanish-owned Canary

Islands. Less prized sherries came from Portugal. The sixteenth-century English pronounciation of Jerez has given us the name "sherry," although until after Shakespeare's death the drink was called "sack" or "sherris sack."

Drunk before meals as an aperitif, with meals, and after meals, in homes and taverns, sack was a favorite of writers, and it inspired dithyrambs of praise from poets. The cup of "rich Canary wine" that made Ben Jonson lyrical was probably the strong full-bodied Canary sack. "The drink of Gods and Angels," Robert Herrick called it. It is Falstaff's favorite and probably the favorite of Shakespeare, who mentions sack forty-four times and Canary wine seven times in the plays, mentioning also its capacity to addle the wits. In *The Merry Wives of Windsor* (Act II, Scene 2), Mistress Quickly plays on Falstaff's amorous gullibility: "You have brought her [Mistress Ford] into such a canaries as 'tis wonderful."

John Taylor, called the "Water Poet" because he earned a living ferrying passengers across the Thames, found sack too strong a drink for him: "for where other wines have scarce strength to make me drunke . . . Sack hath the power to make me mad." Drinking no sack, he says, may be the reason his verses lack vigor. But he offers a double-edged tribute to the virtues of sack for less talented writers: "Is any man so . . . shortwinded, or that his voice failes him, let him drink *Sacke,* it shall make him capable to vent words and speake beyond measures. . . . Sack enables our moderne writers, to versify most ingeniously, without much cudgelling their headpieces . . . whereby they get some portion of credit, a great proportion of windy applause but little money."

Herbs and spices were added to wines to make various cordials, of which the best known was ipocras. And wine was sometimes mixed with ale as a drink; a "gossip's cup" was made of one pint of ipocras to two quarts of ale. Hot wines were also enjoyed and described usually as "burnt" wine. Master Ford, in *The Merry Wives of Windsor* (Act II, Scene 1), offers his tavern keeper a "pottle [two quarts] of burnt sack" if he will introduce him, under an assumed name, to Falstaff. Hot eggnogs, called possets, were made with claret and white wines as well as with sack, and sometimes with ale. Cream, sugar, spices, and eggs were beaten together and cooked until thickened; then the wine was stirred in. Possets, said to be eaten rather than drunk, were not only cheering but they were also thought helpful in alleviating minor discomforts or illness. Lady Anne Clifford, the wife of the earl of Dorset, wrote in her diary on March 9, 1617, "I was not well at night so I ate a posset and went to bed."

To physicians and dietary writers, "hot" as applied to wine did not mean the temperature at which it was drunk but the element to which it belonged, fire. As there were different degrees of fire or heat, some wines were "hotter" than others. Hot wines were those of greater alcoholic content and were sweeter than "small" wines. Claret and Rhenish were small wines; sherry, muscatel, malmsey (a kind of madeira, sweet and brown colored), bastard, and the sweet wines from Greece, the Near East, and Corsica were among the hot wines. William Harrison wrote, "We also use our wines by degrees, so that the hottest cometh last to the table."

Medical men warned against drinking "hot" wines in quantity and suggested that it would be prudent to mix them with water. "All wine," said Dr. Boorde, "is full of fumosyte [vapors or fumes that went to the head and confused the brain], it is good, therefore to alay it with water." Hot wines were especially bad for choleric people, whose temperaments were already over-heated, the dietaries admonished. Thomas Elyot, in *The Castle of Health*, warned that deep red and sweet wines caused melancholia and were "hurtfull to the eyes." Boorde recommended eating some food before taking any wine, and drinking light wines such as claret and Rhenish with meals. "Sweet and heavy wines made a man fat," he said, and only old men might drink "hyghe wynes at theyr pleasure." He also objected to any wine-drinking by young children, especially girls. "In hyghe Almayne [southern Germany]," he wrote, girls were supposed to drink only water before they were married. If a girl drank wine before that, she was "common."

The most prestigious of the previously mentioned spiced wines was ipocras. (The recipe for red ipocras is on page 47, for white ipocras on page 409.) Like so many other names in this age of unstandardized spelling, it was spelled in different ways, among them, hypocras, ipocrasse, and hipocras. Its name came from the conical bag through which the wine was filtered, presumably because the bag resembled the sleeves of the gown worn by the Greek "father of medicine," Hippocrates.

Ipocras was the ceremonial wine used at royal coronations. In

Silver-gilt wine cup (1617)

The Progresses and Public Processions of Queen Elizabeth, John Nichols describes its role in her coronation. "At the serving up of the wafers the Lord Mayor of London went to the cupboorde, and filling a cup of gold with ipocrasse, bare it to the Queene, and kneeling before her, tooke the assaie [assayed or tasted of it to make sure that it was not poisoned], and she receiving it of him, drinking of it, gave the cup with the cover unto the Lord Maior for his fee."

It was with ipocras also that the lord mayor of London, in 1583, drank to a newly elected sheriff of the city and of Middlesex county. Nichols, who also described this event, wrote that two feasts were held simultaneously—one at the Haberdashers Hall, where the lord mayor, the recorder, and some of the alderman were dining, a second at the Grocers Hall, where Alderman Massam and others were dining. "After the second course was served at the Haberdashers Hall, the Lord Mayor took the great standing cup of the Haberdashers, being full of hypocrasse; and silence being commanded through all the tables, all men being bareheaded, my Lord openly, with a convenient loud voice, used these words: 'Mr. Recorder of London, and you my good brethren, the Aldermen, bear witness that I drink unto Mr. Alderman Massam, as Sheriff of London and Middlesex, from Michaelmas next coming, for one whole yeare.' The mayor's nomination having been approved by all there, the Sword-bearer in haste went to the Grocers' feast where Alderman Massam was at dinner, and did openly declare the words my Lord Mayor had used."

Spoiled and spoiling wines were a continuing problem for the butlers, the servants in charge of the care and distribution of alcoholic drinks in the household [the word "butler" is derived from the casks or butts in which wine, ale, and beer were stored], and for the cooks, who needed good wine for their dishes. Numerous suggestions for preventing wine from spoiling, as well as reviving wines that were spoiled or about to spoil, were offered by dietaries and occasionally by cookbooks. William Vaughan's suggestion for wine that had begun to ferment ("reboyleth") was to put a piece of cheese into the barrel "or else put a bunch of Pennyroyall, Organy [oregano], or Calamint, about the hole at which the new wine commeth forth; but if your wine be new, and you will have it quickly purged, you must put halfe a pint of vinegar to every fifteen quarts of new wine."

Knowing how to choose wines was useful, but though some individuals no doubt had their particular ways of judging wines, few suggestions appear in cookbooks or dietaries. William Turner told his readers to be sure, when they purchased or drank Rhenish wine, that it was clear and light-bodied. Beyond that, his words comparing good with bad wine were doubtless acceptable in Elizabethan days, but they are too scatological for our tastes. Gervase Markham's advice on how to buy claret was to choose one that was "fair coloured, and bright as a Ruby, not deep as Amythyst . . . also let it be sweet as a Rose or a Violet, and in any case let it be short, for if it be long [syrupy or ropy] then in no case meddle with it." Muscadine, he said, "must be great, pleasant, strong, with a sweet scent and amber colour."

Adulteration of wines by vintners and innkeepers was common, though sale of wine, like that of beer and bread, was officially regulated. Wine was adulterated in numerous ways: lime was added to make it look brighter, honey to make it taste sweeter or cover up souring, and water might be added to make it go farther. Vintners, said Vaughan, "in these days are wont to juggle and sophistically to abuse Wine." To test whether the wine had been adulterated with honey, he recommended that a few drops of the wine be poured "upon a hot plate of yron, and the wine being resolved [separated], the honey will remain and thicken." If the wine was suspected of being watered, he said, "you shall discerne the same by putting a Peare into it; for if the Peare swimme upon the face of the wine, and sinke not to the bottom, then it is perfect . . . but if it sinke to the bottome, water without doubt is added unto it."

Shakespeare was well aware of the ways in which wine could be adulterated. In *Henry IV, Part I* (Act II, Scene 4), Falstaff, having called for "a cup of sack" at his favorite tavern, tastes it and denounces the serving boy, "You rogue, here's lime in this sack too!"

"In old time," said William Harrison, "the best wine was called *theologicum,* because it was had from the clergy and religious men, unto whose houses many of the laity would often send for bottles filled with the same, being sure that they would neither drink nor be served of the worst, or such as was anyways mingled or brewed by the vintner."

Drinking glasses were becoming chic. "As for drink," said Harrison, "it is usually filled in pots, goblets, bowls of silver in noblemen's houses, also in fine Venice glasses of all forms." Glasses make a shining appearance in the letters of John Chamberlain, who has been called the most interesting letter-writer of the early seventeenth century. To the sister of his friend Dudley Carleton, who is with him on his diplomatic mission in Venice, he writes in 1615, "I cannot follow your advice to sell the glasses you sent me, for I have not one left within three days after they came . . . having disposed of them all so soon as might be. . . . I brought the Lady Winwood and the Lady Fanshawe to see in one room and in one view above eight hundred dozen of glasses that came all in the same ship with mine, whereby you may see that this town [London] is thoroughly furnished of that commodity, and not great estimation to be made of them unless they be somewhat extraordinary and rare." Wine bottles, however, were still being made of stoneware. Some fine glass was being produced in England by Venetian glass-blowers, who had been induced to bring their skills to England by Queen Elizabeth, but most English glassware was of inferior quality.

In Shakespeare's plays, glasses usually meant mirrors, but there are also several references to drinking glasses. In *Henry IV, Part II* (Act II, Scene 1), Falstaff says exuberantly, "Glasses, glasses, is the only drinking." In *Henry VIII* (Act I, Scene 1), Buckingham denounces the recent treaty with France as one "that swallow'd so much treasure, and like a glass did break i' the rinsing."

Droeshout portrait of William Shakespeare, from the First Folio of the plays (1623)

A Dinner to Honor Mistress Shakespeare, Anne Hathaway

Go, sirrah, trudge about
Through fair Verona; find those persons out
Whose names are written there, and to them say,
My house and welcome on their pleasure stay.
Romeo and Juliet, Act I, Scene 2 (*Capulet*)

SHERRY

Nor other satisfaction do I crave,
But only, with your patience, that we may
Taste of your wine.
Henry VI, Part I, Act II, Scene 3 (*Talbot*)

WHITE RADISHES

If I fought not with fifty of them, I
am a bunch of radish.
Henry IV, Part I, Act II, Scene 4 (*Falstaff*)

STEWED COCKLES

'How should I your true love know
From another one?
By his cockle hat and staff,
And his sandal shoon.'
Hamlet, Act IV, Scene 5 (*Ophelia*)

ONION POTTAGE

Mine eyes smell onions; I shall weep anon.
All's Well That Ends Well, Act V, Scene 3 (Lafeu)

BROOK TROUT IN ORANGE
AND WINE SAUCE

Here comes the trout that must be caught with tickling.
Twelfth Night, Act II, Scene 5 (Maria)

A FILLET OF BEEF IN CLARET SAUCE

O! my sweet beef, I must still be good angel to thee.
Henry IV, Part I, Act III, Scene 3 (Prince Hal)

OLIVES OF VEAL

'Veal,' quoth the Dutchman. Is not 'veal' a calf?
Love's Labour's Lost, Act V, Scene 2 (Katharine)

A VENISON PIE

I'll be a park, and thou shalt be my deer.
Venus and Adonis, Line 231 (Venus)

SPINACH FRITTERS

'Seese' and 'patter'! have I lived to stand at
the taunt of one that makes fritters of English?
The Merry Wives of Windsor, Act V, Scene 5 (Falstaff)

A COMPOUND SALAD

I remember one said there were no sallets in the
lines to make the matter savoury.
Hamlet, Act II, Scene 2 (Hamlet)

FINE CHEATE BREAD

O monstrous! but one half-pennyworth of bread to
this intolerable deal of sack!
Henry IV, Part I, Act II, Scene 4 (Prince Hal)

RHINE AND CLARET WINES

I pray you, do not fall in love with me,
For I am falser than vows made in wine.
As You Like It, Act III, Scene 5 (Rosalind)

JOHN MURRELL'S QUINCE PIE

I will get Peter Quince to write a ballad of
this dream.
A Midsummer-Night's Dream, Act IV, Scene 1 (*Bottom*)

SIR KENELME DIGBIE'S CAKE

He that will have a cake out of the wheat
must tarry the grinding.
Troilus and Cressida, Act I, Scene 1 (*Pandarus*)

CHEDDAR CHEESE

Much like a cheese, consumes itself to the very paring.
All's Well That Ends Well, Act I, Scene 1 (*Parolles*)

APPLES

Nay, you shall see mine orchard, where, in an arbour,
we will eat a last year's pippin of my own graffing.
Henry IV, Part II, Act V, Scene 3 (*Shallow*)

Now we sit to chat as well as eat.
The Taming of the Shrew, Act V, Scene 2 (*Lucentio*)

Gervase Markham places radishes among the "simple salads" and says they may be eaten uncooked with or without a dressing of oil, vinegar, and sugar. William Vaughan insists that it is better "to seethe [boil] Radish, and to put oyle, vinegar, and sugar, or honey unto it rather than to eat it raw."

Gervase Markham calls radishes "a sauce for cloyed stomachs, as are Capers, Olives and Cucumbers." If there was no kitchen garden to supply radishes, they could be had from the street peddlers, who walked up and down calling:

> White raddish, white young lettis,
>
> . . . .
> You hear me cry, come mistris buy,
> To make my burden light.

TO STEW COCKLES BEING
TAKEN OUT OF THE SHELLS

Wash them well with vinegar, broil or broth them before you take them out of the shells, then put them in a dish with a little claret, vinegar, a handful of capers, mace, pepper, a little grated bread, minced tyme, salt, and the yolks of two or three hard eggs minced, stew all together till you think them enough; then put in a good piece of butter, shake them well together, heat the dish, rub it with a clove of garlick, and put two or three toasts of white bread in the bottom, laying the meat on them.

Robert May, *The Accomplisht Cook*

THE WORKING VERSION:

½ pint shelled cockles
½ cup claret
2 tablespoons red wine vinegar
1 garlic bud, peeled
½ teaspoon capers
½ teaspoon mace
⅛ teaspoon salt
⅛ teaspoon pepper
¼ teaspoon thyme
2 hard-boiled egg yolks, mashed
2 teaspoons grated bread crumbs
2 tablespoons butter
2 slices hot buttered toast, quartered

If you use fresh cockles, which may be difficult to find, scrub the shells well in cold water, and steam them in one cup of boiling water, to which one tablespoon of vinegar has been added, until the shells open. Remove the cockles from the shells and set them aside, covered, until needed. If you use canned cockles, as I did, rinse them in a sieve under cold water to remove the brine, and set them aside, covered.

In a small saucepan simmer the claret, wine vinegar, garlic, capers, mace, salt, pepper, and thyme for ten minutes. Remove the garlic and add the mashed egg yolks, bread crumbs, and butter, and stir until the butter melts. Add the cockles and simmer for two minutes.

Arrange the quarters of toast in a warmed serving dish, spoon the cockles and the sauce over them, and serve immediately.

Cockles are a member of the clam family, and if you cannot find them, substitute the smallest clams available. The English firm of Severnside Foods, Bristol, markets the cockles in brine, which is what I used. I found them on the "gourmet shelf" of one of the local chain grocery stores, so they should be available in shops handling gourmet foods under other brand names as well.

In Shakespeare's day live cockles were hawked through the streets by fishwives. Not only did housewives listen to the calls of "new, new cockles!" and "cockles nye," but composers found the street vendors' cries interesting and often incorporated them into songs.

ONION POTTAGE

Fry good store of slic't onions, then have a pipkin of boiling liquor over the fire, when the liquor boils put in the fryed onions, butter and all, with pepper and salt: being well stewed together, serve in on sops of French bread.

Robert May, *The Accomplisht Cook*

THE WORKING VERSION:

3 tablespoons butter
½ pound onions, peeled and sliced ¼ inch thick
4 cups beef broth, fresh or canned*

1 teaspoon salt
⅛ teaspoon pepper
4 slices French bread, toasted**

* A good fresh beef broth can be made in a pressure cooker in less than an hour: to one quart of water add 1½ pounds chuck, a large onion, a large carrot scrubbed clean, one bay leaf, and four large sprigs parsley. Cook at fifteen pounds pressure for forty-five minutes; remove the cooker from the heat but do not open it until the pressure has gone down. Strain the broth and skim off the fat. (For another fresh broth recipe, see page 143.)

** The recipe for Robert May's French bread is on page 111, if you would like to use the French bread he doubtless used for this recipe.

Melt the butter in a large skillet. Add the sliced onions and sauté them for about ten minutes, or until they are golden brown, stirring them occasionally to prevent their burning.

Bring the broth to a boil, add it to the onions, and cook over medium heat for ten minutes. If you are using fresh, homemade broth, add the salt and pepper—taste the broth and add more seasoning if needed. If you use canned broth, taste before seasoning and add the salt and pepper only if needed.

Put the toasted bread in individual soup bowls. Pour the broth and onions over it and serve immediately.

Pottage could be anything from a thin broth to a thick stew. It was served at both dinner and supper as part of the first course, or as the entire meal in modest homes or for servants. Grains, vegetables, meat, fish, and poultry were all used in making pottage, sometimes with the addition of dried prunes, raisins, or currants. Among the poor, pottage was most likely to be made of some kind of grain.

Boiling was the most common and easiest method of cooking. In well-equipped households a large kettle was always simmering with beef or mutton. Broth from the kettle was thus available for making soups, stews, and sauces. It was also used as the cooking liquid for fowl and other meats; even game birds were boiled. The great kettles for cooking large pieces of meat or whole small animals such as young pigs were sometimes kept boiling all through the night.

TO STEW TROUT

Take the trout . . . and boil it whole in a stew-pan with white-wine, put to it also some whole cloves, large mace, slic't ginger, a bay leaf or two, a bundle of sweet herbs well and hard bound up, some whole pepper, salt, some butter and vinegar, and an orange in halves; stew all together, and being well stewed, dish them in a clean scowred dish with carved sippets, lay on the spices and slic't lemon, and run it over with beaten butter, and some of the gravy it was stewed in.

Robert May, *The Accomplisht Cook*

THE WORKING VERSION:

4 brook trout, each 10 to
   12 inches long
1 medium orange
1 cup white wine
½ cup white wine vinegar
4 tablespoons butter
2½ teaspoons salt
12 peppercorns
1 tablespoon minced chives

¼ teaspoon thyme
2 bay leaves
2 cloves
1 large piece whole mace
1 lemon, sliced thin and
   seeded
4 slices hot buttered toast,
   cut into triangles

Eviscerate and scale the trout if they are not already cleaned, and wash them under cold running water. Place the fish side by side in a baking dish just large enough to hold them.

With a sharp knife sliver off the outer rind (zest) of the orange and set aside. Cut the orange in half, remove the meat, and dice it. Scatter the orange meat over the top of the trout.

In a small saucepan bring the orange zest, wine, wine vinegar, butter, salt, peppercorns, herbs, and spices to a boil. Lower the heat and simmer, covered, for fifteen minutes. Pour the hot broth through a strainer directly onto the trout. Cover the pan with aluminum foil and bake at 400° for twelve to fifteen minutes—when you can feel the flakes separate with a slight pressure of your fingers, the fish is done.

Arrange the trout on a warmed serving dish and garnish with alternate slices of lemon and toast. Pour half the sauce over the fish and serve the remaining sauce separately.

Most estates had artificial ponds called stews or stew ponds, which were kept stocked with young fresh-water fish of various kinds. Stock supplies could be purchased from fish hatcheries maintained for this purpose. But friends often exchanged varieties of young fishes. To keep the water in the stew ponds sweet, to repair the ponds, or to build new ones, "pond-makers" and "pond-casters" were employed. Carp ponds were probably the most successful stew ponds since warm and quiet water suits the carp's feeding habits.

To fill all family needs for fish some still had to be purchased, and it was important to know who were the best fishermen in the area for they were the source of fresh fish. This was the responsibility of the "acater" who purchased the food supplies not produced on the estate. He was one of the most important servants in the household.

TO STEW FILLETS OF BEEFE

Take a rawe fillet of beefe and cut it in thin slices half as broad as your hand and fry them till they bee halfe fried in a frying-panne with sweet butter uppon each side with a soaft fire, then powre them into a dish or pipkin putting in a pint of claret-wine, a faggot of sweet herbes, and two or three blades of whole mace, a little salt, the meate of a Lemon cut in slices, then stewe these all together very softly for the space of two or three houres till it be halfe boyled away, then dish it upon sippets and throwe salt upon it, and serve it to the table hot.

John Murrell, *A Booke of Cookerie*

THE WORKING VERSION:

1 ¼ pounds tenderloin steak
2 tablespoons butter
¼ lemon
¾ cup claret
2 tablespoons minced parsley
2 tablespoons minced chives
1 teaspoon salt
1 bay leaf
⅛ teaspoon mace
1 egg yolk
4 slices hot buttered toast, cut into triangles

Slice the meat into ¼-inch-thick slices, or ask your butcher to do this. Melt the butter in a large skillet, add the slices of meat and brown them lightly on each side over moderate heat.

Halve the lemon, remove and dice its meat, and add this along with all the remaining ingredients except the egg yolk and toast to the skillet. Cover, lower the heat to simmer, and cook until the beef is tender—from eight to ten minutes.

Beat two tablespoons of the sauce into the egg yolk, return the mixture to the skillet, and stir gently until it begins to thicken.

Put the toast into a heated serving dish, arrange the meat over it, and pour the sauce over the meat. Serve immediately.

Except for the finest cuts, such as the tenderloin and the saddle roasts, beef was considered "gross" meat and not usually served at important feasts. But it was exceedingly popular.

Shakespeare makes frequent use of the well-known English fondness for beef. Before the battle of Agincourt in *Henry V* (Act III, Scene 7), the duke of Orleans and the constable of France are discussing the English invaders. "Give them great meals of beef and iron and steel, they will eat like wolves and fight like devils," says the constable. So they fought at Agincourt, though they were out of beef.

TO ROAST OLIVES OF VEAL

You shall take a legg of Veal, and cut the flesh from the bones, and cut it into thinn long slices: then take sweet herbs, and the white part of Scallions, and chop them well together with the yolks of eggs, then role it up within the slices of Veal, and so spit them and roast them: Then boyle Verjuice, Butter, Sugar, Cinnamon, Currants and sweet herbs together, and being seasoned with a little salt, serve the Olives up upon the Sawce with salt cast over them.

Gervase Markham, *The English Hus-wife*

THE WORKING VERSION:

1 pound veal round steak, sliced ½ inch thick
2 hard-boiled egg yolks
¼ cup minced parsley
3 scallions, minced, white part only
½ teaspoon thyme
1 teaspoon salt
3 tablespoons butter

THE SAUCE
1 cup white wine vinegar
1 tablespoon butter
1 tablespoon currants, parboiled
1 teaspoon brown sugar
¼ teaspoon rosemary
¼ teaspoon cinnamon

Remove bone and fat from the veal and cut it into approximately three- by four-inch pieces. Flatten the pieces with the side of a cleaver or a meat tenderizer. Make a paste of the egg yolks, parsley, scallions, thyme, and salt. Divide the paste into as many parts as you have pieces of meat, and spread the paste evenly over them. Roll up each piece and secure it with a toothpick or tie it with heavy white thread.

Melt the butter in a heavy casserole or skillet. Lay the veal rolls side by side in the pan and brown them lightly on all sides. Lower the heat to simmer, cover the pan, and cook from twelve to fifteen minutes—check after twelve minutes, for overcooking toughens the veal.

To make the sauce, combine all the ingredients and bring them to a boil in a small saucepan. Lower the heat to simmer and cook for ten minutes. Pour the sauce over the veal rolls and cook two minutes longer. Serve immediately.

Verjuice was vinegar made from either crab apples or sour grapes. If you have white wine but no wine vinegar on hand, you can approximate white wine vinegar by mixing equal parts of wine and distilled vinegar.

Markham's recipe calls for roasting the "olives," which in his day meant broiling on a spit in front of a fire. But veal is somewhat dry, and broiling or grilling tends to dry out the meat rolls before they are fully cooked; sautéeing avoids this problem.

Today we know these little meat rolls mostly as veal birds. In Markham's day they were called by a number of different names. Robert May called them "Olines," while A. W., in *A Booke of Cookerie,* called them "Aloes." Other cookbook writers called them variously "olios," "Alows," and "Olavs." Beef, mutton, lamb, and fish were also used, and sometimes the rolls were arranged in a double-crust pie and baked. They must have been popular, for they appear in most of the cookbooks of the period.

The origin of the name is probably French. The earliest English recipe is from the fifteenth century and is called "Alows de Beef or de Moutoun," which is clearly from the French. Perhaps English cooks, having no French-language cookbooks to guide them, simply spelled the names they heard phonetically. Today in France these little meat rolls are often called *alouettes sans têtes,* which means "larks without heads."

TO BAKE RED DEARE

Take a hand full of time, and a hand full of rosemarie, a hand full of winter savorie, a hand full of bay leaves and a hand full of fennel, and when your liquor seeths that you perboyle your Venison in, put in your hearbes also and perboyle your venison untill it be halfe enoughe, then take it out and lay it upon a faire boorde that the water may runne out from it, then take a knife and pricke it full of holes, and while it is warme have a faire traye with vinegar therein, and so put your venison therein from morning until night, and ever nowe and then turne it upside downe, an then at night have your coffin [piecrust] ready, and this done season it with synamome, ginger, and nutmegges, pepper and salte, and when you have seasoned it, put it into your coffin, and put a good quantitie of sweete butter into it, and then put it into the Oven at night, when you goe to bedde, and in the morning drawe it forth, and put in a saucer full of vinegar into your pye at a hole above in the toppe of it, so that the vineger may runne into everie place of it, and then stop the whole againe and turne the bottome upward and so serve it in.

Thomas Dawson, *The good huswifes Jewell*

THE WORKING VERSION:

1½ pounds boned venison
  steak or backstrap
½ cup red wine vinegar
1½ teaspoons salt
¼ teaspoon pepper
¼ teaspoon savory
¼ teaspoon fennel
¼ teaspoon rosemary
¼ teaspoon thyme
⅛ teaspoon cinnamon
⅛ teaspoon nutmeg
⅛ teaspoon ginger

1 bay leaf
3 tablespoons butter, diced

THE PASTRY
2 cups sifted unbleached
  flour
1 teaspoon salt
¾ cup cold butter
½ cup clear beef broth,
  approximately
1 egg, separated

Remove any gristle from the venison. Make a marinade of the vinegar and all the seasonings, stir the meat around in it, then cover the bowl closely and marinate the venison in the refrigerator for at least six hours.

See page 31 for the basic method of mixing the pastry.

Sprinkle your work surface with flour and turn the ball of dough onto it. Toss the ball lightly between your hands until it has taken on enough flour to make it easy to handle, then roll the dough into a rectangle approximately twelve by sixteen inches.

Loosen the pastry by sliding a long, narrow steel spatula under it from the outside to the center of the pastry sheet on each side. Fit the pastry into a low-sided rectangular baking dish that can also be used for serving.

Drain the marinating liquid from the venison and reserve the marinade. Place the meat on the pastry and dot it with the butter. Bring the two short sides of the pastry up over the meat and brush their edges with egg white, then bring the two long sides up and pinch the edges to seal the pie.

Carefully turn the pie over in the baking dish. Brush the top with the remaining egg white and bake at 450° for twenty minutes, lower the heat to 350°, and bake for twenty-five minutes longer.

A few minutes before removing the pie from the oven, bring the marinade to a boil. Remove the pie from the oven and make a small hole in the top crust. Carefully pour the hot marinade through the hole, then shake the pie gently from side to side to distribute the marinade. Serve hot.

If you like a thicker sauce, beat an egg yolk into the hot marinade before pouring it into the pie.

This pie has a rich, tender crust because it is meant to be eaten immediately. Large venison pies, meant to last for many meals, would have been baked in thick, moist crusts that also served as storage containers.

Various liquids were used for making pastry for meat pies, although broth was not often specified. I found this pastry recipe in *A Proper newe Booke of Cokerye:* "Take the fattest of broathe of powdered [salt] beyfe, and yf you will have paest royall, take butter and yolkes of egges and so temper the flowre to make the paste." This little volume of only twenty-six pages was among the collection of books and manuscripts that Matthew

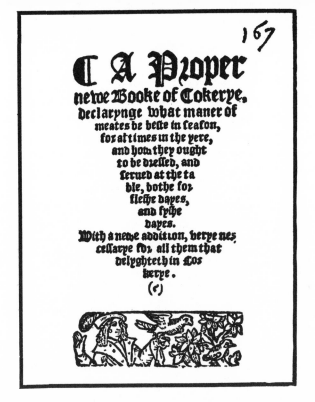

Title page of A Proper newe Booke of Cokerye (*Anonymous: 16th century*)

Parker, archbishop of Canterbury and master of Corpus Christi College, Cambridge, left to the college on his death in 1575. The copy was undated and the earliest known edition of the book is dated 1545.

Venison was not for ordinary people. Only upper-class families with forest land could lawfully enjoy it. In yet an earlier day, it was reserved for royalty and the nobility. But for centuries the poor poached on the animals of the great noble "parks" and deer forests, and of the royal forests until their enclosure. Some of the picturesque details from documents of the period appear in Alan Everitt's interesting chapter on farm laborers in *The Agrarian History of England and Wales, 1500–1640,* edited by Joan Thirsk. For example, a complaint from the papers of Henry VIII stated that in Hatfield Chase, on the border between Yorkshire and Lincolnshire, the poor "almost lived" off the illicit hunting of deer and rabbits.

Families with forest lands could, in Shakespeare's day, hunt deer at will and were often generous with gifts of venison to their friends. Gifts of a whole deer were most likely when a friend or relative was preparing for a wedding or for the entertainment of important visitors. More often a haunch of venison or venison pies or pasties were given. When Sir William Petre (Queen Elizabeth's secretary) was preparing for the wedding of his stepdaughter, Catherine Tyrell, his friends sent, among other gifts of food, "three bucks and one stag" to help feed the four hundred guests who had been invited.

FRITTORS OF SPINAGE

Take a good deal of Spinnage, and wash it cleane, and boyle it in faire water, and when it is boyled, put it in a Collender, and let it coole. Then wring all the water out of it as neere as ye can, lay it upon a board, and chop it with the back of a chopping knife verie smal, and put it in a platter, and put to it four whites of Egs, and two yolks, and the crums of halfe a manchet grated, and a litle Synamon & Ginger, and styre them well together with a spoon and take a frying pan and a dish of sweete [fresh] Butter in it, when it is molten put handsomely in your pan halfe a spoonefull of your stuffe, and so bestowe the rest after, fry them on a soft fyre, and turn them when time is, lay them in a platter and cast sugar on them.

John Partridge, *The good Huswifes Handmaide for the Kitchin*

THE WORKING VERSION:

1 pound fresh spinach	3 tablespoons grated bread
2 eggs	crumbs
½ teaspoon salt	4 tablespoons butter
⅛ teaspoon cinnamon	2 tablespoons brown sugar
⅛ teaspoon ginger	

Wash the spinach in cool water several times to remove any sand, and snap off the root ends of the leaves. Shake off as much water as you can and put the spinach into a saucepan or large skillet with a close-fitting lid. Cover the pot and cook over low heat only until the leaves wilt—about five minutes. Then drain and purée the spinach.

Add the eggs, salt, cinnamon, ginger, and bread crumbs to the puréed spinach and mix until blended. Cover and set aside for ½ hour to allow the mixture to become firm.

Preheat a griddle or large skillet. Melt the butter in it, and, when the butter sizzles, drop in heaping tablespoons of the spinach mixture spaced about two inches apart. Flatten them with the back of a spoon to make three- to four-inch patties. Brown the patties on one side, then turn and brown them on the other.

As they are baked put them into a heated serving dish and keep warm. Sprinkle with the sugar just before serving, or serve the sugar separately.

The spinach mixture can be made up to three days ahead of time and refrigerated until needed.

Robert May's recipe for spinach fritters includes currants and a little cream, although he says that the cream is optional.

Fritters were popular, easy to prepare, and useful as quick dishes for filling out a menu. This kind of fritter was also made with cooked carrots, beets, or other available vegetables.

The frying medium was rendered beef suet, lard, oil, or butter. Butter gave the best flavor and was more often used than any of the other fats. Elegant cooks like John Murrell thought nothing of calling for a gallon of butter for frying fritters, but it was not as extravagant then as it would be today.

Most recipes were for deep-fat-fried fritters. As is done today, pieces of fruit, vegetables, and sometimes meat were dipped in batter and fried. Then, as now, apple fritters were popular.

A COMPOUND SALAD

*Your compound Sallets, are all manner of wholesome Herbes
. . . as Lettice and many others mixed together, and then served
up to the Table with Vinegar, Sallet-Oyl, and Sugar.*

Gervase Markham, *The English Hus-wife*

THE WORKING VERSION:

4 large leaves of crisp leaf lettuce	4 tablespoons olive oil
4 large fresh spinach leaves	3 tablespoons red wine vinegar
4 large leaves of romaine or Boston lettuce	½ teaspoon brown sugar
	½ teaspoon salt

Wash the greens thoroughly in cold water. Shake off the surplus water and roll the greens in a clean towel or put them into a cloth bag and refrigerate until needed.

A few minutes before the salad is to be served, put the oil, vinegar, sugar, and salt into a salad bowl and beat until blended. Tear or cut the salad greens into fairly small pieces and drop them into the dressing. Toss until the greens are nicely coated. Serve immediately, for greens go limp very quickly.

Green salads helped to vary a diet that was weighty and often difficult to digest. After a long period of neglect, their freshness and crispness were again appreciated in Shakespeare's day.

English diet was becoming more varied, and vegetables were returning to the table as dishes of worth rather than as mere seasonings for pottages and stews. Englishmen had enjoyed eating vegetables at least since the days of the Romans, who brought vegetables and a taste for them from Italy. But by the fifteenth century they had, according to William Harrison, fallen into sad disfavor and were considered by all but the poor as "food more meet for hogs and savage beasts to feed upon than mankind. Whereas in my time," continued Harrison in his 1577 work, "their use is not only resumed among the poor commons [common people], I mean of melons, pompions, gourds [squash], cucumbers, radishes, skirrets, parsnips, carrots, cabbages, navews, turnips, and all kinds of salad herbs—but also fed upon as dainty dishes at the tables of delicate merchants, gentlemen, and the nobility, who make their provision yearly for new seeds out of strange countries."

Englishmen who were stationed abroad, or planning to travel on the Continent, were likely to receive requests from friends to look out for seeds for new and choice kinds of vegetables. John Chamberlain forwarded such a request from a mutual friend to Dudley Carleton in Venice; "I am to intreat a favor of you for Sir Henry Fanshawe, that you would inquire for the best and choisest sorts of salletts in those parts, and send him some seeds of them by the first opportunitie."

FINE CHEATE BREAD

To bake the best cheate bread, which is also simply of wheate onely, you shal after your meale is drest and boulted through a more course boulter [sifter] than was used for your manchets, and put also into a cleane tub, trough, or kimnell; take a sowre leaven, that is a peece of such like leaven saved from a former batch, and well fild with salt, and so laid up to sower, and this sowre leaven you shall breake into small peeces into warme water, and then straine [mix] it, which done make a deep hollow hole, as was before said, in the middest of your flower, and therein power your strained liquor, then with your hand mixe some part of the flower therewith till the liquor bee as thicke as pancake batter, then cover it all over with meale, and so let it stand all that night, the next morning stirre it, and all the rest of the meale wel together, and with a little more warme water, barme [yeast], and salt to season it with, bring it to a perfect leaven, stiffe, and firme, then kneade it, breake it, and tread it, as was beforesaid in the manchets, and so mould it up into reasonable bigge loves, and then bake it with an indifferent [average] good heat.

Gervase Markham, *The English Hus-wife*

THE WORKING VERSION:

1 cup sour cheate dough	THE SOURDOUGH
1½ cups warm water	½ cup warm water
2 cakes fresh yeast or 2	¼ teaspoon salt
tablespoons dry yeast	½ tablespoon dry yeast or
1 tablespoon salt	½ cake fresh yeast
1 cup whole-wheat flour	1 cup whole-wheat flour
4 cups unbleached flour	

Make the sourdough two days before you plan to make the cheate bread. Pour the water into a quart bowl. Add the salt and sprinkle or crumble the yeast into the water. When the yeast has softened and expanded, stir in the flour. Cover the bowl closely and set in a warm place or an unheated oven for two days. It will rise, fall, and then sour.

Pour the water for the bread into a large mixing bowl and crumble or sprinkle the yeast into it. When the yeast softens and expands, stir in the salt, sour dough, and the whole-wheat flour. Then stir in three cups of the unbleached flour, one cupful at a time.

Sprinkle the remaining cup of flour on your work surface and turn the bread dough out onto it. Toss the dough between your hands until it is coated with flour and then knead it for five minutes.

Put the dough into a clean, warmed mixing bowl large enough to allow the dough to double in size. Cover it with a clean towel or plastic bowl cover and set the bowl in a warm place or in an unheated oven until it has doubled in bulk—for 1 to 1½ hours.

Turn the dough out on a floured work surface and knead it into a ball. Divide the ball into twelve more or less equal parts and knead each one into a ball. Sprinkle a large cookie sheet with whole-wheat flour. Flatten each ball with the palm of your hand to a thickness of ½ inch. With a sharp knife cut around the circumference of each roll ⅛ inch deep, halfway between top and bottom.

Place the rolls on the floured cookie sheet two inches apart, and punch fork holes into the tops. Set the rolls to rise until they have doubled in size—forty-five minutes to one hour. Bake at 400° for twenty minutes, or until browned. Cool on a wire grille.

Fine cheate was the next in quality to manchet. Coarser cheate was made with flour that had less of the bran removed when the wheat was bolted [sifted].

No bread in Shakespeare's day was as white as modern white bread. The bolting cloths, through which the ground wheat was sifted, were not fine enough to remove all the bran, and the idea that flour could be chemically bleached whiter had, fortunately, not yet been conceived. Until the eighteenth century bolting was done through woolen, linen, or hair cloths. Often some of the millstone dust that wore off during the grinding worked its way through the finest bolting cloths. It was not until silk gauze bolting cloths were developed, in the middle of the eighteenth century, that the smallest particles of bran and the millstone dust could be effectively removed.

TO MAKE A GOOD QUINCE PIE

Pare them, and coare them (the best of the Quince is next unto the skinne, therefore pare it as thinne as is possible) stuff them with Sugar, then with as much other sugar as they weigh, put them with peeces of sliced Ginger in a Coffin, sprinkle on a little Rose-water before you close your Pie. Bake it, and let stand long a soaking in the Oven, Ice it, and serve it in.

John Murrell, *A New Booke of Cookerie*

THE WORKING VERSION:

2 pounds ripe, fragrant quinces
½ cup sugar
¼ cup brown sugar
1 tablespoon grated fresh ginger
2 tablespoons rose water

THE PASTRY
2 cups sifted unbleached flour
1 teaspoon salt
¾ cup cold butter
½ cup cold water (approximately)
1 egg, separated

THE ICING
2 tablespoons sugar
½ tablespoon rose water

Use a potato peeler to peel the quinces—it is easier and faster than a paring knife. Slice off the fruit in small chunks, stopping as soon as the meat begins to look grainy. Cover and set aside until needed.

Make the pastry according to the instructions given on page 31. Divide the pastry into two parts, the part for the bottom crust a little larger than the piece for the top crust. Roll out the larger piece to fit an eight-inch pie dish, and fit the sheet of pastry into the dish. Then roll out the piece for the top crust.

Mix the sugars, grated ginger, and rose water into the quinces and spoon the mixture evenly into the pie dish. Cover the fruit with the top crust and seal the edges by pressing them down with the tines of a wet fork. Slice off the surplus pastry and brush the top of the pie with the egg white.

Bake at 450° for twenty minutes, then lower the heat to 350° and bake twenty-five minutes longer. Mix the sugar and rose water for the icing, spread it over the top of the pie, and return the pie to the oven for five minutes to glaze it. Serve slightly warm.

Some recipes called for dotting the fruit with pieces of butter. This does add flavor to the pie, and if you wish, you may dice two tablespoons of butter and spread them over the fruit before closing the pie. Quinces were also mixed with apples or with pears, sometimes with both.

Quince pies were rightly considered a delicacy worthy of a queen, and Queen Elizabeth's pastry cooks often presented her with them as New Year's gifts. Because all the New Year's gifts the queen received, as well as those she gave, were meticulously recorded, we know that in 1562 "John Betts, Servaunte of the Pastrye," gave the queen a "pye of quinces." In 1578 Dudley, her serjeant of the pastry, gave her "a great pie of quynses and wardyns (guilte)," which was a pie of quinces and winter pears decorated with gold leaf. Dudley must have been a good pastry cook, for he was still baking for the queen in 1589, when he gave her a "fayre pye of quinces oringed"—made with candied orange peel. By 1600 his name was missing, and Thomas French and Ralph Batty, serjeants of the pastry, each presented her with a "Pye of Orengado [candied orange peel]."

KENELME DIGBIE'S ALMOND CAKE

Take four quarts of fine flower, two pound and half of butter, three quarters of a pound of Sugar, four Nutmegs; a little Mace; a pound of Almonds finely beaten, half a pint of Sack, a pint of good Aleyest, a pint of boiled cream, twelve yolks and four whites of Eggs; four pound of Currants. When you have wrought all these into a very fine past, let it be kept warm before the fire half an hour, before you set it in the oven. If you please, you may put into it, two pound of Raisins of the Sun stoned and quartered. Let your oven be of temperate heat, and let your Cake stand therein two hours and a half, before you Ice it; and afterwards only to harden the Ice. The Ice for this Cake is made thus: Take the whites of three new laid Eggs, and three quarters of a pound of fine Sugar finely beaten; beat it well together with the whites of the Eggs, and Ice the Cake. If you please you may add a little Musk or Ambergreece.

Sir Kenelme Digbie, *The Closet of the Eminently Learned Sir Kenelme Digbie, Kt., Opened*

THE WORKING VERSION:

2 cups sifted unbleached flour
½ cup cold butter
½ cup sugar
½ cup blanched almonds, grated
½ cup currants
½ cup seeded raisins
½ tablespoon nutmeg
¼ teaspoon mace
1 cake fresh yeast
¼ cup light cream

¼ cup ale
2 tablespoons sherry
2 whole eggs
1 egg yolk

THE ICING
½ cup sugar
1 egg white
1 drop essence of musk or ambergris

In a large mixing bowl, crumble the flour and butter together until they are like fine meal. Stir in six tablespoons of the sugar, the almonds, currants, raisins, nutmeg, and mace.

Stir the yeast in the remaining sugar until it melts, then blend in the cream, ale, sherry, two eggs, and one egg yolk. Add this to the flour mixture and stir into a smooth dough.

Butter a one-quart ring mold or a deep cake pan generously, and dust it with flour. Spoon the dough evenly into the baking pan. Cover it and set it to rise for one hour in a warm place or an unheated oven. Bake at 350° for one hour. If the cake starts to brown too soon, cover it with a piece of clean brown wrapping paper. Remove the cake from the oven and turn it out onto a cake grille for ten minutes before frosting.

To make the icing, beat together the sugar, egg white, and musk or ambergris until smooth. Place the cake, still on the grille, on a cookie sheet and ice it, allowing the icing to run down the sides of the cake. To set the icing, return the cake, without removing it from the grille and cookie sheet, to the oven for about five minutes. Cool on the grille.

Do not substitute dry yeast for the fresh yeast. Dry yeast must be softened in water, which would upset the liquid-dry balance of the ingredients.

Ambergris and musk were favorite scents for perfuming elegant desserts as well as elegant ladies. Today they are mainly used as perfume fixatives. Essence of ambergris and of musk can be obtained by mail from Caswell-Massey Company Ltd., 518 Lexington Avenue, New York, New York 10017.

All cakes that were leavened were leavened with yeast obtained from the top froth of working beer, ale, or wine. This yeast, which was variously known as yest, barm, and God's good, was the only form of leavening known; compressed yeast and baking powder were not developed until the nineteenth century.

The sweet cakes of earlier times were made of bread dough to which sugar and occasionally currants or raisins were added.

Cheese and fruit, usually apples, were a proper ending to a meal. As Sir Hugh, the Welsh parson in *The Merry Wives of Windsor* (Act I, Scene 2), tells his servant in a thick Welsh accent, "I will make an end of my dinner; there's pippins and seese to come."

In addition to being enjoyed for itself, cheese was considered a digestive by many people. Ben Jonson, in his poem "Inviting a Friend to Supper," as a final touch promises his guest "digestive cheese and fruit." John Harington said,

All sorts eate cheese; but how? there is the question.
The poore for food, the rich for good digestion.

The dietaries, however, warned that cheese, especially aged cheese, was difficult to digest. In *The Castle of Health*, Thomas Elyot wrote, "Cheese by the whole sentence of all auncient writers, letteth [hinders] digestion, & is an enemy unto the stomacke. Also it ingendreth ill humors, and breedeth the stone. That cheese," he said, "which doth least harm is soft cheese

reasonablie salted, which some men do suppose nourisheth much."
William Vaughan also disapproved of aged cheese, "which by the
acrimony thereof makes the body bound and stipticke." But, he
added, "it is nourishing."

Shakespeare accepted cheese as a digestive. In *Troilus and
Cressida* (Act II, Scene 3), Achilles greets Thersites with "Why,
my cheese, my digestion, why hast thou not served thyself in to
my table so many meals?"

Apples had been introduced into England by the Romans. By
Shakespeare's day the noisy cries of the costermongers—originally, sellers of costard apples, the earliest known apples in England, but by this time peddling other fruit as well—were familiar
sounds in city streets. The pippin was a comparative newcomer.
Henry VIII's fruiterer, Richard Hermes, grafted slips from
French pippin trees onto some of the king's apple trees.

Many noblemen, as well as members of the gentry and yeoman
farmers, took keen interest in their orchards and were proud of
their skill in grafting fruit. Sir William Petre's gardeners not
only experimented with grafting various kinds of apples on one
tree at Ingatestone Manor, but tried grafting apples onto pear
trees. Lord Burghley, Queen Elizabeth's principal secretary, took
a personal interest in the workings of his extensive orchards.
Justice Shallow, a typical member of the lesser gentry, proud of
his skill in grafting fruit, ends his invitation to Falstaff with the
promise of a "pippin of my own graffing" after dinner.

ON ALE, BEER, METHEGLIN, AND CIDER

Ale, which had been known for millennia in the Mediterranean
world, was brewed in England during the centuries of Roman
rule. By Anglo-Saxon times it was firmly established as a beverage. As a drink it was greatly improved by the Normans, who,
after the conquest of England, brought in Continental monks
with their more advanced brewing skills. Each monastery the
Normans built had its own brewery, and soon many householders,
innkeepers, and tavern keepers were obtaining their supplies of
ale from the monasteries. With the dissolution of the monasteries
in the 1530's, many inns and households no longer able to obtain
their ale from the monasteries began to brew their own. In the

seventeenth century large breweries were established that supplied the inns and taverns with ale and beer.

Ale and beer, like many other words, have changed in meaning since Shakespeare wrote and the first Elizabeth ruled. Each word was, at one time or another, the all-inclusive generic term.

The older drink, ale, was made from barley mash, yeast, and water. Beer and hops came to England from the Low Countries in the fifteenth century. By Shakespeare's day the old fermented malt liquor *without* hops was ale, and the newer liquor *with* hops was beer. Later (by the eighteenth century), this distinction disappeared as ale too came to be made with hops, for hops preserved the product longer against deterioration and the effects of heat and the moving about of barrels in distribution. Now the term "beer" has become generic, and in England it generally includes ale as well as the newer, darker, heavier drinks of stout and porter.

Until the early sixteenth century, ale had no rival as the common drink in city or country. Then beer challenged it, first in the cities. But beer and hops aroused protest, probably because of the touch of bitterness that the hops gave to ale. The opponents of hops petitioned Parliament to forbid the "wicked weed" that would "spoil the taste of ale and endanger the people." To Andrewe Boorde, ale was the "natural drink" for an Englishman, as beer was for a Dutchman. He also worried about the effects of beer on the health of his countrymen. "Nowe of late dayes it is moche used in Englande to the detryment of many Englysshe men; specyally it killeth them the which be troubled with the colycke and the stone." But he conceded that if the beer was "fyned [properly cleared]," and not new but aged, it did no harm and could even "qualify the liver." Moreover, ale too might be harmful: "Newe ale is unwholesome for all men, and sowre ale, and deade ale . . . is good for no man."

William Harrison, who called the English a "nation of malt bugs," himself preferred beer to ale but knew some "aleknights so much addicted thereunto that they will not cease from morrow to even [evening] to visit the same cleansing house [tavern] after house, till they . . . either fall quite under the board [table], or else . . . sit pinking [eyes half shut] . . . till the fume of their adversary be quite digested that they may go at it afresh."

Poetry and drama continued to acclaim the virtues of ale. A

drinking song in *Gammer Gurton's Needle,* a popular sixteenth-century play, begins:

> Back and side go bare, go bare,
> Both hand and foot go cold;
> But belly, God send thee good Ale enough,
> Whether it be new or old.

In rural England ale was to hold its own as the main alcoholic drink until early in the eighteenth century. When times were too hard, or the barley crop too poor, to make real ale, the rural poor were advised by Sir Hugh Plat to distill their drinks from the seeds of anise, fennel, or caraway, or from the birch trees or gorse flowers.

In the country an ale was an affair at which ale flowed. Bride ales were weddings; soul or dirge ales were funerals. At church ales the drink was sold in the church or churchyard, usually on feast days, to raise money for church needs. Help ales celebrated the completion of work done with the help of friends and neighbors, and harvest ales celebrated the bringing in of the harvest.

March ale—named after the month in which it was brewed—was aged for two years in wealthy households before it was drunk. But that was an upper-class luxury; most ale was not even two months old, let alone two years, when it was drunk. Small ale or penny ale was so weak it was little more than a thirst quencher; dagger ale was sharp and potent. Lambs' wool was a popular drink of hot ale to which an apple, roasted until the skin burst, was added.

The quality and price of ale and beer were important enough for the royal government and city authorities to try to prevent adulteration, and, intermittently, to try to prevent or punish price-gouging. Public officials inspected breweries, alehouses, taverns, and inns. It was as one of the city's two elected "ale tasters" that John Shakespeare, William Shakespeare's father, in 1556 started his political career in Stratford-on-Avon. The duties of the ale tasters were to see that the brewers did not add "hops nor other subtle things" to ale when they were brewing it. They also kept watch on the observance of the price regulations and on the sale of ale and beer to see that only sealed pots of it were sold or served. As with wine, however, the authorities did not have the administrative machinery to prevent widespread violations of the regulations. Shakespeare comments on such

A black jack (leather pitcher) (16–17th century)

violations in *The Taming of the Shrew* (Induction, Scene 2). As part of the hoax being played on the drunkard Sly, he is told that for fifteen years he has been mad, and that in his madness he talked like a drunkard:

> Yet would you say ye were beaten out of door,
> And rail upon the hostess of the house,
> And say you would present [bring charges against] her at
>   the leet [local court],
> Because she brought stone jugs and no seal'd quarts.

Andrewe Boorde stated the problem of adulteration simply and firmly: "Ale is made of malte and water; and they the which do put any other thynge to ale then is rehersed [proper], except yest [yeast] . . . do sophysticate [adulterate] theyr ale." Ale-wives, Harrison complained, sometimes added rosin and salt to their ale to make it taste stronger, and to make drinkers thirsty. "If you heat a knife red-hot and quench it in the ale so near the bottom of the pot as you can put it, you shall see the rosin come forth hanging on the knife."

William Vaughan, who praised the drink in its pure form— "Ale, made of Barley malt and good water, doth make a man strong"—complained of its adulteration. "Now adaies," he said, "few Brewers doe brew it as they ought, for they adde slimy and heavy baggage unto it, thinking thereby to please tosspots [tipplers] and to increase the vigor of it."

Adulteration was not the only problem. Many were the methods offered to prevent ale from going sour or dead, and to save it if it was already going bad. Vaughan suggested that adding a handful or two of oatmeal or ground malt to ale that was going bad and stirring it in well could save it. He also had a method for "aging" it within two or three days, which was to bury the ale in jugs or pots "somewhat deepe in the ground in a shady place." But, he warned, "this unnaturall drinke proves windy if it be often used."

By Shakespeare's day, although beer had superseded ale as the most common beverage for all classes, a ballad could sing the praises of both as the drinks of the poor:

> Some say good wine can ner want [lack] sale,
> But God send poore folks Beere and Ale
> Enough until they die.

Tankard, leather with silver rim (16th–17th century)

Another ballad is more specific in its rejection of wine in favor of malt beverages:

> The old renowned Ipocrist
> And Raspie doth excell;
> But never any wine could yet
> My humour please so well!
> The rhenish wine, or muscadine,
> Sweet malmsie is too fulsome;
> No! Give me a cup of barlie broth
> For that is very wholesome.
> Twill make me sing, I cannot go home,
> 'Its long of the oyle of barley,'
> I'll tarry all night for my delight
> And go home in the morning early.

"A healthe to all Good-Fellowes." Woodcut from broadsheet (or broadside) ballad (Roxburghe Ballads: 16th century)

Indeed, the English were well known for their enjoyment of drinking. The average Englishman rather liked this reputation, judging from the popularity of drinking songs, which were sold in the streets, printed on single sheets of wide paper called "broadsides" or "broadsheets," and often illustrated with charming woodcuts. "In England . . . they are most potent in potting [drinking]; your Dane, your German, and your swag-bellied Hollander . . . are nothing to your English," Iago tells Cassio in *Othello* (Act II, Scene III).

For most of England beer was the ordinary, indispensable drink because of the poor quality of the water—neither tea nor coffee had yet come into use. In rural areas (and most of England was still rural), local resources determined what poorer people drank. Milk, buttermilk, or whey might be the thirst-quencher or, in apple-growing areas, cider. Where bees were kept, people could drink the mead or metheglin made of fermented honey.

Beer was drunk at all meals and between meals. "Hath thy ale virtue or thy beer strength, that the tongue of man may be tickled, and his palate pleased in the morning?" Justice Overdo asks the tapster in Ben Jonson's *Bartholomew Fair* (Part I, Act 2). Household beer was generally low in alcoholic content, else little work would have been accomplished in the household.

All ages drank beer, even young children. When her infant daughter was ill with "an extreme fit of the ague," Lady Anne Clifford wrote in her diary, the doctor gave her a salt powder to put into the baby's beer.

Most large households and many medium and small ones brewed all or most of the beer that they consumed. But even those households occasionally had to purchase some. At Grimsthorpe, the home of the duchess of Suffolk, the household accounts show purchases of both strong and small (weak) beer. In 1561, for example, they show seven shillings a barrel paid for strong beer and four shillings sixpence a barrel for small beer. Purchases of hops, malt, and casks, as well as payments to the cooper (maker and repairer of barrels and casks), were also listed in the accounts for the brewhouse and the buttery, which were responsible for the care and serving of all alcoholic drinks.

At Ingatestone, the lovely country home of Sir William Petre, in Essex, some 576 gallons of beer were brewed every two weeks. During festive seasons and during haymaking and the harvest seasons (when hired hands were paid in part in drink), brewing was done weekly. Even here, however, there were times when beer was purchased. F. G. Emmison, in his interesting book on Ingatestone in Petre's time, *Tudor Food and Pastimes,* estimates that each person at Ingatestone drank an average of about a gallon of beer a day during "normal days."

The royal household in Queen Elizabeth's reign consumed about 600,000 gallons of beer a year. The task of supplying this vast amount was in the hands of fifty-eight to sixty brewers.

Even in William Harrison's modest home—he was rector of a small Essex village church—two hundred gallons of beer were brewed and consumed each month. Harrison was proud of his wife's skill in the complicated process of brewing, which he describes, and of her ability to make two hundred gallons of beer for only twenty shillings, or a little over a penny per gallon. His calculations include the servants' wages and food, wood for the fire, and even wear and tear on the vats.

Thomas Tusser, in his popular *Five Hundred Points of Good Husbandry,* advises the country wife to brew her own beer, not only for quality but also for economy, and to use the mash as swill for her pigs:

> Where brewer is needful be brewer thyself. . . .
> In buying thy drink by the firkin or pot
> the score [cost] doth arise, the hogge profiteth not.

Beer and ale were drunk from any available drinking vessel, including stoneware, leather, pewter, and sometimes wood. But there were areas of England where tankards were used for other drinks as well. In 1599 Thomas Platter, a traveler from Germany, expressed considerable surprise that "in some parts of England, we were given but milk to drink in tankards instead of beer."

"Drinke," said Gervase Markham, "is in everie house more generally spent [consumed] then bread . . . being indeed made the very sobstance [substance] of all entertainment." Beer and ale he lists as the most important drinks, to which he adds cider and perry, mead and metheglin, "two compound drinks of honie and herbes which in the places where they are made, in Wales and the marches [the Welsh border] are renouned for exceeding wholesome and cordial."

Leather bottles (16th–17th century)

Metheglin, although commonly made in England, was considered a Welsh beverage. The name comes from the Welsh words "meddyg" for healing, and "llyn" for liquor. Both mead and metheglin are basically fermented honey, metheglin being mead flavored with herbs and spices. (A recipe for metheglin is on page 42.) The drink is well worth the time it takes to make and mature it.

Andrewe Boorde said of it, that "made of hony and water, and herbes boyled and sodden together, yf it be fyned [clarified] and stale [aged], it is better in the regyment [regime] of health than meade." Metheglin was so esteemed in Wales, said Harrison, that of it Welshmen "make no less account (and not without cause, if it be well handled) than the Greeks did of their ambrosia or nectar, which for the pleasantness thereof was supposed to be such as the gods themselves did delight in." He was scornful of "swish-swash," made in his own Essex and elsewhere "with honeycombs and water, which the homely country wives, putting some pepper and a little other spice among, call mead." This was good only "for such as love to be loosebodied at large or a little eased of the cough; otherwise it differeth so much from the true metheglin as chalk from cheese."

Metheglin was a popular drink not only among modest country people but also among the upper classes. It was one of Queen Elizabeth's favorite drinks. A large collection of metheglin recipes is part of *The Closet of the Eminently Learned Sir Kenelme Digbie, Kt., Opened:* about fifty recipes each for metheglin and for mead. The sources for his recipes are usually the noble ladies and gentlemen who were his friends. His own recipe, Sir Kenelme said, "was composed by myself out of Sundry [various] Receipts." There is little to distinguish between metheglin and mead recipes in the book; both include spices and/or herbs in the ingredients, and by the beginning of the seventeenth century, the difference between the two seems to be blurred.

Cider, a drink the Normans are also credited with introducing into England, was an important beverage in apple-growing country, in East Anglia, the south and the west of England. In Herefordshire, which grew excellent cooking apples but had difficulty in selling its cider because it lacked river transport, part of the staple diet of farm hands was bread and cider. Their breakfasts and suppers were usually composed of toast and hot cider, sometimes spiced with rosemary and sugar. In pear-growing country, perry, a drink made from pears, might take the place of apple cider. The west country and Kent were considered to make the best perry. Like cider, it was marketed in cities to which transportation was available.

Cider, in Shakespeare's time, was made much as it is today. The fruit was mashed and the juice extracted in fruit presses, allowed to stand until the heavy particles settled, whereupon the clear juice was drawn off, sometimes sweetened, and allowed to ferment to a controlled point. "The foundation of making perfect Cyder," says Digbie, "consisteth in not having it work much, scarce ever at all; but at least, no second time; which ordinary Cider doth often, upon change of weather, and upon motion; and upon every working it grows harder."

The English still make a delicious, delicately fermented cider, and one may get a descendant of Digbie's "perfect Cyder" at almost any English pub. With good English cheese and bread, it makes an excellent simple lunch.

A Feast for Beatrice
& Benedick

Give me your hand;
We must needs dine together.
Timon of Athens, Act I, Scene 1 (*Timon*)

SHERRY

With excellent endeavour of drinking good
and good store of fertile sherris.
Henry IV, Part II, Act IV, Scene 3 (*Falstaff*)

A CHICKEN GUSSET (BROTH)

And sauc'd our broths as Juno had been sick
And he her dieter.
Cymbeline, Act IV, Scene 2 (*Guiderius*)

ROBERT MAY'S MARINATED SALMON

Here's another ballad of a fish that
appeared upon the coast.
The Winter's Tale, Act IV, Scene 3 (*Autolycus*)

A ROAST FILLET OF BEEF

The case of a treble hautboy was a mansion
for him . . . and now has he land and beefs.
Henry IV, Part II, Act III, Scene 2 (*Falstaff*)

JOHN MURRELL'S
BUTTERED CAULIFLOWER

No more shall trenching war channel her fields,
Nor bruise her flowerets.
                    Henry IV, Part I, Act I, Scene 1 (*Henry*)

PORK SAUSAGES WITHOUT SKINS

This making of Christians will raise the price of
hogs: if we grow all to be pork-eaters, we shall not
shortly have a rasher on the coals for money.
        The Merchant of Venice, Act III, Scene 5 (*Launcelot*)

APPLES STEWED WITH AMBERGRIS

Do not you know my lady's foot by the squire,
And laugh upon the apple of her eye?
            Love's Labour's Lost, Act V, Scene 2 (*Berowne*)

POACHED PIGEONS WITH GOOSEBERRIES

He eats nothing but doves, love; and that breeds
hot blood, and hot blood begets hot thoughts, and
hot thoughts beget hot deeds, and hot deeds is love.
            Troilus and Cressida, Act III, Scene 1 (*Paris*)

A SALAD OF BEETS AND GREENS

Here's the challenge; read it: I warrant
there's vinegar and pepper in't.
            Twelfth Night, Act III, Scene 4 (*Sir Andrew*)

ROBERT MAY'S FRENCH BREAD

Easy it is of a cut loaf to steal
a shive [slice].
            Titus Andronicus, Act II, Scene 1 (*Demetrius*)

RED AND WHITE WINES

Wine, wine, wine! What service is here!
I think our fellows are asleep.
            Coriolanus, Act IV, Scene 5 (*First Servingman*)

AN ITALIAN CREAM

The story is extant, and writ in
very choice Italian.

Hamlet, Act III, Scene 2 (*Hamlet*)

A MARROW PUDDING

Lo! as at English feasts, so I regreet
The daintiest last, to make the end most sweet.

Richard II, Act I, Scene 3 (*Bolingbroke*)

Let all the number of the stars give light
To thy fair way!

Antony and Cleopatra, Act III, Scene 2 (*Lepidus*)

FOR A GUSSET THAT
MAY BE ANOTHER POTTAGE

Take the broathe of the Capons and put in a fayre chafer, then
take a dosen or syxtene egges and stere them all together whyte
and all, then grate a farthynge whyte loafe as small as ye canne,
and mynce it wyth the egges all together, and putte thereto salte
and a good quantitie of safiron [saffron], and or [before] ye
putte in youre egges, putte into youre brothe, tyme, saverye,
margeron and parseley small choppd, and when ye are redye to
your dynner, set the chafer upon the fyre wyth the brothe, and
lette it boyle a lyttle and putte in your egges and stere it up well
for quayling [curdling] the less. The less boylynge it hathe the
more tender it wyll be, and then serve it forthe two or three
slyces upon a dysshe.

Anonymous, *A Proper newe Booke of Cokerye*

THE WORKING VERSION:

4 cups fresh, clear chicken broth
1 tablespoon minced parsley
1 teaspoon salt
⅛ teaspoon saffron
⅛ teaspoon marjoram
⅛ teaspoon thyme
⅛ teaspoon savory
2 eggs

2 teaspoons bread crumbs
3 slices hot buttered toast, quartered

THE BROTH
2½ pounds chicken backs and necks
4½ cups water

To make the broth, rinse the chicken backs and necks. Put them with the water into a pressure cooker and cook at ten pounds pressure for forty-five minutes. Let the pressure go down before opening the cooker. Strain the broth through a fine sieve into a saucepan.

Add the parsley, salt, saffron, marjoram, thyme, and savory and simmer for fifteen minutes. Beat the eggs with the bread crumbs and stir them into the broth. Turn off the heat and let the broth simmer for a minute or two, stirring constantly. Divide the toast among individual soup bowls and pour the hot broth over it. Serve immediately.

If you do not have a pressure cooker, use five cups of water and simmer the chicken parts in a tightly covered pot for three hours.

When a recipe called for "a farthynge whyte loaf," or a penny or halfpenny loaf of bread, the cook had to use his best judgment on how much bread to use, since loaves of bread weighed different amounts at different times, although the officially regulated price per loaf remained the same. The size of the loaf depended on the price of wheat at the time. In addition, the weights of bread, also set by law, were different in the provinces from those set for London.

Pottage, said Andrewe Boorde, "is nat so much used in al christendom as it is used in England." About chicken broth he said, "The flesh of a cocke, is harde of dygestyon; but the broth or gely made of a cocke is restorative." The term "gusset" does not appear in any other cookbook. Broth and pottage were interchangeable terms in this period.

TO MARRINATE SALMON TO BE EATEN
HOT OR COLD

Take a Salmon, cut it into joles [thick slices] and rands [filleted strips], and fry them in good sweet sallet oyl or clarified butter, then set them by in a charger [large serving dish], and have some white or claret-wine, and wine-vinegar as much as will cover it, put the wine and vinegar into a pipkin [pot, usually with three legs] with all manner of sweet herbs bound up in a bundle, as rosemary, tyme, sweet marjoram, parsley, winter savory, bay-leaves, sorrel, and sage, as much of one as the other, large mace, slic't ginger, gross pepper, slic't nutmeg, whole cloves, and salt; being well boild together, pour it on the fish, spices and all, being cold, then lay on slic't lemons and lemon-peel, and cover it up close; so keep it for present spending [use], and serve it hot or cold with the same liquor it is soust in, with the spices, herbs, and lemons on it.

Robert May, *The Accomplisht Cook*

THE WORKING VERSION:

One 1½-pound piece of thick
    salmon fillet
  4 tablespoons butter
  ¼ cup minced parsley
  1 teaspoon grated fresh
    ginger
  1 teaspoon salt
  ½ teaspoon peppercorns
  4 cloves
  1 bay leaf
  ½ nutmeg, broken up

  1 large piece of whole mace
  ¼ teaspoon thyme
  ¼ teaspoon rosemary
  ¼ teaspoon marjoram
  ¼ teaspoon savory
  ¼ teaspoon sage
  6 tablespoons wine vinegar
1¼ cups claret
  1 lemon, sliced thin and
    seeded

Rinse the salmon fillet under cold running water and pat it dry with paper towels or a clean white cloth. Cut into approximately 2½-inch squares. Melt the butter in a skillet large enough to hold all the fish in a single layer. Arrange the fish pieces in the skillet and sauté over low heat only until the flesh is no longer translucent, turning once—about four minutes on each side. Remove the skillet from the heat and set aside, covered, until the sousing liquid is ready.

Add the herbs, spices, and wine vinegar to the claret and bring the mixture to a boil. Lower the heat to simmer and cook ten minutes.

Layer the pieces of salmon in a small, deep bowl—a 1½-quart stainless steel or glass bowl is a good size. Pour the hot marinade, including the seasonings, over the salmon. Arrange the lemon slices over the top, pushing a few down into the liquid at the sides of the bowl. Cover and set aside until the marinade has cooled.

Refrigerate until needed. Serve the salmon cold with some of the marinade poured over it.

This dish keeps well for a week to ten days; after that the fish begins to toughen. But if you plan to keep it that long, peel the lemon before slicing it, since the peel tends to give the fish a slightly bitter taste if left more than a day or two in the marinade.

We preferred the salmon cold, but if you wish to serve it warm, reheat it in the marinade in the top of a double boiler.

The sorrel called for in the original recipe is difficult to find in most markets, so I have increased the amount of lemon to compensate for its absence.

Salmon was a delicacy and a luxury and even salt salmon was considered fit for the royal table. Salmon were protected by a statute that forbade fishing for them in certain seasons even though the Thames and other large rivers were well supplied.

The difference in price between fresh and salt salmon was considerable. The accounts of the meals provided for the judges of the Court of the Star Chamber note that in February, 1576, a side of salt salmon and one of calvered salmon were purchased (calvered salmon was soused salmon made from fresh fish). The salt salmon cost twenty pence while the calvered salmon cost twelve shillings, over seven times as much.

TO ROAST A FILLET OF BEEF

Take a fillet which is the tenderest part of the beef, and lieth in the inner part of the surloyn, cut it as big as you can, broach it on a broach not too big, and be careful not to broach it through the best of the meat; roast it leisurely, and baste it with sweet butter, set a dish to save the gravy while it roasts, then prepare sauce for it of good store of parsley, with a few sweet herbs chopped small, the yolkes of three or four eggs, sometimes gross pepper minced amongst them with the peel of an orange, and a little onion; boil these together, and put in a little butter, vinegar, gravy, a spoonful of strong broth, and put it to the beef.

Robert May, *The Accomplisht Cook*

THE WORKING VERSION:

One	2-pound piece of beef tenderloin	⅛	teaspoon pepper
6	tablespoons butter, melted	1	teaspoon salt
¼	cup minced parsley	1	teaspoon grated fresh orange peel
¼	cup minced chives		
¼	teaspoon thyme	¾	cup clear beef broth
¼	teaspoon savory	¼	cup red wine vinegar
		2	egg yolks

Turn under the thin tail of the tenderloin, if there is one, and tie the roast. Heat the oven to 500°. Set aside two tablespoons of the butter for the sauce. Brush the meat with some of the remaining butter and place it in an open baking dish. Put the roast into the oven and immediately turn the heat down to 350°. Roast for thirty minutes, basting with butter every five minutes.

To make the sauce, put all the remaining ingredients except the egg yolks into a small saucepan and bring to a boil. Lower the heat to simmer and cook for fifteen minutes. Add ¼ cup of the sauce to the egg yolks and beat until blended. Return the egg yolks to the sauce and cook, stirring constantly, until the sauce begins to thicken. Stir whatever gravy there is in the baking dish into the sauce.

Remove the string from the meat and slice it into ½-inch slices. Arrange them on a heated serving dish and pour the gravy over them. Serve immediately.

If you have a rotisserie and wish to use it, spit the tenderloin lengthwise, brush it with butter, and broil for forty minutes, basting every five minutes with butter.

The English were renowned for their fine beef, for its excellent preparation, and for the large amounts of it they consumed. Fynes Moryson, in his *Itinerary,* wrote, "England abounds in Cattel of all kinds, and particularly hath very great Oxen, the flesh whereof is so tender, as no meate is more desired." And he added, "the English Cookes, in comparison with other Nations, are most commended for roast meates."

As an Englishman, Moryson might have been expressing national pride, but Paul Hentzner, a German who accompanied a young nobleman of his country as a tutor on a visit to England, was equally impressed. "The soil is fruitful," he wrote in *A Journey into England,* "and abounds with Cattle. . . . The English are more polite in Eating than the French, devouring less Bread, but more Meat, which they roast to Perfection." Levinus Lemnius, a Dutch physician, was also impressed by the quality of English meat. "And this do I thinck," he wrote, "to be the cause that Englishmen, lyving by such holesome and exquisite meate, and in so holesome and healthful ayre to be so fresh and cleane coloured."

HOW TO BUTTER A COLLEFLOWRE

Take a ripe Colle-floure and cut off the buddes, boyle them in milke with a little Mace while [until] they be very tender, then poure them into a Cullender, and let the Milke runne cleane from them, then take a ladle full of Creame, being boyled with a little whole Mace, putting to it a Ladlefull of thicke butter, mingle them together with a little Sugar, dish up your flowres upon sippets, poure your butter and cream hot upon it strowing on a little slicst Nutmeg and salt, and serve it to the Table hot.

John Murrell, *A Booke of Cookerie*

THE WORKING VERSION:

1 cauliflower, about 5 inches in diameter	1 tablespoon butter
2½ cups milk	¼ teaspoon salt
1 large piece of whole mace	⅛ teaspoon nutmeg
	⅛ teaspoon sugar
THE SAUCE	3 slices hot buttered toast, cut into triangles
½ cup light cream	

Choose a cauliflower that is white and in which the flowerets have not begun to separate. Remove the green leaves and the thick base, rinse the head in cold water, and separate into flowerets.

Heat the milk to just below the boiling point and add the mace and cauliflowerets. Lower the heat to simmer, and cook until the cauliflowerets are tender but still crisp—from twelve to fifteen minutes. While the cauliflower is cooking, bring the cream, butter, salt, nutmeg, and sugar to a point just below boiling.

Arrange the toast in a heated serving bowl. Remove the cauliflowerets from the milk with a slotted spoon and place them on the toast. Pour the sauce over them and serve hot.

John Murrell and Robert May were the only ones to offer recipes for serving cauliflower as a separate vegetable. Both have several ways of preparing it.

Cauliflower is a member of the cabbage family and may have been known as one of the "white coleworts." Gervase Markham tells the English housewife that she may "at all times of the moneth and the moon generally, sow . . . Coleworts." In February and March, he said, "cole Cabbage, white Cole [which may have been cauliflower], green cole [which may have been broccoli], and Cabbage" should be sowed under the old moon.

Michael Drayton, in *Poly-Olbion,* begins his listing of the vegetables grown in English counties with:

> And since these
> Foods fall out so fitly in my way,
> A little while to them I will convert my lay.
> The Colewort, Colifloure, and Cabidge
> In their season.

TO MAKE MOST RARE SAUSAGES WITHOUT SKINS

Take a leg of young pork, cut off all the lean, and mince it very small, but leave none of the strings or skin amongst it; then take two pound of beef suet shred small, two handfulls of red sage, a little pepper, salt, and nutmeg, with a small piece of an onion; mince them together with the flesh and suet, and being finely minced, put the yolks of two or three eggs, and mix all together, make it into a paste, and when you will use it, roul out as many pieces as you please in the form of an ordinary sausage, and fry them, this paste will keep a fortnight upon occasion.

Robert May, *The Accomplisht Cook*

THE WORKING VERSION:

2 pounds boned lean pork	½ teaspoon pepper
¼ pound beef suet	½ teaspoon sage
1 small onion, grated	¼ teaspoon nutmeg
1 teaspoon salt	1 egg yolk

Ask your butcher to grind the pork and suet together. Mix the meat with the rest of the ingredients until well blended. Cover and refrigerate for at least six hours to allow the flavors to blend.

Form the sausage mixture into small rolls—about four inches long and one inch in diameter. Pan-fry over medium heat, turning the rolls so that they brown evenly on all sides, for about ten minutes. Serve immediately—sausage meat dries out very quickly.

Usually, sausage meat was stuffed into casings of animal intestines. The sausages were then either boiled for immediate eating or hung in the chimney space of a fireplace and smoked for later use.

Pork was the preferred meat for sausage, and the best cuts were usually used to make it. May did, however, say that these sausages could be made of mutton or veal. Rabisha said that he had made "rich Sassages of Capons and Rabbits," but "none were as savoury as those of Pork." Sausage was also referred to as puddings.

HOW TO STEW PIPPINS

Pare your Pippins, cut them into halves and coare them, and lay them into a stewing-pan with faire [fresh and clean] water, Rose-water, a little Verjuice, Sugar, Orange-peel, Ambergriece, or Musk; if you eat them hot put Butter on them being beat up

Title page of Michael Drayton's Poly-Olbion (*1612*)

thick; if you eat them cold, put not any in; sippit them, scraping Sugar on the top and serve it up.

Joseph Cooper, *The Art of Cookery Refin'd and Augmented*

THE WORKING VERSION:

1½ pounds tart cooking apples	1 teaspoon rose water
½ cup water	2 drops essence of amber-
¼ cup white wine vinegar	gris or musk
¼ cup brown sugar	2 slices buttered toast, cut
4 tablespoons butter	into triangles
1 tablespoon grated fresh	Brown sugar for garnish
orange peel (zest)	(optional)

If the apples are large, quarter them, otherwise cut them into halves, core, and peel them. Put the water, vinegar, brown sugar, butter, orange zest, rose water, and ambergris or musk into a large skillet and bring to a boil. Lower the heat to simmer, and cook for ten minutes.

Arrange the apples side by side in the sauce. Cover the skillet with a lid or a piece of aluminum foil and simmer until the apples are tender—fifteen to twenty minutes—turning them carefully every five minutes. Put the toast triangles in a heated serving bowl, arrange the apples over them, and pour the sauce over the apples. If you wish, you may also sprinkle a little brown sugar over them.

Apples had been eaten both cooked and raw for centuries in England. The earliest written record of them goes back to 1296, when a hundred "costards" were bought for one shilling. In Shakespeare's day costards were the most popular of the great variety of native apples, and the costermongers did a thriving business.

Apples could be a source of great annoyance, however, in the theater, for one of the pastimes of the young dandies who came to the playhouse to be seen rather than to see the play was to take a bite out of an apple and throw the rest into the pit, where it was picked up and eaten by less affluent playgoers. This practice must have irritated Shakespeare, for in *Henry VIII* (Act V, Scene 4), the porter says of the throng of young lads trying to get in to see the christening of the future Queen Elizabeth, "These are the youths that thunder at a playhouse, and fight for bitten apples."

TO BOYLE PIDGEONS WITH GOOSEBERRIES OR GRAPES

Boile them with Mutton-broth and white Wine, a peece of whole Mace, put into the bellies of them sweet Hearbs: when they be tender thicken it with a peece of Maunchet, and two hard yolkes strained with the same broth. Then put some of the same broth into a boild-meat dish, with Vergis, Butter, and Sugar, and so boyle your Grapes or Gooseberries in the dish close covered, till they be tender, and poure it on the brest of your dish.

John Murrell, *A New Booke of Cookerie*

THE WORKING VERSION:

Two 1-pound squab pigeons, dressed weight
2 large sprigs of parsley
2 small sprigs of thyme
1 large piece of whole mace
3½ cups chicken or mutton broth
⅔ cup white wine
2 teaspoons salt, if the broth you use is unseasoned

½ slice white bread
1 tablespoon white wine vinegar
2 teaspoons butter
½ teaspoon brown sugar
2 hard-boiled egg yolks
¼ cup gooseberries or white grapes

Remove and reserve the giblets, if any are in the squabs, and rinse the birds under cold running water. Into each of the squabs put a sprig of parsley, a sprig of thyme, ½ of the piece of mace, and the squab liver, if there was one. Truss the birds with string, bringing the legs and wings close to the body.

Put the broth, wine, and salt, if the broth is unseasoned, into a saucepan in which the squabs fit fairly snugly, and bring to a boil. Put the squabs into the broth, breast side up, and bring the broth to a boil again. Lower the heat to simmer, cover, and cook the squabs for twenty minutes. Turn them over carefully and continue cooking until tender—ten to twenty minutes longer, but test with a fork after ten minutes.

Remove and reserve ½ cup of the poaching broth for the sauce. Keep the squabs hot in the remaining broth until needed. Remove the crusts from the bread and crumble the center part. Put the reserved ½ cup of broth, the vinegar, butter, sugar, egg yolks, and bread crumbs into a small saucepan and cook, stirring until the egg yolks and the bread crumbs are blended in. Add the gooseberries or grapes and cook five minutes longer. Taste and add salt if needed.

Remove the squabs from the poaching broth, remove the strings, and divide the birds in half lengthwise. Discard the parsley, thyme, and mace. Arrange the squabs on a heated serving platter and pour the sauce over them. Serve immediately.

Pigeons were eaten and enjoyed by most English families, from the lowly agricultural worker and his family, who could raise a few of them in the rafters of their tiny cottage for holiday feasts, to the lordly landowner, whose manor dovecotes provided ample supplies. Wild pigeons were also eaten, but in comparatively small numbers. "No Kingdome in the World hath so many dove houses," wrote Fynes Moryson. Farmers raised pigeons as a source of ready money—sometimes they were the only fresh meat available during the winter months, and they were easily marketed. But, as William Harrison wrote, many were "spent [eaten] at home in good company amongst . . . neighbors."

A GRAND SALLET OF BEETS, CURRANTS AND GREENS

Take the youngest and smallest leaves of spinage, the smallest also of sorrel, well washed currans, and red beets round the center being finely carved, oyl and vinegar, and the dish garnished with lemon and beets.

Robert May, *The Accomplisht Cook*

THE WORKING VERSION:

¼ pound fresh, crisp spinach
¼ pound sorrel
4 tablespoons olive oil
3 tablespoons red wine vinegar
½ teaspoon salt
⅛ teaspoon pepper

⅛ teaspoon brown sugar
4 fresh beets, boiled, peeled, and sliced thin
¼ cup currants, parboiled
½ lemon, peeled, sliced thin, and seeded

Wash the spinach and sorrel in cold water until clean—if sorrel is not available, increase the amount of spinach to ½ pound and the vinegar to four tablespoons. Remove the roots and coarse stems from the greens and tear or cut them into bite-size pieces.

Mix the oil, vinegar, salt, pepper, and sugar until blended. Toss the greens in the dressing, then transfer them to a shallow serving bowl. Add the beets to the dressing and arrange them around the greens, alternating every three or four slices with a slice of lemon. Stir the currants into the remaining dressing, then spoon them over the salad. Pour any remaining dressing over it. Serve immediately.

What Robert May called "grand salads," for which he offered sixteen recipes, and what Gervase Markham called "compound salads" were both combinations of various ingredients. Sometimes they were elaborate combinations of various meats, vegetables, and fruits. Both writers displayed the Renaissance love of color and design in their directions for serving the salads. To meals heavy with meat and bread, salads brought a welcome lightness and savor.

Most cookbooks that provided menus included salads in them, but few of the early cookbooks gave specific recipes. Thomas Dawson, in Part I of *The good huswifes Jewell,* published in 1587, suggested only two salads, one of which was simply sliced lemons sprinkled with sugar; the other was similar to Robert May's salad, but used cucumbers instead of beets.

Markham found salads of sufficient importance to devote several pages to them. He divided them into five categories:

"simple and plain, compound, boiled, preserved, and sallets for shew [show].

"Your simple Sallets," he said, "are Chibols [shallots] pilled [peeled], washt clean, and half the green tops cut clean away, so served on a fruit dish; or Chives, Scallions, Radish-roots, boyled Carrets, Skirrets, and Turnips . . . served up simply; Also, all young Lettice, Cabbage-lettice, Purslan, and divers other herbs, which may be served simply without anything but a little Vinegar, Sallet-Oyl, and Sugar: Camphire, Onions boyled and stripd from their rind, and served up with Vinegar and Oyle and Pepper is a good simple Sallet; so is Camphire, Bean-cods, Asparagus, and Cucumbers served . . . likewise."

Camphire is samphire, a member of the parsley family, with thick roundish leaves of deep green, and a spicy, hot flavor. It grows on rocks washed by the sea, as Shakespeare knew in giving verisimilitude to the landscape Edgar invents (in *King Lear,* Act IV, Scene 6) to persuade his father, Gloucester, that he is indeed on the edge of a cliff by the sea from which he can jump to his desired death: "Half way down hangs one that gathers samphire, dreadful trade!"

"Your preserved Sallets," Markham continued, "are either pickled, as are cucumbers, Samphire [spelled camphire in his previous paragraph] . . . and such like; or preserved with Vinegar, as Violets, Primroses, Cowslips, gillyflowers [pinks] . . . and for the most part any wholsome flower whatsoever." He suggested using distilled vinegar to preserve the colors of flowers to be pickled. They were used, as they came from the pickling liquid, as salads or added to other dishes. As salads, they should be, he suggested, arranged on the serving plates to look like flowers as they appeared in nature. "Thus you may set . . . some full bloom, some half blown, and some in bud, which will be pretty and curious [interesting]. And if you will set forth yellow flowers, take the pots of primroses and cowslips. If blue Flowers, then the pots of Violets, or Bugloss flowers."

Salads for "shew" were also meant to adorn the table and give it color and variety. "They be those which are made of Carret roots of sundry Colours well boyled, and cut into many shapes and proportions, as some in Knots, some in the manner of scutchions [escutcheons], and Arms, some like Birds, some like wild-beasts, according to the Art and cunning of the workman;

and these for the most part are seasoned with Vinegar, Oyl, and a little Pepper."

TO MAKE FRENCH BREAD THE BEST WAY

Take a gallon of fine flour, and a pint of good new ale barm or yeast, and put it to the flour, with the whites of six new laid eggs well beaten in a dish, and mixt with the barm in the middle of the flour, also three spoonfuls of fine salt; then warm some milk and fair water, and put to it, and make it up pretty stiff, being well wrought and worked up, cover it in a boul or tray with a warm cloth till your oven be hot; then make it up either in rouls, or fashion it in little wooden dishes and bake it, being baked in a quick oven, chip it hot.

Robert May, *The Accomplisht Cook*

THE WORKING VERSION:

I cup lukewarm water	I tablespoon salt
2 cakes fresh yeast or 2 tablespoons dried yeast	I egg white
	6 cups sifted unbleached flour
I cup lukewarm milk	

Pour the water into a large mixing bowl. Crumble or sprinkle the yeast into the water and let it stand until the yeast softens and expands. Add the milk, salt, and egg white and beat until the egg white is blended in.

Stir in five cups of the flour, one cup at a time, until all is absorbed. Sprinkle the remaining flour on your work surface and turn the dough out onto it. Pat the dough back and forth between your hands until it is coated with flour. Then knead it for five minutes. Put the dough into a clean, warmed mixing bowl large enough to permit the dough to double in size. Cover with a clean cloth or plastic bowl cover and set to rise in a warm place or an unheated oven. When the dough has doubled in size—in I to I½ hours—turn it out on a floured work surface and knead into a ball.

Divide the ball into twelve more or less equal parts, and knead each one into a ball. Flatten each ball with the palm of your hand to a thickness of ½ inch, and, with a sharp knife, cut around the circumference of the roll ⅛ inch halfway between top and bottom. Place the rolls two inches apart on a floured cookie sheet. Punch holes in the tops and set the rolls to rise—forty-five minutes to one hour—until doubled in size. Bake at 400° for twenty minutes, or until golden brown. Cool on a wire grille.

In Shakespeare's day it was almost impossible to control the heat of the oven, and chipping the burned crusts from bread was a necessary and lowly chore, to be performed by children and servants. In *Henry IV, Part II* (Act II, Scene 4), Prince Hal chides Falstaff for having called him "pantler" and bread-chipper. A pantler was the servant in charge of the bread and the pantry in a great household.

Burned bread was considered bad for the digestion. Thomas Cogan warned, "Burned Bread and hard crustes do engender ill, adjust choler and melancholy. Wherefore the upper cruste above and beneath should be chipped away. Notwithstanding . . . the crustes are wholesome for them that be whole [healthy] and have their stomaches moist, and desire to be leane, but they must eate them after meate, for they must enforce the meate to descend, and to comfort the mouth of the stomach." When the oven cooled off too quickly, however, the bread was likely to be underbaked and doughy.

TO MAKE A CREAM IN THE ITALIAN FASHION TO EAT COLD

Take twenty yolks of eggs, and two quarts of cream, strain it with a little salt, saffron, rosewater, juyce of orange, a little white wine and a pound of sugar; then bake it in a deep dish with some fine cinamon, and some candied pistaches stuck on it, and when it is baked, white muscadines.

Robert May, *The Accomplisht Cook*

THE WORKING VERSION:

5 egg yolks
2 cups light cream
⅓ cup sugar
1 pinch salt
3 tablespoons orange juice
3 tablespoons any sweet white wine

2 tablespoons rose water
⅛ teaspoon saffron
⅛ teaspoon cinnamon
1 tablespoon sugared pistachio nuts (optional)

Mix all the ingredients except the nuts together until blended. Pour the mixture into a quart-size oven-to-table casserole. Set the casserole in a larger and deeper baking pan and pour hot water into the pan around the casserole until it is as high as the top of the cream.

Bake at 350° for about fifty minutes, or until a knife inserted into the center of the cream comes out clean. Remove the casserole from its water bath and cool before serving. If you use the nuts, sprinkle them over the cream just before serving.

Elizabethan and Jacobean ladies distilled their own rose water. True essence of roses is now difficult to find and rarely fresh when it is available. In the amounts called for in sixteenth- and seventeenth-century recipes, the cost would be astronomical. But synthetic rose water can be purchased at pharmacies very reasonably and is an adequate substitute for true rose water.

As an alternative to saffron, the saffron tea sold in health-food stores is adequate for seasoning purposes and much cheaper.

Muscadines were sugar pastilles flavored with musk, ambergris, orrisroot, and rose water and were also called "kissing comfits." A recipe for these is on page 390. Here they would serve merely as decoration and compete with the flavor of the cream, as do the nuts. Neither will be missed if omitted.

TO MAKE A MOST RARE AND EXCELLENT MARROW PUDDING IN A DISH BAKED

Take the marrow of four marrow bones, two pinemolets or french breads, half a pound of raisins of the Sun ready boil'd and

cold, cinamon a quarter of an ounce fine beaten, two grated nut-
megs, sugar a quarter of a pound, dates a quarter of a pound,
sack half a pint, rose water a quarter of a pint, ten eggs, two
grains of ambergreese, and two of musk dissolved: Now have
a fine clean deep large dish, then have a slice of French bread, and
lay a lay [layer] of slic'd bread in the dish, and strew it with
cinamon, nutmeg, and sugar mingled together, & also sprinkle
the slices of bread with sack and Rosewater, and then some
raisins of the sun, and some sliced dates, and good big pieces of
marrow; and thus make two or three lays of the aforesaid in-
gredients, with four ounces of musk, ambergreese, and most mar-
row on the top; then take two quarts of cream, and strain it with
half a quarter of fine sugar, and a little salt (about a spoonful),
and twelve eggs, six of the whites taken away: then set the dish
in the oven, temperate, and not too hot, and bake it very fair and
white, and fill it at two several times, and being baked, scrape
fine sugar on it, and serve it hot.

Robert May, *The Accomplisht Cook*

THE WORKING VERSION:

4 slices good white bread, homemade if you have it	2 tablespoons sugar
¼ cup white raisins, parboiled	1 tablespoon brown sugar
¼ cup sliced dates	1 tablespoon rose water
2 ounces beef marrow, diced	¼ teaspoon nutmeg
3 egg yolks	¼ teaspoon cinnamon
½ cup light cream	¼ teaspoon salt
½ cup sherry	1 drop essence of ambergris
	1 drop essence of musk

Cut the slices of bread into quarters. Arrange a layer of bread in the bottom of an oven-to-table casserole, sprinkle a few raisins, dates, and bits of beef marrow over the bread. Continue layering the bread, raisins, dates, and marrow until all are in the casserole.

Beat together the rest of the ingredients until well blended. Pour the mixture slowly over the ingredients in the casserole and bake at 300° for forty-five minutes. Serve warm.

Served hot out of the oven this pudding needs no sauce, but if you would like to have a sauce for it, mix ½ cup of sherry, ½ cup of light cream, one tablespoon rose water, one tablespoon sugar, and two egg yolks. Cook these over low heat, stirring constantly, until the sauce begins to thicken—it should be only a little thicker than whipping cream.

There is an obvious printer's error in the text of May's recipe; "ounces" was clearly substituted for "grains" of musk and ambergris about ⅔ of the way through the recipe. This is not an error Robert May would have made; musk and ambergris were costly, so costly that some recipes suggest tying a grain of ambergris or musk in a cloth, letting it steep in the ingredients for a while, and then withdrawing it for reuse. The essence is so potent that one should measure it with an eyedropper.

In Shakespeare's day musk and ambergris came in the form of dried granules. Both were used as perfumes, but Shakespeare mentions only musk. In *The Merry Wives of Windsor* (Act II, Scene 2), Dame Quickly is gulling Falstaff into believing that Mistress Ford is head over heels in love with him. She elaborates on the numbers of knights, gentlemen, and lords who have unsuccessfully sought Mistress Ford's favors with "gift after gift; smelling so sweetly—all musk."

The arrival of a ship with ambergris in its cargo was of great interest to many people. John Chamberlain, for example, wrote to his friend Dudley Carleton on August 1, 1613, that a ship that had touched at the Bermudas had "brought thence . . . between 20 and 30 pound waight of amber-greece, worth £900 at least." Nine hundred pounds, needless to say, was an enormous sum in those days.

KITCHENS AND KITCHEN EQUIPMENT

Kitchens and kitchen equipment varied with economic and social status. The very poor were likely to have had little more than a skillet and a pot with which to cook their meals. In winter the cooking would have been done in the single room in which the family lived, over a small iron or brick frame under which a fire was laid; in warm weather the cooking fire might have been set up out of doors. They would have had to buy their bread and, when they could afford it, perhaps a bit of roast meat or meat pie from the commercial cook shops, which were to be found in villages as well as in cities.

The poor were not the only families who patronized the cook

shops. Many families found it easier to purchase some part of their meals at cook shops when their kitchen facilities were limited. Few kitchens, even in wealthy homes, could handle the large amounts of food required for important entertaining.

Even in his comfortable Tower prison, the Earl of Northumberland had kitchen problems. A lavish host, he had to buy a copper pot to boil beef, a pan to boil cockles, a brass pan to boil fish, and a bell-metal device to roast quinces and pears.

Kitchens in the homes of well-to-do families were likely to be fairly well equipped, although lighting facilities might have been poor and the working areas crowded.

Haddon Hall, the Derbyshire manor of the duke of Rutland where the family still maintains its residence, has opened to the public, during part of the year, the lovely great hall with the private dining parlor behind it and the old kitchens. The kitchens, which go back to medieval days, give a rare glimpse of the past.

Originally, there were two large fireplaces, but one was removed when the wall space where it stood was needed for access to a modernized kitchen for the family. Alongside the remaining fireplace is a large woodbox. Under the small windows in the low-ceilinged room are the medieval stone troughs that were used to store water for kitchen use. Along one side of the room stands a long, very thick, wide plank on legs in the top of which are hollowed a series of rounded depressions like large bowls, one of which has been completely worn through with use. This was where the mincing and mixing of ingredients for various dishes were done. On the left of the kitchen are two ovens set in the wall. Several "meal arks," wooden troughs on legs with covers to keep the flour clean and dry, stand along one wall. In an adjoining room, where the butchering was done, is a salting trough, a hanging rack with hooks for meat, and a low chopping block. Several small adjoining rooms, probably used as larders for storing food, contain wooden cupboards on legs with openwork carving in the doors. The carving was not only decorative, but it also served to keep foodstuffs ventilated.

The kitchen in the house that Thomas Qwennell, a prosperous Surrey farmer, left when he died in 1571 was as large as the great hall, the main room of the house. Part of it extended back from the fireplace, which—with the oven—took up one whole side of the room. The rear portion was probably added on to the original kitchen when that became too small for the house-

*Old kitchens in Haddon Hall, the Derbyshire
residence of the Duke of Rutland*

A Dole Cupboard

Larder with Dole Cupboards ▶

Bakery and larder with dole cupboards of Haddon Hall

hold's needs. The extra space may have served as a pantry or larder, or perhaps for storing fuel for the fireplace and oven. But it might equally well have been used for brewing, salting or dressing meats and fish, and baking.

The kitchen garden was alongside the kitchen, and Mistress Qwennell had only to step outside her door for her herbs, vegetables, salad greens, and flowers. The orchard ran conveniently along the back side of the house.

Having bequeathed his soul to God, made several charitable gifts, remembered his servants and farm workers quite generously, and left bequests to various relatives, Thomas Qwennell minutely detailed the goods and rights belonging to the house and farm that his widow was to enjoy during her lifetime.

He apparently expected his widow to carry on farming activities, for he left her the use of land, farm equipment, work animals, stock, poultry, and several riding horses, as well as the garden and orchard. She was to share the house with his brother, but was to have for her own use "the parler in the west syde of my house . . . which adjoynethe to the hawle, there, the chamber over the same parler, the garret above the same chamber, the loft over the hawle and the kytchen lofte with free ingress, egress, and regress . . . and . . . roome and fyer in the said hawle at all times." She was also to have "halfe the kytchen," and firewood "to dress meate, and drinke, bake and brew, and to doe all other necessaryes mete and convenyent in the same kytchen at all tymes." Nothing was left to chance. Thomas Qwennell even stipulates that his wife, Agnys, is to have "halfe my bakon at the beam [*i.e.,* hanging from the rafters, probably in the loft over the kitchen], except the twoe greatest flytches and the twoe leaste flytches" and "two of the best flytches of dryed beefe," as well as "halfe my Lard and greace."

Marjorie and C. H. B. Quennell, in their *History of Everyday Things in England,* discuss the will and reproduce a drawing of the ground-floor plan of the house as it was in 1600. The will gives a picture of the kind of equipment that would have been in a well-equipped kitchen. Mistress Qwennell was, for example, to have "my beste and my leaste two candlestycks, my beste brasse potts, my beste and my leaste kettles, and my kettle which was bound with yron by Hewghe the smythe, my posnet [small saucepan with legs] of belle brasse, my leaste [smallest] Skyllet and the occupation [use] of my Cawdron [cauldron] as often as she

A seventeenth-century kitchen

have nede, so long tyme as she shall be dwellinge at Lyethehill . . . and also halfe of . . . my wodden vessill to be equally divyded except my best vate and my best kyfe [brewing equipment]."

These are only part of the furnishings there must have been in her kitchen to dress meat and drink, to bake and brew with. There would have been spits for roasting meats, fowl, and fish in front of the fire; racks (cobberds or cobards) with hooks at different levels to hold the spits, and dripping pans to catch the juices from the roasting meat. There may have been a device for mechanically turning the spits.

For broiling directly over the fire, there would have been a gridiron. Tripods from which to hand kettles over the coals, or adjustable pothooks, as well as trivets on which small pots or skillets could be rested and a toasting iron, were also likely parts of her kitchen fireplace equipment. In addition to her oven, she may have had a small iron box for baking, which would have been placed in the coals of the fireplace when it was being used.

A pell (a flat, wooden shovel with a long handle) would have been essential for putting Mistress Qwennell's breads and pastries into the oven and removing them when they were baked. Before the bread could be baked, the coals from the fire, which had been set inside the oven to heat the oven bricks to baking temperature, would have had to be raked out and the oven floor wiped clean with a damp huzzy (a mop made of rags tied to a long handle).

The wooden vessels that Mistress Qwennell was to share with her brother-in-law doubtless included a mixing and kneading trough for making bread, tubs for fresh water, watering tubs for soaking the salt out of salt meat and fish, pickling tubs for sousing brawn and other meats and fish, tubs for cheese-making and other dairy activities, as well as brewing equipment. The work surfaces that she used were most likely demountable boards set on trestles that could be taken apart and set out of the way when not in use. She may also have used the tops of chests that contained some of her valued small equipment.

We may think of sixteenth- and seventeenth-century kitchens as rather primitive, but they contained many of the same utensils we find essential today.

On the basis of other household inventories, we can assume that Mistress Qwennell had in her kitchen knives of all sorts: for slicing, chopping, mincing; for cutting the curds in cheese-

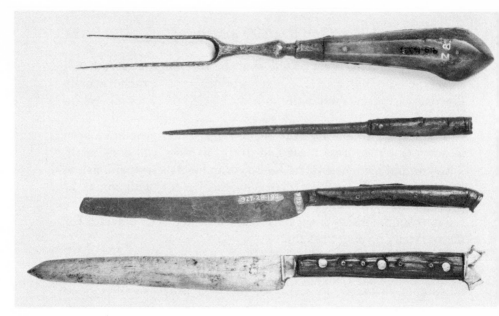

Sixteenth- and seventeenth-century kitchen utensils: knives, larding needle and fork

making; for scraping salt from the solid cakes in which it arrived in her kitchen, as did sugar; chipping knives to remove the burned crusts from bread; a cleaver and boning knives for meat and fish. Other familiar items would have been a grater, a colander, a sieve, ladles, skimmers, a slice (spatula), mixing spoons, and stirring sticks or spoons. A meat hook or a fork to spear pieces of meat from the beef kettle or pottage pot and to remove meat from the spits would also have been part of the basic kitchen utensils.

To grind mustard seed for sauce, there would have been a mustard quern (mill). To pound her precious spices and sugar into powder, her almonds into paste for marchpane, and other ingredients into other pastes, there would have been mortars and pestles made of brass, wood, marble, or earthenware.

Her flour would have been stored in a chest of wood, or kept in a large bag, sometimes made of leather. Spices were stored in small chests or boxes; dried fruits in boxes or earthenware jars, in small wall cupboards or on open shelves. Very likely a large bag would have been hanging from the ceiling to keep the bread out of the reach of rats and mice.

Her kitchen jugs or bottles might have been of earthenware, glass, or leather, perhaps pewter. Fruit and herb cordials for medicinal use would have been stored in glass or earthenware bottles and fruit confections in "gallypots" of glass or earthenware, or perhaps in small wooden boxes.

Her cooking pots and pans were made of iron, brass, copper, tin laten (an alloy of tin with brass in it), and earthenware. She doubtless owned simple distilling equipment in which, when her flowers and herbs were at their most fragrant stages, she would distill "sweet waters."

There is, however, no indication that Mistress Qwennell enjoyed the luxury of having water piped into her kitchen, although an increasing number of wealthy households had water piped into at least the ground floor of their homes. Ingatestone was one of those homes.

As contrast to this amply supplied household, John Trendar, of St. Giles, Oxford, who died in 1582 leaving total possessions valued at "eight pounds one shilling sixpense," had in his cottage —most likely a single room—"3 brasse pottes, 2 Kettles, a posnet and a skimmer, a skillet, 4 candlesticks, two sawcers [bowls to hold sauces], 2 salt sallers, one pewter cuppe, towe paire of Andiernes and a friing pane, a gridierne, a paire of pott houckes [hooks] and hannylls [handles], a broche [broach] . . . a driping pan, and 2 tablecloths."

At Syon House, one of the earl of Northumberland's estates, in Middlesex, only the silverware was itemized in the inventories. The kitchen inventory merely noted: "Potts, panns, spitts, frying panns, gridyrons, tables, and other necessaries." And in the larder were: "2 powdringe [salting] tubbes, 2 tables upon trestles, 1 table and 1 stoole." But listed with the silverware were: a "toasting fork, a culender, a Grater with a case," ladles, skimmers, mortars and pestles, a number of chafing dishes, and a "Posnett with a cover" weighing 84½ ounces and another weighing 35½ ounces.

The fireplaces where food was cooked were called "ranges." Here the boiling, stewing, and frying were done, either in kettles suspended from cranes directly over the fire or in three- or four-legged pots of iron set among the coals in the fire. Except in humble cottages, where the floors were of packed clay or earth, kitchen floors were of stone. Sometimes small fires were made directly on the floor and over them were cooked sauces and perhaps other dishes that could be prepared in small pans or skillets.

The kitchens in even the greatest homes were not always

adequate when royalty was to be entertained. Queen Elizabeth, when she came on a visit, brought with her a retinue of about two hundred people. When she visited Elvetham, one of the smaller manors of the earl of Hertford, in 1591, the earl decided to enlarge the house "with newe roomes . . . for the entertainement of Nobles, Gentlemen, and others" in addition to those for the queen's own use, and set three hundred artisans to work at the job. Although the queen's meals were prepared by her own servants and from her own food supplies, the members of her retinue had to be fed. Since the manor house could not be expanded to meet all the feeding requirements, extra buildings were erected on the grounds of the manor house. These included: "A large Pastery, with five ovens new built, some of them foureteene foote deepe.—A great Kitchin . . . with a boyling place for small boild meates.—An other Kitchin . . . with a Boilinghouse, for the great boiler." Boiling kettles came in all sizes and were made of various metals, the most common being iron, but even earthenware was sometimes used. The palace accounts of the dinners served to the judges of the Star Chamber list several purchases of "earthen boiling kettles" for soups.

Great households usually had two or more kitchens. Those members of the peerage—there were only about sixty families of peers left in England in Elizabeth's time—who still fancied lives of medieval splendor had privy (special) kitchens and cooks to prepare the food for their own tables, distinct from the kitchens and cooks for the household as a whole. In some of these manors, the kitchens were separated from the main building in order to lessen the danger of fire, but that made serving foods hot next to impossible.

At Theobalds, Lord Burghley's magnificent estate, which Queen Elizabeth visited more often than any other place, one of the rooms above the bakehouse was set apart for the use of the queen's privy cook. Theobalds had two kitchens, a boiling room, a "pastry" for baked meats, three larders, a beer buttery, a wine "seller" (cellar), and a scullery.

Ingatestone, which could not compare in size or splendor with Theobalds or the earl of Northumberland's Syon, was still a comparatively large household. Its bakehouse turned out about twenty thousand loaves of bread a year for household use, even counting two manchets as only one loaf.

An itemization of kitchen equipment made at the palace of

Havering, prior to its repair, listed: four dresser boards upon trestles in the "Great Kytchen," two dresser boards in the "new Kytchen," and a kneading trough and four molding boards in the bakehouse. The royal household in London alone kept two bakehouses busy. The privy bakehouse made manchet and fine cheate for the royal table while the "great bakehouse" made the rest of the bread. There were also a privy kitchen, a large kitchen, a boiling room, a scalding room, which did nothing but dress poultry, a pastry kitchen for baked meats, a wafery for cakes and wafers, and a confectionary.

A Repast for Mercutio

Eat with us to-night, the charge and thanking
Shall be for me.

All's Well That Ends Well,
Act III, Scene 5 (*Helena*)

SACK

*Call not me honour, nor lordship; I
ne'er drank sack in my life.*
The Taming of the Shrew, Induction, Scene 2 (*Sly*)

A SUMMER SALAD

*My salad days,
When I was green in judgment.*
Antony and Cleopatra, Act I, Scene 5 (*Cleopatra*)

PETTITOES (PIG'S FEET) IN JELLY

*My clown . . . grew so in love with the wenches'
song that he would not stir his pettitoes till he had both
tune and words.*
The Winter's Tale, Act IV, Scene 3 (*Autolycus*)

A CARP STEWED WITH OYSTERS

Your bait of falsehood takes this carp of truth.
Hamlet, Act II, Scene 1 (*Polonius*)

COLLOPS OF VEAL IN WHITE WINE SAUCE

*Where the bull and cow are both milk-white,
They never do beget a coal-black calf.*
Titus Andronicus, Act V, Scene 1 (*Second Goth*)

STEWED MUSHROOMS

And you, whose pastime
Is to make midnight mushrooms.
The Tempest, Act V, Scene 1 (*Prospero*)

A GAMMON OF BACON (HAM) IN PASTRY

I have a gammon of bacon and two razes of
ginger, to be delivered as far as Charing-cross.
Henry IV, Part I, Act II, Scene 1 (*Second Carrier*)

A FRIED MEAT OF CURDS
(COTTAGE CHEESE) AND APPLES

Upon what meat doth this our Caesar feed,
That he is grown so great?
Julius Caesar, Act I, Scene 2 (*Cassius*)

A FLANK STEAK COLLARED

There is cold meat i' the cave; we'll
browse on that.
Cymbeline, Act III, Scene 6 (*Guiderius*)

SPANISH LAMB MEATBALLS

Why, these balls bound; there's noise
in it.
All's Well That Ends Well, Act II, Scene 3 (*Parolles*)

BUTTERED PEASECODS

Not yet old enough for a man, nor young
enough for a boy; as a squash is before 'tis
a peascod.
Twelfth Night, Act I, Scene 5 (*Malvolio*)

TEMMES BREAD AND MANCHET

Ay, to the leavening; but here's yet in the word
'hereafter' the kneading, the making of the cake, the
heating of the oven, and the baking.
Troilus and Cressida, Act I, Scene 1 (*Pandarus*)

WHITE WINE AND CLARET

He would have all as merry
As, first, good company, good wine, good welcome
Can make good people.

Henry VIII, Act I, Scene 4 (*Guildford*)

ALE

I'll to the alehouse with you presently;
where, for one shot of five pence, thou
shalt have five thousand welcomes.

Two Gentlemen of Verona, Act II, Scene 5 (*Speed*)

A LEACH MADE IN THE FRENCH WAY

Here comes the herald of the French, my liege.

Henry V, Act IV, Scene 7 (*Exeter*)

CHEWETS OF VEAL

Peace, chewet, peace!

Henry IV, Part I, Act V, Scene 1 (*Prince Hal*)

They have done my poor house grace; for which I pay 'em
A thousand thanks, and pray 'em take their pleasures.

Henry VIII, Act I, Scene 4 (*Cardinal Wolsey*)

A SUMMER SALAD

"All herbs [vegetables] should be eaten according to the time of
the year and the property of them," said *William Vaughan,* in
Directions for Health, *"the hot sorts for winter, the cold for*
summer, and the temperate for spring and autumn." Among the
cold herbs he placed lettuce, white endive, succory [chicory or
curly endive].

For old people, he said, it was *"expedient sometimes to boyle*
[lettuce] whole in pottage, and afterwards to eat them with
Sugar, Vinegar and Oyle. In this manner Galen [a Greek physi-

cian of the second century A.D.] *used it in his old age against watchfulnesse [sleeplessness]."*

THE WORKING VERSION:

3 large leaves leaf lettuce	3 tablespoons red wine
3 large leaves chicory (curly	vinegar
endive)	4 tablespoons olive oil
2 heads Belgian endive	½ teaspoon salt
6 blades chives, minced	½ teaspoon brown sugar
	⅛ teaspoon pepper

Wash the lettuce and chicory in cool water and dry in a clean cloth. Wash, dry, and slice the Belgian endive into ½-inch slices.

Put the chives, vinegar, oil, salt, sugar, and pepper in a salad bowl and stir until blended. Tear or cut the lettuce and chicory into bite-size pieces. Toss all the greens in the dressing and serve.

Green leafy vegetables had many virtues according to the health book writers. "Among al hearbes," said Thomas Elyot in *The Castle of Health,* "none hath so good juyce as lettice. Some men doe suppose that it maketh abundance of bloud, albeit not very pure or perfect: it doth set a hot appetite and eaten in the evening it provoketh sleep. Suckory or Cycory," he added, "is like in operation to Lettice and tempereth choler wonderfully."

TO JELLY HOGS OR PORKERS FEET (PETTITOES)

Take twelve feet . . . being finely scalded, & lay them to soke twenty four hours, shift and scrape them very white, then boil them in a fair clean scowered brass pot or pipkin in three gallons of liquor, five quarts of water, three of wine vinegar, or verjuyce, and four of white-wine, boil them from three gallons to four quarts waste, being scummed, put in an ounce of pepper whole, an ounce of nutmegs in quarters, an ounce of ginger slic't, and an ounce of cinnamon, boil them together, as is abovesaid to four quarts.

Then take up the meat and let them cool, divide them into dishes, and run it over with the broth or jelly being a little first setled, take the clearest, and being cold put juice of orange over all, serve it with bay leaves about the dish.

Robert May, *The Accomplisht Cook*

THE WORKING VERSION:

2 fresh pig's feet, halved lengthwise	One 1-inch-thick slice fresh ginger
1 quart water	¼ teaspoon peppercorns
2 cups distilled vinegar	¼ teaspoon nutmeg
1 cup white wine	2 tablespoons orange juice
One 3-inch piece stick cinnamon	Bay leaves (to garnish)

Scrub the pig's feet with a stiff vegetable brush under cold running water. Put all the remaining ingredients except the orange juice and bay leaves into a large saucepan and bring to a boil. Add the pig's feet, lower the heat to simmer, and cook until they are very tender and the liquid is reduced to about one pint—one to two hours. Remove the feet from the cooking broth, bone them, and cut the meat into inch-wide slices.

Put the slices into a bowl just large enough to hold them. Cover and set aside until needed. Strain the cooking broth through a clean white cloth into a small saucepan. Add one tablespoon of the orange juice and continue cooking until the liquid is reduced to one cup. Pour the reduced liquid over the sliced pig's feet. They should be completely covered; if there is not enough liquid to cover them, add equal parts of wine and vinegar to the bowl. Cover and refrigerate until jelled—about eight hours.

Turn the jellied pig's feet out on a flat plate and cut into wedges. Garnish with bay leaves and sprinkle the rest of the orange juice over the wedges.

Calf's feet were usually preferred to pig's feet, or were perhaps more readily available; they appear on more published bills of fare, and more recipes are given for them than for pig's feet. They were sufficiently esteemed to be offered when the guests were members of the nobility, though not so highly esteemed that other guests would be denied them. When Sir Richard Hoghton entertained James I and his retinue at Hoghton Towers, in

White Radish Lettuce.

Street vendor selling radishes and lettuce (16th–17th-century woodcut)

1617, "neats feet" were served at supper. And when the Fairfax family feasted the earl of Rutland and his retinue, "calfes feet boiled" were on the menu. The "Service at Supper" in *A Proper newe Booke of Cokerye* begins with a pottage, a salad, and "a pygges petytoe."

Calf's feet and pig's feet were also soused, fried, and made into pies, generally for a supper dish. Street vendors who sold these were called "tripe wives" because they also sold tripes. "Here's trotters, calf's feet and fine tripes!" they called out to attract buyers.

TO STEW A CARP

Take a Carp, scale and blood him in the tail, garing [fitting] him in a vessel, put to him a quart of Claret-wine, a little Vinegar and Salt, put him into a Pipkin with that liquor, with some Oysters with the liquor, five or six blades of large Mace, whole Pepper and Cloves, the tops of Time, three or four Anchovies, an Onion minced and fryed in brown butter, some grated bread, let all these stew together half an hour, with some Lemmon sliced, till it come to a body to your mind [until you think it is done]; with sippets dish and garnish it as you please.

William Rabisha, *The whole Body of Cookery Dissected*

THE WORKING VERSION:

One 2-pound piece of carp	6 peppercorns
Boiling water	4 cloves
3 tablespoons butter	1 large piece whole mace
1 medium onion, minced	1½ teaspoons salt
1 tablespoon grated bread crumbs	½ lemon, sliced thin and seeded
2 cups claret	8 small oysters in their shells
2 tablespoons vinegar	
1 anchovy fillet, or ¼ teaspoon anchovy paste	3 slices buttered toast, quartered
3 sprigs fresh thyme, or ½ teaspoon dried thyme	

Ask your fish dealer to skin the carp, or, if you want to skin it yourself, wash the carp under cold water and remove any bits of entrails; fill a saucepan with enough water to cover the fish, and bring it to a boil. Lower the carp into the water and cook for one minute. Remove the fish to a plate with a slotted spoon, and, while it is hot, strip the skin off with a sharp knife.

Melt the butter in a saucepan not much larger than the piece of fish. Add the minced onion and bread crumbs and sauté for one minute, stirring constantly. Add all the rest of the ingredients except the oysters and the toast. Lower the heat to simmer and cook for ten minutes, then lower the carp into the sauce, cover the pot, and simmer fifteen to twenty minutes, or until the fish is tender but still firm.

Shuck the oysters, add them with their juice to the fish and simmer five more minutes. Remove the fish from the sauce to a plate and slice the meat from the upper side of the spinal bone, then lift off the bone and slice the lower section. Put the fish into a warmed serving bowl. Bring the sauce to a boil again and spoon it, with the oysters, over the fish. Arrange the toast around the sides of the bowl and serve.

Robert May's cookbook—the largest and most complete of the cookbooks of this period—illustrates the importance of fish in the English diet. Of the 455 pages of recipes, 97 are devoted to ways of preparing fish. Eighteen of these offer "divers ways, and the most excellent, for dressing Carps, either Boiled, Stewed, Broiled, Roasted, or Baked." Carp was sometimes brought alive into the kitchen, and a few recipes begin, "Let your Carpe be alive." Carp were sold, according to William Harrison, by the "inches of clean fish, from the eyes or gills to the crotch of the tails," as were pike and several other large river fish.

London fishwives carried their wares in wide, flat baskets balanced on their heads, or in curved baskets hung over their arms. Noisy and argumentative, the fishwives were a source of constant complaint, but with a reputation as an easygoing lot. Their wares having been sold, it was said, they might spend their day's earnings at an alehouse in the evening, for they had only "to pawn a petticoat the next morning" to buy enough fish to set up in business again.

HOW TO FRY VEALE

Cut a leg of Veale into thin slices, and hack them well with the cleaver, then lay them in a dish and season it with Nutmeg, Ginger, Pepper and Salt, then mix six or eight raw yolks of Eggs with it very well together, and let it stand an houre or more, then fry it in the pan with Butter till it be enough, keeping the pieces with turning; then take it up into a dish, and stew it together with a little white-Wine and a Lemon sliced; and when the dinner is ready, put in a piece of Butter, and shake it well together, and serve it up to the Table with sippits.

Joseph Cooper, *The Art of Cookery Refin'd and Augmented*

THE WORKING VERSION:

1 pound veal round, sliced ½ inch thick	6 tablespoons butter
2 egg yolks	⅔ cup dry white wine
1 teaspoon salt	¼ lemon, peeled, sliced thin, and seeded
¼ teaspoon pepper	3 slices hot buttered toast, quartered
½ teaspoon ginger	
½ teaspoon nutmeg	

Cut the slices of veal into approximately three-inch squares and flatten them with the side of a cleaver or a meat tenderizer.

On a plate mix the egg yolks, salt, pepper, ginger, and nutmeg. Dip the pieces of veal into the mixture and coat them evenly on each side. Melt four tablespoons of butter in a large skillet and sauté the veal over medium heat until tender—about four minutes on each side. When all the pieces are cooked, add the wine and lemon slices and simmer five minutes longer. Then stir in the remaining butter until it melts.

Put the toast on a heated serving dish and arrange the veal over it. Pour the sauce over the meat and serve.

"Veale is nutrytyve meate," said Dr. Boorde, "and doth nurysshe moche a man, for it is soone dygestyd whereupon many men doth holde oppinyon that it is the best flesshe and the most nutrytyve meate that can be for mans sustenance."

Veal was not only considered good for one, it was good eating —and it was properly appreciated. From head to hoof, every part was used, including testicles and udders.

The head was boiled, broiled, stewed, soused, or made into pies and mincemeat tarts. The tongue and brains were cooked separately, or minced together, seasoned, stuffed into the skull cavity, and roasted. Occasionally, oysters would be used as the basis for the stuffing.

The feet were used to make jelly, though mainly for sick people; isinglass was increasingly preferred for desserts since it made a clearer jelly. Calves' feet were also boiled, stewed, fried, roasted, and made into pies.

Kidneys and tongues stewed together were popular, as were small pies of minced kidneys and tongue, mixed with spices and dried fruits and fried in deep fat or baked. Veal sweetbreads and "stones" [testicles] were stewed or fricasseed together; veal udders were boiled and sliced for hot or cold eating, and, because of its richness, minced udder was sometimes used in place of bone marrow when the latter was not available.

The taste for udders has not survived, nor has the taste for animal testicles, although they can still be found in some meat markets. They were, however, considered delicate meat in Shakespeare's day. Robert May includes a dish of "fresh neats tongue and Udder in Stoffado" in one of his feast menus, and Rabisha has "A dish of boyled Udders and Tongues with Cabbage" in one of his feast menus.

TO STEW MUSHROOMS

Peel them, and put them in a clean dish, strow salt on them, and put an onion to them, some sweet herbs, large mace, pepper, butter, salt, and two or three cloves, being tender stewed on a soft fire, put to them some grated bread, and a little white wine, stew them a little more, and dish them (but first rub the dish with a clove of garlick), sippet them, lay slic't orange on them, and run them over with beaten butter.

Robert May, *The Accomplisht Cook*

THE WORKING VERSION:

24 firm, fresh mushrooms about 1 to 1 ½ inches in diameter	¼ teaspoon salt
	¼ teaspoon pepper
	1 teaspoon grated bread crumbs
4 tablespoons butter	
1 small onion, sliced thin	¼ cup dry white wine
1 clove garlic, peeled	2 slices buttered toast, quartered
2 teaspoons minced parsley	
¼ teaspoon marjoram	1 small navel orange, peeled, sliced thin, and seeded
¼ teaspoon mace	
1 pinch of cloves	

Choose mushrooms that have not yet opened. If they are relatively clean, wipe them off with a damp cloth—otherwise wash them under cool running water and dry immediately. Cut off the stems to within an inch of the caps.

Melt the butter in a saucepan or skillet. Add the sliced onion and the garlic and sauté over medium heat until the onion is translucent. Remove and discard the garlic. Add the mushrooms, parsley, marjoram, mace, cloves, salt, and pepper. Cook over medium-low heat for ten minutes, stirring occasionally. Stir in the bread crumbs, add the wine, and continue cooking for five minutes—the mushrooms should remain firm.

Arrange the toast in a heated serving dish and spoon the mushrooms and sauce over them. Garnish the dish with the orange slices and serve.

Most people looked upon new foods with suspicion, and William Harrison was no exception; about mushrooms he was downright alarmed. Having listed with approval all the vegetables of which people had lost fear, he also worried, "Neither do they now stay with such as are wholesome in their kinds, but adventure further upon such as are very dangerous and hurtful, as the verangenes [eggplant], mushrooms, etc., as if Nature had ordained all for the belly or that all things were to be eaten, for whose mischevous operation the Lord in some measure hath given and provided a remedy." His fears were ahead of the facts, as few Englishmen even dreamed of eating mushrooms in Harrison's day. They had not yet become common enough to be discussed in any of the dietaries or described in the herbals.

Few contemporary cookbooks contain recipes for preparing them. Robert May, however, had spent sufficient time in Italy and France to have lost any fears he might have had about mushrooms, and he offers six ways of preparing them. They are commonly called "toad-stools" in English, he says, and adds, perhaps to show his knowledge of Continental foods, that the Italians called them "Fungy" and the French called them "Champignions."

FOR TO BAKE A GAMMON OF BACON

Boyle your gammon of Bacon, and stuffe it with Parsley and Sage, and yolkes of hard Egs, and when it is boyled, stuffe it and let it boile againe, season it with Pepper, Cloves, and Mace, sticke whole Cloves fast in it: Then lay it so in your paste with salte butter, and so bake it.

TO MAKE FINE PASTE ANOTHER WAY

Take Butter and Ale, and seeth them together: Then take your flower, and put thereinto three Egs, Sugar, Saffron, and salt.

John Partridge, *The good Huswifes Handmaide for the Kitchin*

THE WORKING VERSION:

One 2-inch-thick center slice of tenderized ham
2 tablespoons soft butter
2 hard-boiled egg yolks
½ cup minced parsley
¼ teaspoon sage
½ teaspoon mace
⅛ teaspoon cloves
⅛ teaspoon pepper
Prepared mustard (optional)

THE PASTRY
2 cups sifted unbleached flour
1 teaspoon salt
½ teaspoon sugar
⅛ teaspoon saffron
¾ cup cold butter
1 egg, separated
½ cup ale (approximately)

Remove the bone from the center of the ham steak and trim off the fat. Blend the butter, hard-boiled egg yolks, parsley, sage, mace, cloves, and pepper into a paste and spread it over both sides of the ham. Cover and set aside while you make the pastry crust.

To make the pastry, sift together the flour, salt, and sugar, then stir in the saffron. Rub ½ cup of the butter into the flour mixture with your fingers until the mixture is like fine meal. Dice the rest of the butter and stir it in. Stir the egg yolk and ale together until blended and add to the dry mixture. Mix lightly and quickly into a ball—if more liquid is needed add more ale by the tablespoonful. Turn the dough out onto a well-floured work surface, pat into a rectangle, and roll it out to a sheet two inches longer and a little wider than twice the width of the ham.

Loosen the sheet from the work surface, brush it with some of the egg white, and center the slice of ham on the pastry. Bring the two short ends of the sheet of pastry up over the ham and brush the outsides with egg white, then fold over the long sides so that they overlap by about an inch. Press them lightly together to seal the pasty.

Carefully turn the pasty over into a rectangular baking dish. Brush the top with the remaining egg white and bake at 450° for twenty minutes, then lower the heat to 350° and bake twenty-five minutes longer. Serve hot or cold, but not refrigerated, with a side dish of prepared mustard if desired.

If you wish to serve the pasty in the dish in which it was baked, use an oven-to-table baking dish.

English hams and bacon, like cheese, were known by the regions they came from. Yorkshire hams had as fine a reputation in Shakespeare's day as they do today. Some ham was also imported from Westphalia, and both Robert May and William Rabisha call for Westphalian hams in their feast bills of fare.

Flitches—bacon from the sides of the animal—were called by various names: interlarded bacon, streaked bacon, rib bacon, middle bacon. Bacon, but not gammon of bacon (ham), had been the poor man's meat in the Middle Ages and continued as such during, and long after, Shakespeare's lifetime. Although few farm laborers could afford to keep a pig, they sometimes could afford to buy a side of bacon from a better-off neighbor when he slaughtered a pig and smoke it in the cottage chimney.

Smokehouses for curing ham and bacon were common on

larger farms and country estates. Smaller farms, which did not have smokehouses, smoked their meats inside the fireplace, hanging them on the wall away from the fire but where the smoke could envelop the meat. Sometimes fireplaces were built with "smoke holes," that is, small alcoves in the inside walls. Here not only gammons and flitches of bacon but sausages and pieces of Martilmas beef were hung to be smoked. Thomas Tusser, in his "Agricultural Calender," tells farmers:

> For Easter at Martlemas [early in November], hang
>   up a beef,
> For pea fed and stall fed, play Purchase the thief.
> With that and fat bacon, till grass beef come in
> Thy folk shall look cherey when others look thin.

He added:

> He that can rear up a pig in his house [on kitchen
>   scraps]
> Hath cheaper his bacon and sweeter his souse [pickled
>   pork].

And to the housewife he said,

> When Easter comes, who knows not then,
> That Veal and bacon is the man.

Speaking from a higher economic level, Nicholas Breton's countryman boasts of the good things of life in the country: "We have . . . oxen in the stall, sheepe in the pen, hogges in the stie, corne in the garner, cheese in the loft, milke in the dairy, creame in the pot, butter in the dish, ale in the tub, and Acqua vitae in the bottle, beefe in the brine, brawne in the sowce, and bacon in the roofe, hearbs in the garden and water at our doors."

The "Breviate" for a "Nobleman's house" lists bacon as one of the essential meats for the storeroom and kitchen. When Lord North entertained Queen Elizabeth, eight "Gammonds of bacon" were among the meats purchased for the event. And when Sir Richard Hoghton had the expensive honor of being host to James I, ham was served at dinner, supper, and again at breakfast. Hams, usually baked in pies, but sometimes boiled or combined with cured tongue, appear on most of the cookbook feast menus.

Smoked meats did not, however, win favor among the dietary writers. "Bakon," said Andrewe Boorde, "is good for carters

and plowmen the which be ever laborynge . . . but . . . if they
have the stone, and use to eate it they shal synge wo be the pye
[be sorry], wherefore I do saye that coloppes [bacon] and egges,
is as holsome for them, as a talowe candell is good for a horses
mouth, or a peece of poudred befe is good for a blereyed mare."
But, as so often with Andrewe Boorde, the physician yielded to
the tolerant observer of man's nature, and he added, "yet sensuall
appetyde must have a swynge, all these thynges natwithstandynge."

A FRYED MEATE [PANCAKES] IN HASTE
FOR THE SECOND COURSE

*Take a pint of Curds made tender of morning Milk, pressed clean
from the Whey, put to them one handful of flour, six eggs, casting
away three whites, a little Rose-water, Sack, Cinamon, Nutmeg,
Sugar, Salt, and two Pippins minced small, beat this all together
into a thick batter, so that it may not run abroad; if you want
wherewith to temper it, add Cream; when they are fryed, scrape
on Sugar and send them up; if this curd be made with Sack
[sherry], as it may as well as with Rhennet, you may make a
Pudding with the Whey thereof.*

William Rabisha, *The whole Body of Cookery Dissected*

THE WORKING VERSION :

1 cup creamed cottage cheese	⅛ teaspoon salt
1 large, tart cooking apple	⅛ teaspoon nutmeg
3 egg yolks	⅛ teaspoon cinnamon
1 egg white	¼ cup flour
2 tablespoons brown sugar	4 tablespoons butter
1 teaspoon sherry	Additional brown sugar
1 teaspoon rose water	

Drain the liquid from the cheese and press it through a sieve.
Quarter, core, and peel the apple, then mince or grate it through
the large holes of a grater. Beat together all the ingredients
except the butter into a thick batter.

Heat a large skillet or griddle until a drop of water sizzles when dropped on it, then melt the butter on it. Drop spoonfuls of the batter onto the griddle, forming oval-shaped pancakes about four inches long. Cook over medium heat until brown on the underside, then turn the pancakes carefully—they break easily—and brown the other side.

As they are baked, transfer the pancakes to a warmed serving dish and keep warm. Sprinkle brown sugar over them and serve immediately.

Pancakes, which were so popular in all classes, could be made with the simplest kind of equipment. A skillet and a grill over a heap of small coals or wood were all that was needed. For the hurried professional cook, pancakes were a boon. They were easily and quickly prepared. They were also useful to intersperse with the fish and egg dishes for fast- or fish-day meals, as well as to fill menus on meat days.

One of the advantages of such batters, then and now, is that they can be mixed up ahead of time. If you do so, refrigerate the mixture in a covered bowl until half an hour before you plan to make the pancakes, then beat the batter before using it.

TO BAKE A FLANCK OF BEEF IN A COLLAR

Take a flank of beef, and lay it in the pump water four days and nights, shift it twice a day, then take it out and dry it very well with clean clothes, cut it in three layers, and take out the bones and most of the fat; then take three handfuls of salt, and good store of sage chopped very small, mingle them, and strew it betwixt the three layers, and lay them one upon another; then take an ounce of cloves and mace, and another of nutmegs, beat them very well, and strew it between the layers of beef, roul it up close together, then take some packthread and tie it up very hard, put it into a long earthen pot, which are made of purpose for that use, tie up the top of the pot with cap paper, and set it into the oven; let it stand eight hours, when you draw it, and being between hot and cold, bind it up round in a cloth, tie it fast at both ends with packthread, and hang it up for your use.

Robert May, *The Accomplisht Cook*

THE WORKING VERSION:

1½ pounds beef flank steak	⅛ teaspoon ground cloves
1½ teaspoons salt	½ yard cheesecloth
½ teaspoon sage	¼ cup beef broth
¼ teaspoon mace	Prepared mustard
¼ teaspoon nutmeg	

Lay the steak out flat on a plate. Mix together the salt, sage, mace, nutmeg, and cloves and rub the seasoning into the meat on both sides. Roll up the steak into a tight roll and tie it at both ends with heavy white string. Lay the roll on the cheesecloth and roll up the meat in it, then tie both ends of the cheesecloth tightly with string.

Put the meat into an oval baking dish or a large bread pan and pour the broth over it. Cover the pan tightly—if you use a bread pan, cover it with aluminum foil and secure the foil to the pan with string. Bake at 250° for three to four hours, or until a fork goes into the meat easily.

Cool the meat in the broth, then refrigerate it until it is firm enough to slice. Remove the cheesecloth and slice the meat thin for serving. Arrange on a chilled serving dish and garnish with dabs of strong prepared mustard.

Various spices were used to prepare this dish, and sometimes wine or ale substituted for beef broth. Spiced meats were always popular and were served both hot and cold. They were doubtless more often cooked in the boiling kettle than in the oven, but oven cooking made it possible to make use of the heat left in the oven after bread had been baked.

The use of earthenware pans for this sort of cooking was fairly common. Robert May apparently liked them and frequently suggested their use.

TO MAKE SPANISH BALLES

Take a peece of a leg of Mutton, and pare away the skin from the flesh, chop the flesh very small: then take marrow of beefe, and

*cut it as big as a hazel nut, & take as much of marrow in quantity
as ye have of flesh, and put both in a faire platter, and some salt,
and eight yolks of Egs, and stirre them wel together: then take a
little earthen pot, and put in it a pinte and a halfe of beefe broth
that is not salt, or else mutton broth and make it seeth; then make
balles of your stuffe, and put them in boyling broth one after another, and let them stew softly the space of two houres. Then
Lay them on sops three or four in a dish, and of the uppermost
of the broth upon the sops, and make your balles as big as tennis
balles.*

John Partridge, *The good Huswifes Handmaide for the Kitchin*

THE WORKING VERSION:

1 pound boned leg of lamb, ground twice	1 quart well-seasoned clear beef broth
1 teaspoon salt	3 slices hot buttered toast, quartered
3 egg yolks	
4 ounces beef bone marrow, chilled and diced	

Mix the lamb, salt, and egg yolks until well blended, then stir
in the diced beef marrow. Wet your hands with cold water and
form the mixture into twelve meatballs. Arrange them side by
side in a deep skillet—an eight-inch one does nicely.

Heat the broth to boiling and pour it over the meatballs—
there should be just enough broth to cover them. Simmer for
fifteen minutes, turning the meatballs once. Divide the toast
among four individual soup plates and put three meatballs in
each one. Pour the hot broth over them and serve.

I have used less beef marrow than the original recipe called for
because the dish seemed cloyingly rich with equal parts of beef
marrow and meat.

If you cannot find a good canned beef broth, you can make one
from 4 cups water, 1 pound of ground beef, 1 large onion, 4 large
sprigs of parsley, ½ teaspoon of peppercorns, and 1¼ teaspoons
salt. Cook in a pressure cooker for forty-five minutes at ten
pounds pressure, or simmer in a tightly closed saucepan for three

hours. If you use a pressure cooker, let the pressure go down before you open the cooker. Strain the broth. (When I make beef broth this way, I feed the cooked meat to our cat; he is ready to call it a gourmet dish.)

A sharp knife and a strong, skillful wrist could mince meat as fine as any present-day mechanical grinder, and more of the flavor of the meat would have been retained. In a small meat shop in Paris some years ago, in response to my request for ground beef, the butcher told me that he had no grinder but could mince the meat as fine as I wished. Before my skeptical gaze, he proceeded to do so with his chopping knife, and within a minute or so he had reduced a pound of solid beef almost to a paste.

TO BOYLE . . . PEASCODS

Take greene sugar Pease when the pods bee but young, and pull out the string of the backe of the podde, and picke the huske of the stalkes ends, and as many as you can take up in your hand at three several times, put them into the pipkin, with halfe a pound of sweete Butter, a quarter of a pint of faire water, a little grosse Pepper, Salt, and Oyle of Mace, and let them stue very softly until they bee very tender, then put in the yolkes of two or three rawe egges strained with six spoonefuls of Sacke, and as much Vinegar, put it into your Peascods and brew them with a ladle, then dish them up.

John Murrell, *A Booke of Cookerie*

THE WORKING VERSION:

¾ pound edible-pod peas	⅛ teaspoon mace
½ cup water	1 egg yolk
4 tablespoons butter	2 tablespoons sherry
¼ teaspoon salt	2 tablespoons white wine
⅛ teaspoon coarsely ground	vinegar
pepper	

String the pods and rinse them in cool water. Bring the water, butter, salt, pepper, and mace to a boil in a large skillet with a lid. Add the peas, cover, and cook for seven minutes over medium heat, stirring once or twice—the peas should be tender but crisp, so taste after five minutes.

Beat the egg yolk with the sherry and vinegar until blended. Turn the heat under the peas to low and slowly stir in the egg mixture. Simmer for half a minute, watching carefully to see that the sauce does not curdle.

Murrell doubtless used peapods right out of the kitchen garden, as I did. Since it is nearly impossible to find such young peas in the markets, edible-pod or snow peas, as they are sometimes called, are a good substitute.

Green peas were usually a second-course dish, but when they were called a "hot sallett," as in one of Rabisha's menus, they were likely to be served in the first course. Like spinach and other green vegetables, they were also made into pies.

Young peas were a delicacy and often brought by country tenants to their landlords as gifts. Such gifts had a long tradition. In May, 1502, a woman who brought a present of "peesecoddes" to Henry VII's queen received two shillings for her kindness, and in May, 1531, the royal accounts noted, "a man in reward for bringing pescoddes to the King had 4s. 8d."

Shakespeare uses peasecods several times with as many dramatic effects. In *As You Like It* (Act II, Scene 4), Touchstone seeks to console the love-wounded Rosalind. "I remember," he tells her, "the wooing of a peascod instead of her, from whom I took two cods, and giving her them again, said with weeping tears, 'Wear these for my sake.' We that are true lovers run into strange capers." Touchstone is referring to the lovers' tradition of divining whether one was loved or not by jerking a peapod from the vine; if the peas remained in the pod, it was a good omen, and the lover presented the pod to the loved one. Peasecods and love are also coupled in the old Devonshire proverb, "Winter time for shoeing, peascod time for wooing."

TEMMES RYE BREAD

Some mixeth to miller, the rye with the wheat
Temmes loaf on his table to have for to eat.

Thomas Tusser, *Five Hundred Points of Good Husbandry*

THE WORKING VERSION:

2 cups warm water	2 cups whole-wheat flour
2 cakes fresh yeast or 2	2 cups rye flour
tablespoons dry yeast	2 cups unbleached flour
1 tablespoon salt	

Pour the water into a large mixing bowl. Crumble or sprinkle the yeast into the water, and when the yeast has softened and expanded, add the salt. Stir in the whole-wheat flour, one cup at a time, then the rye flour, one cup at a time, and last stir in one cup of the unbleached flour.

Sprinkle your work surface with the remaining unbleached flour and turn the dough out onto it. Pat the dough back and forth between your hands in the flour until it is coated with flour. Then knead for five minutes. Put the dough in a warmed mixing bowl large enough to allow it to double in size. Cover the bowl with a clean towel or a plastic bowl cover and set it in a warm place or in an unheated oven.

When the dough has about doubled in size—in 1 to 1½ hours—turn it out again on a floured surface and knead it into a round loaf. Flatten the loaf to two inches in height and cut about ½ inch deep around the circumference of the loaf halfway between top and bottom.

Sprinkle a cookie sheet or a deep cake pan with whole-wheat flour and place the loaf on it. Punch knife holes over the top of the loaf and set it to rise again until it has nearly doubled in size—about one hour. Bake at 450° for five minutes, lower the heat to 350°, and bake forty minutes longer. Turn out on a wire grille to cool.

This dough can also be baked as flat, round rolls, like manchets. In this case they should be baked at 400° for twenty minutes.

Ovens were lined with firebricks and were heated by placing wood and dry fagots in them. These were set afire and allowed to burn until the oven reached the desired temperature, which usually took about 1½ hours. The coals were then raked out and the floor of the oven swept out. The breads were placed on a peel, a flat wooden shovel with a long handle, and slid into the oven.

ℂ Here begynneth the Boke

amed the Aſſyſe of breade, what it ought to weye
after the pryce of a quarter of Wheete. And al‐
ſo the Aſſyſe of Ale, with all maner of wood
and Cole, Lath, Bowrde, and tymbre, and
the weyght of Butter, and Cheſe.
ℂ Imprynted by me Robert Wyer.

Frontispiece of The Assyse of Bread (*16th century*)

The oven door was attached and bolted shut. The length of time required for baking bread depended on the size and kind of bread, but usually it would bake in about an hour.

Horse bread, *i.e.*, food for horses made of ground peas and beans mixed with liquid and then baked, was also made in household ovens. In times of near famine, the very poor often had to eat horse bread.

A LEACH OF DIVERS COLOURS IN THE FRENCH FASHION

Lay halfe a pound of Jordane *Almonds in colde water, the next day blanch and beate them in a stone morter, put in some good Damaske Rose-water into the beating of them, when they be very fine draw them through a strainer with a quart of sweete milke from the Cowe, and set on a chafing dish of Coales, with a piece of Isinglasse, a piece of whole Mace and Nutmeg quartered, a Graine of Muske tyed in a piece of lawne, when it groweth thick, take off the fire, and take out your whole spices, and let it runne through a strainer into a broad and deepe dish, and when it is colde, you may so slice it and serve it in. If you will colour any of it, Saffron is for yellow, greene Wheat for green, Turnsole is for red, and blew bottles in corne give their own colour.*

John Murrell, *A Daily Exercise for Ladies and Gentlewomen*

THE WORKING VERSION:

¼ pound blanched almonds	1 large piece of whole mace
6 tablespoons rose water	½ nutmeg, cut up
1 tablespoon unflavored gelatin	2 drops essence of musk
2 cups rich milk (or half and half)	2 tablespoons sugar (optional)

Grind the almonds fine and mix with three tablespoons of rose water; soften the gelatin in the remaining rose water. Put the milk, ground almonds, mace, nutmeg, and musk into a quart-size saucepan and bring it to just under a boil. Lower the heat to simmer, and cook for fifteen minutes, stirring every five minutes.

Add the sugar and the softened gelatin and stir until the mixture just begins to thicken.

Remove from heat and strain the leach through a fine-mesh sieve or cheesecloth into a glass cake or pie dish. Set the mixture in the refrigerator until the leach sets firmly.

To serve, cut the leach into small squares or diamonds and pile them lightly in a chilled serving dish.

I added the sugar because I thought it brought out the combination of flavors better. All the other recipes for almond leaches that I saw used some sugar.

If you want multicolored leach, divide the liquid into four parts and add a drop of green vegetable coloring to one part, a drop of blue to the second, and of yellow to the third, leaving one part uncolored. Refrigerate the different colors in different dishes.

We found the leach more attractive in the natural color and served it garnished with rose petals. This was one of the rare unsweetened desserts, and it is possible the sugar was left out inadvertently when the type was set for the book.

The name "leach" is probably derived from the Spanish *leche*, meaning milk. It was a popular jellied dessert and was sometimes made with cream instead of milk.

Cooks were not certain just how much isinglass was needed to jell a particular quantity of liquid, and the proportions of isinglass vary from recipe to recipe, or else no specific amount is given. Only Markham tells how to prepare isinglass for use: "Take Isinglass and lay it two hours in water, shift it and boyl it in fair water, and let it cool." Isinglass, when softened, left a residue, and some cookbooks suggested it be removed by straining through a sieve or through a jelly bag.

"Dry leaches" were sweetmeats made with almond paste or dried fruits such as dates.

TO MAKE CHEWITS OF VEALE

Take a litle Veale and slice it, and perboile it then take it up, and presse it in a fayre cloth, then mince it very fine, take Corante and dates and cut them very small, take some mary [beef marrow] or suet, and the yolkes of three or foure Egges, and pepper, salt, and Mace, fine beaten, and the crums of bread fine grated: then mingle al these together, and put in suet enough, and they will be good pies.

John Partridge, *The good Huswifes Handmaide for the Kitchin*

THE WORKING VERSION:

2 ounces boned veal round
½ cup currants
2 ounces beef suet, diced
½ cup pitted dates
1 teaspoon grated bread crumbs
½ teaspoon mace
¼ teaspoon salt
⅛ teaspoon pepper

1 egg yolk

THE PASTRY
2 cups sifted unbleached flour
1 teaspoon salt
¾ cup cold butter
½ cup cold water (approximately)
1 egg, separated

Cut the veal in pieces and parboil it with the currants for five minutes in one cup of boiling water. Drain and set aside for a few minutes to cool. Mince fine or grind together the veal, currants, suet, and dates. Add the bread crumbs, the seasonings, and the egg yolk and mix until blended. Cover and set aside for an hour to allow the flavors to blend.

Make the pastry according to the instructions given on page 31. Roll the dough out to a rectangle sixteen inches long and eight inches wide. Divide the rectangle into eight four-by-four-inch squares. Divide the filling into eight portions and place one portion on each square. Fold the pastry squares to cover the filling and make rectangles of two by four inches. Seal the edges with the tines of a wet fork and brush the tops of the chewets with egg white.

Place the tarts on a cookie sheet four inches apart. Bake at 450° for twenty minutes or until golden brown. Serve slightly warm.

These can be made ahead of time and reheated in a 350° oven for five to ten minutes just before serving. They also freeze well and can be reheated from the frozen state at 350° in about fifteen minutes.

This is but one of the numerous versions of mincemeat tarts or pies so popular in Shakespeare's day. Apples as part of the ingredients of mincemeat are a later phenomenon, although I did find one fast-day mincemeat tart recipe that contained both apples and pears. The fillings of these tarts were less moist than the kind of mincemeat we are accustomed to, but the tarts were of a more interesting texture. Chewets for fast days were usually made with fish rather than meat. And sometimes the chewets were fried in oil instead of baked.

MEALS AND MENUS

With candles, rush lights, or torches the only sources of artificial light, people retired early. They also got up early, especially in the country. Meal hours were adjusted to these habits, although they varied, depending on social rank and individual responsibilities.

The main meal of the day, dinner, was eaten, or perhaps I should say begun (since three hours at dinner was not unusual in well-to-do homes when there were guests), somewhere between ten o'clock in the morning and one o'clock. "With us the nobility, gentry and students do ordinarily go to dinner at eleven before noon," William Harrison tells us. "The merchants dine . . . seldom before twelve at noon . . . especially in London. The husbandmen [farmers] dine also at high noon as they call it."

Supper was usually a smaller version of dinner. In well-to-do homes it might be equally ample if guests were being entertained but was likely to be much simpler if there were no guests. In modest homes supper might consist only of bread, cheese, and beer, with perhaps eggs or porridge. It was eaten some time between five o'clock and eight o'clock in the evening. "The nobility, gentry, and students," says Harrison, "go to . . . supper at five or between five and six in the afternoon. . . . The merchants . . . sup seldom before six at night, especially in London. . . . The husbandmen . . . sup at seven or eight."

Breakfast was often omitted; there were those who considered it unhealthful. But when eaten, it usually consisted of bread and beer. In wealthy homes, meat or, on fish days, fish was provided for breakfast, sometimes with wine as well as beer. Breakfast in the household of Henry Percy, ninth earl of Northumberland, according to the household accounts from 1564 to 1632, for the earl and his lady on a "flesh day" was "a loofe of bred in trenchors, 2 manchets, 1 quart bere, 1 quart wyne, a Chyne of Muton or Chyne of Beef Boilid." (On fish days, of course, no meat was served.) For the two older sons, the menu was less generous, consisting of "½ loaf of household Breid, a Manchet, 1 Potell [two quarts] of Bere, a Chekynge [chicken] or ells 3 mutton Bonys [bones, with meat on them, of course] boyled." The younger children had much simpler breakfasts, which, nevertheless, included beer.

Queen Elizabeth's maids of honor breakfasted on flesh days on bread, beer, and beef. On fast days they ate herrings instead of beef.

Servants' breakfasts, if any, were likely to be a piece of bread with, occasionally, a bowl of porridge. Nicholas Breton pictures the early-morning activities in a country household: "The cock calls the servants to their day's work. The milkmaids begin to look towards their dairy, and the good housewife begins to look about the house. The porridge-pot is on for the servants' breakfast, and hungry stomacks will soon be ready for their victuals."

Refreshments between meals were likely to be simple—a piece of bread and a glass of beer, or whey, or perhaps wine. When important personages were being entertained, the refreshments ranged from a simple collation of manchet and wine to a lavish banquet of sweetmeats. Wye Saltonstall, in *Picturae Loquentes,* describes "A Gentlemans House in the Countrey." Between meals, he says, "there's bread and Beer for all commers, and for a stranger a napkin, and colde meate in the buttery may be obtained."

"Scrambling meals" were hastily gotten together meals known even to the nobility. In her diary, Lady Anne Clifford noted that, after a visit to the Court, she "went up . . . and ate a scrambling supper with my Lady Pembroke at my Lord Duke's Lodgings."

Claudius Hollyband, in the section of his French-English conversation manual titled "The Citizen at Home," gives us a glimpse into the home of a prosperous London merchant at the dinner hour. His host is a hale and hearty Englishman who likes food, drink, and friends, goes daily to prayers, and expects his children to know their manners and his servants to know their duties. His wife is the kind of English housewife who sees to it herself that the kitchen is run properly but who does not worry overmuch about the order in which the dishes for dinner are brought into the dining room.

Neighbors dining together (16th-century woodcut)

Our merchant, having picked up another guest for dinner on his way home from the morning service at church—there are already twelve or thirteen guests for dinner—is chided by his wife for his lateness. "The meat mareth [is getting overdone]," she complains, and the guests are waiting in the hall to be asked to sit down to table. As for herself, she says, she must go to the kitchen "to cause to serve the boorde [table]."

Having apologized to his guests for being late, the host suggests that they wash their hands before sitting down to table. The page is told to ring the bell to announce that dinner is ready, to call the children in "to bless the boorde [say grace]," and to "brynge us some meate." He also asks the butler to bring up some of the best wine from the cellar. Then he drinks to his guests: "Sirs, I pray you make good cheere: yee bee welcome: cosin [a country nephew who is visiting], I drinke to you with such a good hart as ever I did when I have been very drie."

What is there for dinner in the home of this prosperous

London merchant? First come the boiled dishes, which include the inevitable powdered [salt] beef with mustard, capon with leeks, mutton stuffed with garlic—which last our host refuses, saying, "geeve mee rather of that Capon boyled with leeks: for I should smell of garlicke three days after." The boiled cabbage, our host's favorite dish, cannot be eaten, his wife says, "for they be to much peppered and salted." Upon which our host exclaims, "God sendeth us meate, and the Devil cookes." Even an immigrant like Hollyband knew this old English proverb. The hostess urges her husband to try the boiled turnips instead.

The boiled meats are removed, and the roast meats are put on the table. Unfortunately, the chickens are overdone for our host's taste, and one of the meat pies is overbaked. The venison pasty is good, however, and apparently so are a shoulder of veal, a capon, a turkey cock, blackbirds, larks, woodcocks, partridges, and "loynes of Hare with Black sauce [a sauce made with bread crumbs that have been toasted until black]." Only two fish dishes are served, a stewed carp and a pike with a "high [highly seasoned] Dutch sauce."

The hostess watches to see that all the guests are well cared for. When her husband seems to be overlooking his neighbor at table, she says, "Husband, I pray you pull in peeces that Capon, and help your neighbour: truly he eateth nothyng."

The main dishes having been "read over," as the English phrase went, our merchant calls for the desserts. "Now serve the fruite," he tells the servants, "laye here those rosted paires, and the scrapped cheese; set those appels lower: they be pepins, as it seemeth unto me." He complains that the tarts and the egg pies are cold, and denounces the baker; "Maistris [mistress], will you have some cake? Trulie it is but dow [dough], I would the baker had been backed [baked] when he did heat the oven." But he cannot stay angry long and, dinner being over, he calls for some singing.

Important Elizabethan feasts could, in sheer number of dishes served, have made lavish Victorian dinner parties seem modest. But the enormous variety of dishes, as I noted earlier, was meant to cater to many different tastes; one ate only of those dishes that appealed to one. Not even Falstaff would have attempted to try all the dishes provided at a great feast. John Murrell's "Bill of Service for an extraordinary Feast for a Summer Season" is a three-course menu of fifty dishes, twenty

First Course.

1 A Dish of fowl with ingredients, for a grand boyled meat.
2 Chines of Mutton and Veal in pieces, roasted with Oysters, and larded
3 A grand Sallet in plates on a Charger.
4 An Olue of Puddings.
5 A dish of Pheasants.
6 A Pattee, or Pie of ingredients.
7 Hares larded.
8 A chine of Pork boyled and carbonadoed with Turnips.
9 A Venison pasty of a Doe
10 Two hen Turkies larded
11 A Hash.
12 A chine of roast Beef.
13 A Marrow Pudding.
14 A Frigasie of Chickens.
15 A dish of collops of Veal larded.
16 A dish of collered Pork.
17 A dish of Capons.
18 A Made dish.
19 A stewed meat with pottage.
20 A baked meat of Rabbets.
21 Two Geese in a dish.
22 A leg or fillets of Veal farced and larded.

Second Course.

1 Partridges.
2 Quails.
3 An Amulet of preserved Lemmon.
4 A dish of rich Taffatee Tarts.
5 A Sallet of Lemmon, Caveer, Anchovies, and other of that nature, to corroborate the palate, and cause appetite.
6 A dish of Curlews.
7 Godwithes.
8 Warden pie.
9 A dish of Rabbets larded
10 A dish of Leach and Jelly
11 A dish of cram'd Chickens.
12 A dish of tame Pigeons.
13 A laid Tart of preserves
14 A dish of Skeerits fryed.
15 Stewed Peaches.
16 A dish of Red-shanks.
17 A dish of Teal if good, or other wild fowl.
18 A dish of collered Geese
19 Of Westphalie Bacon and Tongues.
20 A coll baked meat of red Dear.
21 A set Custard.
22 Of baked Apples with Orangado.

First Course.

1 A Coller of Brawn.
2 A brown Bisk or Olue.
3 A chine of Mutton or Veal in a Dish larded.
4 A grand Sallet of pickles.
5 A baked meat of small wild fowl, with ingredients.
6 Pheasants larded.
7 A Frigasy of great Chickens, or Rabbets larded.
8 An Almond Pudding baked in a dish, with a garnish of Puff-paste.
9 A dish of stewed broth, if at *Christmas.*
10 A dish of Hens with eggs
11 A Pasty of Venison.
12 A Hash.
13 A chine of beef.
14 A forced baked meat with artificial fowl.
15 A dish of minced Pies.
16 A Swan or Geese.
17 Capons and white broth.
18 Chines of Pork roasted.
19 Olives of Veal roasted.
20 A Brawns head soused.

Second Course.

1 Six Cocks.
2 Twelve Snites.
3 A dish of Anchovies.
4 A Bacon Tart.
5 A dish of Jelly.
6 A Potatoe pie.
7 Six Plovers
8 Six Teal.
9 Two dozen of Larks with Lard.
10 A dish of rich Tarts, in Puff-paste.
11 A Lamb in joints.
12 A dish of Leach and Blamaing.
13 Wild Goose pie cold.
14 Wild Ducks roasted.
15 A dish of tame Pigeons.
16 An Orangado pie.
17 A Frigasie of Pistaches and Pine-apple curnels.
18 A dish of Wigeons larded.
19 A set Custard.
20 A cold baked meat of Venison.

Page of menus, in William Rabisha's The whole Body of Cookery Dissected

in each of the first two courses and ten in the third. William Rabisha's "Bill of Fare for an Extraordinary Feast on a Flesh day in Spring" is only two courses, but each contains thirty-five dishes. *A Proper newe Booke of Cokerye* offers a "Flesh-day" feast and a "Fast-day" meal of feast proportions, as well as several modest menus. All are two-course meals. The first course of a modest dinner starts with "Pottage or stewed broath." It continues with "Bolde [boiled] meate or stewed meate, Chekins [chickens] and Bacon, Powdred beyfe, Pyes [meat pies], Goose, Pygge, Roosted beyfe, Roosted veale, Custarde." The second course begins with "Roosted Lamb" and continues with "Capons, Roosted Connies [rabbits], Chekins, Pehennes [peahens], Baken Veneson [pie], Tarte."

Robert May offers the largest selection of menus, all of which are two-course meals. They range from twenty-dish courses to very modest six-dish courses. He also offers a small menu for each month of the year. The first course of his bill of fare for February includes: "Eggs and Collops [bacon], Brawn and mustard, A hash of Rabbits, A grand Fricase, A grand Sallet, A Chine of roast Pork." The second course is: "A whole Lamb roast, Three widgeons [a kind of small crane], A Pippin Pie, A Jole of Sturgeon. A Bacon Tart. A cold Turkey Pie." For the banquet or dessert dishes he adds "Jellies and Ginger-bread, and Tarts Royal."

John Murrell offers a two-course menu of twelve dishes each "to direct them [young cooks] which are unperfect to bring them to further knowledge of greater Service."

Most menus included a custard in one of the courses and a tart in the other. Both were likely to be served hot or warm.

Traditionally, in formal serving, certain kinds of food were considered proper for particular courses. However, "proper" was defined differently by the few authors who provided sample menus. Nor do many cookbooks offer advice on where a particular recipe would be used in a menu of several courses, although William Rabisha will occasionally say, "This will do for a second course," or "for a first course."

Gervase Markham intends to be practical. He first teaches his English housewife how to compose a menu for a feast for a prince, then, moving from this lofty region, he says, "In the case it be for much humbler men, then lesser care and fewer dishes may discharge. . . . Now for a more humble Feast of an ordinary proportion, which any good man may keep in his Family, for the entertainment of his true and worthy friends, it must hold limitation with his provision, and the season of the year."

This "humble" feast is of heroic proportions by any modern standard, even though many of the dishes are not what Markham calls dishes "of substance." He suggests, "It is good . . . for him that intends to Feast, to set down the full number of his full dishes, that is dishes of meat that are of substance, and not empty or for shew [decoration]; and of these sixteen is a good proportion, for one course . . . as for example; First a shield of Brawn with mustard; Secondly, a boyl'd Capon; Thirdly, a boyl'd piece of Beef; Fourthly, a chine of Beef rosted; Fifthly, a Neats [beef or veal] tongue rosted; Sixthly, a Pigg rosted; Seventhly, Chewets bak'd; Eighthly, a Goose rosted; Ninthly, a Swan rosted; Tenthly, a Turkey rosted; The eleventh, a haunch of Venison rosted; the Twelfth, a Pasty of Venison; the Thirteenth, a Kid with a Pudding in the belly; the Fourteenth, an Olive-pye [of little meat rolls]; the Fifteenth, a Couple of Capons; the Sixteenth a Custard or Dousets [usually small tarts].

"Now to these full dishes," he continues, "may be added Sallets, Fricases, Quelquechoses, and devised paste, as many dishes more as will make the full service no less than two and thirty dishes." These are "as many as can conveniently stand on one Table . . . and after this manner you may proportion both your second and third course, holding fullness in one half of the dishes and shew [for example, pies empty of meat] in the other, which will be both frugall in the spender, contentment to the guest, and much pleasure and delight to the beholders."

A Christmas-day dinner menu at Ingatestone included: "six boiled and 3 roast pieces of beef, a neck of mutton, a loin and breast of pork, a goose, 4 coneys [rabbits] and 8 warden pies [pear pies colored with saffron]." For supper "5 joints of mutton, a neck of pork, 2 coneys, a woodcock and a venison pasty" were served. This was a modest menu indeed compared with the feast that celebrated the marriage of Petre's stepdaughter and the meals that were served when Queen Elizabeth visited Ingatestone.

In 1599, Thomas Platter, a traveler from Germany, dined at the home of the lord mayor of London and wrote a detailed account of the event. He described the service at dinner as dignified, and the food copious and of high quality, "all most perfectly and richly prepared and served with delightful sauces, whiles diverse other dishes to stimulate the appetite surrounded one. . . . After two helpings [courses] of roasts, stews, and other things, dessert was served consisting only of sweetmeats, tarts, and pastries," but these "were not to be compared in delicacy with the entrees." The drinks, he noted, consisted of "the best beer and all manner of heavy and light wines to follow . . . Greek, Spanish, Malmsey, Languedoc, French and German."

A May Day Feast

This night I hold an old accustom'd feast,
Whereto I have invited many a guest
Such as I love.
> *Romeo and Juliet,* Act I, Scene 2 *(Capulet)*

HOT MADEIRA WINE

*I am known to be a humorous patrician, and one
that loves a cup of hot wine with not a drop of
allaying Tiber in 't.*
> *Coriolanus,* Act II, Scene 1 *(Menenius)*

PICKLED EELS

*You might have thrust him and all his apparel
into an eel-skin.*
> *Henry IV, Part II,* Act III, Scene 2 *(Falstaff)*

A SALAD OF HERBS AND FLOWERS

*She was the sweet-marjoram of the salad, or,
rather the herb of grace.*
> *All's Well That Ends Well,* Act IV, Scene 5 *(Clown)*

STURGEON IN CLARET SAUCE

*Here's nothing to be got now-a-days unless
thou canst fish for 't.*
> *Pericles,* Act II, Scene 1 *(Second Fisherman)*

PIGEONS WITH RICE
IN THE FRENCH FASHION

Who are arriv'd?
The French, my lord; men's mouths are full of it.
King John, Act IV, Scene 2 (*King and Bastard*)

FRESH BEEF TONGUE
IN ORANGE AND CLARET SAUCE

Tell her, Emilia,
I'll use that tongue I have.
The Winter's Tale, Act II, Scene 2 (*Paulina*)

A RABBIT PIE

But if thou needs wilt hunt, be rul'd by me;
Uncouple at the timorous flying hare.
Venus and Adonis, Lines 673–74 (*Venus*)

APPLEMOYSE

I think he will carry this island home in his
pocket, and give it his son for an apple.
The Tempest, Act II, Scene 1 (*Sebastian*)

JOHN MURRELL'S STEWED TURNIPS

Why should you want? Behold, the
earth hath roots.
Timon of Athens, Act IV, Scene 3 (*Timon*)

VEAL STEAKS STEWED
IN THE FRENCH FASHION

Calf-like, they my lowing follow'd through
Tooth'd briers, sharp furzes, pricking goss and thorns.
The Tempest, Act IV, Scene 1 (*Ariel*)

CHEATE AND ROBERT MAY'S
FRENCH BREAD

A good shallow young fellow: a' would have made
a good pantler, a' would have chipped bread well.
Henry IV, Part II, Act II, Scene 4 (*Falstaff*)

RED AND WHITE WINES AND BEER

We'll teach you to drink deep ere you depart.
Hamlet, Act I, Scene 2 (*Hamlet*)

CURDS AND CREAM

He tells her something
That makes her blood look out. Good sooth, she is
The queen of curds and cream.
The Winter's Tale, Act IV, Scene 3 (*Camillo*)

A GOOSEBERRY TART

I'll shew thee the best springs; I'll
pluck thee berries.
The Tempest, Act II, Scene 2 (*Caliban*)

"So are you to my thoughts as food to life."
Sonnet 75

HOT MADEIRA WINE

THE WORKING VERSION:

Heat the wine over moderate heat to just under the boiling point. Serve in cups. (If madeira is not available, substitute a cream sherry.)

Burned sack, which was a favorite of Falstaff's, was hot sherry sack.

Cookbooks said nothing about the simple heating of wines, although they gave many recipes for hot drinks made with wine that were similar to what we know as eggnogs.

TO PICKLE A CONGER EELE

You must scald your Eele, and scrape it till the outward skin is scraped off, then boyle your Eele, being cut in pieces and bound with Tape, in water, salt, and Vinegar, and an handful of green Fennel, and when it is boyled, put it into your Sowsing pan, with some of the same liquor and Beer-Vinegar, with an handful of Fennel on the top of the fish, so serve it up cold to the Table.

William Rabisha, *The whole Body of Cookery Dissected*

THE WORKING VERSION:

1 fresh eel, weighing 1 ¼ to 1 ½ pounds
2 cups water
1 ¼ cups vinegar
1 ½ teaspoons salt
1 large sprig green fennel or ½ teaspoon dried fennel
½ cup beer
1 large sprig parsley (optional)

Cut off the head, remove the viscera from the body of the eel, and rinse it under cold water. Then scald the eel for one minute in enough boiling water to cover. While it is still warm, scrape off the skin and rinse it again under cold water. Then cut the eel into four-inch pieces.

Bring the water, vinegar, salt, and fennel to a boil, lower the heat and simmer for five minutes. Add the pieces of eel and simmer, covered, for about twenty minutes, or until tender. Put the pieces of eel into a quart-size bowl and cover them with two cups of the cooking liquid, including the fennel and the beer.

Cover and chill for several days before serving. Serve garnished with a sprig of fresh fennel, or, if you used dried fennel to prepare the eel, with a sprig of parsley.

Eels take to sousing (pickling) very well because their flesh is firm, and they will keep well for several months. Congers are marine eels which attain enormous size. They are much larger than river eels.

Lampreys, which are like eels, were favored for pies but were also served boiled, stewed, roasted, grilled, and fried. "In July," wrote Nicholas Breton in *Wits Trenchmour,* "the Lamprey out of the River leaps into a Pye." They apparently made good pies in April too, for "lampreies bakt" were on the menu four days during the week in 1591 that the earl of Northumberland was keeping house in Bath while taking the water cure there.

Cooks, it seems, were not always successful in preparing congers and eels to Breton's taste. In *Pasquils Passe, and passeth not,* he prays,

> From raw sodde [half-cooked] cunger, and ill rosted eeles,
> The blessed Lord of Heav'n deliver me.

William Harrison reported that some people believed that if you cut a piece of turf from marshy land alongside a river and laid it with the grass downwards "in such sort as the water may touch it . . . you shall have a brood of eels."

TO MAKE A SALLET
OF ALL KINDS OF HEARBES AND FLOWERS

Take your hearbes and picke them very fine into faire water, and picke your flowers by themselves, and wash them all cleane, and swing them in a strainer, and when you put them into a dish, mingle them with Cowcumbers or Lemmans payred and sliced, and scrape Suger, and put in vineger and Oyle, and throw the flowers on the top of the Sallet, and of every sorte of the aforesaid thinges, and garnish the dish about with the foresaide thinges, and hard Egges boyled and laid about the dish and upon the Sallet.

Thomas Dawson, *The good huswifes Jewell*

THE WORKING VERSION:

4 large leaves leaf or butter lettuce
1 ½ cups watercress
¼ cup fresh mint leaves
¼ cup fresh tarragon leaves
¼ cup flower petals—roses, primroses, nasturtiums, calendulas, or a combination of these

One 6-inch cucumber
2 hard-boiled eggs
4 tablespoons salad oil
3 tablespoons white wine vinegar
½ teaspoon salt
⅛ teaspoon pepper
½ teaspoon brown sugar

Wash the lettuce, watercress, and herb leaves in cold water and remove any coarse stems. Pat the greens dry in a clean towel and refrigerate until needed. Drop the flower petals into a bowl of cold water for a moment, shake the water from them, put the petals into a small bowl, cover and refrigerate. Pare and slice the cucumber thin; peel and cut the eggs into eighths lengthwise and set aside, covered.

Put the oil, vinegar, salt, pepper, and sugar into a large salad bowl and stir until blended. Tear the lettuce into bite-size pieces and add, with the mint, tarragon, watercress, and sliced cucumber, to the dressing. Toss these until well coated, then gently mix in the flower petals, saving a few to garnish the salad. Surround the greens and flowers with the egg sections and serve.

If you would prefer lemon to cucumber, slice the lemon in half crossways and, with a sharp paring knife, remove the meat from the sections and dice it.

Green salads such as this one were available only in the growing season. In cold weather salads would be made of whatever root vegetables were available, such as turnips, carrots, and beets, and usually served as boiled salads. Or pickled vegetables, olives, capers, pickled berries, and flower petals would be served as cold salads. Flower petals and berries were usually pickled in wine vinegar and sugar.

John Gerard, like other herbalists, was interested in the dietary aspects of herbs and vegetables. Lettuce, he wrote, "maketh a pleasant sallad, being raw with vinegar, oile, and a little salt;

but if it be boiled it is sooner digested and nourisheth more."
Like Harrison, he noted that salads started the evening meal in
England. "Salad is served in these daies in the beginning of supper
and eaten first before any other meat." But, he adds, it may be
eaten at either end of the meal, "for being taken before meat it
doth many times stir up appetite: and eaten after supper it
keepeth away drunkennesse which commeth by the wine; and that
is the reason it staieth the vapours from rising to the head."

TO FRY STURGEON

*Take a rand of fresh sturgeon, and cut it into slices of half an
inch thick, hack it, and being fried, it will look as if it were ribbed,
fry it brown with clarified butter; then take it up, make the pan
clean, and put it in again with some claret wine, an anchove,
salt, and beaten saffron; fry it till half be consumed, and then put
in a piece of butter, some grated nutmeg, grated ginger, and some
minced lemon; garnish the dish with lemon, dish it, the dish being
first rubbed with a clove of garlick.*

Robert May, *The Accomplisht Cook*

THE WORKING VERSION:

Four ½-inch-thick slices of fresh sturgeon
6 tablespoons butter
2 teaspoons anchovy paste
1 teaspoon nutmeg
1 tablespoon fresh ginger, grated
½ teaspoon saffron
1 cup claret
1 large lemon
1 garlic clove, peeled and quartered
¼ teaspoon salt (optional)

Remove the skin, cartilage, and bone from the sturgeon and,
with a sharp knife, score the slices on both sides. Melt four
tablespoons of the butter in a skillet large enough so that the
fish slices won't overlap, and brown the sturgeon for three
minutes on each side.

Stir the anchovy paste, nutmeg, ginger, and saffron into several
spoonfuls of the claret until blended. Add the rest of the claret,

pour the mixture over the fish, and simmer uncovered until half the liquid has evaporated, basting the fish every few minutes with the sauce.

Cut the lemon in half crossways, slice one half thin and remove the seeds. Remove the meat from the other half and mince it. Add the remaining butter, the minced lemon, and the garlic to the sturgeon and cook five more minutes. Taste the sauce at this point and add the salt if needed.

Remove the pieces of garlic, arrange the sturgeon on a heated serving dish, pour the sauce over the fish, and garnish with the slices of lemon. Serve immediately.

A rand was what we call a fillet, or a piece of a fillet. Large fish were usually cleaned, split, boned, and cut up in various shapes and sizes, depending on what was to be done with them. Fish whose heads were considered good eating, such as salmon, were jowled, that is, the head with a good-size piece of solid meat attached to it would be cut off first. The center of the fish would then be sliced crosswise or filleted and the tail left in a single piece.

Sturgeon can be very large. One of Robert May's recipes begins, "If the sturgeon be nine foot in length, two firkins [a firkin was sixty-four pounds] will serve." A large part of such a sturgeon would most likely be soused. Because its texture is similar to veal—some people find the flavor similar also—sturgeon is excellent for pickling.

At one period in English history, sturgeon was reserved for use by the royal family and those caught were supposed to be brought to the royal kitchens. In Shakespeare's day this was no longer mandatory, although fishermen still brought gifts of sturgeon to the palace. Generally, the royal household purchased its sturgeon as it purchased other fish not available from the royal stew ponds.

For the wedding feast of Catherine Tyrell at Ingatestone, one firkin of sturgeon was purchased. Two firkins were purchased for the visit of Queen Elizabeth. These were bought in London and delivered to Ingatestone. They cost twenty-three shillings, fourpence a firkin and the delivery charge was fivepence, the accounts noted.

TO BOYLE PIDGEONS WITH RICE,
ON THE FRENCH FASHION

Fit them to boyle, and put into their bellies sweet Hearbs, viz,
Parsly, tops of young Time: and put them into a Pipkin, with
as much Mutton broth as will cover them, a peece of whole Mace,
a little whole Pepper: boyle all these together until your Pidgeons
be tender. Then take them off the fire, and scum off the fat cleane
from the broth, with a spoone, for otherwise it will make it to
taste ranke. Put in a peece of sweet Butter: season it with Vergis,
Nutmegge, and a little Sugar: thicken it with Ryce boyled in sweet
Creame. Garnish your Dish with preserved Barberries, and
Skirret rootes, being boyled with Vergis and butter.

John Murrell, *A New Booke of Cookerie*

THE WORKING VERSION:

- 2 squab pigeons, 1 pound each, dressed weight
- 2 large sprigs of parsley
- 4 small sprigs fresh thyme or ½ teaspoon dried thyme
- 5 cups fresh unseasoned chicken broth, approximately
- 1¼ teaspoons salt
- 1 teaspoon peppercorns
- 1 large piece whole mace
- ¼ teaspoon nutmeg
- 7 tablespoons white wine vinegar
- 2 tablespoons butter
- ½ pound oyster plant (salsify), or parsnips, peeled and cut into sticks ½ inch by 2 inches long
- 1 cup light cream
- ½ cup long-grain rice
- 2 slices of buttered toast, cut into triangles
- ½ cup stewed or canned gooseberries, drained

Remove any pinfeathers there may be on the squabs, and the giblets, if there are any. Rinse the birds under cold water and wipe them dry with a paper towel. Into each squab put a sprig of parsley, two sprigs of thyme, or ¼ teaspoon of dried thyme, and a squab liver, if any.

Tie the wings and legs to the bodies of the birds with clean string. Put the squabs into a saucepan with a tight-fitting lid, breast side up. Pour four cups of the chicken broth over them—they should be completely covered—and add one teaspoon salt, the peppercorns, and the mace. Cover the pot and bring the broth to a boil, lower the heat to simmer, and poach the birds for twenty minutes. Carefully turn the squabs over and continue cooking until the thighs are tender when pierced with a fork—fifteen to twenty minutes longer.

While the squabs are poaching, bring the remaining cup of broth, four tablespoons of vinegar, ¼ teaspoon of salt, and one tablespoon of butter to a boil in a small saucepan. Add the vegetable sticks, cover the pan, lower the heat to medium, and cook until the vegetable sticks are tender but still crisp—twenty to thirty minutes. Turn off the heat but leave the vegetables in the broth until needed.

In the top of a small double boiler, heat the cream to just under the boiling point. Stir in the rice, cover the pot, and cook over simmering water until the rice has absorbed the cream—from fifteen to twenty minutes.

Remove the squabs from the poaching broth, cut away the strings, and remove the herbs from the inside of the birds. With a sharp scissors, cut the squabs in half lengthways, cutting down the backbone first, then through the center of the breast, and set aside, covered, to keep warm.

Remove the peppercorns and mace from the broth, add the nutmeg, the three remaining tablespoons of vinegar, and the remaining tablespoon of butter. Stir in the cooked rice and simmer for two minutes.

Place the toast in a warmed serving bowl, and arrange the squabs over them skin side up. Spoon the rice and broth over them, dot the gooseberries over the rice, and serve.

A recipe for making chicken broth is on page 98. If you have difficulty finding squab pigeons—and except in larger cities they may be hard to find—you may, with Murrell's permission, substitute a three-pound frying chicken. A chicken will need from 1 to 1¼ hours to poach.

Most cookbooks called for broth of some kind for boiling pigeons; sometimes a particular broth would be specified, sometimes just "a good broth." Occasionally, wine would be added to the broth to vary the flavor. I used chicken broth because it retains more of the natural flavor of the squabs.

Skirrets, a vegetable much appreciated in Shakespeare's day, are barely known today. I could not find them in any of our local markets and substituted oyster plant (also called salsify) or parsnips as the closest in flavor. Skirret seeds can be purchased from English, if not American, seed companies if you have garden space and are curious about their flavor. The roots should be left in the ground over the winter and dug up the following spring—in May, one of the cookbooks advised.

NEATS TONGUE STEWED

Take them being tender boild, and fry them whole or in halves, put them in a pipkin with some gravy or mutton-broth, large mace, slic't nutmeg, pepper, claret, a little wine vinegar, butter and salt; stew them well together, and being almost stewed, put to the meat two or three slices of orange, sparagus, skirrets, or chestnuts, and serve them on fine sippets; run them over with beaten butter, slic't lemon, and boil'd marrow over all.

Sometimes for the broth put some yolks of eggs, beaten with grape-verjuyce.

Robert May, *The Accomplisht Cook*

THE WORKING VERSION:

One 1½-pound fresh beef or veal tongue
2 quarts water (approximately)
1 medium-size onion, quartered
2 teaspoons salt
6 peppercorns
2 bay leaves
¾ cup broth in which the tongue cooked
¾ cup claret
3 tablespoons butter
1 navel orange, peeled, sectioned, and the meat diced
¼ teaspoon nutmeg
¼ teaspoon mace
⅛ teaspoon cloves
¼ teaspoon pepper
3 egg yolks
2 tablespoons red wine vinegar
2 ounces beef marrow
3 slices buttered toast, quartered
½ lemon, peeled, sliced thin, and seeded

Rinse the tongue under running water. Fill a large pot with sufficient water to cover the tongue by one inch—if you use a pressure cooker, 2½ cups will be sufficient. Add the onion, one teaspoon of the salt, the peppercorns and bay leaves, and bring to a boil. Lower the tongue into the pot, cover, and cook over low heat until the meat is easily pierced with a fork—about two hours. If you use a pressure cooker, cook at fifteen pounds pressure for forty-five minutes, and allow the pressure to go down before opening the cooker. Cool the tongue in its cooking liquid. Then strain the broth and set it aside until needed.

When the tongue is cool enough to handle comfortably, slit the skin down the top side of the tongue and pull it off. Remove the gristle and fat from the root end and slice the tongue into ½-inch-thick slices. Cover and set aside until needed.

Bring ¾ cup of the broth, the claret, butter, diced meat of the orange, and the seasonings to a boil in a large skillet or saucepan. Add the tongue, lower the heat to simmer, and cook uncovered for thirty minutes, turning the meat occasionally.

Beat the egg yolks with the vinegar, add to the ingredients in the saucepan, and stir gently until the sauce begins to thicken. Keep warm until needed. Slice the beef marrow into ½-inch slices and poach them in one cup of the remaining broth for five minutes. Remove from the broth carefully so as not to break them.

Place the slices of toast in a warmed serving bowl, arrange the tongue slices over them, pour the sauce over the meat, and garnish with the pieces of beef marrow and lemon. Serve hot.

Beef tongue is preferable to veal tongue as it has a more pronounced flavor.

This is a good dish to include in a feast menu because it can be prepared several days in advance, except for thickening the sauce and poaching the beef marrow, and refrigerated. The beef marrow may be eliminated if you wish, although it does add richness to the dish. Elizabethan cooks frequently used it as garnish and sometimes served it as a separate dish on buttered toast.

TO BAKE A HARE

Take your Hare and perboile him, and mince him, & then beat him in a morter verie fine, liver and all if you will, and season him with all kind of spice and salt, and doe him together with the yolks of seven or eight egges, when you have made him up together, draw Lard very thicke through him, or cut Lard and mingle them altogether and put him in a Pye, and put butter before you close him up.

Thomas Dawson, *The good huswifes Jewell*

THE WORKING VERSION:

One 3-pound frying rabbit, dressed weight
2 slices lean bacon
5 egg yolks
2 teaspoons salt
½ teaspoon mace
¼ teaspoon ginger
¼ teaspoon cloves
4 tablespoons butter, diced

FOR THE PASTRY
2 cups sifted unbleached flour
1 teaspoon salt
¾ cup cold butter
½ cup beer or ale (approximately)
1 egg, separated

With a sharp knife cut and scrape the meat of the rabbit from the bones. Cut the meat, the rabbit liver, and the bacon into small pieces and grind them together. Add the egg yolks, salt, mace, ginger, and cloves to the ground meat and mix until blended. Then lightly stir in the diced butter. Cover and set aside while you make the pastry, following directions given on page 31.

Make the pie in any shape that pleases your fancy. (This amount of dough is sufficient for an eight-inch pie, a six-to-seven-inch spring-form pan, or a rectangular pie about six by ten inches.) Spread the meat mixture evenly over the bottom crust and cover with the top crust, sealing the edges with the tines of a wet fork. Then slice off any surplus pastry from the edges of the pie.

If you have pastry dough left over, roll it out and, with a small rabbit cookie cutter, cut out pastry rabbits. Brush the top of the pie with egg white, arrange the pastry rabbits on it, and brush them with egg white. Bake at 450° for twenty minutes, then lower the heat to 350° and bake twenty-five minutes longer.

Serve either hot or cold, but not refrigerated.

Compared to the great number of domesticated rabbits consumed in Elizabethan times, few wild rabbits or hares were eaten. There were very few recipes for preparing hare, and most of these were for minced meat pies to be eaten cold. In 1580 the Fairfax family, who entertained a good deal, consumed 1,308 rabbits and conies. During one year the royal household purchased 1,428 dozen conies and 605 dozen rabbit-suckers. Rabbit suckers (or rabbet-runners) were suckling rabbits. Conies were rabbits a year or older. In 1572 the best rabbit sold for fourpence a piece in London; rabbet-runners were twopence each. Since the feast menu in *A Proper newe Booke of Cokerye* calls for "Two connies, or half a dozen Rabbets," it apparently took three suckling rabbits to equal the flesh of one cony.

Hare the dietary writers considered dry meat and likely to cause melancholia, especially in those whose natural temperament was already melancholic. About hare Andrewe Boorde had strong opinions: "A hare," he said, "doth no harm nor dyspleasure to man: yf the flesshe be not eaten, it maketh a gentleman good pastyme. And better is for the houndes or dogges to eat the hare after they have kylled . . . than man should eate it; for it is nat praysed, nother in the olde Testament, nother in physycke [medicine]; for the byble sayth the hare is an unclene beeste, and physycke sayth hares flesshe is drye, and dothe ingender melancholy humours." Conies, however, were approved of, and suckling rabbits highly recommended by the dietaries.

TO MAKE APPLEMOYSE

Take a dosen apples and ether rooste or boyle them and drawe them thorowe a streyner, and the yolkes of three or foure egges withal, and as ye strayne them, temper them wyth three or foure sponefull of damaske water yf ye wyll, than take and season it with sugar and halfe a dyshe of sweete butter, and boyle them

upon a chaffyng-dysche in a platter, and caste byskettes or
synamon and ginger upon them and so serve them forthe.

Anonymous, *A Proper newe Booke of Cokerye*

THE WORKING VERSION:

1½ pounds tart cooking apples	1 tablespoon rose water
¼ cup water	⅛ teaspoon ginger
1 tablespoon butter	⅛ teaspoon cinnamon
2 tablespoons sugar	1 egg yolk
	Brown sugar (optional)

Quarter, core, and peel the apples, and cut them into small
pieces. Cook the apples in the water in a covered saucepan until
the apples are soft—about ten to fifteen minutes. Purée the
apples and return them to the saucepan, add the butter, sugar,
rose water, ginger, and cinnamon, and return to the heat.
Lower the heat to simmer and cook, stirring constantly, until the
butter melts and the seasonings are blended in. Beat in the egg
yolk and remove the sauce from the heat.

Spread evenly in a warmed shallow bowl and score the top in
a crisscross pattern with the point of a knife. If you wish,
sprinkle a little brown sugar over the sauce before serving.
Serve warm.

There are numerous variations on this recipe. The earliest
one with a similar name is from a fifteenth-century cookbook for
a dish called "Apple Moyle." That recipe, however, was more
like a rice-apple pudding than a sauce. The current German term
for apple sauce is *Apfelmus,* and the name "applemoyse" was
of German derivation.

TO MAKE A DISH OF TURNIPS

Pare your Turnepes as you would pare a Pippin [apple] then
cut them in square pieces an ynch and a halfe long and as thicke
as a Butchers pricke or skewet, put them into a pipkin with a
pound of butter and three or foure spoonefuls of strong broath,

and a quarter of a pint of Vineger seasoned with a little Pepper, Ginger, Salt and Sugar, and let them stue very easily upon a soft fire, for the space of two houres or more, now and then turning them with a spoone, as occasion shall serve, but by all meanes take heede you breake them not, then dish them up upon Sippets, and serve them to the Table hot.

John Murrell, *A Booke of Cookerie*

THE WORKING VERSION:

1½ pounds young turnips	¼ teaspoon salt
4 tablespoons butter	1 tablespoon sugar
1½ cups chicken broth	⅛ teaspoon pepper
¼ cup white wine vinegar	2 slices hot buttered toast,
¼ teaspoon ginger	cut in triangles

Peel the turnips with a potato peeler, slice them crossways, ¼ inch thick, then divide the slices into quarters. Bring the butter, broth, vinegar, and seasonings to boil in a saucepan, add the turnips, and bring back to a boil. Lower the heat to simmer, cover the pot, and cook until the turnips are almost tender—about one hour—stirring them carefully every fifteen minutes.

Uncover the pot and continue cooking until most of the broth has been absorbed and the turnips are tender. Arrange the toast slices in a warmed serving dish, spoon the turnips over them, and serve hot.

Turnips were sometimes used as garnish over a boiled fowl or meat, but usually they were part of the seasoning for stewed meats and pottages—Joseph Cooper adds them to the cooking liquid for stewing a loin or leg of mutton. When used as a garnish, they were cooked separately. Murrell, however, seems to be the only cookbook writer who thought turnips worthy of serving as a separate dish, and even he suggests that a "ladelful of the foresaid stued Turneps" could be spooned over the top of boiled rabbit, capon, or chicken.

TO BOYLE A RACKE OF VEAL
ON THE FRENCH FASHION

Cut it into Steakes, cut a Carrot, or Turnup in pieces like Diamonds, and put them into a Pipkin with a pinte of White-wine, Parsley bound in a Fagot, a little Rosemary and large Mace, and a sticke of Sinamon: pare a Lemmon, or Orenge, and take a little grose Pepper, halfe a pound of Butter: boyle all together untill they be enough; when you have done, put in a little Sugar and Vergis. Garnish your dish as you list.

John Murrell, *A New Booke of Cookerie*

THE WORKING VERSION:

1¼	pounds veal cutlet, sliced ¼ inch thick	1	lemon
¾	cup white wine	⅛	teaspoon rosemary
2	tablespoons white wine vinegar	1	large piece of whole mace
2	small carrots, scraped, washed, and diced	1	small stick of cinnamon
¼	cup minced parsley	1	teaspoon salt
		⅛	teaspoon pepper
		4	tablespoons butter
		½	teaspoon brown sugar

Cut the veal into approximately three-inch pieces and flatten them with the side of a meat tenderizer or a cleaver to a thickness of ⅛ inch. Combine the wine, wine vinegar, carrots, parsley, the grated outer peel of the lemon, rosemary, mace, cinnamon, salt, and pepper in a bowl just large enough to hold the meat and marinade. Add the meat and marinate for one hour, turning it after ½ hour.

Cut the lemon in half crossways, slice half the lemon in thin slices and remove the seeds, then remove the meat from the other half and mince it. Drain the marinade from the veal and bring it to a boil in a small saucepan. Lower the heat to simmer, cover the pan, and cook until the carrots are tender but still firm— ten to fifteen minutes.

Melt the butter in a large skillet, and when it sizzles add the pieces of veal in a single layer. Sauté for one minute on each side. Add the marinade and simmer, uncovered, for five minutes, turning the meat once. Stir in the minced lemon and the sugar and continue to cook for five minutes more.

Remove the mace and cinnamon and arrange the veal in a warmed serving dish, pour the sauce over it, and garnish with the slices of lemon.

Veal was prepared in much the same ways that beef was, from sousing to mincemeat tarts and minced meat pies. Veal dishes appear on all the published bills of fare for flesh days, often in several different forms. Rabisha, in his menu for a spring-day feast, suggests "a chine of veal with oysters, a dish of olives of veal roasted, and a dish of collared Veal soused and sliced."

For the cook's information, "A Breviate . . . of a Nobleman's House," which includes veal in some form in all the flesh-day menus, also tells how various kinds of meat carcasses should be divided: "There bee in a Large Veale twelve services, vidz, 2 Shoulders, 2 Brestes, 2 Racks, 4 Loynnes, 2 Legges." The front legs were considered part of the shoulders and were cut with them. How many each piece would serve, the "Breviate" says, depends on the discretion of the "officers," meaning the clerk of the kitchen and the master cook.

The recipe for fine cheate bread is on page 77, and for Robert May's French bread on page 111.

Richard Braithwaite outlined the duties of a yeoman baker in *Some Rules and Orders for the Government of the House of an Earl.* The skillful yeoman baker, he said, made his manchets "white, light, well seasoned and crusted; his sippet bread in high loaves, set in the oven close together, that on the sides they have little or noe crust, and as small bottomes and toppes as may be, for they are to cutt into sippets and to dredge [crumb] meat withall."

Little is known of Braithwaite other than that he was born in 1588, that he said he wrote this book of rules at the request of a friend, from memory, when he was sixty years old, and that he died in 1673. Some historians think he was the steward in the household of a noble family. The book was found after his death and was not published until 1821.

About cheate bread, John Taylor said in his satire, *A Navy of Land Ships,* "Their bread and drink I had almost forgotten; indeed it was not rusk as the Spaniards use, or oaten-cakes, or bannocks, as in North Britain, nor biscuit as Englishmen eat; but it was a bread which they called *Cheat-bread,* and a mad fellow once told me, it was so called, because the baker was never like to be paid for it." Like Shakespeare, Taylor could not resist an opening for a pun.

TO MAKE CHEESE AND CREAM

When you have run your morning milk with about one pottle of fresh Cream to a gallon and a half, your Curds being cleansed from the Whey season it with fine beaten Cinamon, Sugar and Rosewater; fill five or six dishes, about half a pint a piece with the said Curd; then lay trenchers on the top of them, and a board thereon, and press them until they come into a body like Cheeses; then turn them out whole into your dish (which you may do the better by buttering the bottom of your dish) and having a pottle of Cream boyled up, with whole Cinamon, large Mace, and a Nutmeg quartered; with the yolks of Eggs beaten with Rose water, stirred in a little before it comes off the fire, seasoned with fine Sugar; you may add one grain of Musk in the boyling, which will serve for the same purpose another time; when it is almost cold put it in with your ladle between the fair Cheeses; scrape thereon Sugar, and serve it up.

William Rabisha, *The Whole Body of Cookery Dissected*

THE WORKING VERSION:

½ tablet rennet
7 cups whole milk
1 cup light cream
4 teaspoons sugar
1 tablespoon rose water
⅛ teaspoon cinnamon
   Unsalted butter to grease
   the molds

THE SAUCE
1 cup light cream
2 egg yolks
1 teaspoon rose water
2 teaspoons sugar
⅛ teaspoon cinnamon
⅛ teaspoon mace
⅛ teaspoon nutmeg
1 drop essence of musk

Melt the rennet in one tablespoon of milk. Heat the rest of the milk and the cream to lukewarm. Remove from the heat and stir in the rennet, mixing thoroughly. Cover the pan with a clean cloth and set it in a warm place to solidify for six hours.

Spread a clean white cloth over a colander and spoon the curds into it. When the whey has ceased to drip—you can speed the separation of the curds from the whey by occasionally raising one edge of the cloth and spooning the curds toward the bottom of the colander—put the curds into a mixing bowl and beat until smooth; then stir in the sugar, rose water, and cinnamon.

Butter individual gelatin dessert molds or custard cups lightly with unsalted butter, and smooth the top of the curds; do not press down on them. Cover the molds with waxed paper or plastic wrap and chill for twenty-four hours.

An hour or so before serving, beat together all of the sauce ingredients and cook in a double boiler, stirring constantly, until the sauce begins to thicken. Remove from the heat and set the sauce aside to cool, but do not refrigerate it.

Run the tip of a pointed knife gently around the edges of the molds to loosen the curds and turn them out into a shallow serving bowl, leaving a little space between each one. Spoon the sauce over them and, if you wish, sprinkle a little sugar over the curds before serving. Garnish the dish with flower petals.

Rennet, sometimes spelled "runnet," was usually used to solidify milk for cheese-making. I have used a little more rennet than is actually needed to speed up the coagulating process.

The texture of these curds is somewhat like *coeur de la crème*, the French dessert cheese, but the flavorings and the sauce change it into an exotic dessert.

Nicholas Breton may have been thinking of the prospect of such a dish when he wrote, in "Friar Bacon's Brasenheads-Prophesces," "Ale and Spice, and Curdes and Creame Would make a scholler make a Theame."

A GOOSEBERRY TART

Pick the stalkes of your Gooseberries, and the pips in the tops; put them in good Paste, with a little greene Ginger sliced in slices: cast on good store of Sugar and Rose-water, and so close them.

John Murrell, *A Booke of Cookerie*

THE WORKING VERSION:

1 quart large gooseberries
1 ¼ cups sugar
1 tablespoon rose water
1 tablespoon fresh ginger, peeled and grated

THE PASTRY

2 cups sifted unbleached flour
1 teaspoon salt
¾ cup cold butter
½ cup cold water (approximately)
1 egg, separated

Pinch off the stems and flower ends of the gooseberries. Rinse them in cold water and dry in a towel. Mix the berries with the sugar, rose water, and ginger and set aside while you make up the pastry according to the directions given on page 31.

Sprinkle your work surface with flour. Divide the dough into two parts, one, which will serve as the bottom crust, a little larger than the other. Roll out the larger piece to fit an eight-inch pie dish. Fit it into the dish, then roll out the top crust.

Spoon the seasoned berries into the dish evenly, and cover with the top crust. Seal the edges of the pie by pressing down on them with the tines of a wet fork. Slice off the surplus crust with a sharp knife. Make fork holes in the top and brush with the egg white. Bake at 450° for twenty minutes, then lower the heat to 350° and bake twenty-five minutes longer. Serve slightly warm.

Small gooseberries are difficult to stem, so if you can find the large English-type gooseberries, use them.

In Murrell's day baking decisions had to be made by guess and by prayer, since there was no effective way of controlling the temperature of the ovens. Murrell warns his readers to use coarse crusts when making tarts of fruits that take comparatively long to bake, such as apples, "else your Apples will be hard when your Crust will be burnt and dryed away." Gooseberries, however, cook quickly enough to be baked in "good Paste."

SETTING THE TABLE AND SERVING

"Go to thy fellows; bid them cover the table, serve in the meat, and we will come in to dinner," Lorenzo tells Launcelot in *The Merchant of Venice* (Act III, Scene 5). The style in which meals were served varied with the social and economic standing of the family and the guests. The rituals of serving had been greatly simplified by Shakespeare's day except at court and in a few families of the nobility who still fancied the serving rituals of medieval days.

Eating utensils, until late in the seventeenth century, consisted of one's fingers, a spoon, and a knife. Knives, however, were not in great supply and most people carried theirs with them when they went out to dine—sheathed and tucked in a man's belt and sheathed and hung from a lady's waistband.

Household inventories of even very wealthy families show surprisingly few knives, although there are often fabulous amounts of silver and pewter tableware. Silver spoons were in greater supply. The household inventory of Sir Thomas Ramsey, a wealthy grocer and former lord mayor of London, made in 1590, listed a little over ten dozen silver spoons, but only two "cases with 16 knives; a pair of knives graven and guilt [gold plated]; and a guilt Scot's dagger." Only five "chopping knives" were listed with the kitchen ironware.

"If they be of the degree of barons, bishops and upwards," said William Harrison, "the chief part of . . . their daily provision is brought in before them in silver vessels." The silverware, however, did not include forks. Except for a single gold or jeweled fork, clearly a collector's item, forks do not appear in the inventories of even the wealthiest homes of Shakespeare's day.

Thomas Coryate, one of the many young men who dined at the table of the crown prince, Henry, James I's son (who did not live to inherit the crown), is credited with introducing the fork into

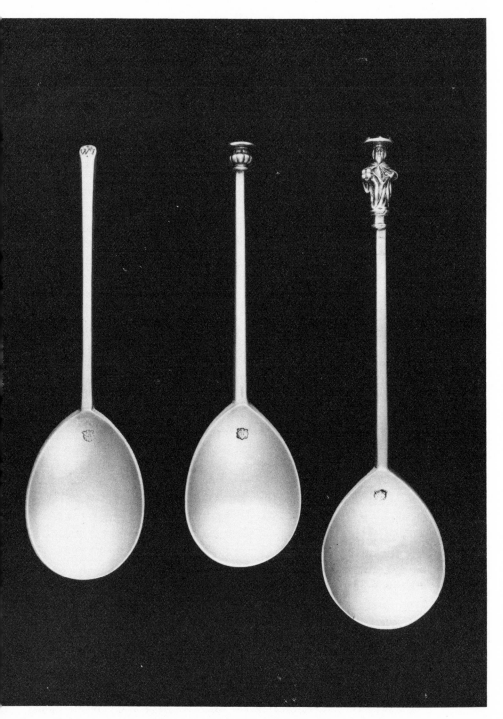

Silver spoons (16th century)

England. In 1610, after several months of traveling on the Continent, he returned to England the proud possessor of a curious, but very practical, table utensil that he had seen in common use in Italy. And he brought the fork and used it when he dined at Prince Henry's, despite the teasing he took from the other young wits who frequented the prince's table.

Coryate published a sort of travelogue after his return from the Continent which he called *Coryates crudities*. In it he told of the sarcasms he had endured. One of them was to dub him "furcifer" (a combination of "furca," Latin for "fork," and Lucifer) "for using my fork at feeding." More fastidious than his friends, Coryate explained that the use of the fork protected everyone, since everyone's hands were not equally clean. "I observed a custome in all those Italian cities and townes through the which I passed," said Coryate, "that is not used in any other country that I saw in my travels. . . . The Italian and also most strangers that are commorant [living or sojourning] in Italy, do alwaies at their meales use a little forke when they cut their meate. For while with their knife which they hold in one hand they cut the meate out of the dish, they fasten their forke which they hold in their other hand upon the same dish, so that whatsoever he be that sitting in the company of any others at meale, should unadvisedly touch the dish of meate with his fingers from which all at the table doe cut, he will give occasion of offense unto the company, as having transgressed the laws of good manners. . . .

"This forme of feeding, I understand is generally used in all places of Italy; their forkes being for the most part made of yron or steele, and some of silver, but those are used only by Gentlemen."

Playwrights, as well as courtiers, exercised their wits against the poor fork. "It doth express th' enamoured courtier. As full as your fork-carving traveller," Beaumont and Fletcher remarked in *The Queen of Corinth* (Act IV, Scene 1). Shakespeare, however, was silent on the fork as an eating utensil.

If courtiers could not yet appreciate the usefulness of the fork, it was not surprising that in the country as a whole it was disdained. Nicholas Breton gives a countryman's feelings about forks: "For us in the Country, when we have washed our hands, after no foule work, nor handling any unwholesome thing, we neede no little Forkes to make hay with our mouths, to throw our meat into them."

Napkins were used even in rather simple homes, and table-cloths in many relatively modest ones. Clothes were expensive and difficult to clean; napkins saved wear and tear on them. But the laundering of table linens could also be a problem, especially for large households. Linen was sometimes saved up for several months before it was either sent out to be laundered or a laundress hired to come in and wash it. This was perhaps part of the explanation for the huge stocks of linens possessed by some families.

The Ramsey family's household linen was valued at almost 152 pounds—an enormous sum for those days. The household made do with sixty-four tablecloths, ranging in length from four to six yards, and sixty-two dozen napkins, in size a little over a yard square. In addition there were for the ewery, which was responsible for the basins and pitchers used for hand-washing at mealtimes, "16 damaske towels each three yards long; 15 diaper [linen huck] towels, each three yards long; 12 towels of half-holland cloth and 1 holland towel, which measured 4¼ ells [an ell is forty-nine inches], as well as 1 fine diaper towel 6 yards long, and 15 damaske towells each 6⅓ yards long."

The England of Queen Elizabeth's day was more fastidious than that of her father, Henry VIII. People not only washed

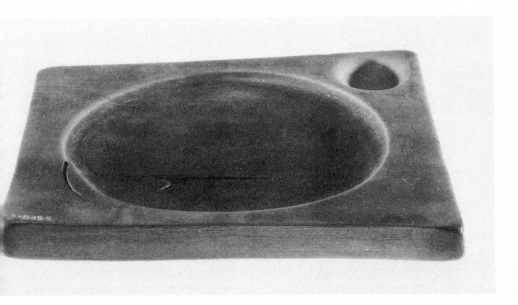

Sycamore trencher with depression for salt (16th–17th century)

their hands before sitting down to eat and after eating, but in elegant homes a serving man might bring around hot, moist towels or napkins during the meal to wash off sticky fingers.

The basic place setting, after the cloth had been laid, was a napkin, a spoon, a trencher [plate], and in wealthy homes perhaps a knife. Drinking vessels were kept on a separate serving table. If one of the diners felt the need of a drink either to quench his thirst or to offer a toast to his host or another guest, he called a serving man to bring the desired drink. It was drunk and the glass or goblet was returned to the servant, who took it to a tub of water, rinsed it, and replaced it on the "cupboard" for the next request. At feasts the table ordinarily was so covered with dishes of food that there was no room for drinking glasses, even if there were enough to go around. William Harrison approved of this: "By this device, much idle tippling is furthermore cut off, for if the full pots should continually stand at the elbow or near the trencher, divers would always be dealing with them, whereas now they drink seldom, and only when necessity urgeth, and so avoid the note of great drinking or often troubling of the servitors with filling of their bowls."

Treen (wooden) tableware was still in common use in Shakespeare's day and long after, although it was gradually being replaced by tin, pewter, and occasionally silver. Leather jugs and mugs were still in common use as well. In *The Taming of the Shrew* (Act IV, Scene 1), Grumio, who has preceded Petruchio and Katharina to see that the house is ready for his master and new mistress, calls out to Curtis, "Where's the cook? is supper ready, the house trimmed, rushes strewed, cobwebs swept; the serving-men in their new fustian, their white stockings . . . ? Be the Jacks fair within, the Jills fair without, and carpets laid, and everything in order?" Blackjacks or jacks were jugs made of waxed leather, coated with pitch on the outside.

There was still a shortage of furniture. Most people sat on benches or stools, sometimes made more comfortable with pillows. What chairs there were were reserved to the master of the house and to esteemed guests. John Harington complained about the hardness of the benches at court. Even London merchants, he said, had more comfortable seating equipment. But even in the royal palaces, furniture was in short supply, and when Queen Elizabeth moved from one of her many castles to another, furniture often moved with her. Joint stools resembled tables and were sometimes used as such. When they were not in use, the legs were turned inwards and they could be stacked out of the way, sometimes under the tables. "Away with the joint-stools, remove the court-cupboard [where the family silver is displayed in the dining hall while the feast is in progress], look to the plate," a serving man calls out to his fellow servants, to clear the hall for the dance that is to follow Lord Capulet's supper in *Romeo and Juliet* (Act I, Scene 5).

Permanently joined tables, some with draw leaves, were beginning to appear in wealthy homes, but most dining tables were still trestle tables, the legs of which were attached to flat planks with pegs that could be withdrawn so that the top could be lifted off and the whole piece stacked against a wall to make more room. "A hall! a hall!" Capulet shouts to the servants (in the same scene), "give room, and foot it, girls. More light, ye knaves! and turn the tables up."

Until private dining parlors became fashionable, even in the homes of the great nobility, the whole household, including the servants, dined in the hall that was the main room in the house. The family and their guests, however, ate at a table set apart from the others, often on a platform built into the far end of the room (probably the origin of the phrase, the "high table"). A fine example is the raised platform in the old dining hall at Knole, the ancestral home of the Sackville family, in Kent. Knole also has kept the carved oak screen across the width of the hall at the entrance side, and behind it the gallery for the musicians; music was an important adjunct of Elizabethan dining.

The dining room was usually lighted by candles in wooden or iron circles suspended from the ceiling—in earlier days by torch lights fixed in iron brackets on the walls. Candles were also used on the tables.

Guests, as well as servants, were seated at the table in order of their rank. At the master's table the closer one sat to him the higher the guest's rank could be presumed to be. At the other tables the position of the salt cellar indicated the relative rank of the diners. To be seated "above the salt," that is, closer to the host's table, proclaimed a higher rank than to sit "below the salt." In *Coriolanus* (Act IV, Scene 5), one of the serving men describes Coriolanus (Caius Marcius) being honored "as if he were son and heir to Mars; set at upper end o' the table."

In wealthy homes the steward or chamberlain saw to it that the

Standing salt, silver-gilt and mother-of-pearl (late 16th century)

servants knew their responsibilities and that meals were properly served. Before the diners were asked to come to the table, all the dishes for the first course were placed on the table together. When that course had been eaten, the dishes were removed and all the dishes for the second course were brought in to the table.

In noble homes gentlemen servants carved for the master of the house, his family, and esteemed guests. The rest of the diners carved for themselves, although sometimes one diner would graciously offer to carve for another. When a servant carved he took the desired dish of meat or fish from the table to a carving table, where he would cut off a serving-size piece and then cut this into bite-size pieces. These would then be taken by a server back to the table and placed before the diner.

Thomas Platter described the service at a dinner at the home of the lord mayor of London when he was a guest. It began at his lodgings: "As it drew near to lunch time two men of distinction came to our lodging from the Mayor, to advise that the gentlemen were foregathered. On arrival . . . we were received and let through the house to a handsome apartment, where the gentlemen bade us a warm welcome, and the women received us with a kiss. Then we were handed scented water . . . to wash our hands" before being seated at the table. After the mayor's son had said grace, Platter went on, "straightways all manner of lavish dishes were served most decorously. . . . There were two servers or carvers who removed one plate after another from the table to another covered table near by, and they did nothing else but carve and serve." The food, said Platter, was served in small pewter bowls, placed on plates before each guest.

The medieval rituals of serving were still maintained in the royal palace when serving the queen or king. Paul Hentzner, a German visitor in 1598 who was permitted to watch the ritual of setting the royal table, gave this account. "It is very seldom that any Body, Foreigner or Native, is admitted [to watch while the queen dined] but while the Queen was still at prayers [in the chapel], we saw her Table set out with the following Solemnity. A Gentleman entered the Room bearing a Rod, and along with him another who had a Table-cloth, which, after they had both kneeled three Times with the utmost Veneration, he spread upon the Table and after kneeling again they both retired." The same ceremony was then repeated with a salt cellar, a plate, and bread.

Following them came two of the queen's ladies-in-waiting, one of whom carried a tasting knife. The other "prostrated herself three Times in the most graceful Manner, approached the Table, and rubbed the Plates and Bread and Salt, with as much Awe, as if the Queen were present.

"When they had waited there a little while, the Yeomen of the Guard entered, bareheaded, cloathed in Scarlet, with a Golden Rose upon their Backs, bringing in at each Turn a Course of twenty-four Dishes, served in Plate [silver], most of it gild [gold-plated]; these Dishes were received by a Gentleman in the same Order they were brought, and placed upon the Table, while the Lady-taster gave to each of the Guards a mouthful to eat, of the particular dish he had brought, for Fear of any Poison." At the end of this ceremony, he continued, "a number of unmarried Ladies [ladies-in-waiting] appeared, who, with particular Solemnity, lifted the Meat off the Table, and conveyed it into the Queen's inner and more private Chamber, where, after she had chosen for herself, the rest goes to the Ladies of the Court."

On December 27, 1584, Lupold von Wedel, another German visitor, was privileged to watch the queen dine in state after she returned from a Christmas service in her chapel. He also wrote a detailed account of his observations: "While she was in church, a long table was made ready [on a dais] under a canopy of cloth of gold. On her return from Church there were served at this table forty large and silver dishes, all of gilt silver, with various meats.

"She alone took her seat at the table. . . . A young gentleman habited in black carved the meats for the Queen," he continued, "and a gentleman of about the same age arrayed in green served her beverages. This gentleman had to remain kneeling as long as she was drinking; when she had finished, he rose and removed the goblet.

"At the table, to her right stood gentlemen of rank . . . white staffs in their hands [the symbols of their high rank as household officers]." When the queen summoned one of them, von Wedel noted, he kneeled until commanded to rise, bowed, went to the center of the room and bowed again, then ordered the servers to bring the next course. "Four Gentlemen with scepters also walked before the dish bearers," who, von Wedel said, were knights and nobles, and on each side of the room knights and ladies stood near those who were in charge of "the magnificent drinking vessels." During all this time the queen's musicians "discoursed [played] excellent music."

Portrait of Queen Elizabeth I (Artist unknown)

Queen Elizabeth was a fastidious eater and dined sparingly. After she had tasted a few of the dishes in the first course and a few in the second, von Wedel continued, she rose from the table. "Just before she did so, five . . . countesses [who had been sitting at a small table near the door] arose from their table and having twice made a deep courtesy to the Queen, passed over to the other side. The Queen arose and turned her back upon the table, whereupon two bishops stepped forward and said grace. After them came three earls. . . . These three then took a large basin, which was covered like a meat dish and of gilt silver, and two of the old gentlemen held the towel. The five of them then advanced to the Queen and knelt down before her. They then raised the lid from the basin. . . . A third poured water over the Queen's hands, who before washing her hands drew off a ring and handed it to the . . . Lord Chamberlain. After washing her hands she again drew on the ring."

Elizabeth's successor, James I, already James VI of Scotland, did not share Elizabeth's dislike of being observed at table. He enjoyed having people around him more than he did the food. Sir Henry Wooten, who visited Scotland in 1601, described a dinner scene at that court. "Anyone may enter the King's presence while he is at dinner, and as he eats he converses with those about him. . . . Dinner finished, he remains at table for a time before he retires, listening to banter and merry jests in which he takes delight." As king of Scotland, James ruled over a rougher and far poorer people than the English, and his own eating habits changed little when he became king of England. Unfortunately, his unusually narrow jaws made it difficult for him to eat with royal dignity.

The Taming of the Shrew makes use of such dining rituals for its introductory comic scene. Sly, found dead drunk in the gutter by a lord and his companions, is made the butt of a practical joke. "Sirs, I will practise on this drunken man. What think you, if he were convey'd to bed, wrapp'd in sweet clothes, rings put upon his fingers, A most delicious banquet by his bed, And brave attendants near him when he wakes . . . ? Let one attend him with a silver basin Full of rose-water, and bestrew'd with flowers; Another bear the ewer, the third a diaper, And say, 'Will 't please your lordship cool your hands?' " Poor Sly is properly bewildered, to the amusement of his tormentors.

In Gervase Markham's *The English Hus-wife*, he points out

Court cupboard (for display of family silver), English oak (early 17th century)

that the mistress of the house might on occasion have to or want to take over the ordinary responsibilities of the steward. He gives her detailed instructions on the manner of "setting forth of meat for a great Feast, and from it to derive meaner [more modest] menues, making due proportion of all things." For what, he asks, "avails it our good *Huswife* to be never so skilful in the parts of Cookery, if she want skill to marshall the dishes, and set everyone in his due place, giving precedency according to fashion and custome?" He then shows her how to "marshall" the dishes for a princely feast in their traditional order, as they are to go from the cook to the table, from servant to servant, until each dish is finally set in its proper place on the table, so that the table will have "a most comely beauty" and provide "very great contentment to the Guests." Although the dishes for each course were to travel from the kitchen in a prescribed order, they were to be placed on the table, not as the Sewer [server] received them, but set down "so that before every Trencher may stand a Sallet, a Fricases, a boyl'd meat, a rost meat, a baked meat [pie], and a carbonado. . . . And for made Dishes and Quelquechoses, which rely on the invention of the Cook, they are to be thrust in into every place that is empty, and so sprinkled all over the Table."

A Twelfth Night Feast

Madam, the guests are come, supper served up, you called, my young lady asked for, the nurse cursed in the pantry, and everything in extremity. I must hence to wait [serve the guests]; I beseech you, follow straight.

Romeo and Juliet, Act I, Scene 3 (*Servant*)

SHERRY

There's never none of these demure boys come to any proof; for thin drink doth so over-cool their blood . . . and then, when they marry, they get wenches.

Henry IV, Part II, Act IV, Scene 3 (*Falstaff*)

TURNIP CHIPS

This is my father's choice. . . .
Alas! I had rather be set quick i' the earth,
and bowl'd to death with turnips.

The Merry Wives of Windsor, Act III, Scene 4 (*Anne*)

OYSTERS STEWED IN WHITE WINE SAUCE

'Say, the firm Roman to great Egypt sends
This treasure of an oyster.'

Antony and Cleopatra, Act I, Scene 5 (*Alexas*)

BRAWN (PICKLED PORK)

'I know not love,' quoth he, 'nor will not know it
Unless it be a boar, and then I chase it.'

Venus and Adonis, Lines 409–10 (*Adonis*)

A HOT VENISON PASTY

Wife, bid these gentlemen welcome. Come,
we have a hot venison pasty to dinner.
                    The Merry Wives of Windsor,
                    Act I, Scene 1 (*Master Page*)

RED WHEAT FURMENTY

Shall we sow the headland with wheat?
With red wheat, Davy.
Henry IV, Part II, Act V, Scene 1 (*Davy and Shallow*)

ROAST PIGEONS WITH
MARROW AND LIVER DRESSING

As the ox hath his bow . . . so man hath his desires;
and as pigeons bill, so wedlock would be nibbling.
                    As You Like It, Act III, Scene 3 (*Touchstone*)

A LETTUCE TANSIE

If we will plant nettles or sow lettuce . . .
the power . . . lies in our wills.
                    Othello, Act I, Scene 3 (*Iago*)

A STOFFADO OF KID

As full of spirit as the month of May . . .
Wanton as youthful goats.
                    Henry IV, Part I, Act IV, Scene 1 (*Vernon*)

A DISH OF SWEET POTATOES

Earth, yield me roots!
Timon of Athens, Act IV, Scene 3 (*Timon*)

A SALAD OF LEMONS

How tartly that gentleman looks! I never can
see him but I am heart-burned an hour after.
                    Much Ado About Nothing, Act II, Scene 1 (*Beatrice*)

MESLIN RYE BREAD AND MANCHET

Lord Angelo . . . scarce confesses
That his blood flows, or that his appetite
Is more to bread than stone.
                    Measure for Measure, Act I, Scene 3 (*The Duke*)

WINE—RED AND WHITE

Fill the cup, and let it come;
I'll pledge you a mile to the bottom.
Henry IV, Part II, Act V, Scene 3 (*Silence*)

ALE

For a quart of ale is a dish for a king.
The Winter's Tale, Act IV, Scene 2 (*Autolycus*)

AN ALMOND PUDDING

I have sat in the stocks for puddings he hath
stolen.
Two Gentlemen of Verona, Act IV, Scene 4 (*Launce*)

A MINCEMEAT TART

I know no ways to mince it in love,
but directly to say 'I love you.'
Henry V, Act V, Scene 2 (*King Henry*)

When we have stuff'd
These pipes and these conveyances of our blood
With wine and feeding, we have suppler souls
Than in our priest-like fasts.
Coriolanus, Act V, Scene 1 (*Menenius*)

A SIMPLE SALAD OF TURNIPS

Your simple Sallets are . . . Turnips, pilled and served up sim-
ply.

Gervase Markham, *The English Hus-wife*

THE WORKING VERSION:

½ pound fresh young turnips
Ice water

Peel the turnips with a potato peeler and slice them very thin crosswise. Chill in ice water for half an hour before serving.

Dr. Boorde also approved of raw turnips. If eaten in moderate amounts, he said, "it doth provoke a good apetyde;" and he added, "boyled and eaten with flesshe [meat] they augmenteth the sede of man."

HOW TO STEW OYSTERS

Straine the liquor from the Oysters, then wash them very clean, and put them into a pipkin with the liquor, a pinte of Wine to a quart of Oysters, two or three whole Onions, large Mace, Pepper, Ginger; let all the spices be whole, they will stew the whiter; put in Salt, a little Vinegar, a piece of butter and sweet Herbs; stew all these together till you think them enough, then take out some of that liquor and put to it a quarter of a pound of butter, a Lemmond minced, and beat it up thick, setting it on the fire, but let it not boyle; dreine the rest of the liquor from the Oysters thorow [through] a culender, and dish them; pour this sauce over them; garnish your dish with searced [sieved] Ginger, Lemmon, Orange, Barberries, or Grapes scalded; sippit it, and serve it up.

Joseph Cooper, *The Art of Cookery Refin'd and Augmented*

THE WORKING VERSION:

1 pint fresh-shelled oysters with their juice
1 cup dry white wine
2 tablespoons white wine vinegar
¼ teaspoon rosemary
2 sprigs washed and drained parsley

½ teaspoon peppercorns
¼ teaspoon salt
2 small onions, peeled
5 tablespoons butter
1 lemon
2 slices buttered toast, cut into triangles

Cut the oysters in half if they are large ones. Simmer the wine, wine vinegar, herbs, spices, onions, and one tablespoon of the butter for ten minutes in a small saucepan. Add the oysters with their juice to the sauce and simmer for three minutes, turning the oysters once.

Cut the lemon in half crossways, slice one half in thin slices and seed them. Then remove the segments of meat from the other half with a sharp knife and mince them. Dice the remaining four tablespoons of butter.

Remove the oysters from the sauce to a warmed bowl. Strain the seasonings from the sauce and return the sauce to the saucepan. Add the minced lemon and the diced butter to the sauce and simmer, stirring vigorously until it begins to thicken. Return the oysters to the pan and heat just long enough to make sure the oysters are hot.

Arrange the slices of toast in a warmed serving dish, spoon the oysters over the toast, and pour the sauce over them. Garnish with the slices of lemon and serve immediately.

Oysters were not only popular but, by all accounts, they were of excellent quality. In Shakespeare's time the Thames was clear and sparkling and its oyster beds provided ample supplies. "The best Oysters are sold here in great quantities," wrote the German Paul Hentzner in 1598. Another Continental, Thomas Platter, was also impressed: "A great many oysters are caught in England too, better than the French and Italian ones, small but very perfect."

Oysters were usually purchased for home eating by weight, either in pecks or bushels. They were also eaten directly off oyster carts in the streets, as well as at inns and taverns.

Despite the difficulties of transportation and the danger of spoilage, oysters were sent inland, usually from London, which was both the chief market and a great center for food distribution. The household accounts of Milton Abbey, the Norfolk home of Sir William Fitzwilliam, show a purchase of 3,300 oysters, at eight pence a hundred, which were transported from London. These must have graced an important occasion, for nearly a hundred pounds of butter and large amounts of spices, as well as sweetmeats for "the banquet," were among the items purchased at the same time. Lord North bought two horseloads of oysters for Queen Elizabeth's visit in 1577.

TO SOWCE A PIGGE

Take white Wine and a little sweet broth, and halfe a score nutmegs cut into quarters, then take Rosemarie, Baies, Time, and sweet margerum, and let them boyle altogether, skum them very cleane, and when they be boyled, put them in an earthen pan, and the syrop also, and when yee serve them, a quarter of a pig in a dish, and the Bays and nutmegs on the top.

Thomas Dawson, *The good Huswifes Jewell*

THE WORKING VERSION:

One 1½-pound piece of boned loin of pork
⅓ yard cheesecloth
2½ cups veal or chicken broth
2 cups dry white wine
3 bay leaves

1 nutmeg, broken up
½ teaspoon thyme
½ teaspoon rosemary
½ teaspoon marjoram
1½ teaspoons salt

Remove all but a thin covering of fat from the pork. Roll the meat up tightly in the cheesecloth and tie it as you would a roast, then make a knot in the cheesecloth at each end.

Put the broth, one cup of wine, and the seasonings into a two-quart saucepan with a tight-fitting lid and bring to a boil. Add the pork roll, lower the heat to simmer, and cook, covered, until a fork will easily penetrate the meat—2 to 2½ hours. Remove the meat from the cooking broth and put it into a glass or stainless-steel bowl. Pour the second cup of wine over it, add the herbs from the cooking broth, and as much of the broth as is needed to completely cover the roll. Cover the bowl with a plastic bowl cover, set aside until cold, then refrigerate.

Marinate the pork for at least one week, turning it once a day. To serve, remove the cheesecloth covering and slice the meat about ¼ inch thick. Arrange the slices on a shallow serving dish and spoon a little of the sousing liquid over them with some of the spices. Serve with a sauce of prepared mustard to which a little vinegar has been added.

Pickled pork (brawn) was considered best when made of wild boar, but as wild boars had practically disappeared from England by the sixteenth century, domesticated boars (pigs) were perforce substituted. Occasionally, however, a wild boar was caught. The Petre family accounts indicated that it had received one as a gift; from that boar, ten pasties were made, and the boar's head, suitably prepared, was served at the "master's table."

Brawn was a cold-weather dish. "It is accounted a great piece of service at the table from November until February be ended," wrote Harrison, "but chiefly in the Christmas time. . . . With the same also we begin our dinners each day and because it is somewhat hard of digestion a draught of malvesey [malmsey], bastard or muscatel is usually drunk after it, where either of them are conveniently to be had; otherwise the meaner [poorer] sort content themselves with their own drink [beer] which at that season is generally very strong."

Cookbook bills of fare for winter feasts all begin with a dish of brawn. *A Proper newe Booke of Cokerye* specifies "Brawne and mustarde"; Murrell uses a "Shield or collar of Brawne"; Robert May's menu for All-Saints' Day begins with "A collar of brawne and mustard"; and Rabisha starts his menu with "a Coller of Brawne."

TO BAKE RED DEER (VENISON PASTY)

Take a side of red deer, bone it and season it, then take out the back sinnew and the skin, and lard the fillets or back with great lard as big as your middle finger; being first seasoned with nutmeg and pepper: then take four ounces of pepper, four ounces of nutmeg, and six ounces of salt, mix them well together, and season the side of venison; being well slashed with a knife in the inside for to make the seasoning enter; being seasoned, and a pye made according to these forms [in Robert May's cookbook various illustrations of possible shapes and decorations follow the recipe], put some butter in the bottom of the pye, a quarter of an ounce of cloves, and a bay leaf or two, lay on the flesh, season it, and coat it deep, then put on a few cloves, and good store of butter, close it up and bake it the space of eight or nine hours, but first baste the pye with six or seven eggs beaten well together.

If you bake it to eat hot, give it but half the seasoning, and liquor it with claret-wine and good butter.

TO MAKE A PASTE FOR IT

Take a peck of flour by weight, and lay it on the pastery board, make a hole in the midst of the flour, and put to it five pound of good fresh butter, the yolks of six eggs and but four whites, work up the butter and eggs into the flour, and being well wrought to-gether put some fair water to it, and make it into a stiff paste. In this fashion of fallow deer you may bake goat, doe, or pasty of venison.

Robert May, *The Accomplisht Cook*

THE WORKING VERSION:

1½ pounds boned venison steak	1 strip lean bacon, diced
¾ cup claret	
1 teaspoon salt	**THE PASTRY**
¼ teaspoon pepper	2 cups sifted unbleached flour
⅛ teaspoon cloves	1 teaspoon salt
½ teaspoon nutmeg	¾ cup cold butter
¼ teaspoon powdered bay leaves	½ cup cold water (approximately)
2 egg yolks	1 egg, separated
5 tablespoons butter, diced	

Remove any gristle from the venison. Mix the claret, salt, pepper, cloves, nutmeg, and bay leaves together in a shallow bowl, and place the meat in the marinade, turning it over several times to coat it well with the mixture. Cover the bowl and refrigerate the meat for six hours, turning it after three hours.

Make the pastry dough according to instructions given on page 31. Turn the dough out on a floured work surface and form it into a rectangle. Roll this out to a sheet one inch wider than twice the width of the steak and six inches longer than its length. From the longer end of the sheet of pastry cut out four arrows to decorate the pasty. Straighten out the edge from which you cut the arrows and drape the sheet in a low, rectangular oven-to-table baking dish with the extra pastry hanging over the sides of the dish.

Drain the venison, saving the marinade for the sauce. Beat one egg yolk and brush both sides of the meat with it. Dot half the diced butter and half the bacon over the pastry, arrange the meat over it, and dot the top with the rest of the butter and bacon. Bring the two shorter sides of the pastry up over the steak and brush the edges with egg white. Then bring the two longer sides over and pinch the edges together to seal the pasty. Carefully turn the pasty over in the baking dish. Brush the top of it with egg white and arrange the arrow decorations on it with two of the arrows facing one direction and two the opposite direction. Brush these with egg white. Bake at 450° for twenty minutes, then lower the heat to 350° and bake fifteen minutes longer.

While the pasty is baking, bring the reserved marinade to a boil in a small saucepan. Lower the heat to simmer and cook for ten minutes. Remove the saucepan from the heat and beat in the remaining egg yolk. Return the pan to the heat and cook, stirring constantly, until the sauce begins to thicken. To serve, pour a spoonful of the sauce over each slice of the pasty.

Robert May would have poured the sauce (the English called it lear) through a hole made in the top of the pasty. But with a pasty as small as this one, his method is impractical.

Meat pies meant to be eaten cold required more seasoning, as May pointed out, and a crust that was strong enough to hold up and stay moist, to keep the meat from drying out. Very large pies might continue to be eaten from for as long as three months. Their crusts were called coffins, an apt name for some of these pies which must have been deadly by the time the last bit of them was eaten. Mercutio, in *Romeo and Juliet* (Act II, Scene 4), describes just such a pie—a Lenten pie—as "something stale and hoar ere it be spent [eaten]."

Gervase Markham instructs the housewife on the kind of pastry crusts needed for various kinds of pies. "Our English huswife," he says, "must be skillful in Pastery, and know how and in what manner to bake all sorts of meat, and what Paste is fit for

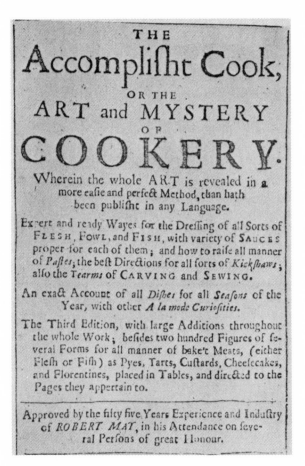

Title page of Robert May's The Accomplisht Cook

every meat, and how to handle and compound such Pastes. As for
example, Red Deer Venison, Wild-Boar, Gammons of Bacon
[hams], Swans, Elkes, Porpus [porpoise], and such like standing
dishes, which must be kept long, would be bak'd in a moyst, thick,
tough, course and long lasting crust, and therefore of all other
your Rye paste is best for that Purpose; your Turkey, Capon,
Pheasant, Partridge, Veal, Peacocks, Lamb and all sorts of Water Fowl, which are to come to the table more than once (yet not
many days), would be bak't in a good white crust, somewhat
thick; therefore your Wheat is fit for them; your Chickens,
Calves-feet, Olives [of meat], Potatoes, Quinces, Fallow Deer,
and such like; which are most commonly eaten hot, would be in
the finest, shortest, and thinnest crust, therefore your fine Wheat-
flower, which is a little baked in the oven [to dry the flour if it
was damp], before it is kneaded, is best for that purpose."

TO MAKE FURMENTY

Take wheat and wet it, then beat it in a sack with the wash-beetle, being finely hulled and cleaned from the dust and hulls, boil it over night, and let it soak on a soft fire all night; then next morning take as much as will serve the turn, put it in a pipkin, pan or skillet, and put it a boiling in cream or milk, with mace, salt, whole cinamon, and saffron, or yolkes of eggs, boil it thick and serve it in a clean scowred dish, scrape on sugar, and trim the dish.

Robert May, *The Accomplisht Cook*

THE WORKING VERSION:

1 cup whole-grain red wheat	¼ teaspoon mace
4 cups water	1 three-inch stick of cinnamon
1½ cups light cream	1 tablespoon brown sugar
½ teaspoon salt	2 egg yolks

Rinse the wheat in a coarse sieve to remove any chaff. In the top of a double boiler, bring the water to a boil. Add the wheat, remove the pot from the heat, cover it and set aside for eight hours or overnight to soften. Return the pot to direct heat and bring to a boil. Lower the heat to simmer and cook the wheat for ½ hour.

Drain off the water, add the cream, salt, mace, and cinnamon, and heat to just below the boiling point. Fill the lower part of the double boiler with boiling water to within an inch of the top pot. Cover the furmenty pot and place it over the boiling water. Lower the heat to simmer, and cook, stirring occasionally, until the wheat has absorbed most of the cream—about five hours.

Beat the sugar and egg yolks together. Stir them into the furmenty and continue cooking for five minutes. Remove the cinnamon stick and serve in a warmed dish with a little brown sugar sprinkled over the top or in a separate saucer.

Whole-grain red wheat can be purchased in most health-food shops.

Furmenty—or fermenty, fromenty, frumenty, or formenty—had been popular for more than a hundred years when Shakespeare was born. It was eaten with venison by the fortunate few, but appreciated without it by those to whom venison was just a word. A "mynstrals Sollem Song" of about 1575 goes, "A boll of furmenty and in the midst of it sticking a dozen hornspoons [spoons made of horn] in a bunch" are "the instruments meetest to eate furmenty porage withall."

May's recipe varies very little from the recipe for "Venyson with Furmenty" given in a Harleian (British Museum) manuscript of about 1430 that reads: "Take whete and pyke it clene, and do it in a morter, and caste a lytel water ther-on; and stampe with a pestel tyl it loses the husks; then blow owt the husks, and put it in a potte, and let seethe tyl it breke; then set yt douun, and sone after set it over the fyre, and stere it wyl; an whan thow hast boylid it wyl, put therinne swete mylke, and seethe it to-gederys, and stere it wyl; and whan it is y-now, coloure it wyth safron, and salt it evenly, and dress it forth, and the venyson in a-nother dyshe with fayre hot water."

AN EXCELLENT WAY TO ROAST PIGEONS

Prepare them to trusse; then make a farcing-meat with Marrow or Beefe-suet, with the liver of the Fowle minced very small; and mixe with it grated Bread, the yolkes of hard Eggs minced, Mace and Nutmeg beat, the tops of Thyme minced small, and Salt; incorporate all these together with hard Eggs and a little Verjuice, then cut the skin off the Fowle betwixt the legs and the body, before it is trussed, and put in your finger to raise the skin from the flesh, but take care you break not the skin; then farce it full with this meat, and trusse the leggs close to keep in the meat; then spit them and roast them, setting a dish under to save the Gravy, which mixe with a little Claret, sliced Nutmeg, a little of that farced meat, and Salt; then give it two or three walms on the fire, and beat it up thick with a yolk of raw Egg and a piece of Butter, with a little minc'd Lemmon, and serve it up in the dish with the Fowle.

Joseph Cooper, *The Art of Cookery Refin'd and Augmented*

THE WORKING VERSION:

Two 1-pound squab pigeons, dressed weight
1 chicken liver or the livers from the squabs
2 ounces beef marrow, minced
2 tablespoons grated bread crumbs
2 hard-boiled egg yolks
1 teaspoon red wine vinegar
½ teaspoon salt
¼ teaspoon nutmeg
¼ teaspoon mace
½ teaspoon thyme

THE MARINADE
1 tablespoon olive oil
1 teaspoon salt
¼ teaspoon nutmeg

THE SAUCE
¼ lemon
½ cup claret
1 tablespoon butter
¼ teaspoon salt
¼ teaspoon nutmeg
1 egg yolk
2 teaspoons of the dressing from the pigeons

Cut off the wing tips and remove the giblets—if any—from the squabs. Rinse the pigeons under cold water and wipe them dry with a paper towel or clean white cloth. Mince the liver and mix with the beef marrow, bread crumbs, hard-boiled egg yolks, vinegar, and the seasonings.

Loosen the skin from the breasts and thighs of the birds by sliding two fingers under it and gently pushing the skin upwards. Push the dressing, a spoonful at a time, up into the loosened area. Close the necks with steel pins or sew them closed with thread.

Mix all the marinade ingredients into a paste and spread it over the outside of the birds. Tie the wings and legs loosely to the bodies of the squabs. Roast at 425° for thirty minutes—rotisserie roasting will take a little longer.

When the pigeons are tender, remove a teaspoonful of dressing from each one and reserve, turn off the oven heat, and return the birds to the oven to keep warm. Peel and mince the lemon. In a small saucepan bring the claret, lemon, butter, salt, and nutmeg to a boil. Lower the heat and simmer for five minutes. Then add the egg yolk, the reserved dressing, and any pan gravy there may be. Cook, stirring constantly, until the sauce begins to thicken.

Remove the pins or string from the squabs. Cut the birds in half lengthways, cutting down the back first and then down the breast. Arrange them in a warmed serving dish, pour the sauce over them, and serve.

Cooper says that this method can also be used for roasting chickens. So if you are unable to obtain squabs, these ingredients will serve for a three-pound chicken.

"Pygions yf they be younge be ever good," notes the anonymous author of *A Proper newe Booke of Cokerye,* and vast numbers of them were eaten throughout the year, at humble feasts as well as at important ones. When Queen Elizabeth visited Lord North in 1577, 217 dozen pigeons were served up to the guests during her stay of several days.

FOR A TANSIE

Take either walnut tree leaves or lettice alone, or all other good hearbes, stamp them and strain them, and take a little Creame and grated bread, nutmeg, pepper and Sugar, fower Egges two of the whites: beat them together and so frye it in a pan.

Anonymous, *The Good Hous-wives Treasurie*

THE WORKING VERSION:

1¼	pounds crisp leaf lettuce	¼	teaspoon pepper
¼	cup minced parsley	¼	teaspoon nutmeg
2	tablespoons light cream	¼	teaspoon brown sugar
4	egg yolks	2	egg whites
¼	cup grated bread crumbs	4	tablespoons butter
¼	teaspoon salt		

Separate the lettuce leaves, wash them in cool water, and pat them dry in a clean cloth. Put the lettuce and parsley in a large saucepan without any water, cover, and cook over low heat only until the greens wilt; then purée them.

Add the cream, egg yolks, bread crumbs, salt, pepper, nutmeg, and sugar, and beat until blended. Whip the egg whites until stiff and fold into the mixture. Melt the butter on a griddle or in a large saucepan. When the butter sizzles, drop spoonfuls of the mixture, large enough to make three-inch pancakes, onto the griddle. Fry until lightly brown on the underside, then turn and brown the other side.

Arrange the pancakes on a warmed serving dish, sprinkled, if you wish, with a little brown sugar. Serve immediately.

Most tansies were a cross between an omelet and a pancake, with eggs as the basic ingredient. Originally, tansies were made with the herb tansy as one of the ingredients and eaten in the spring, especially during Lent. Tansy is a handsome herb with lovely clusters of buttonlike flowers, but it is very bitter. This bitterness, according to some writers, gave tansies a religious significance when eaten during Lent. The bitterness was related to the bitter days of the Hebrews during their bondage to the Egyptians.

Because of its bitterness, the herb was usually mixed with other herbs, or the leaves were crushed, the juice extracted, and a little of the juice used to season the tansies. As often as not other herbs were substituted. "Some use to put of the herb Tansey into it [tansies]," said Markham, "but the Walnut-tree-buds do give better taste or rellish." Rabisha has a recipe for a tansy of cowslips or violets, as well as one for spinach, neither of which contains the tansy herb.

A STOFFADO OF KID

Bone and lard it with great lard as big as your finger, being first seasoned with pepper and nutmegs, and being larded, lay it in steep in an earthen pan or pipkin in a quart of white-wine, and half as much wine-vinegar, some twenty whole cloves, half an ounce of mace, an ounce of beaten pepper, three races [roots] of slic't ginger, half a handful of salt, half an ounce of slic't nutmegs, and a ladle full of good mutton broth, and close up the pot with a sheet of course paste, and bake it; it will ask four hours baking; then have a fine clean large dish, with a six-penny French bread slic't in large slices, and then lay them in the bottom of the dish, and steep them with some good strong mutton broth, and the same broth it was baked in, and some roast mutton gravy and . . . garnish it with spices, some sausages, and some kinds of good puddings, and marrow, and carved lemons slic't.

Robert May, *The Accomplisht Cook*

THE WORKING VERSION:

One 3-pound leg of young
   kid, boned
  4 slices lean bacon
1 ½ teaspoons salt
  ¼ teaspoon pepper
  ½ teaspoon nutmeg
  6 cloves
  1 large piece of whole mace
One ½-inch-thick slice
   of fresh ginger, quartered
  ½ cup white wine

  ¼ cup white wine vinegar
  ¼ cup mutton broth
  2 ounces beef marrow,
   diced
  6 slices French bread,
   toasted
  6 small pork sausages, fried
   brown
  1 lemon, sliced thin and
   seeded

With a sharp knife, slash four cuts through the meat equidistant from each other and push a slice of bacon through each cut so that a little extends on each side of the meat. Put the seasonings, wine, and wine vinegar in a bowl, add the meat and marinate for one hour.

In a casserole just large enough to fit the meat comfortably, bring the marinade with the spices and the broth to a boil. Add the meat, cover the casserole, and bake at 300° for about two hours, or until the meat is tender.

When the meat is about three-quarters done, turn it over and dot it with the beef marrow. When done, remove the meat from the pan and slice it into ½-inch-thick slices. Arrange the toast in a warmed serving bowl, put the slices of meat over it, and garnish with the sausages and slices of lemon. Then pour the sauce over the meat and serve.

Kid was a delicacy; in cookbook bills of fare it appears only on feast menus. When the Fairfax family entertained the earl of Rutland in 1579, and later in the year when they were entertaining the archbishop of York, roast kid was served to "their lordships' tables," as well as to the guests of somewhat lower rank "at the board's end," but it was not served to the guests' retinues.

It was customary to serve the best foods to the family and to important guests. Humbler guests accepted this, although they may have grumbled into their beards. In his *Panegerick,* Robert Herrick lauded Sir Lewis Pemberton, sheriff of Northampton-shire in 1621, for his hospitality to the poor as well as to the rich, and like many a lesser poet of his day he denounced the households where "true hospitality" had fallen into decay. At Sir Lewis's table, said Herrick, there was:

> no currish Waiter to affright
> With blasting eye, the appetite,
> Which fain would waste upon thy Cates, but that
>   The *Trencher-creature* marketh what
> Best and more suppling piece he cuts, and by
>   Some private pinch tels danger's nie
> A hand too desp'rate, or a knife that bites
>   Skin deepe into the Porke, or lights
> Upon some part of Kid, as if mistooke,
>   When checked by the Butler's look.

Kid was also highly recommended by the dietaries. Henry Buttes, in *Dyets Dry Dinner,* said, "Red and black kiddes: scarce halfe yeare, lately weaned, not yet wearied is easily and soon digested; of best nourishment . . . wholesomer roast than sodde [boiled]; the hinder quarters, than the fore: because they less abound with excrementitious moysture."

Thomas Elyot ventured cautiously to differ with the ancient Greek physician, Galen, who had said that "kid, in wholesomness and nourishment rates next to pork." Some men, said Elyot, "doe suppose that in health and sicknes they [kids] be much better than porke."

Goat flesh, however, was not high on the list of meats in the dietaries. Elyot warned that goat's flesh, like beef, hare, and boar, "engendered melancholy" and should be avoided by those already of a melancholy nature. Andrewe Boorde recalled that "in physycke . . . old Kydde is nat prayzed." William Vaughan advised against eating the meat of gelded goats, except in winter, because it was "strong meat" and only in winter were people's systems able to digest it properly.

Rabisha is concerned only with the culinary aspects of goat meat. And he offers a recipe for a pasty of "an old Goat," which he seasons as we do venison, except that he uses a good deal of salt: "Let it look grey with Salt. . . . And when it is served," he tells his readers confidently, "it will not be known from Venison, by the generality of men, either in taste or colour."

HOW TO STEW POTATOES

Boyle or roast your Potatoes very tender, and blanch [peel] them; cut them into thin slices, put them into a dish or stewing pan, put to them three or foure Pippins sliced thin, a good quantity of beaten Ginger and Cynamon, Verjuice, Sugar and Butter; stew these together an hour very softly; dish them being stewed enough, putting to them Butter and Verjuice beat together, and stick it full of green Sucket or Orrengado, or some such liquid sweet-meat; sippit it and scrape Sugar on it, and serve it up hot to the Table.

Joseph Cooper, *The Art of Cookery Refin'd and Augmented*

THE WORKING VERSION:

1½	pounds sweet potatoes		4	tablespoons butter, diced
1	pound tart cooking apples		⅓	cup white wine vinegar
5	tablespoons brown sugar		¼	cup candied orange peel,
¼	teaspoon cinnamon			diced
½	teaspoon ginger			

Bake the potatoes in their skins for thirty minutes at 400°. Peel them and cut them into thin slices. Core and peel the apples and slice them thin.

Mix three tablespoons of the sugar with the cinnamon and ginger. Butter a casserole with one tablespoon of the butter and put a layer of sliced apples into it. Sprinkle a little of the sugar-spice mixture and bits of the diced butter over them. Cover with a layer of sliced potatoes, sprinkle them with some of the sugar-spice mixture and dot with butter. Continue layering apples and potatoes as above until all are in the casserole.

Pour the wine vinegar over the top and sprinkle with the remaining two tablespoons of sugar. Cover and bake at 350° for

Title page of John Gerard's The Herball or Generall Historie of Plantes
(*1597*)

forty minutes, or until the potatoes and apples are tender. Dot the dish with the candied orange peel and serve hot.

Few cookbooks gave recipes for preparing sweet potatoes other than as desserts and sweetmeats. They were made into confections similar to the fruit pastes that were so popular, and used for pies. Robert May, however, used sweet potatoes in one of his "grand" salads.

John Gerard, the herbalist, grew them in his garden on the outskirts of London, and he described them as "like unto the roots of Peonies, or rather of the white Asphodill." The plants, he said, were called "Skyrrets of Peru" by some people, and were "ordinarie and common meate among the Spaniards, Italians, Indians, and many other nations." He does not doubt that they are nourishing but finds them somewhat "windie." They were used mainly for making sweetmeats, he said, but were occasionally "roasted in the embers" and sometimes eaten dipped in wine. "Others to give them greater grace in eating, do boile them with prunes and so eate them: likewise others dress them (being first roasted) with oile, vinegar, and salt, every man according to his owne taste and liking."

TO MAKE A SALLET OF LEMMONS

Cut out the slices of the peel of the Lemmons long Waies, a quarter of an inch one piece from an-other, and then slice the lemon very thin, and lay in a dish Crosst, and the peels about the Lemmons, and scrape a good deale of sugar upon them, and so serve them.

Thomas Dawson, *The good huswifes Jewell*

THE WORKING VERSION:

> 4 large, firm lemons
> 4 to 8 tablespoons sugar, according to your taste

Wash and dry the lemons and remove the stem ends. Cut out narrow strips of the peel, half an inch apart, lengthwise, and reserve. Slice the lemons as close to paper thin as you can and remove the seeds.

Arrange the slices on a flat serving dish in the shape of an X, sprinkle four tablespoons of sugar over them, and garnish with the reserved peel. If you prefer a sweeter flavor, pass the remaining sugar separately when serving.

The membrane in lemons can be unpleasantly bitter as well as tough. If you wish, you may cut out the sections of the fruit instead of slicing the lemon. Arrange the sections as a sunburst with the slices of peel between the sections of lemon.

This dish is not as curious as it looks at first glance. Grapefruit are often as sour as lemons, yet we find them refreshing in salads.

Lemons had been known in England since the days of the crusaders, who brought them back from Palestine. By the end of the sixteenth century, lemon trees were appearing in noblemen's gardens and greenhouses. William Harrison assures us that he had seen them growing there. As imported lemons became more available and cheaper, their juice was often used instead of vinegar as a sauce for fish and for some meats. They were regularly purchased for sauce for the dinners of the Court of the Star Chamber.

Sugar was "scraped" onto the lemons because it came in solid cones. Sugar refining was not very advanced and much sugar was of inferior quality. The best sugar, that is, the whitest, was reserved for salads such as this and for sweetmeats and fine cakes.

A sixteenth-century woodcut shows a street vendor of lemons and oranges carrying her wares in a basket and calling:

> Fine sevil [Seville] oranges, fine lemons, fine;
> Round, sound, and tender, inside and rine,
> One pin's prick their virtue show;
> They-ve liquor by their weight, you may know.

MESLIN RYE BREAD

Mestlyne breade is made, halfe of whete and halfe of Rye.

Dr. Andrewe Boorde, *A Compendyous Regyment or a Dyetary of Healthe*

THE WORKING VERSION:

1 cup soured cheate dough (from a previous bread-making)

1½ cups warm water

2 cakes fresh yeast or 2 tablespoons dry yeast

1 tablespoon salt

2½ cups rye flour

2½ cups unbleached flour

If you have no soured dough on hand, start this two days before you plan to make the bread, following the recipe for sour cheate dough given on page 77. The method for making this bread is the same as that for fine cheate bread given on page 77.

The recipe for manchet appears on page 38.

Bread made of mixed flours was considered of lower quality than bread made entirely of wheat flour, although the mixture of wheat and rye was thought to keep fresh longer than all-wheat bread. Dietary writers in general disapproved of bread made entirely of rye flour. It was heavy and hard to digest and fit only for "labourers and such as worke or travail much, and for such as have good stomacks," Thomas Cogan said in his *Haven of Health*. However, William Vaughan, in *Directions for Health,* found that freshly baked rye bread when made of finely ground rye from which the bran had been removed was "in Summer time highly commended, specially in the beginning of meate [the meal], for it keepeth the belly loose and for this cause it is so used at the tables of Princes: It must not be eaten but in small quantitie, rather for diet and health sake, then to satisfie hunger."

The kinds of bread that people ate depended largely on the grains grown in their particular region, although price was also important. In the north of England and in Scotland, where oats was the major grain crop, mostly oat bread was eaten. But most of the bread eaten in England was a mixture of either rye and wheat or barley and wheat. When harvests were very bad, and as a result prices rose sharply, peas, beans, lentils, and even acorns were sometimes ground in with grain for flour to make bread for the poor.

In the Yorkshire home of Henry Best, a member of the minor gentry, bread for the family was made with "messleden," one of the numerous spellings for a mixture of flours. For pies for their own eating, however, the family sent some of their best wheat to be ground into flour, but for the "folkes" [servants' and laborers'] puddings, they sent barley grain to be ground.

TO MAKE AN ALMOND PUDDING

Take a pound of almond paste, some grated bisket-bread, cream, rose-water, yolks of eggs, beaten cinamon, ginger, nutmeg, some boild currans, pistaches, and musk, boil it in a napkin, and serve it in a dish with beaten butter, stick it with some muskedines or wafers, and scraping sugar.

Robert May, *The Accomplisht Cook*

THE WORKING VERSION:

½ cup almond paste	¼ teaspoon ginger
3 egg yolks	¼ teaspoon nutmeg
2 cups light cream	1 drop essence of musk
½ cup crushed Holland rusks or zwieback	¼ cup currants, parboiled
2 tablespoons sugar	1 tablespoon pistachio nuts, chopped
2 tablespoons rose water	3 tablespoons unsalted butter
¼ teaspoon cinnamon	

If the almond paste seems stiff, rub it through the medium-large holes of a grater into your mixing bowl. Beat the egg yolks and cream together, add the rusk crumbs, and set aside for five minutes to soften the crumbs. Add this to the almond paste and stir until blended.

Add one tablespoon of the sugar and one tablespoon of the rose water, the flavorings, the currants, and the chopped pistachios, and stir until blended. Butter a one-quart mold and spoon the mixture into it. Cover the mold tightly—if your mold does not have a lid, make one of either aluminum foil or cooking parchment fastened tightly with rubber bands.

Steam the pudding for one hour over simmering water—if you don't have a steamer, you can make one by setting a small cake tin upside down in a deep saucepan with a lid; or use a pressure cooker without the pressure gauge. When the pudding is done, turn it out onto a heated serving dish, cover, and keep warm over a pan of hot water.

Melt the rest of the butter with the remaining rose water and sugar in a small saucepan, beating until the mixture begins to thicken. Pour the sauce over the pudding and serve.

Like other cooks of his day, Robert May believed in garnishing just about everything he sent in to the table. The garnishes he suggested detract from, rather than add to, the pudding, but if you want to garnish it, stick some small butter wafers into the sides. And if you prefer your desserts sweet, sprinkle a little sugar over the pudding.

Puddings, both sweet and savory, were everyday affairs. But puddings such as this one were likely to find their way only to the tables of the rich. Almonds, while not rare—they were grown in parts of England—were expensive, and musk was both rare and expensive.

A MINC'T PIE

Take a Legg of Mutton, and cut the best of the flesh from the bone, and parboyl it well: Then put to it three pound of the best Mutton suet, and shred it very small; then spread it abroad, and season it with Salt, Cloves, and Mace: Then put in good store of Currants, great Raisins, and Prunes clean washed, and picked, a few Dates sliced, and some Orange pills sliced; then being all well mixt together, put it into a Coffin, or into divers Coffins, and so bake them; And when they are served up, open the lids and strow store of Sugar on the Top of the meat, and upon the Lid. And in this sort, you may also bake Beef or Veal, only the Beef would not be parboyl'd and the Veal will ask a double quantity of Suet.

Gervase Markham, *The English Hus-wife*

THE WORKING VERSION:

½ pound boned leg of lamb or mutton
1 medium navel orange
1 cup currants
¼ pound ground beef suet
2 dates, minced
8 prunes, seeded and minced
1½ cups seedless raisins
½ cup brown sugar
¼ teaspoon salt
1 teaspoon mace

½ teaspoon cloves

THE PASTRY

2 cups sifted unbleached flour
1 teaspoon salt
¾ cup cold butter
½ cup cold water (approximately)
1 egg, separated

2 tablespoons sugar—to glaze the pie

Parboil the meat for five minutes, then mince or grind it. Peel off the thin outer skin of the orange and slice the peel into slivers. Parboil the orange peel with the currants for five minutes and drain.

Combine all of the filling ingredients until well mixed. Cover and set aside for several hours so that the flavors blend.

Make the pastry according to directions given on page 31. Flour your work surface and turn the pastry dough out onto it. Divide the dough into two pieces, one a bit larger than the other for the bottom crust. Pat the larger piece into a rectangle and roll it out to fit a rectangular baking dish six inches by nine inches. Fit the sheet of pastry into the baking dish and roll out the top crust.

Spoon the filling into the pie, spreading it evenly. Cover with the top crust and seal the edges with a fork dipped in cold water. Trim off any surplus dough with a knife, punch fork holes in the top of the pie, and brush with egg white. Bake at 450° for twenty minutes, then lower the heat to 350° and bake twenty-five minutes longer. Remove the pie from the oven, sprinkle it with the sugar, and return the pie to the oven to glaze for five minutes. Serve slightly warm.

Mincemeat pies were eaten throughout the year, but they were a *must* at Christmastime. Numerous traditions were connected with them. An old folk saying popular in Shropshire had it that, as the twelve days between Christmas and Twelfth Night were a mirror of the year, the eater would enjoy one happy month in the coming year for each mince pie consumed at a neighbor's house during the holiday period.

Another tradition was the guarding of the great mince pie against theft after it was baked. Robert Herrick has immortalized several of the traditions in *The Hesperides*:

> Drink now the strong Beer,
> Cut the white loaf here,
> The while the meat is a shredding;
> For the rare Mince-pie
> And the Plums stand by
> To fill the paste that's a kneading."

And when the pie was baked:

> "Come guard this night the Christmas-Pie.
> That the Thiefe, though ne'er so slie,
> With his Flesh-hooks don't come nie
> To catch it,
> From him, who all alone sits there,
> Having his eyes still in his eare,
> And a deale of nightly feare
> To watch it.

These lines rhymed when Herrick wrote them; it is our pronunciation that has changed. The night is Christmas Eve and the flesh-hooks are the hooks from which meat is hung.

These pies and tarts were the cause of an excited religious controversy that lasted for decades. Because they were baked in rectangular "coffins"—all pie shells were called coffins—religious fanatics, including many churchmen, argued that it was sacrilegious to eat them. Their argument was that the rectangular crust represented Christ's sepulcher, and the spice in the filling, the gifts of the Magi. Religious tracts fulminated against the innocent pies, but the effort to forbid their eating was a lost cause with both clergy and laity.

GENTLEMEN SERVANTS AND PAGES

Although the custom was dying out by the late sixteenth century, many children of noble and gentry families were still sent at an early age into the households of families of high rank to learn manners and arts and skills that would be important to them in their later lives. Anne Boleyn, Queen Elizabeth's mother, had been sent when she was about seven years old to live with Margaret of Savoy to learn "courtesie." Margaret, the aunt of Charles V, was acting as regent for him in the Low Countries.

Sir Thomas More was a page in the household of Cardinal Morton and served him at table. The cardinal was fond of the boy and proud of him; he used to tell the nobles who might be dining with him that the child waiting on him at table "would prove a marvellous man." And the learned cardinal, to further his page's education, sent him to Oxford University.

In 1620 the earl of Arundell wrote a letter of instructions for the benefit of his younger son, who was being sent to live with the bishop of Norwich. In it he told the boy, "You shall in all things reverence, honour and obey my Lord Bishop of Norwich, as you would do any of your Parents, esteeminge whatsoever He shall tell or Command you, as if your Grandmother Arundell, your Mother, or my self should say it; and in all things esteem your self as my Lord's page; a breeding which youths of my house far superior to you were accustomed unto, as my Grandfather of *Norfolk,* and his Brother my good Uncle of *Northampton* were both bred as Pages with Bishops."

At least one foreigner did not see this practice in the same light as the English. An Italian, said to have been the secretary of the Venetian ambassador to Henry VII's court, wrote in his description of English life, "The want of affection in the English is strongly manifested towards their children; for after having kept them at home till they arrive at the age of seven or nine years at the utmost, they put them out, both males and females, to hard service in the houses of other people . . . and few are born who are exempted from this fate, for every one, however rich he may be, sends away his children into the houses of others, whilst he in return receives those of strangers into his own. And

James I and his son entertaining the Spanish ambassadors (17th-century print)

on enquiring their reason for this severity, they answered that
they did it in order that their children might learn better manners.
But I, for my part, believe that they do it because they like to
enjoy all their comforts themselves, and that they are better
served by strangers than they would be by their own children."

But not all children of the nobility were sent away to learn
manners, as some instructions in the Percy family household
books show. These read, "A Gentillman . . . shall attend upon
my Lord's Eldest Son . . . and Appoynted Bicause he shall
Always be with my Lord's Sonnes for seynge and Orderynge
them: and My Lord's Second Son [is] to serve as Kerver
[carver], and my Lord's Thurde Son as Sewer." The sewer
placed the dishes of food on the dining table and tasted the food
before it was served, and filled the role of waiter when required.
Where the second and third sons learned these skills is not told,
but they might well have learned them from the gentlemen
servants in the household.

An important part of the pages' skills and arts was related to the dining chambers. To be properly educated, a nobleman's or a gentleman's sons had to know how to set a table, to see that the various dishes for the meal were brought from the kitchen and placed on the table in the proper order. He had to know how to serve a nobleman and bring him his drink gracefully and courteously, as well as how to carve his meat.

To carve well had been considered one of the manly arts from Anglo-Saxon days. Chaucer himself was a page in the household of the countess of Ulster. In *The Canterbury Tales* he notes as one of the accomplishments of his twenty-year-old squire that he could carve for his father ("and carf beforn his fadur") at the table.

It was an honor to be asked to carve by a friend, and a mark of prestige to carve for a great nobleman or for royalty. At the christening supper of the future Charles I, in 1600, according to John Nichols's *Progresses and Public Processions of Queen Elizabeth,* "my Lord Lyon served in his coat at supper; My Lord President served the King [then only James VI of Scotland] at supper as cupper [cupbearer]; my Lord Spynie, Carver; my Lord Roxburg, sewer."

When the sixteen-year-old Prince Henry (James I's first son) was made prince of Wales in 1610, the lords who had attended his investiture and the twenty-five young men who had been made knights of the Bath as part of the investiture ceremonies were Henry's guests at a state supper. There the earl of Pembroke was the prince's sewer, the earl of Montgomery his cupbearer, and the earl of Southampton his carver.

Carving was the most prestigious of the serving skills. If a page aspired to become carver to his lord, he not only had to learn to cut up, slice or mince, and sauce the meat, fish, and fowl, but also to serve it properly. Slices of meat were handed to the diner on a broad knife; meats and fishes in sauces were cut into pieces small enough to be eaten with a spoon. Pages had to learn as well the carving terms for each meat, fowl, fish, or pasty he served. For example, brawn was not sliced, it was *leached;* a lobster was *barbed;* a pasty *bordered;* a pheasant *allayed;* a deer *broken;* an egg *tired;* a salmon *chined;* a pigeon and other small birds, *thighed;* a sturgeon *tranced;* and a crab *taymed.* The thirty-eight "goodly terms" of carving that Wynkyn de Worde listed in his *Boke of Kervynge,* first published in the fifteenth century and frequently reprinted, continued to be used for several

Oak armchair (circa 1620)

centuries. They were reprinted as "Terms of Art for Carving" as late as the 1774 edition of *The Compleat Housewife*.

Nicholas Breton's countryman, in *The Court and Country,* published in 1618, thinks all this rather silly. "I remember," he tells the courtier, "I have heard my father tell of a world of orders hee had seene in divers places, where he had travel'd, where right good Gentlemen, that had followed great Lords and Ladies, had enough to doe to study orders in their Service: A Trencher must not be laid, nor a Napkin folded out of order; a dish set downe out of order, A capon carved, nor a Rabbet unlaced out of order; a Goose broken up, nor a pasty cut up out of order; a Glasse filled, nor a Cup uncovered nor delivered out of order; you must not stand, speake, nor looke out of order: which were such a business for us to goe about, that we should be all out of time ere we should get into any good order. . . . How much more at rest are we in the Country that are not troubled with these duties?" But, he concedes, "there is difference of places, and everyone must have their due. It is meete for good manners to keepe the rules of good orders."

Pages were sometimes worked very hard and given menial tasks, but they acquired skills that stood them in good stead later. Such skills helped younger sons of noble and gentle families, who would not inherit their fathers' titles or the family wealth, and who had not been apprenticed to merchants or professionals, to obtain posts as "gentlemen servants" in noble or richer gentry households.

Such posts were not considered menial. Nor were all the duties of gentlemen servants confined to the dining room. Such servants formed part of their master's retinue when he traveled; they hunted, played billiards, cards, parlor games, and outdoor games with him. They also played musical instruments or sang with him and other members of the family and household for their mutual enjoyment after meals.

The posts were not well paid, but they provided a home, clothing, and a certain amount of social status. Young gentlemen who showed promise or competence might look forward to becoming officers of one of the various household departments, with yeoman servants under their supervision and probably with a personal servant or two of their own. And there was always the shining goal at the top, the steward's or chamberlain's post. In the royal household such officers were usually lords.

Archbishop Matthew Parker had a number of brothers of earls and lords among his servants. In 1566 his gentlemen servants included "fourteen or sixteen gentlemen waiters." In 1578 Lord North's household staff included twenty-four gentlemen and seventy yeomen. The "checkerolle" of the earl of Derby's household at Lathom, in Lancashire, showed seven gentlemen waiters, "whereof the gentleman Usher and not above three more are to attend daily." There were, in addition, thirteen yeoman waiters. The Northumberland household books of the Percy family list as "Gentlemen of the Household: Kervers, Sewers, Cupbearers, and Gentillmen Waiters."

Richard Braithwaite, in his *Some Rules and Orders for the Government of the House of an Earl,* said that the "state of an Earl" required a household staff of over a hundred people, among whom should be ten gentlemen waiters and two gentlemen pages. But by the end of the sixteenth century, gentlemen servants and large staffs of other servants were becoming luxuries that fewer households were able or willing to pay for.

In 1577 Hugh Rhodes published a manual for pages called *The Boke of Nurture, or Schoole of Good maners,* which outlined the duties of a page who was to serve as a waiter to "a Knight, squire or Gentleman." The manual was not written for pages from gentle or noble families, but the rules would also have applied to them. Such manuals were usually written in tortured verse, but Rhodes's manual was in simple, straightforward prose:

First yee must be diligent to know your Maysters' pleasure, and to knowe the order and custome of his house, for dyvers maysters are of sundry condicions and appetytes. When your Mayster will goe to his meate, take a towell aboute your necke, then take a cupbord cloth, a Basen, Ewer, & a Towell, to aray the cupbord; cover your table, set on bread, salt & trenchers, the salt before the bread, and the trenchers before the salte. Set your napkyns and spoones on the cupbord ready, and lay [for] every man a trencher, a napkyn, & a spone. And if you have more messes than one at your maisters table [a mess was usually a group of four people], consider what degree they be of, and thereafter [according to their social rank] ye may serve them: and then set down every thing at that messe as before, except your Carving knives. If ther be many Gentlemen or yomen, then set on bred, salt, trenchers & spoones, after they be set, or els after the custome of the house. . . . See ye have Voyders ready for to avoyd [take away] the Morsels that they doe leave on their Trenchours. Then with your Trenchour knyfe take of [off] such fragmentes, and put them in your Voyder, and sette them downe cleane againe.

When the meal is finished, the page is to:

take up the salte, and make obeysaunce; and marke if your Mayster use to wash at the table, or standing: if he be at table, cast a clean Towell on your table cloth, and set downe your basen and Ewer before your soveraigne [master], and take the ewer in your hand, and give them water. Then voyd your Basen and Ewer, and fold the bord cloth together with your towell therein, and so take them of [off] the boord. And when your soveraygne shall wash, set your towell on the lefte hand of him, and the water before your soveraygne at dinner or supper.

The girls who were sent into other homes for training were under the tutelage of the lady of the house and served as her maids-in-waiting much as the boys served as pages. Girls needed to know how to order a meal properly all the way from the kitchen to the table and to see it served correctly at the table. After marriage they could expect on occasion to take charge of the entire household while their husbands were away at court or war or on other business. They were also taught the ladylike arts of needlework, distillation of flower and herb "waters," preserving, candying, making various banqueting sweetmeats, as well as more everyday kinds of cooking. To prepare them for possible appearances at court, they learned court graces and the singing and dancing that were necessary accomplishments for upper-class social life in Elizabethan and Jacobean England.

This may have been how Lady Anne Clifford, the wife of the earl of Dorset, learned how to make the quince marmalade and the pancakes she offered the friends who came to visit her. Her diary, on October 25, 1617, records that she made "much quince marmalade" about this time. It also tells us that making pancakes was one way to while away an afternoon with friends.

Any young girl of noble parentage could at least dream of becoming one of the queen's maids-of-honor. If she was fortunate enough to be chosen, the social graces she had previously learned would be given a final polishing in the queen's service. Queen Elizabeth's maids-of-honor entertained her with their singing and dancing, attended her in public, served the queen her meals, and usually carved for her, in addition to their other duties.

All children were expected to make themselves useful at mealtimes as soon as they were tall enough to see above the table. Claudius Hollyband in his English-French conversation manual describes a merchant's family at dinner and comments on the duties of the children. Dinner is nearly over and the merchant calls to his children, who have been eating at a separate table, "Henry rise, and your sister also: what, you kepe table as long as wee? serve here: and see whether anye thing be wanting upon the bord."

A Dinner for Rosalind & Orlando

I do feast tonight
My best-esteem'd acquaintance.
The Merchant of Venice,
Act II, Scene 2 (*Bassanio*)

SACK (SHERRY)

*If I had a thousand sons, the first human principle I
would teach them should be, to forswear thin potations
and to addict themselves to sack.*
Henry IV, Part II, Act IV, Scene 3 (*Falstaff*)

GREEN AND RIPE OLIVES

*If you will know my house,
'Tis at the tuft of olives here hard by.*
As You Like It, Act III, Scene 5 (*Rosalind*)

PICKLED CAPERS

*Faith, I can cut a caper.
And I can cut the mutton to't.*
Twelfth Night,
Act I, Scene 3 (*Sir Andrew, Sir Toby*)

A MUTTON PIE

*I, a lost mutton, gave your letter to her, a laced mutton;
and she, a laced mutton, gave me, a lost mutton, nothing for
my labour.*

Two Gentlemen of Verona, Act I, Scene 1 (*Speed*)

A POACHED CHICKEN
WITH CAULIFLOWER

*Davy, a couple of short-legged hens . . . tell William
cook.*

Henry IV, Part II, Act V, Scene 1 (*Shallow*)

A RABBIT STEWED WITH HERBS

*I knew a wench married in an afternoon as she went
to the garden for parsley to stuff a rabbit.*

The Taming of the Shrew, Act IV, Scene 4 (*Biondello*)

A ROAST PHEASANT WITH
ARTICHOKE DRESSING

Advocate's the court-word for a pheasant.

The Winter's Tale, Act IV, Scene 3 (*Clown*)

MANCHET

*There is my pledge; I'll prove it on thy heart,
Ere I taste bread.*

King Lear, Act V, Scene 3 (*Albany*)

WHITE AND RED WINES

*But, i' faith, you have drunk too much canaries, and that's
a marvelous searching wine, and it perfumes the blood ere
one can say, 'What's this?'*

Henry IV, Part II, Act II, Scene 4 (*Dame Quickly*)

A LUMDARDY TART

Praise us as we are tasted, allow us as we prove.

Troilus and Cressida, Act III, Scene 2 (*Troilus*)

CHESHIRE CHEESE

*I will rather trust a Fleming with my butter, Parson
Hugh the Welshman with my cheese, an Irishman with
my aqua-vitae bottle, or a thief to walk my ambling
gelding, than my wife with herself.*
        The Merry Wives of Windsor, Act II, Scene 2 (*Master Ford*)

FRESH FIGS

*Here is a rural fellow
That will not be denied your highness' presence:
He brings you figs.*
        Antony and Cleopatra, Act V, Scene 2 (*Guard*)

*Then let us take a ceremonious leave
And loving farewell of our several friends.*
        Richard II, Act 1, Scene 3 (*Bolingbroke*)

This menu is based on Ben Johnson's delightful poem "Inviting
a Friend to Supper," written in 1612:

To night, grave Sir, both my poore house, and I
    Doe equally desire your companie:
Not that we thinke us worthy such a ghest,
    But that your worth will dignifie our feast,
With those that come; whose grace may make that seeme
    Something, which, else, could hope for no esteeme.
It is the faire acceptance, Sir, creates
    The entertaynment perfect: not the cates.
Yet shall you have, to rectifie your palate,
    An Olive, capers, or some better sallade
Ushring the mutton; with a short-leg'd hen,
    If we can get her, full of egs, and then,
Limons, and wine for sauce: to these a coney
    Is not to be despair'd of, for our money;

And, though fowle, now, be scarce, yet there are clarkes,
The skie not falling, thinke we may have larkes.
Ile tell you of more, and lye, so you will come:
Of partrich, pheasant, wood-cock, of which some
May yet be there; and godwit, if we can:
Knat, raile, and ruffle too. How so ere, my man
Shall reade a piece of *Virgil, Tacitus,*
Livie, or of some better booke to us,
Of which wee'll speake our minds, amidst our meate;
And Ile professe no verses to repeate:

To this, if ought appeare, which I know not of,
That will the pastrie, not my paper, show of.
Digestive cheese, and fruit there sure will bee:
But that, which most doth take my *Muse,* and mee,
Is a pure cup of rich *Canary*-wine,
Which is the *Mermaids,* now, but shall be mine:
Of which had *Horace,* or *Anacreon* tasted,
Their lives, as doe their lines, till now had lasted.
Tabacco, Nectar, or the *Thespian* spring,
Are all but *Luthers* beere, to this I sing.
Of this we will sup free, but moderately.

The Mermaid was a famous London tavern of Shakespeare's day where dramatists, poets, and wits forgathered. "Luther's beer" was German beer, and was considered inferior by the English.

Appetizers were called salads and, like salads, served to give relish to a meal. Olives and capers were considered choice appetizers and were saved for festive occasions.

Queen Elizabeth must have liked them, for they appear frequently on the bills of fare for her table. When the queen was a guest at Ingatestone, Sir William Petre purchased for the event, "1 barrell olives, cont. 1 gallon and 1 pint . . . and one barrell of capers containing 3 lb."

Both green and ripe olives were imported preserved in salt brine. Real capers were not always available, and sometimes other things, such as broom buds and green nasturtium seeds, were pickled and used instead.

When properly prepared, said the dietaries, olives and capers had salutary effects on the digestive system, especially if eaten with vinegar. "Olives condite [preserved] in salt licoure," said Thomas Elyot, "taken at the beginning of a meal doth corroborate [strengthen] the stomacke, stirreth up appetite. . . . They which be ripe are temperately hot, but they which bee greene are cold and dry."

TO MAKE PYES OF MUTTON

Pyes of mutton . . . must be fyne mynced and ceasoned with pepper and salte, a lyttle saffron to coloure it, suet or marrow a good quantitie, a lyttle vynegar, prumes, greate raysins and dates, take the fattest of the broathe of powdred beyfe, and yf you will have paest royall, take butter and yolkes of egges and so tempre the flowre to make the paste.

Anonymous, *A Proper newe Booke of Cokerye*

THE WORKING VERSION:

1¼ pounds ground shoulder of lamb or mutton	2 dates, minced
1 teaspoon salt	¼ teaspoon saffron
½ teaspoon pepper	
5 tablespoons red wine vinegar	FOR THE PASTRY
1 ounce beef marrow or suet, minced	2 cups sifted unbleached flour
1 tablespoon seedless raisins	1 teaspoon salt
2 prunes, minced	¾ cup cold butter
	½ cup clear, chilled beef broth
	1 egg, separated

Mix together lightly but thoroughly all the ingredients for the pie filling. Cover and set aside while you make the pastry for the crust. The directions for making pastry dough are on page 31.

Sprinkle your work surface with flour and turn the pastry dough out onto it. Divide the dough into two parts, that for the bottom crust a little larger than for the top crust. Roll out the pastry for the bottom crust large enough to fit a seven-inch spring-form pan with an overlap of ½ inch.

Fit the sheet into the pan and roll out the dough for the top crust. Spread the filling mixture evenly and cover with the top crust. Seal the edges with the tines of a fork dipped into cold water, then slice off the surplus pastry. Roll out the surplus dough and, with a cookie cutter, cut out pastry lambs to decorate the pie.

Punch fork holes in the top of the pie, then brush it with egg white. Arrange the pastry lambs over the crust and brush them with the remaining egg white. Bake at 450° for twenty minutes, then lower the heat to 350° and bake twenty-five minutes longer. Serve hot or cold, but not refrigerated.

Minced mutton or beef pies, although much enjoyed by the English, were not considered feast fare except in modest homes, and they rarely appear on cookbook bills of fare.

Mutton was considered good eating until it was three years old, after which it was thought too strong for cultivated palates. Its quality also depended upon the season. *A Proper newe Booke of Cokerye* noted that mutton "is good at all tymes, but from Easter to myd Sommer it is worste," and that "Lambe . . . is best between Christmas and lente, and good from Easter to Witsontyde."

Pork, veal, chicken, rabbit, and venison were also made into minced pies. Except for venison pies, the ingredients generally included raisins, prunes, and sometimes dates, although the spices varied with the recipe.

TO BOYLE A CAPON OR CHICKEN WITH COLLE-FLOWRES

Cutt of [off] the budds of your flowres, boile them in milke with a little Mace, till they be very tender: then take the yolkes of two eggs, straine them with a quarter of a pint of Sacke, then take as much thicke butter being drawne, with a little vinegar and a sliced Lemmon, and brue them together, then take the flowers out of the Milke, and put them into the Butter and Sacke, then dish up your Capon being tender boyled, upon sippets, strowing a little salt upon it, and so poure on the sawce upon it and so serve it to the Table hotte.

John Murrell, *A Booke of Cookerie*

THE WORKING VERSION:

THE BROTH	THE SAUCE
5 cups water	5 tablespoons butter
1 tablespoon salt	½ cup sherry
2 pounds chicken backs and necks	1 tablespoon white wine vinegar
One 3-pound frying chicken	¼ teaspoon salt
1 cauliflower, about 1¼ pounds	½ lemon, peeled, seeded, and thinly sliced
2½ cups milk	2 egg yolks
¼ teasoon mace	3 slices buttered toast, quartered
½ teaspoon salt	

To make the broth, bring the water to a boil and add the salt, the chicken backs and necks, and the wing tips and giblets from the whole chicken. Cover closely and simmer for three hours. If you use a pressure cooker, cook at fifteen pounds pressure for one hour. Strain the broth into a three-quart pot and bring it to a boil. Rinse the fryer under cool running water inside and out, and dry it with paper towels or a clean cloth. Lower the chicken into the boiling broth, reduce the heat to simmer, cover the pot, and poach the chicken 1½ hours, or until it is tender. Leave the chicken in the broth until needed.

Remove the green leaves from the cauliflower, separate the head into two-inch flowerets, rinse them under cool water, and drain. Heat the milk, mace, and ½ teaspoon of salt over low heat to just below the boiling point. Add the cauliflower and simmer uncovered until the buds are tender but still firm—twelve to fifteen minutes. Turn off the heat but leave the cauliflower in the milk until needed.

In a small saucepan combine the butter, sherry, vinegar, salt, and lemon, and cook over medium heat, stirring vigorously, for five minutes. Remove the pan from the heat and stir in the egg yolks, then return the pan to the heat and cook, stirring constantly, until the sauce begins to thicken.

Carve the chicken into serving-size pieces. Place half the toast in a deep serving dish and arrange the chicken over it. Spoon the cauliflower over the chicken and pour the sauce over all. Garnish the sides of the dish with the remaining toast. And, as Murrell constantly reminds his readers, serve it up hot.

Vegetables rarely appeared on bills of fare by name, except for cauliflower, green peas, and artichokes, which were considered delicacies. William Rabisha, in his sixty-dish bill of fare for a "flesh-day in the Summer Season," includes in the first course, "A hanch of Venison boyled with collyflowers." In one of his recipes for preparing cauliflower, he also says that the vegetable may be served with boiled "small birds or fowl."

In 1619, while the Shuttleworth family was staying in London, their household accounts showed an expenditure of three shillings for two cauliflowers, a very high price compared with the sixteen artichokes purchased at the same time, which cost only three shillings fourpence, and thirty lettuces for a total of only fourpence.

TO BOYLE A RABBET

Parboyle your Rabbet well, and cut it in peeces: then take strong broth, and a Fagot of Hearbs, a little Parsley, sweet Marjoram, three or four yolkes of Egges, strained with a little white Bread, and put all in a Pipkin with Mace, Cloves, and a little Vergis to make them have a taste.

John Murrell, *A New Booke of Cookerie*

THE WORKING VERSION:

One 3-pound frying rabbit, dressed weight	1 teaspoon salt
1 quart fresh chicken broth	1 large piece of whole mace
¼ cup minced parsley	2 cloves
¼ teaspoon marjoram	1 slice of white bread
½ teaspoon thyme	¼ cup white wine vinegar
1 bay leaf	3 egg yolks

A recipe for making fresh chicken broth is on page 98. Cut the rabbit into serving-size pieces. In a large saucepan with a tight-fitting lid, combine the strained broth, herbs, and spices, and bring to a boil. Add the pieces of rabbit, and bring to a boil again. Lower the heat to simmer, cover the pan, and cook until the rabbit is tender—from forty-five minutes to one hour.

Remove the bay leaf, cloves, and mace from the broth. Soften the bread in ½ cup of the broth, and press it through a sieve with the broth. Beat the vinegar and egg yolks with the puréed bread, and stir the mixture into the stew. Cook over medium heat, stirring constantly, until the sauce begins to thicken.

Arrange the pieces of rabbit in a warmed serving bowl, pour the sauce over them, and serve.

This recipe is from the "English Cookerie" section of Murrell's book. In the French-cookery section, he gives a more elaborate recipe for boiling a rabbit with herbs, which calls for mutton broth and white wine as the poaching liquid, and includes lettuce and spinach with the herbs. He also suggests bruising the greens to make the broth "looke pleasantly green." The French-style rabbit is to be served on sippets and garnished with barberries. Sippets, which, alas, went out of fashion long ago, gathered to themselves much of the sauce, concentrating the flavor in a most satisfying way. With sippets out of fashion, and spooning up the sauce in one's plate too often frowned upon, a lot of gastronomic pleasure has literally gone down the drain.

John Taylor, the "Water Poet," described the delights of eating stew ("pottage" in the vocabulary of the time) in *The Great Eater of Kent*:

> There for your solace you may feed upon
> Whole seas of pottage, hot as Phlegethon,
> And midst those seas, by art, the cook hath laid
> Small Isles of mutton, which you may invade
> With stomack, knife and spoon, or tooth and nail,
> With these, the victory you cannot fail.

TO ROAST A PHEASANT

Roste your Phesant with his head off, his wings and legges on whole: but when you serve him in, sticke one of his feathers upon his breast. And in lyke maner you must roast a Partridge, but stick up no feather.

John Partridge, *The good Huswifes Handmaide for the Kitchin*

The temperature of the fire [must be] quick and sharp without scorching. . . . The meat be Pale and white roasted, and yet throughly roasted; . . . The best bastings . . . is sweet Butter, sweet Oyl, Barrell Butter, or fine rendered seam [suet] with Cinamon, Cloves, and Mace.

Gervase Markham, *The English Hus-wife*

FORCING [DRESSING] FOR ANY DAINTY FOWL . . . AS PHEASANTS

Take minced veal raw, and bacon or beef-suet minced with it; being fine minced, season it with cloves and mace, a few currans, salt, and some boil'd bottoms of artichokes cut in form of dice small, and mingle among the forcing with pine-appleseeds [pine nuts], chesnuts, and some raw eggs, and fill your poultrey.

Robert May, *The Accomplisht Cook*

THE WORKING VERSION:

One 3-pound hen pheasant, dressed weight
4 ounces lean veal
3 ounces Canadian bacon
4 chestnuts, shelled and blanched
1 tablespoon shelled pine nuts (pignolias)
2 cooked artichoke bottoms, diced
1 teaspoon currants, parboiled
1 egg
¼ teaspoon mace
¼ teaspoon cinnamon
⅛ teaspoon cloves
2½ teaspoons salt
1 tablespoon olive oil

Wipe the pheasant inside and out with a clean, damp cloth. Mince or grind together the veal and bacon. Chop the chestnuts and pine nuts together coarsely.

Lightly mix together the minced meats, nuts, diced artichokes, currants, egg, mace, cinnamon, cloves, and ½ teaspoon of the salt. Loosely fill the cavity of the pheasant with the dressing. If there is remaining dressing, loosen the skin at the neck end of the bird by gently sliding your fingers under the skin, and fill the opened space with the remaining dressing. Pull the skin back over the neck bone and fasten with a steel pin or sew up the opening with heavy white thread.

Mix the remaining salt with the olive oil and rub it over the skin, getting it under the wings and thighs as well. Truss the bird with string, bringing the legs and wings close to the body. Roast uncovered at 375° from fifty minutes to one hour—the pheasant should not need basting, but if it looks dry after half an hour, sprinkle a little more olive oil over it. Serve either hot or cold, with or without "one of his feathers upon his breast."

Pine nuts can be purchased in nut shops, health food stores, and in many groceries. Fresh artichoke bottoms are best for this recipe, but canned ones may be substituted if necessary.

Domesticated pheasants are generally available in shops specializing in "gourmet foods," or from game-bird farms that raise and dress them for the market. The flavor of the bred bird is not as distinctive as that of the wild pheasant, and the bird is likely to be larger. Wild pheasant should be hung by the neck in a cool place until the leading tail feather will pull out easily—about four days in warm weather, and from ten to twelve days in winter.

A fine small roasting chicken can be substituted if a pheasant is not available. May's dressing will give the bird a distinctive flavor.

The supply of wild pheasants, even in Shakespeare's day, was small, and many landed families bred pheasants to supplement it. Sir William Petre bred them at Ingatestone, so, although his stepdaughter was married in June, when wild pheasants were out of season for hunting, nineteen pheasants were available for the wedding dinner and supper and nine more were served during the week of festivities that followed.

Not only was pheasant considered elegant eating, it was highly recommended by the dietary writers. "The phesant henne is the chiefe fowle, surpassing all other for health and nourishment," said Vaughan. Thomas Elyot wrote that "Feasant exceedeth all fowles in sweetness and wholesomenes, and is equal to Capon in nourishing: but hee is somewhat drier, and is of some men put in comparison, meane [halfway] between a Henne and a Partriche." Dr. Boorde specified that pheasant "doth comfort the brayne and the stomacke; and doth augment carnail lyst [carnal lust]."

The recipe for manchet appears on page 38.

TO MAKE LUMDARDY TARTES

Take Beets, chop them small, and put to them grated bread and cheese, and mingle them wel in the chopping, take a few Corrans, and a dish of sweet Butter, & melt it then stir al these in the Butter, together with three yolks of Eggs, Synamon, ginger, and sugar, and make your Tart as large as you will, and fill it with the stuff, bake it and serve it in.

John Partridge, *The good Huswifes Handmaide for the Kitchin*

THE WORKING VERSION:

1 pound fresh young beets	4 tablespoons butter, melted
2 tablespoons brown sugar	
1 teaspoon grated bread crumbs	THE PASTRY
¾ cup grated mild Cheddar cheese	2 cups sifted unbleached flour
¼ cup currants, parboiled	1 teaspoon salt
¼ teaspoon cinnamon	¾ cup cold butter
¼ teaspoon ginger	½ cup cold water
3 egg yolks	1 egg, separated

Peel the beets—this is best done with a potato peeler—and grate them into a mixing bowl. Add the sugar and stir until it melts. Mix in the bread crumbs, grated cheese, currants, spices, and egg yolks. Then stir in the melted butter. Cover and set aside while you make the pastry. The instructions for making pastry are on page 31.

Divide the dough into two parts, the part for the bottom crust a bit larger than the piece for the top crust. On a floured work surface, roll out the piece for the bottom crust to fit an eight-inch pie dish and fit it into the dish. Then roll out the piece for the top crust.

Spread the filling evenly in the dish and cover it with the top crust. Seal the edges with the tines of a wet fork and trim off the surplus pastry. Punch fork holes in the crust and brush it with egg white. Bake at 450° for twenty minutes, then lower the heat to 350° and bake twenty-five minutes longer. Serve slightly warm.

Beets came to England with the Romans, who first developed the red beet. The leaves of the "greater red Beet or Roman Beet," wrote John Gerard in his *Herball,* made "a most excellent and delicat sallad" when they were boiled and eaten with a dressing of oil, vinegar, and pepper. "But what might be made of the red and beautiful root (which is to be preferred before the leaves, as well in beautie as in goodnesse) I refer unto the curious and cunning cooke, who no doubt when hee had the view there, and is assured that it is both good and wholesome, will make thereof many and divers dishes, both faire and good." And beets were used in many ways by cooks, including beet-root salads, both hot and cold.

White beets, said William Vaughan, should not be eaten raw, but boiled; they "breede good blood." He also offered the advice that beet root eaten after leeks or garlic "takes away their bad smells."

Cheese, which with fruit was the proper ending to a meal, was a staple part of English diet. It was made in all large country houses, and probably in any household that could afford to keep a milk-giving animal—a cow, a ewe, or a goat. The responsibility for making it was the housewife's and her dairymaid's, if there was one.

Cheese-making is not complicated, but it does require a certain amount of skill and attention. Thomas Tusser lists some of the mistakes that could be made in making cheese in a rhymed lesson to his wife's dairymaid, Cisley. The unfortunate Cisley is told:

Gehazi, his sickness was whitish and dry.
Such cheeses good Cisley ye floted [skimmed] to nigh [much].

. . . .

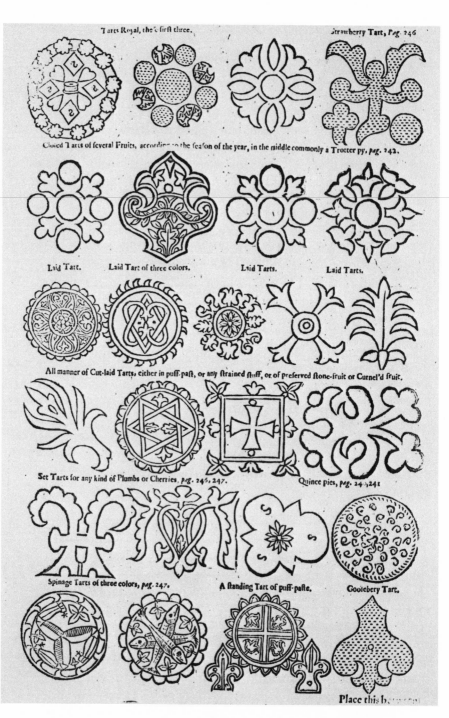

Designs for tarts and pies in Robert May's The Accomplisht Cook

Leave Lot with her pillar good Cisley alone,
Much saltness in white meat [cheese] is ill for the stone.
. . . .
As Maudlin wept so would Cisley be dresst [chided]
For whey in her cheeses not half enough prest.

Figs, since they were imported and expensive, were saved for feasts. The fruit in season in English orchards, mainly apples, were the usual accompaniment to the cheese at the end of the meal.

ON MANNERS

The best gift you could pray for was good manners ("and yif ye shulde at god aske yow a bone [boon] . . . better in noo degree Might yee desire than nurtred [properly brought up] for to be"). So *The Babees Book, or a Lytyl Reporte of How Young People Shoud Behave* told the children of fifteenth-century England.

The little book devoted almost half its pages to lessons on how a child should behave at table, and its precepts were repeated in manuals on manners for several centuries. What children were being told to learn, their elders were presumably practicing. Children were expected to behave at table as much like their parents as possible.

Many of the *Babees Book* precepts are still being urged on today's children: don't talk with your mouth full; don't eat your soup noisily; don't be greedy and reach for the best bits but share them with others; use your napkin, not the tablecloth, if your fingers get sticky; don't chatter throughout the meal: use your knife and spoon properly.

In some homes children had their meals at separate tables, although they were expected to help at the adults' table—clearing or bringing in dishes when the servants were rushed. When the household supplies of stools and benches were limited, the children would take their meals standing.

In the dinner scene at the home of Hollyband's Elizabethan merchant, the mistress of the house calls the servant to see that the children's table has a cloth on it and is set. "Bring their round table," she says, "and make them dine there at the bordes ende [at the lower end of the family table]."

Except in families rich enough to have a household chaplain, the children were expected to say the grace before meals and sometimes after. Herrick's "A Child's Grace" differs from the one usually recited but has more of the child's spirit in it:

> Here a little child I stand
> Heaving up my either hand [both hands];
> Cold as paddocks [frogs] though they be,
> Here I lift them up to thee,
> For a benison to fall
> On our meat and on us all. Amen.

Elizabethans and Jacobeans enjoyed being read to while they were at table. In wealthy homes this task was often assigned to a servant or to a page, but sometimes a child would read to the others during the meal. Usually, the selection would be something from the Bible or from one of his school lessons if it was a child who did the reading. Ben Jonson's "Inviting a Friend to Supper" promises his hoped-for guest not only a good supper but a reading by a servant of "a piece of Virgil, Tacitus, Livie, or of some better booke."

Francis Seager's *The Schoole of Vertue,* which followed the earlier manuals on manners very closely, was typical of the manuals of Shakespeare's lifetime. Seager's manual is in rather dreadful doggerel, and his tortured rhyming must have been hard on the defenseless children. It was printed in double columns, as below, but was meant to be read straight across. He starts the section on table manners with:

O Chyldren! geve eare   your duties to learne,
Howe at the table   you may your selves governe.
Presume not to hyghe   . . . .
In syttynge downe,   to thy betters geve place.
Suffer eche man [others]   Fyrste served to be,
For that is a poynte   Of good curtesie.
when they are served   then pause a space,
For that is a sygne   of nourture and grace.
Saulte with thy knyfe   then reache and take,
The breade cut fayre,   And do not it breake.
Thy spone with pottage   to full do not fyll,
For fylyng the cloth   If thou fortune to spyll,

For rudness it is thy pottage to sup,
Or speak to any, his head in the cup [while he is
    drinking].

Thy knyfe se [make sure] be to cut fayre thy meate;
    sharpe
Thy mouth not to full when thou dost eate;
Not smackynge thy lyppes, As comonly do hogges,
Nor gnawynge the bones As it were dogges;

. . . .

At the table behave thy self manerly.
Thy fingers se cleane that thou ever kepe,
Havynge a Napkyn thereon them to wype;
Thy mouth therwith Cleane do thou make,
The cup to drynke In hande yf thou take,
Let not thy tongue At the table walke,
And of no matter Neyther reason nor talke.
Temper thy tongue and belly alway.
For 'measure is treasure,' the proverbe doth say,

. . . .

For silence kepynge thou shalt not be shent
    [scolded],
where as thy speache May cause thee repent.
Bothe speache and silence are commendable,
But sylence is metest [most
    fitting] In a chylde at the table.
And Cato doth saye, that 'in olde and yonge
The fyrst of vertue Is to kepe thy tonge.'
Pyke not thy teethe at the table syttnge,
Nor use at thy meate Over muche spytynge;
this rudnes of youth Is to be abhorede;
thy selfe manerly Behave at the borde [table].
If occasion of laughter At the table thou se,
Beware [be sure] that thou use the same moderately.
Of good maners learne So much as thou can;
It wyll thee preferre when thou art a man.

Claudius Hollyband's well-to-do merchant and the school-master breathe life into some of these precepts. When, at dinner, the merchant's country nephew suggests to his young city cousin that he blow on his porridge to cool it, the merchant says in disgust, "Are those your good manners to blow your porage at the boorde [table]: where have you learned that? at your village?"

The schoolmaster concerns himself with his pupils' table manners nearly as much as with their reading and writing. "Wipe not thy mouth with thy hand, nor sleeve," he tells the boys, "but with a napkin, for that cause it is layed before thee." And he adds, "Touche not any part of the meate, saving that which thou wilt cut of [off], for thyself." Then he says scornfully, "You fine gentlemen, do you lean on the table: Where have you learned this goodly fashion? in some hogstie?"

Graciousness was part of good manners. "Why do you not welcome your ghest?" the boys are reminded when they fail to make a visiting Flemish lad welcome at their table. Although the English could be rough and rude at times, they often impressed foreign visitors with their graciousness and courtesy when they entertained. Hentzner, the German visitor to London, reported with wonderment that the Lord Mayor's traditional hospitality was so magnificent that anyone, "Foreigner or Native, without any Expence, is free, if he can find a chair empty, to dine at his Table."

Two benches (16th–17th century)

In wealthy homes musicians played during meals, especially at feasts and banquets. Quiet conversation was considered permissible, but not excited discussions and loud talking. William Harrison spoke of "the great silence that is used at the tables of the honorable and wiser sort, generally over all the realm (albeit that too deserveth no commendation, for it belongeth to guests neither to be *muti* nor *loquaces* [mute nor loquacious]."

In Archbishop Parker's household, table conversation, not surprisingly, was supposed to be confined to questions of religion or other sober matters. There was a monitor of the hall at mealtimes, and if anyone spoke too loudly, or about subjects not considered suitable to the archbishop's table, he cried out, "Silence." Shakespeare, of course, did not share the belief that silence was a good thing in itself. In *The Merchant of Venice* (Act I, Scene 1), Gratiano tells Antonio, "Silence is only commendable In a neat's tongue dried and a maid not vendible."

Hats were worn by some men and boys at table, although many did not follow this fashion. Those who wore them would lift their hats from their heads when proposing a toast to their hosts or another guest. Hollyband offered a practical reason for the custom of wearing hats at meals in the student usher's reminder to the boys not to remove their caps during the meal "lest some heare [hair] might fall into the dishes."

Women kept their napkins on their laps, but men often wore them folded over a shoulder. When the meal was over, the knives (which the guests often brought with them) were wiped clean on the napkins, which were then folded and placed on the table.

Removing bits of food from one's teeth during meals was considered proper if it was done discreetly. Using the point of one's knife to do so, however, was bad manners. Hollyband's schoolmaster tells his pupils that they are not to use their penknives as toothpicks, but to "make a tooth-picke of a little quill, or of a litle piece of wood with a sharp point," and to use it carefully lest they make their gums bleed. In some circles permanent toothpicks were fashionable; often these were made of ivory, silver, or gold, and sometimes they were ornately decorated. Queen Elizabeth received a toothpick of "gold, garnished with diamonds, etc.," as a New Year's gift from the captain of the Isle of Wight in 1579. Doubtless she possessed many others equally ornate. The toothpicks were carried in small cases hung from the waist, as were knives.

Using a toothpick ostentatiously, especially an ornate one, became known as the mark of the young man who had traveled on the Continent. In *King John* (Act I, Scene 1), Philip the Bastard learns from Queen Elinor that he is her grandson and he amuses himself with imagining the new roles that his "foot of honour" will permit him to play. For example, wasting an afternoon in meaningless chitchat with a supercilious young traveler, "he and his toothpick at my worship's mess." In *Much Ado About Nothing* (Act II, Scene 1), Benedick tells Don Pedro, "I will go on the slightest errand . . . you can devise to send me on; I will fetch you a toothpicker now from the furthest inch of Asia."

Toothpicks may, however, have gone out of fashion for a time, for in *All's Well That Ends Well* (Act I, Scene 1), Parolles tells Helena, "Virginity, like an old courtier, wears her cap out of fashion; richly suited, but unsuitable: just like the brooch and the tooth-pick, which wear not now."

At the end of the meal, as at the beginning, water was brought around for the diners to wash their hands. Very often the family and guests continued to sit at the table entertaining each other with music. Most guests expected to be asked to sing or play a musical instrument, and many households had a stock of instruments on which guests could show their talents.

As dinner comes to an end at the home of Hollyband's merchant, the host says to his son, "Shall we have a song? Where bee your bookes of musick? for they bee the best corrected." And to his daughter he says, "Fetche the songes," and "Behold, therbee fair songes at fouer partes." The afternoon moves on pleasantly until one of the guests realizes that the bells have already rung for evening prayers, so the guests make their adieus. To their thanks the merchant replies, "I drinke unto all the companie: thanking you that you have shewen unto me so much curtesie as to have come to my house: I am sorie that I am not able to make you better cheer." The guests respond politely, "What better cheere could you wishe?"

A Fast-Day Menu

Come, thou shalt go home, and we'll have flesh for holidays, fish for fasting-days, and moreo'er puddings and flap-jacks; and thou shalt be welcome.

Pericles, Act II, Scene I *(First Fisherman)*

A CUCUMBER SALAD

*So much as will serve to be prologue
to an egg and butter.*

Henry IV, Part I, Act I, Scene 2 *(Falstaff)*

JOHN MURRELL'S BUTTERED EGGS

Thy head is as full of quarrels as an egg is full of meat.

Romeo and Juliet, Act III, Scene I *(Mercutio)*

A DISH OF UNSALTED BUTTER

They are up already and call for eggs and butter.

Henry IV, Part I, Act II, Scene I *(Chamberlain)*

RIVER BASS WITH HERBS

Bait the hook well: this fish will bite.

Much Ado About Nothing, Act II, Scene 3 *(Claudio)*

A PIE OF LING COD

*I have no mind to Isbel since I was at court. Our old ling
and our Isbels o' the country are nothing like your old ling
and your Isbels o' the court.*

All's Well That Ends Well, Act III, Scene 2 *(Clown)*

SPICED APPLES

How like Eve's apple doth thy beauty grow,
If thy sweet virtue answer not thy show!

Sonnet 93

COTTAGE CHEESE PANCAKES

The shepherd's homely curds,
His cold thin drink out of his leather bottle,
. . . .
All which secure and sweetly he enjoys,
Is far beyond a prince's delicates.

Henry VI, Part III, Act II, Scene 5 (King Henry)

STEWED FLOUNDER

Give me mine angle; we'll to the river: there—
My music playing far off—I will betray
Tawny-finn'd fishes.

Antony and Cleopatra, Act II, Scene 5 (Cleopatra)

EELS SPITCHCOCKED

Is the adder better than the eel
Because his painted skin contents the eye?

The Taming of the Shrew, Act IV, Scene 3 (Petruchio)

SOOPS OF CARROTS

Remember, William; focative is caret.
And that's a good root.

The Merry Wives of Windsor,
Act IV, Scene 1 (Evans and Mistress Quickly)

CHEATE BREAD

An honest soul, i' faith, sir; by my troth he is,
as ever broke bread.

Much Ado About Nothing, Act III, Scene 4 (Dogberry)

BEER

There shall be in England seven halfpenny loaves sold for
a penny . . . and I will make it felony to drink small beer.

Henry VI, Part II, Act IV, Scene 2 (Jack Cade)

WATER

Here's that which is too weak to be a sinner,
Honest water, which ne'er left man i' the mire.
Timon of Athens, Act I, Scene 2 (*Apemantus*)

A QUAKING PUDDING

When I do stare, see how the subject quakes.
King Lear, Act IV, Scene 6 (*Lear*)

A TART OF RICE

Let me see; what am I to buy for our sheep-shearing feast?
'Three pound of sugar; five pound of currants; rice,' what
will this sister of mine do with rice?
The Winter's Tale, Act IV, Scene 2 (*Clown*)

To-morrow, if you please to speak with me,
I will come home to you.
Julius Caesar, Act I, Scene 2 (*Brutus*)

A SALLET OF ALL KINDS OF
HEARBES AND CUCUMBERS

Take your hearbes and picke them very fine into faire water, and
wash them all clean, and swing them in a strainer, and when you
put them into a dish, mingle them with Cowcumbers or Lemmans
payred and sliced, and scrape Sugar, and put in Vinegar and Oyle
and hard Egges boyled and laid about the dish and upon the
Sallet.

Thomas Dawson, *The good huswifes Jewell*

THE WORKING VERSION:

3 large leaves leaf lettuce	3 tablespoons red wine
3 large leaves Boston or	vinegar
butter lettuce	½ teaspoon salt
1 medium-size cucumber	⅛ teaspoon brown sugar
4 tablespoons olive oil	1 egg, hard-boiled

Wash the lettuce leaves in cold water, pat them dry in a clean cloth, and tear them into bite-size pieces. Peel and thinly slice the cucumber. Blend the oil, vinegar, salt, and sugar in a large salad bowl. Peel and cut the eggs into wedges.

Toss the lettuce and cucumber in the dressing, and garnish the bowl with the egg wedges. Serve immediately.

During the growing season cucumbers were used fresh and raw. They were also pickled, much as we pickle them today, with dill and spices. These were eaten alone as simple salads, or as part of the ingredients of compound salads. Thomas Tusser includes cucumbers in his list of "herbs and Roots for Sallads and Sauce."

The dietaries, however, were on the cautious side in their advice about cucumbers. Vaughan said, "If used now and then with oyle, vinegar, and pepper," cucumbers "doe further digestion; but it is unwholesome for them which feare the approach of any watry or windy sicknesse." Other writers agreed. Andrewe Boorde added that "cocumbers, restrayneth veneryousnes or lassyvyousnes, or luxuryousness." But in an age that read eagerly about aphrodisiacs, restraint of "lassyvyousnes" was not necessarily appreciated.

Although easily grown in kitchen gardens, cucumbers were fairly expensive to buy. Two cucumbers purchased by the Shuttleworths during a London stay, in September, 1597, cost one penny —but a worker's wage for a whole day was then often no more than sixpence.

TO BUTTER EGGES OF THE BEST FASHION

Boyle your Egges very hard, and then blanch them in cold water, then slice them as thinne as wafer, then you may take sweet butter drawne thicke with faire water, then season your Egges with a little grose pepper, and salt, and then put them into your thicke butter, and so set them upon a Chafindish of char-coales, now and then tossing and turning them upside downe, then you may dish them up in a very fayre dish, and prick fryed toasts about them: then strew on them a little grose pepper and salt, and so you may serve them to the Table hot.

John Murrell, *A Booke of Cookerie*

THE WORKING VERSION:

8 large eggs, hard-boiled and peeled	¼ teaspoon salt
	¼ teaspoon pepper
¼ pound butter	2 slices hot buttered toast,
4 tablespoons water	cut into triangles

Wait until the eggs are completely cold before slicing them thin. Set aside, covered, until the sauce is ready. Put the butter, water, and salt into a saucepan over medium-low heat, and, as the butter begins to melt, beat the mixture with a wire whisk until it begins to thicken—it should come to the consistency of whipping cream.

Add the sliced eggs and stir them about gently until they are coated with the sauce and are hot. Spoon the eggs into a warmed serving dish, sprinkle with pepper, garnish with the triangles of toast, and serve immediately.

The term "buttered eggs" was elastic; it was sometimes used for fried eggs as well as for scrambled eggs. Eggs in some form were a part of most meals and were particularly important in fish day meals. "On fish days," said William Harrison, "we begin our meals with butter and eggs." "The Service for Fyshe Dayes" in *A Proper newe Booke of Cokerye* starts with "Butter . . .

any other thing, nor ſleepe within three houres after. To conclude, Milke muſt not in any caſe be taken of them which are ſub-ieƈt to feauers, head-aches, or fluxes; accor-ding to that vulgar ſaying : *Dare lac aut vi-num febricitantibus & capite dolentibus,eſt dare venenum.*

What is the vſe of Butter?

Butter, whether it be freſh or ſalt purgeth mildely, and helpeth the roughneſſe of the throat: freſh Butter being taken faſting with a little Sugar,hindreth the engendring of the ſtone,by making the vrine-paſſage ſlippery : and cureth the ſhortneſſe of breath.It makes a man to ſpit, by ripening the matter. That Butter is beſt which is made in *May.*

What is the vſe of Cheeſe?

Cheeſe being the thickeſt part of the milk, is very nouriſhing : but old Cheeſe, by the acrimony thereof, makes the body bound and ſtipticke.But it is a thing worthy of ob-ſeruation , to ſet downe the diuerſities of Cheeſe,accordingto the nature of the beaſts, the Cow,Ewe, and Goate : the nature of the ground, hilly,meadow,and marſhie : the na-ture of the time, for the Summer is better then

then Winter : but aboue all, the cunning of the Dairy-woman is moſt to be regarded.

What is the vſe of Egges?

There are three things worthy of conſide-ration to be marked in Egges, as the Author of *The Countrey-Farme* noteth : The firſt is, their proper ſubſtance and qualitie;for egges of ſome Fowles are better then of ſome others.Henne-Egges are the beſt,and of bet-ter nouriſhment, then the egges of Duckes, Geeſe, or other Fowle. The ſecond thing re-markable in Egges is the time,*to wit*,whether they be freſh or ſtale, whether they be layed of a young Henne, or of an olde Henne;for experience teacheth vs, that theſe laſt doe quickly corrupt within the ſtomacke,and be nothing ſo good to nouriſh. Likewiſe it hath beene noted that Egges layed after the new of the Moone, in the Moneth of *Auguſt*, or in the wane of the Moone, in the Moneth of *Nouember*, as thoſe likewiſe which are layed about *Chriſtmaſſe* or *Witſontide*, are laſting and durable, & not eaſily corrupted:where-of there cannot be deuiſed any other reaſon, then that in ſome of them the ſhell is made hard, and not to be pierced through of the ayre,

Pages from *William Vaughan's* Directions for Health *on use of butter, cheese and eggs*

and A sallet with harde Egges." Robert May's menu for fasting days and Lent starts with butter and eggs and goes on to an additional dish of "buttered eggs on toasts." Rabisha's "Fish Dinner in the Spring" calls for "a rock of Butter" and a dish of buttered eggs in the first course. Butter and eggs, occasionally roasted, are on all the fish-day menus in "A Breviate . . . of a Nobleman's House."

Most sixteenth- and seventeenth-century cookbooks included some recipes for preparing eggs. Robert May gives more than seventy-five ways of "Dressing Eggs." Most of them are omelets, which range from a simple omelet seasoned with salt and fried in butter to elaborate and often exotic combinations of eggs with fish, meats, poultry, game, and dried fruit. Rose water, musk, ambergris, and spices of various kinds are used for flavoring these. Eggs in "Moneshyne" were egg yolks poached in a syrup made of rose water and sugar and served sprinkled with sugar and cinnamon, or poached in sweetened sack or other white wine and flavored with ambergris. Egg pies and tarts were also popular. A typical filling for these was made of egg yolks, butter, sugar, and rose water.

Eggs were hard-boiled, but they were also roasted among the coals in the fireplace, which must have been a tricky thing to do. In *As You Like It* (Act III, Scene 2), Touchstone tells Corin, "Truly thou art damned like an ill-roasted egg, all on one side."

Hens' eggs were, of course, most common, but duck, goose, partridge, and pheasant eggs were also eaten. Partridge and pheasant eggs were especially recommended by the dietaries; duck and goose eggs were not. "The yolkes of hens egges be cordialles, for it is temporately hote," wrote Andrewe Boorde, "but the white of an egge is viscus & colde & slacke of digestion, and doth nat ingender good blode, wherefore whosoever that wyl eate an egge, let the egge be newe & roste him reare [rare] & eate him, or els potch [poach] him for potched egges be best at night, and new reare rosted egges be good in the mornynge so it be tired [seasoned] with a litle salt & suger that they be nutrytyve, but harde egges be slowe and slacke of digestion. Rosted egges be better than sodden [boiled], fryed egges be nought [worthless]."

Butter, or butter with honey or sugar, was also recommended by the dietaries for breaking one's fast in the morning. And it was given to children for growing pains. Salted butter, according to Sir Thomas Elyot, was better in the diet than unsalted butter, for "it heateth and clenseth . . . more."

Butter was comparatively cheap and was used in cookbook recipes more often than any other cooking fat. Professional cooks thought nothing of using butter for deep-fat frying. It was almost always used for pie crusts, even for those "coffins" that were to serve merely as the storage containers of cold baked meats. The latter, however, would have been made with melted, rather than solid, butter.

TO BROIL BACE

Take a bace, draw it and wash it clean, broil it with the scales on, or without the scales, and lay it in a dish with some good sallet oyl, wine-vinegar, salt, some sprigs of rosemary, tyme, and parsley, then heat the gridiron and lay on the fish, broil it on a soft fire on the embers, and baste it with the sauce it was steeped in, being broild serve it in a clean warm dish with the sauce it was steeped in, and the herbs on it, and about the dish, cast on salt, and so serve it with slices of orange, lemon, or barberries.

Or broil it in butter and vinegar with herbs as above-said and make sauce with beaten butter and vinegar.

Sometimes for change, with grape-verjuice [vinegar], juice of sorrel, beaten butter and the herbs.

Robert May, *The Accomplisht Cook*

THE WORKING VERSION:

One 2-pound fresh-water bass	¼ cup minced parsley
½ cup white wine vinegar	4 tablespoons butter, melted
1 teaspoon salt	½ lemon or sour orange,
½ teaspoon thyme	peeled, sliced thin, and
¼ teaspoon rosemary	seeded

Scale the fish, cut off the fins, and, if you wish, the head, but leave on the tail. Remove the viscera and wash the fish under cold running water. Make a marinade of the vinegar, salt, thyme, rosemary, and parsley.

Place the fish in a shallow baking dish, pour the marinade over it, and marinate it for ½ hour. Sprinkle ½ of the melted butter over the fish and bake in the marinade for twenty to twenty-five minutes at 350°, basting three times during the baking. The fish is done when you can feel the flakes separate when pressed lightly with the fingers.

Remove the skin from the upper side of the fish, spoon the sauce with the herbs over it, pour on the remaining butter, and serve immediately in the dish in which it baked, garnished with slices of the lemon or orange.

May's recipe requires double cooking. He broils the fish without seasoning on a gridiron over the coals and then cooks it a second time in the marinade. I simplified the process to avoid overcooking the fish.

Bass, which was also spelled "base," was fried, boiled, pickled, or made into pies.

TO BAKE A JOLL OF LING IN A PIE

Let your Ling be almost boyled, then season it with pepper only (the skin being first taken off), strow the bottom of your Coffin with an Onion or two minced small, close your Pie, and bake it; then take the yolks and whites of about a dozen eggs, not boyld altogether hard, mince them small with your knife, and put them into drawn Butter, toss them together, draw your Pie, and pour in this lear [sauce] all over, and shake it together; so put on your lid, and dish your pie.

William Rabisha, *The whole Body of Cookery Dissected*

THE WORKING VERSION:

One 2½-pound piece of ling, or rock, cod
2 quarts water
4 teaspoons salt
½ cup minced onions
½ cup butter, melted
¼ teaspoon pepper
2 eggs, coddled for 10 minutes

THE PASTRY
2 cups sifted unbleached flour
1 teaspoon salt
¾ cup cold butter
½ cup cold water (approximately)
1 egg, separated
1 teaspoon of the minced onion (above)

Wash the fish under cold running water. Bring the two quarts of water to a boil in a large saucepan. Add three teaspoons of the salt and the fish. Lower the heat to simmer, and poach the fish for five minutes.

Remove the fish to a large plate or a cutting board and, while it is still hot, scrape off the skin—this becomes very difficult if the fish gets cold. Slide a boning knife or a long, narrow, sharp paring knife under the flesh and over the backbone—using a sliding-cutting motion—and loosen the flesh from the backbone. Transfer this piece to a plate. Slide the knife under the bone, this time lifting off the bone, and remove the rest of the fish to the plate. Reserve one teaspoonful of the minced onion for the pastry and mix together the remaining onions, half the butter, the pepper, and the remaining salt. Set aside, covered, until needed.

Make the pastry following instructions on page 31, adding the reserved teaspoonful of minced onion to the water and egg mixture. Divide the dough into two pieces, with the piece for the bottom crust a little larger than the other. Roll out the larger piece to fit a rectangular baking dish approximately nine inches by six inches. Drape the sheet of pastry in the dish and roll out the other piece.

Divide the onion mixture into two equal parts and spread one part evenly in the pie dish. Place the two pieces of fish side by side over the seasoning and spread the rest of the mixture over the top of the fish. Fit the top crust onto the pie, seal the edges with the tines of a fork dipped in cold water, and slice off the surplus pastry. If there is enough surplus pastry to roll out, cut small pastry fishes from it, either freehand or with a fish-shaped cookie cutter.

Brush the top of the pie with egg white, arrange the pastry fishes over it, and brush them with the remaining egg white. Bake at 450° for twenty minutes, then lower the heat to 350° and bake for fifteen minutes longer.

While the pie is baking, peel and mince the eggs and mix them

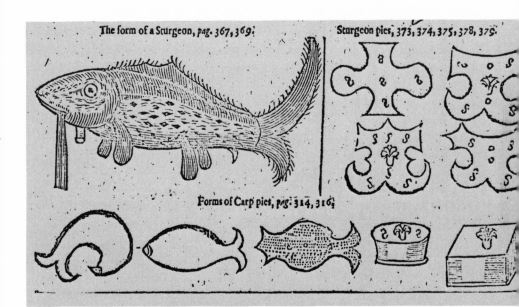

Pastry designs for fish pies, in Robert May's The Accomplisht Cook

with the remaining butter. Cut the top crust loose around the sides of the finished pie and carefully lift it off. Spread the egg mixture over the fish and replace the crust on the pie. Serve immediately.

Rabisha's recipe calls only for pepper to season the fish, so he was probably using salt ling for the pie. Markham's recipe for a ling pie is clearly for the salt fish, as he specifies a "Jowl of the best Ling that is not much watered [soaked in water to remove the salt]."

The slang phrase for salt cod was "poor-john," a phrase that Shakespeare uses in several plays. In *The Tempest* (Act II, Scene 2), Trinculo, escaped from the storm, comes upon Caliban. In his drunken state he is unable to make out who or what the creature is. "What have we here?" he asks himself, "a man or a fish? . . . he smells like a fish; a very ancient and fish-like smell; a kind of not of the newest Poor-John." Most people must have been very tired of salt cod by the time spring arrived and with it the possibility of fresh fish.

SPICED APPLES

Apples if they be dressed with fresh Butter, Sugar, Saffron, Cinnamon, and Annise-seede, they will restore nature . . . and make a man of lively spirit.

William Vaughan, *Directions for Health*

THE WORKING VERSION:

2 pounds tart cooking apples	⅛ teaspoon saffron
¼ cup sugar	4 tablespoons butter, diced
¼ teaspoon cinnamon	2 tablespoons water
¼ teaspoon anise seeds	

Core and peel the apples and cut them into ¼-inch-thick slices. Mix together the sugar, cinnamon, anise seeds, and saffron, and sprinkle over the apples.

Arrange the slices of apples overlapping each other, in a round oven-to-table baking dish. Dot the butter over them and add the water. Cover and bake at 350° until tender—from thirty minutes to one hour. Serve warm directly from the baking dish.

Anise seeds were rarely used to flavor foods, although they occasionally appeared in recipes for small cakes such as the almond cookies that Robert May, for some unexplained reason, calls "Bean Bread." They were, however, very popular as "comfits"—that is, candied—and were nibbled both for pleasure and for sweetening the breath.

They were also eaten as an aid to digestion after heavy meals. Vaughan favored them especially during winter weather: "In Autumn . . . when the earth looseth her beauty . . . melancholy is engendered," and by winter, "the cheerful virtues of the body are weakened by the cold air . . . , when we may feede liberally on strong meates, as Beefe, barren Does, gelt [gelded] Goats, and on spiced or baked meates, for whose better digestion, some use to eate Comfits of Anise-seedes presently [immediately] after meales." Apples he recommended as helpful for "swellings [bloating]" when eaten with wine or salt, and for "windinesse" when eaten with comfits.

TO MAKE CURDE FRITTERS

Take the yolks of ten Egs, and breake them in a pan, & put to them one handfull of Curds and one handful of fine flower, and straine them alltogether, and make batter, and if it be not thicke enough, put more Curdes in it, and salt to it. Then set it on the fire in a frying pan, with such stuff as ye will fry them with, and when it is hot, with a ladle take part of your batter, and put of it into your panne, and let it run as small as you can & stir them with a stick and turn them with a scummer, & when they be faire and yellow fried, take them out & cast sugar upon them, and serve them foorth.

John Partridge, *The good Huswifes Handmaide for the Kitchin*

THE WORKING VERSION:

2 cups creamed cottage cheese	½ cup sifted unbleached flour
8 egg yolks	4 tablespoons butter
¼ teaspoon salt	½ cup brown sugar

Beat the cheese with the egg yolks until the mix is nearly smooth. Stir in the salt and the flour and beat for ½ minute. Melt the butter on a heated griddle or in a large skillet.

When the butter starts to bubble, drop large spoonfuls of the batter onto the griddle, leaving space between the fritters so they can be turned easily. Fry until they are lightly browned on the underside. Turn carefully, and brown on the other side. Keep the baked fritters warm until all are finished. Serve on a heated platter, either with the sugar sprinkled over the fritters or served separately in a small bowl.

The batter can be made up ahead of time and refrigerated, but the fritters should not be fried until just before they are to be served, for they lose their delicate flavor and light texture as soon as they get cold.

This was the sort of hurry-up dish that William Rabisha often recommended for the second course. It was quickly and easily prepared—an important consideration when a cook was very busy but still had to produce the required number of dishes for each course.

TO STEW FLOUNDERS

Take two faire Flounders, cut off the heads and the finnes, crosse them overthwart with a sharpe knife two or three cuts, then put them in a pewter dish the white side downeward, put in halfe a pinte of sweete butter, halfe a pint of vinegar, a handfull of shred parsley, three or foure blades of Mace, a faggot of sweete herbes, three or foure whole Onions, strow on a little salt, and let them stewe halfe an houre, then turne them and let them stew halfe an

*houre more, then dish it upon sippets and strew salt upon it, and
then serve it to the table hott.*

John Murrell, *A Booke of Cookerie*

THE WORKING VERSION:

1 ¼ pounds fresh medium-large fillets of flounder	1 teaspoon salt
4 tablespoons butter	2 large pieces of whole mace
1 cup onions, sliced thin	½ teaspoon thyme
1 cup white wine vinegar	½ teaspoon rosemary
½ cup minced parsley	2 slices buttered toast, quartered

Wipe the fillets of flounder with a clean, damp cloth. Put all
the rest of the ingredients except the toast into a large skillet with
a lid. Bring the mixture to a boil, lower the heat to simmer, and
cook for fifteen minutes.

Arrange the fillets side by side in the broth. Cover the skillet
and simmer for twelve to fifteen minutes, turning the fish once
during the poaching. Taste the sauce and, if necessary, add more
salt. Put the slices of toast in a heated serving dish, arrange the
fish fillets over them, pour the sauce with all the seasonings over
the fish, and serve.

If fillets of flounder are not available, fillets of plaice or sole
will do. The unfilleted flounder is a large, flat, ugly fish, with both
its eyes on the same side of its head; it has two sets of bones and
a skin like sandpaper. The first time I tried this recipe I used a
whole flounder, but, even without the head and fins, whole
flounders are usually too large for the pots in most kitchens.
Besides, they are difficult to serve as well as being unattractive.

"New flounders, new!" was the call of the fishwives who sought
to assure housewives or maids that their fish was fresh.

HOW TO SPITCHCOCK AN EELE

*Take a faire Eele, and split him in the back close to the bone,
from the head to the tail, but not through the belly; scour him*

*well with Salt, and wash him, lay him up, and dry him, and cut
the bone through all along the back, that it may have no strength
to double up the Eele, when it is on the Gridiron; then cut him
(if he be large) in six pieces; wash him over in the inside with
Butter, and sprinkle on Salt, and a little minced Time; your
Gridiron being very hot upon the coals, lay him on the inside
downwards, and when he is broyled on that side, turn him, and
let him broyl on the skinny side very well; so dish him up, and
pour all over him drawn Butter, Vinegar, and a grated Nutmeg,
garnish him with Bay leaves.*

William Rabisha, *The whole Body of Cookery Dissected*

THE WORKING VERSION:

One 1½-pound fresh eel
  1 teaspoon salt
  ½ teaspoon thyme
  ¼ teaspoon nutmeg

4 tablespoons butter, melted
¼ cup vinegar
Bay leaves

Ask your fishmonger if he will eviscerate the eel, cut off its
head, and section the eel into three-inch pieces. If you do this
yourself, remember the saying "slippery as an eel," and hold the
fish with a dry cloth while you work on it.

Remove the head and the viscera and wash the eel under cold,
running water. Wipe the eel dry with a clean cloth. Cut the eel
through the bone with a sharp knife into three-inch pieces. Then
loosen the flesh from both sides of the backbone to ½ inch in.

Mix together the salt, thyme, and nutmeg, and rub it into the
pieces of eel. Brush them generously with the melted butter, and
broil for eight minutes. Brush the pieces again with butter, turn
them over, and broil for five minutes.

While the eel is broiling, add the vinegar to any remaining
butter and simmer for five minutes. Arrange the eel in a warmed
serving dish, pour the sauce over it, and garnish with the bay
leaves. Serve immediately.

Robert May, who gives twenty-four recipes for eel, is the only
one who explains how to use salt eels in cooking. They should, he
says, be boiled tender first, the skin removed, and then broiled.

The flesh of eels, when they are getting ready to migrate downstream to the sea, contains a good deal of fat. When fat eels were available, strips of their flesh were sometimes used for larding meats.

SOOPS OF BUTTER'D CARROTS

Take fine young carrots and wash them clean; then have a skillet or pan of fair liquor on the fire, and when it boils, put in the carrots, give it a walm or two [parboil] and take them out into a cullender; let them drain, then mince them small, and put them in a pipkin with some slic't dates, butter, white wine, beaten cinamon, salt, sugar, and some boild currans, stew them well together, and dish them on sippets finely carved.

Robert May, *The Accomplisht Cook*

THE WORKING VERSION:

1½	pounds fresh young carrots	1	tablespoon currants, parboiled
1½	cups water	1	teaspoon brown sugar
¼	teaspoon salt	¼	teaspoon cinnamon
3	tablespoons butter	2	dates, minced
6	tablespoons white wine	2	slices hot buttered toast, cut into triangles

Scrape the carrots, rinse them under cold water, and slice into thin rounds. Bring the water and salt to a boil in a saucepan with a lid. Add the carrots, cover, and cook until tender but still firm—about ten minutes.

Drain and mash the carrots coarsely. Stir the butter into the carrots until it melts, then add all the remaining ingredients except the toast.

Simmer over low heat, stirring constantly, until the carrots and seasonings are blended and the carrots hot. Transfer to a heated serving dish and garnish with the toast.

Carrots were a boon to the cook since they could be left in the ground in the kitchen garden through the winter and thus were available throughout most of the year. They were used mainly to season soups and stews but were also made into fritters and pies. No other cookbook uses the word "soops" for this type of dish, and I was unable to track down its source. May's spelling of carrots is the standard spelling today, but in his day the word was variously spelled "carrets," "carots," and "carets."

CHEATE BREAD OF UNSOURED LEAVEN

Thus according to the example [following the recipe for manchet] you may bake any leavened bread.

Gervase Markham, *The English Hus-wife*

Cheate, or wheaten bread [is] so named because the color thereof resembleth the gray or yellowish wheat, being clean and well dressed, and out of this is the coarsest of the bran (usually called gurgeons or pollard) taken.

William Harrison, *The Description of England*

THE WORKING VERSION:

2 cups lukewarm water	2½ cups whole-wheat flour
2 cakes fresh yeast or	2½ cups sifted unbleached
2 tablespoons dry yeast	flour
1 tablespoon salt	

Pour the water in a large mixing bowl and crumble or sprinkle the yeast over the water. When the yeast has softened and expanded, add the salt and stir in the whole-wheat flour, ½ cup at a time. Then add the unbleached flour one cup at a time.

Flour your work surface and turn the dough out onto it. Pat it back and forth in the flour between your hands until the dough is easy to handle. Knead it for five minutes. Put the dough into a warmed clean bowl large enough to allow the dough to double in size. Cover and set in a warm place or in an unheated oven until it has doubled in bulk—1 to 1½ hours.

When the dough has doubled, turn it out on a floured work surface and knead just long enough to make it into a ball. Divide the ball into twelve pieces and knead each into a ball. Flatten these to rolls ½ inch thick. Cut about ⅛ inch deep around the circumference of each roll with a sharp knife halfway between top and bottom.

Sprinkle a cookie sheet with whole-wheat flour and place the rolls on it spaced two inches apart. Punch fork holes in the tops and set to rise again in a warm place or unheated oven until they have doubled in size. Bake at 400° for twenty minutes. Cool on a wire cooling grille.

If you would like to make this dough into loaves instead of rolls, divide it into two pieces. Knead each piece into a ball and flatten it to about two inches high. Cut around the circumference of the loaves as for the rolls. Set the loaves to rise on a floured cookie sheet four inches apart. Punch holes in the tops, and when they have doubled in size—in 1 to 1½ hours—bake at 400° for twenty minutes. Then lower the heat to 350° and bake twenty minutes longer.

This may have been the "coarse" cheate that was made in the royal bakehouse and served to the lower ranks of courtiers and the higher ranks of servants.

TO MAKE A QUAKING PUDDING, BAKED

Slice the crumbs of a penny manchet, and infuse it three or four hours in a pint of scalding hot cream, covering it close, then break the bread with a spoon very small, and put to it a pound of walnuts beaten small with rosewater in a stone mortar, and season it with sugar, nutmeg, salt, the yolks of six eggs, a quarter of a pound of dates slic't and cut small, a handful of currans boiled, some marrow minced. Beat them all together and bake it. Put to it butter, rosewater, and sugar, and serve it up to the table.

Robert May, *The Accomplisht Cook*

THE WORKING VERSION:

3 egg yolks	2 tablespoons currants,
1 cup light cream	parboiled
2 tablespoons sugar	6 dates, diced
2 tablespoons rose water	½ cup walnuts, grated
⅛ teaspoon salt	
½ teaspoon nutmeg	THE SAUCE
1 cup soft bread crumbs	3 tablespoons butter
2 tablespoons beef marrow,	2 tablespoons rose water
or butter, diced	2 tablespoons brown sugar

Beat the egg yolks into the cream. Add the sugar, rose water, salt, nutmeg, and bread crumbs, and beat until the crumbs are softened. Stir in the beef marrow or butter, the currants, dates, and the walnuts. Cover and set aside to allow the flavors to blend for three hours.

Pour the mixture into a quart-size oven-proof casserole and bake at 350° for forty-five minutes.

While the pudding is baking, make the sauce by simmering the rose water, sugar, and butter together, stirring until the butter melts, for five minutes. Keep the sauce warm. Serve the pudding in the dish in which it was baked and pour the sauce over it.

As this menu is for a fast-day meal, the dish should logically be made with butter rather than with beef marrow. The beef marrow, however, gives the pudding a more exotic flavor, which we prefer to that of the pudding made with butter. The choice is yours.

Like most bread puddings this one is best when served fresh from the oven. Bread puddings, like other puddings, were usually boiled in a floured cloth, but baked puddings were not unusual in seventeenth-century cookbooks. Hasty puddings were close kin to our cornstarch puddings today, and just as awful.

Puddings were not usually considered fare for feasts. May includes only two in his feast bills of fare. Rabisha, however, rates them higher. His bill of fare for a "Flesh-day for the Summer Season" includes a dish of rich "puddings of several colours" and a "marrow Pudding or some other, boyled or baked."

TO MAKE A TART OF RYSE

Boyle your rice, and put in the yolkes of two or three Egges into the Rice, and when it is boyled put it into a dish and season it with sugar, synamon and ginger, and butter, and the juice of two or three Orenges, and set it on the fire againe.

Thomas Dawson, *The good huswifes Jewell*

THE WORKING VERSION:

1¾ cups milk	¾ cup long-grain rice
1 tablespoon butter	2 tablespoons brown sugar
½ teaspoon ginger	½ cup fresh orange juice
½ teaspoon cinnamon	1 egg yolk, lightly beaten

Heat the milk in the top of a double boiler, over moderate heat, until the milk begins to bubble. Add the butter, ginger, and cinnamon, and stir until the butter melts. Then slowly stir in the rice. Cover the pot and cook until the rice has absorbed the milk—about twenty-five minutes—watching it carefully to prevent the milk from burning.

Add the sugar and orange juice and stir until absorbed. Then stir in the egg yolk. Keep warm over hot water until ready to serve, then spoon the rice into a shallow dish and sprinkle a little additional sugar over it.

I used milk to boil the rice in because all other recipes for rice tarts that I saw called for milk or cream in which to cook the rice. Why Dawson called this a tart is hard to tell, unless he assumed that it would be served in a baked tart shell, as other such mixtures often were.

Recipes for rice dishes vary from rice porridge to link puddings in which mixtures similar to bread puddings, but substituting rice for the bread, are stuffed into "washed and scoured guttes," boiled, and cooled before serving. In cookbook bills of fare, rice appeared only on fish-day and fast-day menus, usually as rice milk or porridge. Otherwise, rice does not seem to have been important in the English diet. The Petre, Fairfax, and Shuttleworth accounts show only small and infrequent purchases of rice and rice meal. Rice meal was used as a thickening agent for various dishes. Joseph Cooper, for example, suggested that rice meal be used to thicken a spinach tart if ground almonds were not available.

FAST DAYS AND FASTING

The dishes for this menu are from published fast-day bills of fare. There was a distinct difference between fast days and fish days. Fast days were fixed days of abstinence from meat-eating for religious reasons, ordered by the Church; in this the Anglican Church did not break with Catholic tradition, although it did reduce the prescribed number of fast days. Fish days were, however, set by the government for economic and political reasons. The 1563 statute specifies that its prohibition on flesh-eating is meant "not for any superstition to be maintained" in the choice of food, but "meant politicly for the increase of fishermen and mariners."

This was the argument that William Harrison, a clergyman, stressed in defending the secular fish days. Otherwise, he pointed out, there was no restraint of any kind on the food Englishmen could eat if they had the money to buy it. In the English law of 1563, said Harrison, writing about a dozen years later, the "order is taken only to the end that our numbers of cattle may be better increased and that abundance of fish which the sea yieldeth more generally received." In addition, there was "great consideration had in the making of this law for the preservation of the navy and maintenance of convenient [sufficient] numbers of sea faring men, both of which would otherwise greatly decay."

The eating of meat was proscribed by the Church and government for a combined total of 153 days during the year. This was a large bill of fish to sell the English people. Queen Elizabeth herself refused to abide by the secular fish days, although those who were permitted to dine at court daily were not served meat on those days.

The Elizabethan law made exceptions for young children, old people, and those who were ill, although they still had to get

Portrait of William Cecil, Lord Burghley, who was responsible for instituting statutory secular fish days in England in the latter part of the 16th century

official permits to eat meat on fish days. A limited number of butchers were permitted to kill meat on statutory fish days and during Lent.

There was, of course, much grumbling about the extra fish-eating days forced on people by the secular law, and there was a good deal of breaking of the law, but those caught were punished. In *Henry IV, Part II* (Act II, Scene 4), Falstaff, quarreling with Dame Quickly, tells her, "Marry, there is another indictment upon thee, for suffering flesh to be eaten in thy house, contrary to the law; for the which I think thou wilt howl." But Dame Quickly brushes off the accusation with "All victuallers do so: what's a joint of mutton or two in a whole Lent?" For, like most Tudor laws and regulations, this law, with its severe penalties for violations, could be policed only sporadically.

In the Fairfax household fasting days were kept, although strictly only when Lady Fairfax was at home. A menu for "An ordinary fast day Dinner, for my Master," dated 1572, included: "Greyne [grain] pottage, butter, Sallettes with egges, Linge, Haddock, Coddlyne, Coddes heade, Turbutt in broth; Barbyll [barbel], Trowes [trout]" in the first course, and for the second course, "Fresh lynge, Sawmon chynkes, Bull heades in broth, and wheting [whiting]."

Fast days were observed at Ingatestone Manor, and no supper was served on Fridays. But a light meal, euphemistically called "Drinking at Night," was often served later in the evening. One such "drinking" consisted of: "Egges, 3 cakes of butter, 2 playces, 2 whitinges, and a mudefish." This hospitable household, which was rarely without at least one guest at meals, consumed vast amounts of fish, most of it salt fish. Sir William Petre's orders were to have an ample stock of salt fish on hand for Lent and fish days, as well as for emergencies. His acater (servant responsible for purchasing food) went to nearby markets to buy sole, flounder, whiting, plaice, and occasionally mackerel, bass, salmon, and other fish. Ingatestone also had its own artificial fish ponds, which supplied some of the household needs.

Thomas Tusser gives a thoughtful lesson to farmers on how to buy and store salt fish:

> When Harvest is Ended, Take Shipping or Ride,
> ling, salt-fish, and herring, for Lent to provide:
> . . . .
> Choose skilfully salt-fish, not burnt at the stone,

Portrait of Sir William Petre, Queen Elizabeth's secretary and master of Ingatestone manor

buy such as be good, or else let it alone:
Get home that is bought, and so stack it up dry,
with pease-straw between it, the safer to lie.

It was also important, he said, to move the salt fish around
periodically because otherwise winter dampness could rot it. And
as a last suggestion,

Spend herring first, save salt-fish last,
For salt-fish is good when Lent is past.

Lenten fasting was a popular subject among writers. Nicholas
Breton, in an exuberant sketch of Lent, wrote, "Now . . . the
poore stockfish is sore beaten for his stubborness [stockfish was
air-dried cod that was beaten with a stick to make it tender];
the Herring dominiers like a Lord of Great Service, and the
fruit of the Dairy make a hungry Feast: Fasting and mourning
is the life of the poor, and the Dogges grow leane, with the lack
of bones."

Cob, the water carrier in Ben Jonson's *Every Man in His
Humour* (Act III, Scene 5), in answer to the query "What makes
you so out of love with fasting-days?" replies, "Marry . . .
their bad conditions. . . . First they are of a Flemmish breed
. . . for they raven up more butter than all the dayes of the
week beside: next, they stinke of fish, and leek-porridge miser-
ably: thirdly, the'll keep a man devoutly hungrie all day, and at
night send him supperless to bed."

Those who were looking for arguments other than the Puritan
objection to such "relics of Popery" against fast and fish days
could find them in the dietaries. Andrewe Boorde was especially
concerned about the large amounts of salt fish that were eaten.
(Because of the perishability of fish, most Englishmen ate salt
fish most of the time.) "Salte fysshe the whiche be poudered and
salted with salte, be nat greatly to be praysed specyally if a man
do make his hole refeccion [meal] with it, the qualyte dothe nat
hurte, but the quantyte. . . . All manner of fysshe is cold of
nature, & doth lytle nurysshe."

A Feast for Katharine & Petruchio

He says he'll come;
How shall I feast him? what bestow of him?
Twelfth Night, Act III, Scene 4 (Olivia)

SACK (SHERRY)

Your hearts are mighty, your skins are whole, and let burnt sack
be the issue.
The Merry Wives of Windsor,
Act III, Scene 1 (Host of the Garter Inn)

WHITE RADISHES

He was for all the world like a forked radish, with
a head fantastically carved upon it with a knife.
Henry IV, Part II, Act III, Scene 2 (Falstaff)

BARLEY BROTH

Can sodden water,
A drench for sur-rein'd jades [horses], their barley-broth,
Decoct their cold blood to such valiant heat?
Henry V, Act III, Scene 5 (The Constable of France)

CRAB IN CLARET SAUCE

For you yourself, sir, should be old as I am,
if, like a crab, you could go backward.
Hamlet, Act II, Scene 2 (Hamlet)

BEEF TONGUE STEWED WITH CHESTNUTS

See, what a ready tongue suspicion hath!
Henry IV, Part II, Act I, Scene 1 *(Northumberland)*

A VENISON PIE

'Poor deer,' quoth he, 'thou mak'st a testament
As worldlings do, giving thy sum of more
To that which had too much.'
As You Like It, Act II, Scene 1 *(First Lord)*

BUTTERED ONIONS AND APPLES

And, most dear actors, eat no onions nor garlic,
for we are to utter sweet breath, and I do not doubt
but to hear them say, it is a sweet comedy.
A Midsummer-Night's Dream, Act IV, Scene 2 *(Bottom)*

ROAST BREAST OF VEAL
WITH SAUSAGE DRESSING

It was a brute part of him to kill so capital a calf there.
Hamlet, Act III, Scene 2 *(Hamlet)*

A WATERCRESS SALAD

I climbed into this garden . . . to pick a sallet another
while, which is not amiss to cool a man's stomach.
Henry VI, Part II, Act IV, Scene 10 *(Jack Cade)*

RAVELED BREAD AND
ROBERT MAY'S FRENCH BREAD

A crew of patches, rude mechanicals, that work for bread.
A Midsummer-Night's Dream, Act III, Scene 2 *(Puck)*

RED WINE, WHITE WINE, AND ALE

When the butt is out, we will drink water; not a drop before.
The Tempest, Act III, Scene 2 *(Stephano)*

GERVASE MARKHAM'S BANBURY CAKE

Dost thou think, because thou art virtuous, there
there shall be no more cakes and ale?
Twelfth Night, Act II, Scene 3 *(Sir Toby)*

A PLUM TART

Mass, thou lov'dst plums well, that wouldst venture so.
Henry VI, Part II, Act II, Scene 1 (Gloucester)

A DUTCH CHEESE

Like a man made after supper of a cheese-paring.
Henry IV, Part II, Act III, Scene 2 (Falstaff)

If I like thee no worse after dinner
I will not part from thee yet.
King Lear, Act I, Scene 4 (Lear)

Radishes were probably introduced by the Romans, who liked their pungent flavor with venison and other meats. John Gerard, in his *Herball,* said of radishes, "The root boiled in broth and the decoction drunk is good for the cough" but "eaten raw with bread instead of other food . . . yield very little nourishment and that faulty and ill."

BARLEY BROTH

Boil the Barley first in two waters, and then put to it a knuckle of Veal, and to the broth, Salt, Raisins, Sweet Herbs a faggot [bunch], large Mace, and the quantity of a fine Manchet slic't together. . . . Otherways, without the fruit; Put some good Mutton gravy, Saffron.

Robert May, *The Accomplisht Cook*

THE WORKING VERSION:

¼ cup pearl barley
1 cup water
1 quart mutton or lamb broth
1 pound veal shoulder
1 ½ teaspoons salt
¼ cup minced parsley
⅛ teaspoon marjoram
⅛ teaspoon savory
½ teaspoon thyme
1 large piece of whole mace
1 bay leaf
¼ cup seeded raisins (optional)
3 slices buttered toast, quartered

Parboil the barley in the cup of water for five minutes, drain; then put all the ingredients except ½ teaspoon of the salt, the raisins, and the toast into a large saucepan with a lid. Bring to a boil, cover the pan, lower the heat to simmer, and cook until the barley and veal are tender—about two hours.

Remove the mace, bay leaf, and the veal from the broth and dice the meat. Return the diced meat to the broth. Taste the broth and add the remaining salt, if needed, and the raisins, if desired. Divide the toast into individual soup bowls and ladle the soup into the bowls. Serve hot.

Lamb or mutton broth can be made from two pounds of lamb neck or mutton, five cups of water, one large onion, a carrot, a blade of celery, and a sprig of parsley, in a pressure cooker or simmered in a covered saucepan. If you use a pressure cooker, cook at fifteen pounds pressure for one hour. Let the pressure go down before opening the cooker. If you use a saucepan, add an additional cup of water to allow for evaporation, and simmer for three hours. Strain and skim the fat from the broth. The broth can be made well ahead of time and frozen for later use. Before freezing, chill it until the fat hardens and then skim it.

French pearl barley was also used for sweet puddings—sometimes very rich ones—which were boiled in casings as sausages were. Barley flour was widely used for bread, usually mixed with other grains.

TO STEW CRABS

Being boiled take the meat out of the shells, and put it in a pipkin with some claret wine, and wine vinegar, minced thyme, pepper, grated bread, salt, the yolks of two or three hard eggs strained or minced very small, some sweet butter, capers, and some large mace; stew it finely, rub the shells with a clove or two of garlick, and dish the shells being washed and finely cleansed, the claws and little legs round about them, put the meat into the shells, and so serve them.

Robert May, *The Accomplisht Cook*

THE WORKING VERSION:

One 3-pound fresh-cooked crab or 1¼ pounds fresh crab meat
2 hard-boiled egg yolks
½ cup claret
4 teaspoons red wine vinegar
1 teaspoon fresh thyme leaves or ½ teaspoon dried thyme

⅛ teaspoon pepper
1 teaspoon grated bread crumbs
¼ teaspoon salt
2 tablespoons butter
1 teaspoon capers
1 large piece of whole mace
1 clove of garlic, peeled

If you use a whole crab, scrub the upper shell clean in cold water and save it to serve the crab in. Remove the orange waxy material and the spongy mass from the crab—unless this was done at the fish market—and rinse the crab under cold water. Pick out the meat in as large pieces as possible. Crack the upper legs and joints and remove the meat, saving the small end joints for garnishing.

Mash or press the egg yolks through a sieve. Put all the ingredients except the crab meat into a saucepan and bring to a boil. Lower the heat, cover the pot, and simmer for ten minutes. Stir in the crab meat carefully to avoid breaking the pieces, and simmer for five minutes. Remove the mace and the garlic and spoon the crab into the reserved shell, or into a warmed serving dish. Garnish with the claw ends and serve.

Few cookbooks of Shakespeare's day give any recipes at all for crab, although Robert May offers thirteen ways of preparing it. Crab was probably eaten most often boiled and dipped into vinegar as a sauce.

TO HASH NEATES-TONGUE WITH CHESNUTS

Boyle them and blaunch them, and slice them in pieces, put them into a Pipkin with blauncht Chesnuts, a strong broth, a Fagot of Hearbes, large Mace, washt Endisse [endive], a little Pepper, a few Cloves, and whole Sinamon. Boyle all together with Butter, season them with Salt onely, garnish your Dish as you list.

John Murrell, *A New Book of Cookerie*

THE WORKING VERSION:

One 1½-pound fresh beef tongue
2 quarts water (approximately)
2 bay leaves
1 medium-size onion, quartered
3 teaspoons salt
6 peppercorns
2 cloves
4 leaves curly endive or escarole
1½ cups broth in which the tongue was cooked, strained

2 tablespoons minced parsley
2 tablespoons minced chives
¼ teaspoon marjoram
¼ teaspoon savory
1 large piece whole mace
1 two-inch piece of stick cinnamon
3 tablespoons butter
½ pound chestnuts, peeled and blanched
3 egg yolks (optional)

Wash the tongue under cool running water. Put the water into a large pot with a lid. Add the bay leaves, onion, two teaspoons of the salt, the peppercorns, and cloves, and bring to a boil. Add the tongue—there should be enough water to cover the tongue by one inch; if not, add more water—cover the pot, lower the heat to simmer, and cook until the tongue is tender, two to three hours. Remove the pot from the heat and let the tongue cool in the cooking liquid.

When the tongue is cool enough to handle comfortably, remove it from the broth to a large plate or a cutting board. Strain the broth and set aside two cups of it for the sauce. With a sharp knife, slit the skin down the top center of the tongue from one end to the other. Peel off the skin and trim the fat and gristle from the root (thick) end. Slice the tongue into ½-inch-thick slices and set aside, covered, until needed.

Wash the endive or escarole leaves under running water, press the water from them, and shred them. Put the 1½ cups of reserved tongue broth, the shredded greens, parsley, chives, marjoram, savory, mace, cinnamon, butter, and the remaining teaspoon of salt into a large saucepan and bring to a boil. Add the chestnuts, lower the heat to simmer, cover and cook until the chestnuts are tender—forty-five minutes to one hour.

Add the sliced tongue and simmer for fifteen minutes. If you wish a thicker, smoother sauce, remove ½ cup of the sauce to a small bowl and beat the egg yolks into it. Return this to the saucepan and stir it in gently until the sauce begins to thicken. Remove the stick of cinnamon, the mace, and the cloves, and arrange the tongue in a serving bowl. Spoon the sauce over it and serve.

Murrell gives two recipes for "hashing"—that is, stewing—tongue. In the first recipe he thickens the sauce with egg yolks, and in this recipe he says the tongue is to be treated as it was in the previous one. Since the addition of egg yolks improves both the texture and flavor of the sauce, I suggest using them.

Fresh chestnuts are best, but if they are not available, use either dried or canned ones. Dried chestnuts should be covered with hot water, soaked for eight hours, and cooked in the water in which they soaked until nearly tender—thirty to forty-five minutes.

Tongue, like all other organs of meat animals, was usually considered "gross meat" and not fit for elegant feasts. But it was regularly served at the Star Chamber Court dinners, and "A Breviate . . . of a Nobleman's House" lists among the year's essential provisions for such a household both "neatstongue dried" and "neatstounge greene [fresh]."

TO BAKE VENISON

Take leane Venison, and take out all the sinewes, then chop your flesh verie small, and season it with a little pepper and salt, and beaten Cloves, and a good handful of Fenel seeds, and mingle them all together. Then take your Larde, and cut it of the bignesse of a goose quill, and the length of your finger, and put it in a dish of Vinegar, & all to wash it therein. Then take meale as it doeth come from the mil, and make a paste with colde water, and see that it be very stiff; then take a sheet, and make a laying of the minced flesh upon the sheet, of the breadth that your Larde is of the length, then make a laying of your Larde upon your flesh, and let your Larde be one from another, the breadth of one of the peeces of the Larde, and so make foure layings of Larde, and three layings of flesh one upon another, so press it downe with your hands as hard as you can for breaking [without breaking] the paste and caste in a handful of Pepper and salt; & beaten Cloves, so close up your paste, & let it bake two houres.

John Partridge, *The good Huswifes Handmaide for the Kitchin*

THE WORKING VERSION:

1 pound boneless venison, cut up
2 slices lean bacon
4 slices Canadian bacon, sliced thin
½ cup red wine vinegar
¾ teaspoon salt
¼ teaspoon pepper
½ teaspoon ground fennel seed
1 pinch cloves

THE PASTRY
2 cups sifted unbleached flour
1 teaspoon salt
¾ cup cold butter
½ cup cold water (approximately)
1 egg, separated

Remove any sinews and fat from the venison and cut the meat into small chunks. Cut the bacon into small pieces and the Canadian bacon into ½-inch strips; cover and set aside until needed.

Marinate the venison and the bacon in the wine vinegar for two hours. Drain, but reserve the vinegar, and grind the venison and lean bacon. Reserve the Canadian bacon strips until needed.

Add the salt, pepper, fennel, cloves, and four tablespoons of the reserved wine vinegar to the ground meat and stir until blended. Cover and set aside while you make the pastry according to directions given on page 31.

Sprinkle your work surface with flour and turn the dough out onto it. Pat the dough into a rectangle, then roll it out to a sheet approximately twelve by sixteen inches. From the long end of the pastry sheet, cut out several small pastry deer with a cookie cutter or freehand.

Drape the pastry in a rectangular baking dish approximately nine inches by six inches. Divide the ground meat into three parts and the Canadian bacon strips into four parts. Arrange one part of the bacon strips over the center of the pastry and cover with a layer of ground meat. Continue layering the bacon and meat alternately. Brush the edges of the pastry with egg white and bring the two shorter sides up over the meat. Then bring the long sides of the pastry over the top and pinch the edges together to seal them.

Turn the pastry over quickly in the baking dish. Brush the top with egg white. Arrange the pastry deer over the top and brush them with egg white. Bake at 450° for twenty minutes, then lower the heat to 350° and bake twenty-five minutes longer. Serve hot or cold, but not refrigerated.

As the crust suggested by Partridge was coarse, his pasty was doubtless a large one meant to be eaten over a period of time. This pasty is meant to be eaten fresh, hence the pastry is flaky.

Partridge added that mutton could be used if venison was not available. Deer meat was not easily come by, so mutton and other less "noble" meat masqueraded as venison in many a pie and pasty of Partridge's and Shakespeare's day.

TO BUTTER ONIONS

Take apples and onions, mince the onions and slice the apples,
put them in a pot, but more apples than onions, and bake them
with the household bread, close up the pot with paste or paper;

when you use them, butter them with butter, sugar, and boild
currans, serve them on sippets, and scrape on sugar and cinnamon.

Robert May, *The Accomplisht Cook*

THE WORKING VERSION:

1 pound tart cooking apples	½ teaspoon cinnamon
1 medium-large white onion, minced or grated coarse	2 tablespoons currants, parboiled
3 tablespoons butter	2 slices buttered toast,
1 tablespoon brown sugar	quartered (optional)

Quarter, core, and peel the apples and slice them in ½-inch-thick slices.

In a small saucepan, simmer the onion with two tablespoons of the butter until transparent. Then stir in the sugar, cinnamon, and currants.

Arrange a layer of the apples in a casserole with a cover. Spoon a little of the onion mixture over them. Continue to alternate layers of apples and onions, finishing with a layer of apples. Dot the remaining tablespoon of butter over the top, cover the casserole, and bake at 375° until the apples are soft—about forty-five minutes. Serve hot, over buttered toast or not, as you please.

Those who did not like onions could always refuse them on the grounds that the dietaries warned against them as "engendering choler." And those who enjoyed them could quote Andrewe Boorde, who said that "they maketh a man's apetyde good, and putteth away fastydyousness [squeamishness]." Dr. Boorde added, "Yf a man drynke sondry drynkes it doth rectyfy and reform the varyete of the operation of them." But, he said, they did "provoke a man to veneryous actes, and to somnolence."

TO ROAST A BREAST OF VEAL

Raise up the skin side of your breast of Veal, almost to the end
of it, towards the belly, and likewise almost to the place the
shoulder was cut off; force it with sassage force-meat, good store

of Lard in it: but season it with Time, Wintersavoury and Parslee minced, as also with Cloves, Mace, Nutmeg, Salt and small Pepper; let it not be so hot in your mouth as Sassage-meat: mingle this in two eggs, and farce it between the skin and the Veal: and draw your breast all over with Time, and let your sauce be Butter, Vinegar, a little minced Time, and Nutmeg grated: garnish it with Lemmon, and send it up.

William Rabisha, *The whole Body of Cookery Dissected*

THE WORKING VERSION:

One 3½- to 4-pound breast of veal
1 pound mildly flavored pork sausage
1 egg
¼ cup minced parsley
½ teaspoon winter savory
1 teaspoon thyme
1 teaspoon salt
⅛ teaspoon each of pepper, cloves, mace, and nutmeg

1 tablespoon olive oil
1 lemon, sliced thin and seeded

THE SAUCE
1 tablespoon butter
½ cup white wine vinegar
¼ teaspoon thyme
⅛ teaspoon nutmeg

Ask your butcher to open a deep pocket in the breast of veal. Mix together until well blended the sausage, egg, parsley, savory, ½ teaspoon of the thyme, ½ teaspoon of the salt, the pepper, cloves, mace, and nutmeg. Fill the pocket with this mixture, spreading it evenly throughout the cavity. Sew up the opening with heavy white thread or lace it shut with steel lacing pins.

Stir the remaining salt and thyme into the olive oil and spread the seasoned oil over the outside of the veal. Roast at 325° for 1¾ to 2 hours.

To make the sauce, bring all the ingredients to a boil in a small saucepan, lower the heat to simmer, and cook for ten minutes. Slice the veal before removing the thread or the lacing needles. Arrange the slices on a warmed platter. Add whatever pan gravy there is to the sauce and pour it over the meat. Garnish with the sliced lemon and serve.

You can make your own sausage meat, if you wish, using Robert May's recipe for "sausages without skins" given on page

105. If you do, omit the egg, nutmeg, and half a teaspoon of salt from the stuffing mixture. Rabisha said nothing about basting the roast, but since veal has little fat in the skin, I used the seasoned olive oil to keep it from drying out. Veal was so highly esteemed that even a breast of veal was considered worthy of serving when James I and his retinue were entertained at Hoghton Towers.

A GRAND SALAD OF WATERCRESS

Being finely picked, washed, and laid in the middle of a clean dish, with slic't oranges and lemons finely carved one against the other, in partitions or round the dish, with some Alexander buds boiled or raw, currans, capers, oyle, and vinegar, sugar or none.

Robert May, *The Accomplisht Cook*

THE WORKING VERSION:

1 large bunch of crisp watercress	1 teaspoon brown sugar
1 large navel orange	½ teaspoon salt
1 large lemon	2 tablespoons currants, parboiled
4 tablespoons olive oil	2 tablespoons capers
5 tablespoons red wine vinegar	

Wash the watercress in cool water, and remove any wilted leaves and the coarse part of the stems. Roll the greens in a clean towel and refrigerate until needed.

Wash and dry the orange, slice off ¼-inch-wide strips of the skin, an inch apart lengthways, then slice the orange into thin slices. Peel the lemon down to the meat and, with a sharp knife, separate the sections whole. Remove the seeds and set aside with the oranges, covered, until needed.

Just before serving, blend the oil, vinegar, sugar, and salt in a shallow salad bowl, mix in the currants and capers and toss the greens in the dressing. Alternate slices of orange and sections of lemon around the sides of the bowl and serve.

Alexander buds came from an herb called black lovage. Lovage has a slightly bitter celery flavor and is probably impossible to find in shops, but seeds for planting are available from English seed companies. If you wish the celery flavoring, add two table-spoons of minced celery leaves to the greens.

You may find some weeds among the watercress; I usually do. But, as Nicholas Breton said, "Who loves to feede upon a Sallet dish, Among his Herbes some wicked weede may have."

RAVELED BREAD

Raveled is a kind of cheat bread also, but it retaineth more of the gross and less of the pure substance of the wheat.

William Harrison, *The Description of England*

THE WORKING VERSION:

1 cup soured cheate dough	1 tablespoon salt
1½ cups warm water	2 cups whole-wheat flour
2 cakes fresh yeast or	2 cups unbleached flour
2 tablespoons dry yeast	

Prepare the soured cheate dough two days ahead according to instructions given on page 77. Then follow the instructions for making fine cheate bread, given on page 77, to make raveled bread.

Wheat bread, said Thomas Cogan, ought to have five prop-erties: "First it must be well leavened, for bread without leaven is good for no man. . . . Next it ought to be light, for thereby it is known that the clamminess thereof is gone. Thirdly it ought to be well baked, for bread that is ill baked is of ill digestion, and sore grieveth the stomacke. Fourthly it must be temperately salted. . . . The fifth thing is that bread should be made of the best wheate."

Raveled bread, when it was purchased, would have been bought from a "browne-baker." Brown-bakers were limited by govern-ment statute to making breads of coarser flour and grains, as "white-bakers" were limited to making white breads and rolls.

In many places housewives could make up their own bread and

take it to a baker's shop to be baked for a small fee. One of the chores of the baker's apprentice might be to walk through the streets calling out that the baker's oven was hot and that whoever had bread to be baked should bring it immediately.

Some villages had public ovens where housewives could bring their bread to be baked, also for a modest charge. There may still have been, even in Shakespeare's day, some communities in which the only bake oven belonged to the lord of the manor, who charged a fee for its use. This was a vestige of feudal times, when one of the sources of income for the lord of the manor was the ownership of such an oven with the right to require all villagers in the manor to use it and pay him for its use.

BANBURY CAKE

To make a very good Banbury Cake, *take four pounds of Currants and wash and pick them very clean, and dry them in a cloth; then take three Eggs, and put away one yolk, and beat them, and strain them with Barm, putting thereto Cloves, Mace, Cinamon, and Nutmeggs, then take a pint of Cream, and as much mornings milk, and set it on the fire till the cold be taken away; then take Flower, and put in good store of cold butter and sugar; then put in your eggs, barm, and meal, and work them all together an hour or more; then save a part of the paste, and the rest break in pieces, and work in your Currants; which done, mould your Cake of whatever quantity you please, and then with that paste which hath not any Currants, cover it very thin, both underneath, and aloft. And so bake it according to bigness.*

Gervase Markham, *The English Hus-wife*

THE WORKING VERSION:

2 cups sifted unbleached flour	1 cake of fresh yeast
½ teaspoon cinnamon	½ cup sugar
¼ teaspoon mace	2 egg yolks
¼ teaspoon cloves	¾ cup light cream
¼ teaspoon nutmeg	½ cup currants, parboiled
½ cup cold butter	

Sift together the flour and the spices. Add the butter and work it into the flour until it is like fine meal. In a large mixing bowl, mash the yeast into two tablespoons of the sugar until it liquefies. Add the egg yolks, cream, and the rest of the sugar, and beat until blended. Stir the flour, butter, and spice mixture into the liquid mixture, then spoon the dough up against the side of the bowl, turn it over, and let it drop back into the bowl, giving the bowl a quarter turn after each spoonful is raised (this is called spoon-kneading). Five minutes is sufficient time to knead the dough. Cover the bowl and set it in a warm place to rise until the dough has doubled in size—forty-five minutes to one hour.

When the rising is completed, generously butter a nine- or ten-inch cake pan. Stir down the dough, spread a thin layer of it in the pan, and set aside enough of the remaining dough to make a thin top layer. Add the currants to the dough still remaining in the bowl and spread this evenly over the dough in the pan, then cover this layer with the dough that had been set aside. Set it to rise until the dough has almost reached the top of the pan— about ½ hour.

Bake at 400° for ten minutes, then lower the heat to 350° and bake twenty-five minutes longer—if the cake seems to be browning too fast, cover it with a piece of clean brown paper or kitchen parchment. Cool in the pan for five minutes, then carefully turn it out onto a wire grille to finish cooling. This is a delicate cake and breaks easily.

Later recipes for Banbury cakes were quite different. They were usually made from a rich yeast sponge dough into which candied fruits as well as currants were mixed, and spoonfuls of this were then sealed into pastry or puff-pastry cases to be baked. Markham's is the only recipe for Banbury cake I found in the cookbooks of the period, although Banbury was already famous for its cakes by Elizabethan days. The Shuttleworth accounts for 1612 note that a servant was given thirty shillings—a large amount—to purchase Banbury cakes, probably for some festive occasion. Ben Jonson also mentions them with evident appreciation.

TO MAKE A TART OF PRUNES

Take prunes and set them upon a chafer wyth a little red wyne and putte thereto a manshet, and let them boyle together, then drawe them thorowe a streyner with the yolkes of four egges and season it up wyth suger and so bake it.

Anonymous, *A Proper newe Booke of Cokerye*

THE WORKING VERSION:

1½ pounds Italian plums	**THE PASTRY**
1 slice manchet, crumbed	2 cups sifted unbleached flour
¼ cup red wine	1 teaspoon salt
3 tablespoons butter	¾ cup cold butter
½ teaspoon cinnamon	½ cup cold water (approximately)
½ teaspoon ginger	1 egg, separated
½ cup brown sugar	
¼ cup sugar	
2 egg yolks	

Wash, pit, and quarter the plums. Put them into a saucepan with the bread crumbs, wine, cinnamon, ginger, and one tablespoon of the butter, and simmer until the fruit is very soft—about twenty minutes. Purée the mixture and add the sugars and the egg yolks and beat until blended. Cover and set aside while you make the pastry for the crust according to the directions on page 31.

Divide the dough into two parts, the piece for the bottom crust a little larger than that for the top crust. On a floured work surface roll out the larger piece to fit an eight-inch pie pan and fit it into the pan. Then roll out the top crust.

Spoon the filling evenly into the pan and dot with the remaining two tablespoons of butter. Cover with the top crust and seal the edges with the tines of a wet fork. Slice off the surplus pastry and punch fork holes into the top. Brush the pie with the egg white and bake at 450° for twenty minutes, then lower the heat to 350° and bake twenty minutes longer. Serve slightly warm.

From the same book's recipe for a damson plum tart, I borrowed the use of butter to give the pie additional flavor. Cinnamon and ginger were the spices used in other recipes to flavor fruit pies, so I used them also.

A fruit tart was traditionally part of the second course of a meal, as a custard was of the first course. Not only do cookbook bills of fare follow this rule, but menus given in household accounts do too.

Tarts were also made from dried fruits, and this pie can be made from dried Italian prunes soaked overnight in warm water. They do not, however, make as tasty a pie as the fresh prunes. Not all fruit pies and tarts were double-crust ones. Uncooked fruits or berries were often seasoned, sweetened, and spread in baked shells for serving. "Laid tarts" were sheets of baked rich pastry or puff pastry on which either fresh or preserved fruits were arranged in various designs. Eggs and bread crumbs were often used, separately or together, to thicken fruit mixtures for pies.

England produced large quantities of cheeses, many of them excellent, but the English also ate large quantities of foreign, especially Dutch, cheeses. Lord North, for example, preparing for the impending visit of Queen Elizabeth and her retinue, purchased six "holland Cheeses"—a total of approximately seventy pounds.

FEASTS AND FEASTING

Having pointed out the advantages of moderation, the old man in Nicholas Breton's *An Olde Man's Lesson: and a Young Man's Love* tells his son, "Without offense, I thinke I may say, that Feasts are as necessarie as fasts: for as the one doth pull downe the flesh from rebelling against the Spirit, so doth the other give the Spirit more life in rejoycing upon a just cause of joy . . . a little too much is better than much too little; furthermore the varieties of meates and drinkes, as Ale, Beere, Wine, Sugar and Spices, are the better knowne, wherein God is Glorified and praised for his blessings, and the Vintner, the Grocer, the Comfitmaker, the Cooke, the Brewer and the Butcher, doe by the venting [selling] of their wares the better maintain their trades: so that

I thinke I may well say, that monye in the provision of Feasts and banquets, is to be employed as a servant of necessitie."

A nice rationalization, but few Englishmen felt the need for such a rationalization. If a feast was in the offing, they enjoyed the prospect, and when it was in being, they made the most of it.

True, those with strong Low Church Protestant views made dour comments about feasting, but they also made dour comments about the fast days in the Church calendar. Of the official Church festival days, Christmas was clearly the most important. Christmas festivities continued through Twelfth-day, with New Year's as the day on which most people exchanged gifts. But New Year's was not considered a holy day, and if it chanced to fall on a Friday, it was a fast day, whereas Christmas was a feast day regardless of the day on which it fell.

"Prepare for mirth, for mirth becomes a feast," Simonides says in *Pericles* (Act II, Scene 3). And genial Thomas Tusser expresses the countryman's feelings about Christmas:

> At Christmas we banquet the rich with the poor,
> Who then, but the miser, but openeth his door:
>
> . . . .
>
> Good husband and huswife, now chiefly be glad
> Things handsome to have, as they ought to be had.
> They both do provide, against Christmas do come,
> To welcome good neighbour, good cheer to have some.
>
> Good bread and good drink, a good fire in the hall
> Brawn, pudding, and souse, and good mustard withall.
> Beef, mutton, and pork, shred pies of the best,
> Pig, veal, goose, and capon, and turkey well drest,
> Cheese, apples and nuts, joly carols to hear,
> As then in the country is counted good cheer.

Christenings, engagements, weddings, even funerals were all occasions for feasting. And rural communities added feasts to celebrate important farming events. These Tusser calls "feasts of the plough": Plough Monday, the Monday after Twelfth-night, when the ploughing started; sowing the wheat; shearing the sheep; and bringing in the harvest were all celebrated with feasting. To the farm housewife, Tusser says:

> Good huswives whom God hath enriched enough,
> forget not the feasts that belong to the Plough,

Gentlemen feasting (old print, circa 1600)

The meaning is onely to joy and be glad,
  for comfort with labor should sometimes be had.

Tusser then enumerates the farm events that the housewife
must be ready to help celebrate:

Wife, sometime this weeke if that all things go cleare,
an end of wheat sowing we make for this yeare,
Remember you therefore though I do it not
the Seede Cake, the Pasties, and Furmenty pot.

At sheep-shearing time, Tusser says,

Wife make us a feast, spare fleshe neither corne,
make wafers and cakes, for our shepe must be shorne.
At sheep shearing neighbours no other thing crave
but good cheer and welcome like neighbours to have.

If the harvest was that of the lord of the manor, he was expected to offer a feast to the harvesters. Robert Herrick describes
the gaiety of such an occasion:

Well, on brave boyes, to your Lords Hearth,
Glittering with fire; where, for your mirth,
Ye shall see first the large and cheefe

Foundation of your Feast, Fat Beefe:
With Upper Stories, Mutton, Veale,
And Bacon, Pork (which makes full the meale)
With sev'rall dishes standing by,
As here a Custard, there a Pie,
And here all tempting Frumentie.
And for to make the merry cheere,
If smirking [sparkling] Wine be wanting here,
There's that, which drowns all care, stout Beere;
Which freely drink to your Lords health.

There were also the traditional feast days kept by the various artisans' guilds and by the great merchant guilds. Of the London merchants' feasts Harrison writes: "At such time as the merchants do make their ordinary feasts [officially required by the rules of the guild] or voluntary [private feasts], it is a world to see what great provision is made of all manner of delicate meats from every quarter of the country, wherein, beside that they are often comparable herein to the nobility of the land, they will seldom regard anything that the butcher usually killeth, but reject the same as not worthy to come in place. In such cases also [for the banquet part of the feast or special banquets of sweet meats] geliffes [jellies] of all colors, mixed with a variety in the representation of sundry flowers, herbs, trees, forms of beasts, fish, fowls, and fruits, and thereunto marchpane wrought with no small curiosity [imagination], tarts of divers hues and sundry denominations [kinds], conserves of old fruits, foreign and home-bred suckets, codiniacs [quince marmalades], marmalades . . . sugarbread [small cakes], gingerbread, florentines [pies], wild fowl, venison of all sorts, and sundry outlandish [foreign] confections, altogether seasoned with sugar . . . do generally bear the sway."

The guilds of city artisans—tailors, shoemakers, carpenters, cooks, bakers, butchers—were more modest in their feasts than were the merchant guilds. Whatever the master artisans had, the journeymen and apprentices were happy with simpler fare. Their ideas of what would constitute a great feast were likely to correspond with those of Firk, in Thomas Dekker's comedy *The Shoemakers' Holiday,* of 1599. Simon Eyre, a happy-go-lucky master shoemaker, finds himself elected mayor of London and announces he will feast all the apprentices of London at a breakfast. His journeyman, Firk, is delighted with the prospect and envisions the feast: "There's cheer for the heav'ns," he exclaims, "venison-pasties walk up and down piping hot, like sergeants; beef and brewes [slices of bread in broth] comes marching in dry-vats [barrels], fritters and pancakes come trowling in wheel-barrows: hens and oranges hopping in porter's baskets, collops and eggs in scuttles, and tarts and custards comes quaverying in malt-shovels."

Commencements at the two universities were also occasions for feasting. John Chamberlain reports on one in October, 1602: "The commencement at Oxford was very famous for plentie of Doctors . . . for store of venison whereof Doctor Kinge had 27 bucks for his part; for royal cheer . . . the exceeding as-semblie of gentles, but especially for the great confluence of cut-purses."

Christmas-day activities at the Inner Temple, one of the Lon-don Inns of Court, where young men, generally of noble or gentle parentage, went to study law, followed a traditional pattern. In 1561 the rules read: "Service in the Church ended, the Gentle-men presently [immediately] repair into the Hall to breakfast, with [on] brawn, mustard, and malmsey.

"At dinner, the Butler, appointed for the Grand Christmas, is to see the tables covered and furnished and the Ordinary Butlers of the House are decently to set bread, napkins, and trenchers, in good form, at every table; with spoones and knives. At the first course is served in a fair and large bore's-head, upon a silver platter with [accompanied by] the minstralsye [music]. Two Gentlemen in gownes are to attend at supper, and to bear two fair torches of wax, next before the Musicians and Trumpetters, and stand . . . with the musick, till the first course be served in through the Hall. Which performed, they with the musick [musicians], are to return to the buttery."

Feasting at country weddings for the daughters of wealthy gentry families and rich yeoman farmers could be costly. Various household accounts record lavish preparations and extended festivities. When Sir William Petre married off his stepdaughter, close to four hundred guests came and stayed for at least two days. To take charge of the food preparations, Sir William brought down to Ingatestone from London a master cook and four undercooks. But even these and the Ingatestone cooks to-gether were apparently insufficient to meet all needs because the

Silver-gilt pepper pots (1581)

accounts for the wedding show that Wilcocks, the master cook, paid out five shillings "for baking a conger [eel]," and that a hundred "marchpane breads" were bought.

When important feasts were being planned, friends and neighbors often helped out, not only with gifts of food but also with the occasional loan of a cook or other servants. Among less wealthy families, friends would often bring a prepared dish for the wedding feast or would provide some of the drinks.

James I, like Queen Elizabeth before him, was extravagant and spent vast sums of money on feasts and entertainment. But James preferred drinking to feasting, and Elizabeth was an abstemious eater. James's physician, Mayerne, said of him, "He was temperate in eating being rather indifferent to food but ate what he pleased, roast meats with no bread, and great quantities of fruit of which he was very fond. . . . In drinking His Majesty errs as to quality, quantity, frequency, time and order."

Funeral feasts, although they did not last as long as wedding feasts, could also be lavish. But lavish funerals sometimes provided food and drink for many poor people. Between three and four thousand of the poor, it was said, fed on the leavings of the funeral feast of the Earl of Rutland in 1587.

Sir Thomas Ramsey, a member of the Grocers' Company, provided in his will for two feasts the day of his funeral. One was to be held at the Grocers' Hall for the warden and wealthier members of the Grocers' Company; the other at his home, to which were to be invited "the Lorde Mayor and all my brethren the alderman and their wyves my deputie and his wife and all my neighboures and such other as my executor shall thinke good."

Wakes were originally parts of funeral or church functions. The meaning of the word had expanded to include parties and fair-going. Robert Herrick uses the word to indicate the entertainment and feasting at fairs to which country folk flocked:

> Come Anthea let us two
> Go to Feast, as others do.
> Tarts and Custards, Creams and Cakes,
> Are the Junketts [sweetmeats] still at Wakes.

Shrove Tuesday was the day when everyone who could feasted to prepare himself for the long period when "Jack-a-Lent" would be master of his diet. Any fresh meat that still remained in the larder had to be eaten or cut into collops [slices], salted, and put away to purify the house for Lent. In *Jacke-a-Lent,* which John Taylor dedicates to the fishmongers and the butchers, he says, "Always before *Lent* there comes waddling a fat gross butsten-gutted groom, called *Shrove Tuesday,* whose manners show that he is better fed than taught: and indeed he is the only monster for feeding amongst all the days of the year, for he devours more flesh in fourteen hours, than this whole kingdome doth (or at least should do) in six weeks after. . . . Moreover, it is a goodly sight to see how the cooks in great men's kitchens . . . are that day . . . monarchs of the marrow-bones, marquesses of the mutton, lords high regents of the spit and kettle, barons of the gridiron, and the sole commanders of the frying pan, and all this if for no other purpose but to stop the mouth of this land-wheel *Shrove-Tuesday."*

Good Friday was the day when "Flesh and Fish must be banished all stomackes, strong and weak," Nicholas Breton wrote. But for the butchers, it was the day they "happily wash their Boords, make cleane their Aprons, sharpen their knives . . . and cut out their meat for the Easter eve market: Now must the Poulters make ready their Rabbets and Fowles, the Cookes have their ovens cleane, and all for Pies and Tarts against the merry Feast."

When Jack-a-Lent was turned out of doors [that is, when Lent ended], "the Fishermen . . . turn up their nets to dry, while the Calfe and the Lambe walke toward the Kitchen and the Pastry: the velvet heads [deer] of the Forrests fall at the loose of the Crosse-bow; the Sammon Trowt playes with the Fly, and the March Rabbit runnes dead into the dish: The Indian commodities [spices from the East Indies] pay the Merchants adventure [repay the investments in voyages]; and Barbary sugar puts Honey out of Countenance . . . and he that hath money, will be no meane man in his mansion."

The "Progresses" of Queen Elizabeth and James I through the realm invariably brought upheavals to the great halls and kitchens, as well as to the purses of their hosts. The royal servants did help out in the hosts' kitchens—and were of course tipped for their services—but even with such extra aid, additional cooks often had to be hired. When Elizabeth visited Lord North in 1577, he paid out "21 pounds to ye cookes of London." Even his enormous household did not possess enough tableware to cope with all the guests; one of the items in the accounts for that visit was "20 shillings for the Hyering of Pewter vessell."

The problems of entertaining royalty were understandably a source of many tales. One, told about Colonel Richard Shuttleworth, then sheriff of Lancashire, said that when the colonel heard, in the summer of 1617, that King James was coming to Barton to pay him a visit, he burned down his house to save himself the greater financial losses of having to entertain the king. The house did burn down about that time, but the tale is doubtless apocryphal.

A Repast for Viola

I will bespeak our diet,
Whiles you beguile the time and feed your knowledge.
Twelfth Night, Act III, Scene 3 (*Antonio*)

SHERRY

It illumineth the face, which, as a beacon, gives warning to
all the rest of this little kingdom, man, to arm; and then the
vital commoners and inland petty spirits muster me all to their
captain, the heart, who, great and puffed up with this retinue,
doth any deed of courage; and this valour comes of sherris.
Henry IV, Part II, Act IV, Scene 3 (*Falstaff*)

A SALAD OF BABY CARROTS

Like madness is the glory of this life,
As this pomp shows to a little oil and root.
Timon of Athens, Act I, Scene 2 (*Apemantus*)

PICKLED OYSTERS

I have been in such a pickle since I saw you last
that, I fear me, will never out of my bones.
The Tempest, Act V, Scene 1 (*Trinculo*)

STEWED CARP

Pray you, sir, use the carp as you may.
All's Well That Ends Well, Act V, Scene 2 (*Clown*)

A "VENISON" PIE OF A FILLET OF BEEF

A borrow'd title hast thou bought too dear.
Henry IV, Part I, Act V, Scene 3 (Douglas)

AN OAT PUDDING

I cannot draw a cart nor eat dried oats;
If it be man's work I will do it.
King Lear, Act V, Scene 3 (Officer)

A CHICKEN STEWED IN WINE AND GINGER SAUCE

She's e'en setting on water to scald such chickens as you are.
Timon of Athens, Act II, Scene 2 (Fool)

SPICED SPINACH

How green you are and fresh in this old world!
King John, Act III, Scene 4 (Pandulph)

BROWN BREAD AND ROBERT MAY'S FRENCH BREAD

Good morrow, gallants! Want ye corn for bread?
Henry VI, Part I, Act III, Scene 2 (Joan of Arc)

CLARET

I charge and command that, of the city's cost, the
pissing-conduit run nothing but claret wine.
Henry VI, Part II, Act IV, Scene 6 (Jack Cade)

ALE

And thereof comes the proverb, 'Blessing of your heart,
you brew good ale.'
Two Gentlemen of Verona, Act III, Scene 1 (Launce)

GOOSEBERRY CREAM

Virtue is of so little regard in these costermonger times
that true valour is turned bear-herd . . . all the other gifts
appertinent to man, as the malice of this age shapes them,
are not worth a gooseberry.
Henry IV, Part II, Act I, Scene 2 (Falstaff)

JOHN MURRELL'S SHREWSBURY CAKES

For these good deserts,
We here create you Earl of Shrewsbury.
> *Henry VI, Part I, Act III, Scene 4 (Henry)*

APPLES AND CHEESE

I will make an end of my dinner; there's pippins and
seese to come.
> *The Merry Wives of Windsor, Act I, Scene 2 (Evans)*

Welcome ever smiles,
And farewell goes out sighing.
> *Troilus and Cressida, Act III, Scene 2 (Ulysses)*

A CARROT SALLAD

Carrets boyled and eaten with vinegar, Oyle, and Pepper serve
for a special good sallad to stirre up appetite, and to purifie
blood.

William Vaughan, *Directions for Health*

THE WORKING VERSION:

1 pound baby carrots, each about 3 inches long	½ cup white wine vinegar
3 cups water	4 tablespoons salad oil
½ teaspoon salt	¼ teaspoon white pepper
¼ teaspoon chervil	1 large sprig parsley

Scrub the carrots under cold water and cut off the greenery.
Bring the water, salt, and chervil to a boil in a saucepan. Add the
carrots, cover the pot, and cook until the carrots are tender but
still crisp—about ten minutes.

In a deep bowl mix together the vinegar, oil, and pepper. Drain the carrots, add them to the dressing, and stir them about until they are nicely coated. Cover the bowl and marinate the carrots in the dressing for at least an hour.

Wash the parsley in cold water, shake off the moisture, and snip off the stems. Make a rosette of the leaves in the center of a dinner plate, arrange the carrots around the parsley like a sunburst, and pour a little of the dressing over the carrots.

If you cannot find baby carrots, which have a delicacy never found in the mature vegetable, buy the long, thin carrots, and cut them into three-inch lengths after washing them. These, however, may need scraping.

The salad can be served as a first-dish appetizer at table or with the sherry before dinner. The carrots will stay crisp for four or five days without refrigeration if kept in a jar with the top screwed on tight. Cover the jar with plastic before screwing on the top or the vinegar will corrode the metal and cause bits of it to fall into the carrots.

Parsley was also considered a salad herb and was eaten raw, usually mixed with other greens or vegetables. Sir Francis Bacon, in *Sylva Sylvarum,* said that parsley, sage, and parsnips were good to eat only after they had been "boyled or passed through the fire, but being young are eaten raw." Queen Elizabeth seems to have enjoyed eating stewed parsley.

Vaughan called parsley one of the temperate herbs: "No garden hearb comes neere unto Parsley, as well for toothsomeness as for health, and eaten in sallads with Endive and Lettice in summer . . . cooles the stomacke and keepes the head in good plight."

HOW TO BARREL UP OYSTERS, SO AS THEY SHALL LAST FOR SIX MONETHS SWEET AND GOOD, AND IN THEIR NATURALL TASTE

Open your oisters, take the liquor of them, and mixe a reasonable proportion of the best white wine vinegar you can get, a little salt and some pepper, barrell the fish up in small caske, covering all the Oysters in this pickle.

Sir Hugh Plat, *Delightes for Ladies*

THE WORKING VERSION:

1 cup white wine vinegar	1 pint medium-size fresh-
1 teaspoon peppercorns	shucked oysters
¼ teaspoon salt	2 medium white onions,
	peeled and sliced thin

Add the vinegar, peppercorns, and salt to the oyster liquor and stir until the salt dissolves. Add the oysters and stir gently until they are coated with the marinade. Cover the bowl with a plastic bowl cover and refrigerate for twenty-four hours.

Serve the oysters on a bed of sliced onions with a little of the pickling liquid poured over them.

Thin slices of brown bread spread with unsalted butter best bring out the flavor of these oysters.

Not only were oysters prepared according to this recipe good over a long period of time, said Plat, but they were "an excellent meanes to convey Oysters unto drie townes, or to carry them in long voyages."

"We eat our oysters, standing at a side-board, a little before dinner, unsanctified without grace," said John Taylor, and, he added, with his customary exuberance, "after it is eaten, it must be well liquored with two or three rouses [full glasses] of sherry or canary sack." In many well-to-do homes oyster tables were part of the kitchen equipment. In some homes an oyster table stood in the entrance room of the house and the oysters were eaten there.

In Pierre Erondell's French-English conversation manual, *The French Garden,* Lady Ri-Millaine, who is entertaining friends at dinner, offers her guests oysters before they go in to the meal. "Set the round table in the midst of the chamber," she orders a servant, "and goe fetch some browne bread . . . sawcers and vinegar, with onyons and pepper." A practical lady, she tells her guests, "Go too, let us wash handes, but let us have our Oysters first, for we should be forced to wash again." When one of her guests refuses the oysters, Lady Ri-Millaine remembers that it is midsummer and says, "Then I will none . . . for indeed it is too hot to eat of them, we are yet in the Dog dayes, when it is naught to eate meates over hotte, and the Physitians holde, that there is nothing hotter than shell-Fish."

HOW TO STEW A CARP

Open your Carp and wash it very cleane with a cloth, all the blood out; doe not scale it . . . but put it into a flat pan, or pipkin; there are things purposely to stew fish in; and put to it a pinte of white Wine, Mace, Ginger, Salt, Vinegar, Oyster-liquor, and sweet Herbs; and when the Carpe is stewed, take some of the liquor and beat it up thick with the yolke of an Egge well beaten, and a piece of Butter, then heat your dish wherein you serve up your Carp, and rub it with a clove of Garlicke; put minced Lemmon in your sauce; dish your Carp with two or three tosts of white Bread in the dish; sippet it, and serve it up with what garnish you please.

Joseph Cooper, *The Art of Cookery Refin'd and Augmented*

THE WORKING VERSION:

One 2-pound piece of fresh
    carp
  2 cups dry white wine
  ½ cup vinegar
  ½ cup oyster liquor or clam
    juice
  1 large sprig of parsley
  1 bay leaf
  1 clove of garlic, peeled

  2 teaspoons salt
  1 large piece whole mace
  ⅛ teaspoon ginger
  ¼ lemon
  3 tablespoons butter
  2 egg yolks
  3 slices buttered toast,
    quartered

Wash the carp under cold running water. In a large saucepan bring to a boil the wine, vinegar, oyster liquor or clam juice, parsley, bay leaf, garlic, salt, mace, and ginger. Lower the fish into the pot, cover it, and simmer until the carp is tender—from fifteen to twenty-five minutes, depending on the thickness of the piece of fish.

Remove the meat of the lemon and dice it. Strain one cup of the cooking liquid, heat it to the boiling point in a small saucepan, and stir in the butter until it melts. Remove the pan from the heat and beat in the egg yolks. Lower the heat to simmer and return the pan to the heat. Stir the sauce until it begins to thicken, then stir in the diced lemon. Keep the sauce warm over boiling water until needed.

Put the fish on a large flat plate or a cutting board and peel the skin from the top of the fish. Slice the meat down to the bone and remove the slices to a heated dish. Lift off the spinal bone and slice the rest of the fish. Place half the toast in a warmed serving dish and arrange the slices of fish over it. Pour the sauce over the fish, garnish the dish with the rest of the toast, and serve.

I skinned the carp for serving because it is both easier to serve and more attractive when skinned.

Carp was more appreciated in Shakespeare's time than it is today, and it is sometimes difficult to find in American fish markets, except in cities that have a sizable group of people of European background. In the sixteenth and seventeenth centuries, carp was likely to be found on most fish-day menus, whether stewed, boiled, pickled, or made into pies, including minced meat pies—more accurately, perhaps, minced fish pies. But it also appeared on flesh-day bills of fare. It was always on the fish-day menus for the judges of the Star Chamber, and it was regularly served at court but only occasionally to the queen.

The perishability of fish and the poor state of English roads meant that only towns situated on or near the sea, rivers, lakes, or ponds could have fresh fish more or less regularly. England's rivers and lakes were still well stocked at that time and were regularly fished. The city of Cambridge, said William Harrison, "was excellently well served with fresh-water fish . . . by reason of the river [Cam] that passeth thereby."

The fresh-water fish served most frequently at the table of the earl of Rutland were carp, pike, tench, and bream. Since none of these was listed among the fish purchased, they probably came from the estate stew ponds or from rivers on the earl's land. There were carp ponds also on the royal lands in Southwark, at Stains near Windsor, and in Cambridge. These, however, were apparently not adequate to supply all the requirements of the royal household, for carp is listed among the fish regularly purchased by the royal purveyors [purchasers].

The dietaries, which generally took a dim view of fish as food, recognized the facts of life in England and offered their readers advice on how at least to be on the safe side with the fish they ate.

They were unanimous in the opinion that fish from running water were preferable to those from stew ponds and convinced that they had "greater store of victual" in them, as Vaughan put it. He recommended that fish in stew ponds be given special foods to enhance their nutritiousness and to keep them healthy: "Sometimes . . . cast upon the pooles and ponds, the fresh leaves of Parsley, for those leaves doe rejoyce and refresh the fishes that are sick." Carp he recommended as the most wholesome of all fish, but, he added, "this note I give unto all such as feede on fish, that they drinke a draft of Claret-wine after their fish. But let sicke persons temper their appetite as much as they can from both."

TO BAKE FILLETS OF BEEF OR CLODS, INSTEAD OF RED DEER

First take your Beefe and Larde it verie thicke, and then season it with Pepper and Salt, Sinamome and Ginger, Cloves and Mace good store, with a great deale more quantitie of Pepper and Salt, then you would a peece of Venison, and put it in covered Paste, and when it is baked, take vinegar and suger, Sinamom and Ginger, and put in, and shake the Pastrie, and stop it close, and let it stand almost a fortnight before you cut it up.

Thomas Dawson, *The good huswifes Jewell*

THE WORKING VERSION:

One 2-pound piece of beef tenderloin or boned rib roast
3 slices lean bacon
2 teaspoons salt
¼ teaspoon pepper
¼ teaspoon cinnamon
¼ teaspoon mace
⅛ teaspoon cloves
¾ cup red wine vinegar

2 teaspoons brown sugar

THE PASTRY
2 cups sifted unbleached flour
1 teaspoon salt
¾ cup cold butter
½ cup beer (approximately)
1 egg, separated

Remove any fat or gristle from the meat and, with the point of a sharp knife, slash cuts the width of the bacon through the meat about two inches apart. Weave the slices of bacon through the cuts.

In a bowl just large enough to hold the meat, make a marinade of the rest of the ingredients. Put the meat into the marinade and press it down so that it is covered by the marinade. Cover the bowl and marinate the beef for twenty-four hours, turning it several times during this period.

Make the pastry according to directions given on page 31. Turn the dough out on a floured surface and roll it out to a rectangular sheet large enough to envelop the meat with a small overlap. Drape the pastry over a rectangular oven-to-table baking dish.

Drain the meat from the marinade, reserving the marinade for the sauce. Place the meat in the center of the pastry and bring the two short sides up over it. Brush the edges of the pastry with egg white, then bring the two long sides up over these. Pinch the edges together to seal the pie, then turn it over in the dish and brush the top with egg white.

If you have extra pastry dough, roll it out and cut small deer figures from it with a cookie cutter or freehand. Arrange these over the pie and brush them with egg white. Bake at 450° for twenty minutes, then lower the heat to 350° and bake twenty minutes longer.

Strain the reserved marinade and bring ½ cup of it to a boil in a small saucepan. Lower the heat to simmer and cook until about ¼ cup of sauce remains—ten to fifteen minutes. When you take the pie from the oven, make a small opening in the top crust and pour the sauce slowly through a small funnel into the pie. Tilt the dish back and forth gently to distribute the sauce and serve hot or cold, but not refrigerated.

This pie is best eaten fresh.

Many cookbooks offered recipes for making venison pies from other meats. The readers were always assured that the meat would be indistinguishable from venison. One of the cook's problems in counterfeiting venison was the color—venison has a slight bluish tinge. To give the substitute meats the desired bluish tinge, turnsole, a coloring obtained from heliotrope flowers, was added to the marinating liquid. Gervase Markham's recipe for "venison" pies made from beef or mutton says that the meat should be parboiled and marinated in the same sort of marinade used for venison, to which a little turnsole has been added. If the meat is given this treatment, he assures his readers, "A very good judgment shall not be able to say otherwise, then that it is of it self perfect Venison, both in taste, Colour, and the manner of cutting."

Robert May said that the venison color could be counterfeited in beef and mutton by parboiling the meat in a mixture of weak beer and vinegar with a little turnsole in it and steeping the meat in the mixture overnight. He was equally positive that "a good judgement shall not discern it from red or fallow deer." To give lamb, mutton, or kid the bluish tinge, it was sometimes soaked in fresh animal blood. The seasonings were always the conventional ones used for venison.

OATMEAL PUDDINGS OTHERWISE [THAN] OF FISH OR BLOOD

Take a quart of whole oatmeal, steep it in warm milk over night, and then drain the groats from it, boil them in a quart or three pints of good cream; then the oatmeal being boild and cold, have tyme, penniroyal, parsleys, spinage, savory, endive, marjoram, sorrel, succory, and strawberry leaves, of each a little quantity, chop them fine, and put them to the oatmeal, with some fennil-seed, pepper, cloves, mace, and salt, boil it in a napkin, or bake it in a dish, pie, or guts.

Sometimes of the former pudding you may leave out some of the herbs, and add these, penniroyal, savory, leeks, a good big onion, sage, ginger, nutmeg, pepper, salt, either for fish or flesh days, with butter or beef suet, boild or baked in a dish, napkin, or pye.

Robert May, *The Accomplisht Cook*

THE WORKING VERSION:

1 cup whole-grain oats	⅛ teaspoon pepper
2 cups milk	¼ teaspoon pennyroyal, or
1¼ cups light cream	any other mint
2 tablespoons butter	¼ teaspoon savory
1 leek, white part only, well	¼ teaspoon sage
washed and minced	⅛ teaspoon ginger
1 small onion, minced	¼ teaspoon nutmeg
½ teaspoon salt	

Rinse the oats under cold running water and drain. Heat the milk to just below boiling. Add the oats, cover the pot, and steep, off the heat, for four hours.

Drain off the milk, add the cream, cover and cook in the top of a double boiler, over simmering water, until the oats are tender but have not split—from forty minutes to an hour. Stir in the butter until it melts. Cover the pot and set aside until needed.

About ½ hour before you plan to serve, stir in all the rest of the ingredients. Butter a shallow baking dish and spread the oat mixture evenly in it. Bake in a 325° oven for fifteen to twenty minutes and serve hot.

Whole grains are perishable and should be stored in tightly closed jars in the refrigerator.

Most oat-pudding recipes are for blood puddings, that is, puddings in which animal blood was the liquid ingredient. Black puddings were ordinarily blood puddings, although the recipe in *The Good Hous-wives Treasurie* entitled "How to make blacke Puddings" uses milk instead: "Take Otmeale and steepe it in sodden Milke, then take Hogges suet & good hearbes and chop them small, then put in Fennell seed, pepper and Salt." The rest is left to the cook's discretion. Nutmeg, mace, cinnamon, salt, and pepper were the usual seasonings for oat puddings, with currants and sugar occasionally added.

Shakespeare mentions puddings in eight of his plays, usually in a humorous context. Falstaff, with his great belly, is a perfect butt for such humor. In *The Merry Wives of Windsor* (Act II, Scene 1), Mistress Page, indignant at Falstaff's love letter to her, explodes, "How shall I be revenged on him? for revenged I will be, as sure as his guts are made of puddings."

In *Henry V* (Act II, Scene 1), however, the word is a last jest in a sad and affectionate farewell to a friend. Falstaff's page has come to the Boar's Head Tavern seeking help for his dying master. Mistress Quickly, when she hears the news, says, "By my troth, he'll yield the crow a pudding one of these days. The king has killed his heart."

TO FRIE CHICKINS

Take your Chickins and let them boyle in verie good sweet broath a pretie while, and take the Chickens out & quarter them in peeces, and then put them into a frying pan with sweete Butter, and let them stewe in the pan, but you must not let them be browne with frying, and then put out the butter out of the pan, and then take a little sweet broath and as much vergice, and the yolkes of 2 egges, and beat them together, and put in a little Nutmegges, Synamon and Ginger, and Pepper into the sauce, and then put them all into the pan to the Chickens, and stirre them together in the pan, and put them into a dish and serve them up.

Thomas Dawson, *The good huswifes Jewell*

THE WORKING VERSION:

One 3- to 3½-pound frying chicken	½ cup white wine vinegar
2 cups water	⅛ teaspoon nutmeg
2 teaspoons salt	⅛ teaspoon cinnamon
¼ teaspoon pepper	⅛ teaspoon ginger
3 tablespoons butter	2 egg yolks

Have the chickens cut up for frying. Use the back, wing tips, neck, and giblets to make a poaching broth by pressure-cooking them in two cups of water for forty-five minutes, or increase the amount of water to 2½ cups and simmer them in a tightly covered saucepan for two to three hours. Strain the broth into a saucepan just large enough to hold the chicken and the broth comfortably.

Add the salt, pepper, and pieces of chicken. Cover the pot and simmer until the chicken is tender—from forty-five minutes to one hour. Melt the butter in a large skillet, arrange the pieces of chicken in it so that they do not overlap, and brown them on both sides.

Put ¾ cup of the poaching broth, the vinegar, and the rest of the seasonings into a small saucepan and bring to a boil. Lower the heat to simmer and cook for ten minutes. Remove the saucepan from the heat, beat in the egg yolks, then return the pan to the heat and cook, stirring constantly, until the sauce begins to thicken.

Pour the sauce over the chicken in the skillet and stir to coat all the pieces evenly. Arrange the chicken in a heated serving dish, pour the remaining sauce over it, and serve hot.

Chickens were not in the same class as game birds, but they found important space on the feast tables of wealthy families and in official entertaining. Eight different dishes of chicken were served in the first course of Sunday dinner, and three in the second course, when James I was entertained at Hoghton Towers. It appeared on working-class tables only on very special occasions. Artisans and laborers earning as little as sixpence a day could hardly afford to buy chickens at a shilling and a half each, let alone to pay three shillings for a fine, fat capon.

Capons were sold in two grades, capons "of greace" [fat] and coarse capons. The royal household purchased both grades. Very young chickens, what Robert May called "chicken-peepers," were often used whole in pies; the larger, fatter birds were saved for roasting and boiling.

A fat capon was often a country tenant's gift to his landlord at New Year's, and chickens made acceptable gifts to friends and neighbors at any time. When the news of Queen Elizabeth's coming to visit Ingatestone spread in the vicinity, among the gifts of food that were received by the Petres were: two capons, twenty caponets [small capons], and three dozen chickens.

The dietaries were unanimous in their approval of chicken. "The Capon is above all other foules praised," said *The Castle of Health,* "for as much as it is easily digested. . . . Hennes in winter are almost equall unto the Capon, but they do not make so

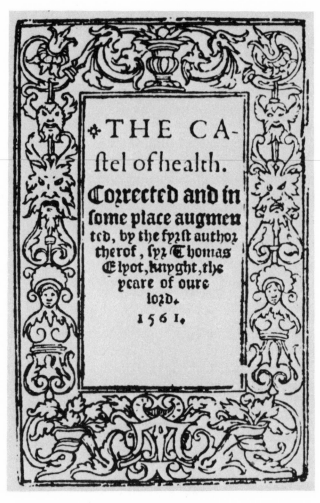

Title page from William Elyot's The Castel of Health (*1561*)

strong nourishment. . . . Chickens in summer, especially if they be cockrels [young cocks], are very convenient for a weake stomacke, and nourisheth a little." Though the meat of a cock was hard to digest, the dietaries said, the broth made from one could relieve a multitude of pains.

BOILED SALLET OF SPINAGE

Parboil Spinage, and chop it fine, with the edges of two hard Trenchers upon a board, or the backs of two Chopping-Knives: then set them on a Chafingdish of coals with Butter and Vinegar, Season it with Sinamon, Ginger, Sugar, and a few parboyld Currans. Then cut hard Egges into quarters to garnish it withall, and serve it upon Sippets.

John Murrell, *A New Booke of Cookerie*

THE WORKING VERSION:

1 ¼ pounds fresh spinach
2 tablespoons water
3 tablespoons butter
1 tablespoon white wine vinegar
4 teaspoons currants, parboiled

½ teaspoon brown sugar
⅛ teaspoon ginger
⅛ teaspoon cinnamon
2 slices buttered toast, cut into triangles
3 hard-boiled eggs, peeled and quartered

Wash the spinach in cool water until it is free of sand and cut off the roots and the coarse part of the stems. Drain it and shake off as much of the water as possible. Put the spinach and two tablespoons of water into a large saucepan, cover, and cook over low heat until the leaves wilt—about five minutes.

Drain the spinach and purée the greens or mince them very fine. Add the butter, vinegar, currants, sugar, and spices, and simmer, stirring constantly, until the butter melts and the spinach is hot.

Put half the toast triangles in a warm serving dish, spoon the spinach over them, garnish the dish with the hard-boiled eggs and the remaining toast, and serve.

On cookbook menus spinach usually appeared in the form of a tart or a boiled salad. Robert May called his often exotic recipes for cooked spinach "soops" or "buttered meats of spinach." One of these combines cooked spinach with almond paste, egg yolks, cream, and musk as a tart. The tart was then sprinkled with sugar and preserved barberries, "red and white biskets [cookies], or red and white muskedines [fondant pastilles flavored with musk]."

Spinach, said Gervase Markham, was one of the herbs that should be grown in the kitchen garden. "It can be sowed at all times of the moneth," he tells the housewife, except that "in March it should be sowed at the wane of the moone."

TO MAKE BROWN BREAD

Brown bread, of the colour, of which we have two sorts, one baked up as it cometh from the mill, so that neither the bran nor the flour are any whit diminished. . . . The other hath little or no flour left therein at all . . . it is not only the worst and weakest of all the other sorts, but also appointed in old time for servants, slaves, and inferior kind of people to feed upon. Hereunto likewise, because it is dry and brickle (for it will hardly be made up handsomely into loaves), some add a portion of rye meal in our time.

William Harrison, *The Description of England*

THE WORKING VERSION:

1 cup soured whole-wheat dough	1 tablespoon salt
1 ¾ cups warm water	4 cups whole-wheat flour
2 cakes fresh yeast or	½ cup cracked-wheat flour
2 tablespoons dry yeast	

Make the soured dough two days ahead according to the directions and ingredients given on page 78. Pour the water into a large mixing bowl and crumble or sprinkle the yeast into it.

When the yeast softens and expands, add the salt, one cup of the whole-wheat flour, and the cracked-wheat flour, and stir until the flours are absorbed. Then stir in the soured dough and two cups of the remaining whole-wheat flour.

Sprinkle the remaining cup of flour on your work surface and turn the dough out onto it. Knead for five minutes. Put the dough into a warmed mixing bowl large enough to allow the dough to nearly double in size. Cover and set to rise in a warm place or in an unheated oven.

When it has doubled in size—in 1½ to 2 hours—turn the dough out on a floured work surface and knead into a ball. Divide this into two parts and knead each of them into a ball. Flatten them to a thickness of about two inches and cut around the circumference of each ⅛ inch deep with a knife. Sprinkle whole-wheat flour over a cookie sheet and place the two loaves on the sheet about four inches apart. Punch fork holes in the top of each loaf and set to rise in a warm place until nearly doubled in size—1 to 1½ hours.

Bake at 400° for ten minutes, then lower the heat to 350° and bake twenty to twenty-five minutes longer or until browned. Remove from the oven and cool on a wire grille.

The recipe for Robert May's French bread appears on page 111.

Bread was so important in the English diet that control of its quality, weight, and price had been a concern of the English government for centuries. The price of bread was nationally regulated for the first time by the Assize of Bread of 1266, which set forth the number of loaves of the various sizes of commercially sold bread that the baker was permitted to make from a "quarter" of wheat (approximately eight bushels).

Breads were sold in farthing (a fourth of a penny), halfpenny, and penny loaves. Their prices were fixed, but when the price of grain rose, the bakers were permitted to decrease the weight of the different loaves of bread accordingly. The sliding scale of bread-loaf sizes in relation to grain prices as decided by the Assize of Bread of 1540 is shown in the illustration on the following page. In August, 1593, for example, the approved weight for a penny wheaten loaf was twenty-two ounces; in January, 1594, as a result of the increase in grain prices, bakers

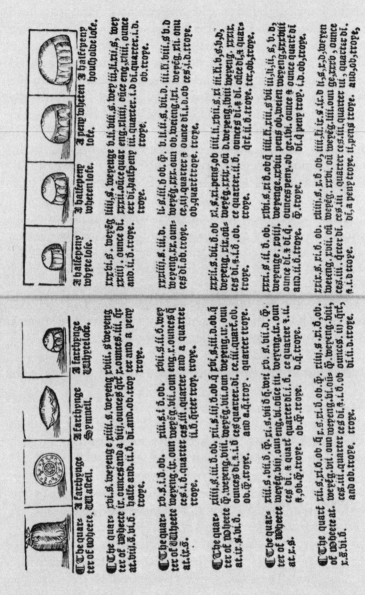

Page from The Assyse of Bread *showing shapes of breads commonly made in the sixteenth and seventeenth centuries*

were permitted to reduce the weight of a penny wheaten loaf to twenty ounces.

Bakers caught cheating on either the weight or quality of their bread were punished, usually by confiscation of the offending loaves and a fine, imprisonment or, occasionally, other punishments. There was no lack of complaints about bakers making bad bread or short-weight loaves.

> In pillory put the Baker's head
> For making of such little bread,
> Good conscience now-a-dayes is dead

was the plaint of one of the popular ballads of the period. An "enquest for the Clarke of the Markett" of Norwich, in 1565, found that "the Cittie hathe neyther common beame, ballaunces nor waightes." And "the common bakers, viz John Pye [and eleven others] do bake ther brede under the syse [assize] and contrary to ther charge."

John Taylor was cynical about the long-term effects of the punishments meted out to bakers caught cheating. In *Jack-a-Lent* he comments, "Their [bakers'] light bread brings in heavy gains, where if by chance, a batch or a basket full being examined by the scales of justice, and the bread committed to Newgate [the debtors' prison] for want of weight, and the baker to the Counter [the prison sometimes attached to the mayor's Court of Justice] for lack of conscience, yet he knows he shall out again, and with a trick that he hath, in one week he will recover the consumption of his purse again, by his moderate light handling of the medicine of meal, yeast, and water."

Andrewe Boorde called on the bakers to make good bread: "Gentyll bakers, sophystycate [adulterate] nat your bread made of pure whete, but yf you do . . . I would you shuld shake out the remnaunt of your sacks, standynge in the Temmes [Thames River] up to the harde chynne, and three ynches above, that whan you do come out of the water you myght shake your eares as a spanyell that veryly commeth out of the water." Ducking in the river was one ancient punishment for bakers and brewers who made and sold substandard bread or beer. But fines and confiscation of the offending product, which was then distributed to the poor, were the usual punishments when the law managed to overtake offending bakers.

TO MAKE GOOSEBERRY CREAM

Codle them green, and boil them up with sugar, being preserved put them into the cream strain'd or whole, scrape sugar on them, & so serve them cold in boild or raw cream.

Robert May, *The Accomplisht Cook*

THE WORKING VERSION:

1 quart fresh goose-berries	¾ cup whipping cream
1 cup sugar	2 to 3 tablespoons sugar (optional)
1 cup water	

Buy the largest gooseberries that you can find, since small ones are a nuisance to clean. Pick off the stem and flower ends, wash the berries in cool water, and drain them. Make a syrup by cooking the cup of sugar with the water over medium-high heat for five minutes, watching carefully to see that the syrup does not boil over. Add the gooseberries, lower the heat to simmer, and cook until the berries are tender but not broken—about ten minutes.

Remove a few of the berries with enough syrup to cover them and set aside to garnish the dish. Purée the rest of the berries with half of the remaining syrup—it should make a rather thick purée. If seeds bother you, strain the purée through a fine sieve.

An hour before you plan to serve, whip the cream until it is stiff. Taste the puréed berries; if you think more sweetening is needed, stir in the additional two tablespoons of sugar, ½ spoonful at a time. Fold the puréed berries into the cream and spoon the mixture into a chilled serving bowl. Garnish with the reserved whole gooseberries.

"Boil'd cream" is a light custard sauce flavored with rose water and ambergris. If you would prefer this to the whipped cream, cook the cream with one egg yolk, two tablespoons of sugar, one teaspoon of rose water, and one drop of ambergris, using an eyedropper to measure the ambergris, in a double boiler to the point of boiling. Remove the sauce from the heat and stir until the cream is cold. Drain the berries from their syrup and pour the cream over them.

These fruit creams were popular and easy to make and must have been refreshing after heavy meals. For winter use, gooseberries were usually pickled in vinegar and sugar. They were then used as a garnish on meat and poultry dishes as well as for sauces and pies.

TO MAKE SHREWSBURY CAKES

Take a quart of very fine flower, eight ounces of fine sugar beaten and cersed [sieved], twelve ounces of sweete butter, a Nutmegge grated, two or three spoonefuls of damaske rose-water, worke all these together with your hands as hard as you can for the space of halfe an houre, then roule it in little round Cakes, about the thicknesse of three shillings one upon another, then take a silver Cup or glasse some foure or three inches over, and cut the cakes in them, then strowe some flower upon white papers & lay them upon them, and bake them in an Oven as hot as for Manchet, set up your lid [keep the oven door closed] till you may tell a hundreth [count to one hundred slowly], then you shall see them white, if any of them rise up clap them downe with some cleane thing, and if your Oven be not too hot set up your lid again, and in a quarter of an houre they will be baked enough, but in any case take heede your Oven be not too hot, for they must not looke browne but white, and so draw them foorth & lay them one upon another till they be could, and you may keep them halfe a yeare, the new baked are best.

John Murrell,
A Delightfull daily exercise for Ladies and Gentlewomen

THE WORKING VERSION:

¼ cup sugar	1½ teaspoons nutmeg
½ cup butter	½ tablespoon rose water
1 cup sifted unbleached flour	

Cream the sugar and butter together until fluffy. Sift the flour with the nutmeg. Add the rose water to the sugar-butter mixture and stir in the dry ingredients only until blended; then chill the dough for ten minutes. Sprinkle your work surface with flour and turn the dough out onto it. Pat the dough into a ball, then roll it out gently to ¼ inch thick.

Cut out the cakes with a two- or three-inch round cookie cutter. Place them on an unbuttered cookie sheet an inch apart and bake at 350° until slightly brown around the edges—from twelve to fifteen minutes. Cool on a wire grille and store in an airtight tin.

If John Murrell had worked the dough less, he would have avoided the "rising up" of the cakes and hence the need to "clap them downe."

There were a good many versions of Shrewsbury cakes. Some were butter cookies made with eggs and, occasionally, with caraway seeds. When caraway seeds were added, the cookies were, naturally enough, called seed cookies.

On August 16, 1602, twenty-year-old Lord Herbert of Cherbury sent his guardian, Sir George More, a gift of Shrewsbury cakes with this message: "Lest you think this countrey ruder than it is, I have sent you some of the bread which I am sure will be dainty, howsoever it be not pleasinge: it is a kind of cake which our countrey people use and make in no place in England but in Shrewsbury; if you vouchsafe to tast of them, you enworthy the countrey and sender. Measure my love not by the substance of it which is brittle, but by the form of it which is circular." The circle was a symbol of eternity.

In 1561 the town council of Shrewsbury presented Lord Stafford with "a dossen of fyen kakys." These, the bailiff's accounts noted, cost the town two shillings.

"Shrewsbury cakes," says a circular distributed by the town council of Shrewsbury, England, "are more like a particularly delicious shortbread with a flavor all their own, the secret of which is jealously preserved." It must have been an open secret, for John Murrell's Shrewsbury cakes certainly fit the council's description.

"Short [rich] as a Shrewsbury cake" was a common saying in England in the eighteenth century, and may still be. But cakes were not Shrewsbury's only specialty; the town was also known for its brawn and its ale.

PROFESSIONAL COOKS
IN SHAKESPEARE'S TIME

"The Art of Cookery is much esteemed in England," wrote Fynes Moryson in his *Itinerary,* "neither doe any sooner find a Master, then men of that profession, and they are most esteemed, which . . . are most exquisite in that Art."

Good cooks were clearly sought after, but even the great cooks of Moryson's day may not have been as elegantly attired as was, a century earlier, the master cook for Cardinal Wolsey's privy (personal) kitchen, who "went about daily in damask satin, or velvet, with a chain of gold about his neck." Servants, including cooks, in Shakespeare's day still wore the traditional blue clothing of woolen or worsted, and they did so in his plays. In *The Taming of the Shrew* (Act IV, Scene 1), Grumio arrives to see that the servants of the household are ready for their master's return and prepares to inspect them. "Call forth Nathaniel, Joseph, Nicholas, Philip, Walter, Sugarsop, and the rest," he orders; "let their heads be sleekly combed, their blue coats brushed." Ben Jonson also confirms the blue of servants' clothing in *The Case is Altered.* Onion, the hall groom (Act I, Scene 2), exclaims, "Does he find fault with please your honour? 'Swounds, it has been a servingman's speech ever since I belonged to the blue order!"

The status of master cook was not easily attained. Like the members of other apprenticed trades, cooks had to serve apprenticeships of seven years before they were accredited as journeymen, and they had to accumulate years more of experience before—if ever—they could attain the rank of master cook.

In addition, wages were low, hours were long, and cooks, like other workers, were bound by harsh statutory regulations that set maximum wages and limited the possibilities for changing jobs. A servant who accepted more than the maximum wage was to "suffer one and twenty days imprisonment without baile."

In 1550 Sir William Petre paid his cook forty shillings (two pounds) a year. In 1560 Lady Suffolk paid her cooks one hundred shillings (five pounds) a year. Wages had been slowly rising, but Archbishop Parker, in 1566, paid his master cook only four

A cook in his kitchen (from a 16th-century print)

nobles (one pound, six shillings, sixpence) a year. The highest
wages were paid by the royal household. Wages, however, included, as a rule, room, board, and an allowance for clothing—
usually about ten shillings a year.

These were hardly exciting financial prospects, but there were
other satisfactions, such as the creative possibilities in preparing
for an important feast. Ben Jonson, in "Neptune's Triumph," describes a master cook at work:

> He designs, he draws,
> He paints, he carves, he builds, he fortifies.
> Makes citadels of curious fowl and fish,
> Some he dry-ditches, some moats round with broths;
> Rears bulwark pies; and for his outer works,
> He raiseth ramparts of immortal crusts.

Whether these crusts were immortal because of their toughness
or their delicacy, Jonson does not say.

Valued cooks were often taken abroad by their masters when
they were sent on diplomatic or trade missions. From the point
of view of the cook, what better way was there to pick up knowl-

edge on how to prepare the foreign dishes so popular among the well-to-do in England, knowledge that in turn made a cook's services more valuable and sought after? The cooks who wrote cookbooks usually told their readers that they had learned to make the foreign dishes in their cookbooks while living abroad.

Sometimes the traveling was only to or from London or to some other English city, but this too provided a change. Occasionally, the household servants were moved from one manor house to another of the family's estates. Lady Anne Clifford has several entries in her diary of this kind of moving; for example, in March, 1617, "All the household were sent down from London to Knole. The 15th my Lord sent for John Cook to come to Buckhurst to make broths for him." Most servants were referred to by the kind of work they performed, and the "John Cook" of whom Lady Anne wrote in her diary was doubtless John Elnor, one of the four cooks at Knole.

Richard Heath's traveling was unusual. His employer, the earl of Northumberland, was imprisoned in the Tower of London from 1605 to 1621 for concealment of treason in the Gunpowder Plot against James I and the members of Parliament. The earl was given a suite of rooms that he did not like, and he soon succeeded in getting himself moved to a larger and better suite. Then he obtained permission to increase the number of servants he had originally been permitted to keep and sent for his master cook, Richard Heath, among others. Heath answered the call to serve his master in prison.

In very large households the master cook could suggest dishes for the menus, but he was still subject to the authority of the clerk of the kitchen. The steward or chamberlain of the household might plan the menu for an important feast with the master cook, or leave the planning to him and the clerk of the kitchen.

Some of the books of rules and orders that various noblemen wrote as guides for their servants have been reprinted. There are great similarities in most of these, which suggests that models of such books might have been circulated. The *Booke of Orders and Rules* that Anthony Viscount Montague prepared when he was only twenty-one years old, three years after he had succeeded to his father's title and property, was probably copied in part from other such books.

For the guidance of the "Chiefe Cooke and his Office," the young viscount wrote, "I will that the Chief Cooke be att the appoyntmente and direction of the Clark of my Kytchin for orderinge of ytt: and that he have the speciall regarde and care in dressinge of the fare, and dyett for myne owne table, as well in boylde meates, as pasterye (not exemptinge the inferioure [lower rank] Cookes from workeinge with him, and assisteinge of him in the same, neither himself from lookeinge also to the raunge [fireplaces where the cooking was done] especially where myne owne meate is dressed) and that he see every thinge wholesomely and cleanely handeled, and with as little expence of spyce as conveniently may be."

The new Viscount Montague must have been served some badly plucked fowl in his youth, for he continues, "and that he looke that all manner of poultre or wylde fowle, that comes to myne owne table be well pulde that there remayne no kynde of fethers or stumpes uppon them." His next direction also reflects poorly on the kitchens of one of the richest households in England: "I will also that he serve owte my meate in cleane vessels and well scowered and such as be nott, that he returne to the Scullerye man to be amended." In defense of the kitchen and the scullery servants, it must be admitted that they had to work in cramped quarters and in poor light in most households.

The second cook and any other undercooks are to be responsible for preparing all meals except the viscount's own. But they are to give a helping hand to the master cook if called upon, "as he shall doe the like for them, if they required." They, too, are subject to the orders of the clerk of the kitchen, not of the master cook.

Pilfering food was a problem at the royal palace where some cooks, like some courtiers, helped themselves to foodstuffs meant for the royal family. This was a long-standing problem to which James I hoped to make an end with his Ordinances of 1604. The ordinances charged, "Whereas the Master Cooke for ourselfe, and our deare Wife the Queene's Majestie, having an honourable allowance of diett, doe presume, contrary to all auncient and good orders, and to the dishonour of our service, to take rawe meate out of dishes in nature of their assaies [i.e., of tasting to detect poisons], some quantity of all kindes of provisions contained in the said dishes, by which the danger of our person can in no sort be prevented. . . . Our pleasure and will therefore is, that our diett in all sortes be daily served for us by our Cookes out of our Kitchens, in as large and ample manner as they receive the same into their handes." The ordinances, however, failed to solve the problem.

The king's master cook, regardless of any chicanery he may have practiced in the kitchen, had a ceremonial role in the elaborate induction of the knights of the early order of the Bath, established in 1610. The ceremonies came to a close in the royal chapel, where the knights, having offered their swords at the altar, redeemed them with gold coins. As the knights filed out of the chapel into the hall, they were met by the king's master cook. In his white apron and sleeves, holding a gilded chopping knife, he challenged each new knight's spurs. These they also redeemed with a coin, but of lesser value. The cook, nevertheless, warned each of them: "Sir Knight, looke that you be true and loyall to the King my master: or else I must hew these Spurres from your heeles."

A cook was also part of the traditional Shrove Tuesday pancake scramble at Westminster School for Boys in London. On "Pancake Day" he was ushered into the schoolroom, holding a long-handled skillet with a pancake in it, by the school beadle. After twirling the skillet several times, he tossed the pancake over the bar that divided the upper and lower grades while the boys scrambled over the bar to snatch the pancake or at least a piece of it. Whoever got the whole pancake, or the largest piece of it, was rewarded with some money. This tradition was still very much alive as recently as 1938.

Cooks who were able to set up in business for themselves as private caterers, or who ran cookshops where they sold prepared foods, could do very well financially. London cooks, who were considered the best in England, were in demand not only in the capital but also in wealthy country homes for important entertaining. Extra cooks were always required for the great feasts given by the lord mayor of London and by the great merchant guilds and the artisans' guilds on special occasions during the year. They were in demand for marriages, christenings, and funerals, and whenever important personages were being entertained or important occasions celebrated.

Shakespeare was well aware of the practice of hiring extra cooks for special occasions. In *Romeo and Juliet* (Act IV, Scene 2), Lord Capulet, making the arrangements for Juliet's marriage to Paris, tells a servant, "Sirrah, go hire me twenty cunning cooks."

Lord North's accounts of the expenses of entertaining Queen Elizabeth included "£21, Paid to the Cookes of London." An item in his 1578 accounts notes the payment of four pounds "to my L[ord] of Lestors [Leicester's] Cookes." Sir William Petre also brought cooks from London to Ingatestone for special occasions. "Mr. Wilcocks the cook" was brought down several times to supervise food preparations for important entertaining. Mr. Wilcocks may have been a private caterer, for he brought with him some of his own equipment and a man to help him. On one occasion—the visit of Queen Elizabeth and her retinue— at least six extra cooks were hired.

Such jobs meant hard work, but they also enlivened the cook's life. Toward the end of his working days, the professional cook, especially one who had been abroad, might try his hand at writing a cookbook, although very few did so. For one thing, the Cooks' Company, or guild, frowned on its members' giving away the secrets of their trade.

Most cooking naturally was done by housewives rather than by hired cooks. And occasionally some of their cherished recipes found their way into cookbooks written by men. Thomas Dawson, Gervase Markham, John Murrell all give credit for some of their recipes to ladies from whom they had first received them. Sir Kenelme Digbie exchanged recipes with many of the ladies at Court and he thanks many of them for the recipes in his collection. Even great ladies were often familiar with the kitchens in their households, and prepared dishes there from time to time. It was in her kitchen that Lady Dormer noticed the young Robert May's promise and decided to send him to Paris to learn about French cooking.

A Feast for Bottom

Thou seest how diligent I am,
To dress thy meat myself and bring it thee.
The Taming of the Shrew,
Act IV, Scene 3 (*Petruchio*)

SHERRY

A good sherris-sack . . . ascends me into the brain; dries me there all the foolish and dull and crudy vapours which environ it.
Henry IV, Part II, Act IV, Scene 3 (*Falstaff*)

STEAMED MUSSELS

Thy food shall be the fresh-brook muscles.
The Tempest, Act I, Scene 2 (*Prospero*)

A FRIGACY OF SHRIMPS

And, when he was a babe, a child, a shrimp,
Thus did he strangle serpents.
Love's Labour's Lost, Act V, Scene 2 (*Holofernes*)

CHEDDAR PANCAKES

Why, my cheese, my digestion, why hast thou not served thyself in to my table so many meals?
Troilus and Cressida, Act II, Scene 3 (*Achilles*)

WILLIAM RABISHA'S PORK AND VEAL PIE

No man's pie is freed
From his ambitious finger.
Henry VIII, Act I, Scene 1 (Buckingham)

APPLE PUFFS

How have you made division of yourself?
An apple cleft in two is not more twin.
Twelfth Night, Act V, Scene I (Antonio)

SIR KENELME DIGBIE'S CHICKEN FRICASSEE

Lord have mercy on thee for a hen!
All's Well That Ends Well, Act II, Scene 3 (Lafeu)

ROBERT MAY'S LUPINS, BOILED (FRENCH BEANS)

Go, give 'em welcome; you can speak the French tongue.
Henry VIII, Act I, Scene 4 (Wolsey)

A SALAD OF RED CABBAGE AND HERBS

In such a night
Medea gather'd the enchanted herbs
That did renew old Aeson.
The Merchant of Venice, Act V, Scene 1 (Jessica)

JANNOCKS (OAT BREAD) AND MANCHET

His kissing is as full of sanctity as the touch of holy bread.
As You Like It, Act III, Scene 4 (Rosalind)

A GREEK WINE

I'll heat his blood with Greekish wine to-night.
Troilus and Cressida, Act V, Scene 1 (Achilles)

A RHINE WINE

The king doth wake to-night and takes his rouse . . .
And, as he drains his draughts of Rhenish down,
The kettle-drum and trumpet thus bray out
The triumph of his pledge.
Hamlet, Act I, Scene 4 (Hamlet)

ALE

Would I were in an alehouse in London! I would give all my fame for a pot of ale, and safety.
Henry V, Act III, Scene 2 (*Boy*)

AN ALMOND CUSTARD

You have made shift to run into 't, boots and spurs and all, like him that leaped into the custard.
All's Well That Ends Well, Act II, Scene 5 (*Lafeu*)

ROBERT MAY'S PEAR PIE

I warrant they would whip me with their fine wits till I were as crest-fallen as a dried pear.
The Merry Wives of Windsor, Act IV, Scene 5 (*Falstaff*)

You have done our pleasures much grace . . .
You have added worth unto 't and lustre . . .
I am to thank you for 't.
Timon of Athens, Act I, Scene 2 (Timon)

TO BOYLE MUSKLES

Take water and yest, and a good dish of butter, and Onions chopt, and a little pepper, & when it hath boyled a litle while, then see that your Muskles be cleane washed, then put them into the broth shels and all, and when they be boiled wel then serve them broth and all.

Thomas Dawson, *The good huswifes Jewell*

THE WORKING VERSION:

2 quarts fresh mussels, in their shells	¼ cup thinly sliced onions
	¼ cup butter
½ cup water	½ teaspoon peppercorns
½ cup beer	

Scrub the mussels thoroughly under cold water. Put them into a bowl of fresh cold water and let stand for one hour. Combine the water, beer, onions, butter, and peppercorns in a pot large enough to hold the mussels and simmer for five minutes.

Drain the mussels, add them to the other ingredients, cover the pot, and cook over medium heat until all the mussels have opened—twelve to fifteen minutes. Divide the mussels into individual soup plates. Pour some of the broth with the seasonings over them and serve immediately.

There were numerous way of preparing mussels. One was to steam them, remove the meat from the shells, and serve in a rich sauce. Steamed, shelled mussels were also rolled in flour, fried in deep fat and served in a sauce of butter and orange juice. Savory pies of steamed minced mussels were also made, usually for fast-day meals.

Both salt- and fresh-water mussels were available and popular. Fortunately, England's shores were well supplied with shellfish, including, Harrison noted, a variety of "mussels and cockles . . . great whelks, scallops and periwinkles." (England still consumes an enormous quantity of mussels—as of about 1970, eighty million pounds of them a year.)

HOW TO FRIGACY SHRIMPS

To these you must put a little Claret-wine, an Onion or two cut in pieces, a couple or two of Anchovies, and a faggot of sweet herbs: stew them or any one of them up together with a little Ginger and Nutmeg; toss them up with the yolk of an egg, a little Vinegar and drawn butter; you may put them into little Coffins; like Hearts or Diamonds, to garnish a bisk or Olie; otherwise to be dished upon sippets, for a second course dish.

William Rabisha, *The whole Body of Cookery Dissected*

THE WORKING VERSION:

1½ pounds raw shrimp	¼ teaspoon nutmeg
3 tablespoons butter	¼ teaspoon ginger
2 teaspoons anchovy paste	1¼ cups claret
1 medium-size onion, grated	2 tablespoons red wine vinegar
1 tablespoon minced parsley	½ teaspoon salt (optional)
½ teaspoon thyme	3 egg yolks
1 bay leaf	3 slices hot buttered toast, quartered
⅛ teaspoon pepper	

Peel the shrimp and remove the black intestines that run along the back. Rinse them under cold water and dry in paper towels.

Melt the butter in a small saucepan, add the anchovy paste, grated onion, parsley, thyme, bay leaf, pepper, nutmeg, and ginger, and simmer for one minute. Add the cleaned shrimp and stir them about in the seasonings until well coated, then add the claret and vinegar and simmer ten minutes more. Taste the sauce and add the salt if needed.

Beat the egg yolks together with ¼ cup of the sauce from the pot. Then stir this back into the sauce until it thickens. Place half the toast in a warmed serving dish, spoon the shrimp and the sauce over it, and garnish with the rest of the toast.

Shrimp, boiled in their shells, then peeled and dipped in vinegar, were popular as snacks. "Shrimpes are pretty picking meate for idle people," wrote Nicholas Breton, and added, "new sodden [freshly boiled] are served in their best kinde."

Shrimp and vinegar also give added tang to a scene in *Henry IV, Part II* (Act II, Scene 1). Mistress Quickly has called in the law because Falstaff has not only failed to pay his bills at her tavern but has borrowed money from her and not repaid it. When Falstaff denies this, she reminds him angrily that she had dunned him for the money he owed her on the day that "goodwife Keech, the butcher's wife" came in "to borrow a mess of vinegar; telling us she had a good dish of prawns," and that Sir John had then brushed aside her demand for repayment by implying that he intended to make her his wife. "And didst thou not, when she was gone down stairs, desire me to be no more so familiarity with such poor people; saying that ere long they should call me madam?"

HOW TO FRY A DISH OF CHEESE

Take a quarter of a pound of good Cheese, or Parmysant, and grate it and put to it a little grated bread, a few Caraway seeds beaten, the yolks of as many eggs as will make it into a stiff batter, so it will not run, fry it brown in Butter, and pour on drawn Butter with Claret wine when they are dished.

William Rabisha, *The whole Body of Cookery Dissected*

THE WORKING VERSION:

1 tablespoon caraway seeds	½ teaspoon salt
4 cups coarsely grated sharp Cheddar cheese	¼ cup grated bread crumbs
	½ cup butter
6 egg yolks	1 cup claret

Pound the caraway seeds with the side of a meat tenderizer to break the shells. Mix the cheese, egg yolks, caraway seeds, salt, and three tablespoons of the bread crumbs into a thick paste. Form this into ½-inch-thick cakes about four inches in diameter.

Melt six tablespoons of the butter in a large skillet and, when it starts to bubble, slide the pancakes in carefully—they break easily. Brown them on both sides over medium-high heat. Remove the pancakes to a warmed dish. Add the wine, the rest of the butter, and the remaining bread crumbs to the butter in the skillet and cook, stirring constantly, until the sauce begins to thicken. Pour the sauce over the pancakes and serve immediately.

The pancake mixture may be made several hours ahead of time and refrigerated, but the pancakes should not be fried until just before you are ready to serve them.

Pancakes were usually of the dessert type, like French *crêpes* and Swedish rolled pancakes, and were made of a thin batter of cream, egg yolks, sugar, spices, and flour. Sometimes ale was used as part of the liquid. The pancakes were fried in butter and served sprinkled with sugar.

TO BAKE PORK TO BE EATEN COLD

Take a Loin of Pork and bone it, and cut thereof into thin collops beaten with the Clever, also take as many collops of Veal thin beaten; season your Pork with Pepper, Salt, and minced Sage, season your Veal with Cloves, Mace, Nutmeg, and minced Time; put yolks of Eggs to each of your meats, and mingle them together, with their several seasonings, then a laying of Pork, in the form you intend to make your Pye, either round or otherwise; and then a laying of your Veal thereon, so continue till you have laid all your meat, then take a Rolling-pin and beat it well into a body, put it in your Coffin made for that purpose, close it, indore [glaze] it, bake it: when it is cold, fill it with clarified butter; let your Pork be the end of the Loyn, and both undermost and uppermost in your pye.

William Rabisha, *The whole Body of Cookery Dissected*

TO MAKE A PASTE

Take to every peck of flour five pound of butter, the white of six eggs, and work it well together with cold spring water; you must bestow a great deal of pains, and but little water. . . . Sometimes for this paste put in eight yolks of eggs, and but two white, and six pound of butter.

Robert May, *The Accomplisht Cook*

THE WORKING VERSION:

¾ pound boned loin of pork
½ pound boned veal loin
⅛ teaspoon pepper
¼ teaspoon sage
¼ teaspoon thyme
½ teaspoon salt
2 egg yolks
⅛ teaspoon mace
¼ teaspoon nutmeg
⅛ teaspoon ground cloves

3 tablespoons butter, diced

FOR THE PASTRY

2 cups sifted unbleached flour
1 teaspoon salt
¾ cup cold butter
½ cup cold water (approximately)
1 egg, separated

Remove any fat from the pork and veal, and with a sharp knife slice both as thin as you can, keeping the meats separate. Mix the pepper, sage, thyme, and ¼ teaspoon of salt with one of the egg yolks and stir the slices of pork around in this until they are coated with the mixture. Cover and set aside until needed.

Mix the mace, nutmeg, cloves, and the remaining ¼ teaspoon of salt with the other egg yolk and stir the slices of veal around in this until coated. Make the pastry according to directions given on page 31.

Divide the ball of pastry into two pieces, the piece for the lower crust a bit larger than the other. On a floured work surface roll out the bottom crust to fit a six-to-seven-inch round springform pan. Fit the sheet into the pan, then roll out the top crust.

Divide the pork into two equal parts and layer one part in the pan. Dot with ⅓ of the diced butter. Arrange the slices of veal over the pork and dot them with another ⅓ of the butter. Then spread the remaining slices of pork over the veal and dot them with the remaining butter.

Cover with the top sheet of pastry, seal the edges with the tines of a wet fork, and slice off the surplus pastry. If there is enough pastry left, roll it out again and, with a cookie cutter, cut out small pigs or cows. Punch fork holes in the top crust and brush with egg white, then arrange the pastry cutouts over the pie and brush them with egg white. Bake at 450° for twenty minutes, then lower the heat to 350° and bake twenty-five minutes longer. Serve hot or cold, but not refrigerated.

This pie is best eaten hot, but it is also good cold. Because the pastry crusts of a meat pie become soggy when cold, I remove the meat from the pie and reheat the crust when we eat it as a leftover. Rabisha's pie was a very large one and meant to last for a good while. It would, therefore, have been baked in a coarse, tough crust; there was no need for him to have specified this, as all cooks would have known it.

If you cannot find veal, make the pie entirely of pork, seasoning two-thirds of the slices with the pork seasoning and the remaining third with the veal seasoning. Unless you tell your guests what you have done, they will most likely, as Elizabethan cookbook writers often said, not know the difference. (I tell my guests.)

TO MAKE APPLE-PUFFES

Take a Pomewater, or any other Apple that is not hard, or harsh in taste: mince it small with a dozen or twenty Razins of the Sunne; wet the Apples in two Egges, beate them all together with the back of a knife or a Spoone. Season them with Nutmeg, Rose-water, Sugar, and Ginger: drop them into a frying pan with a spoone, frye them like Egges, wring on the juyce of an Orenge or Lemmon, and serve them in.

John Murrell, *A New Booke of Cookerie*

THE WORKING VERSION:

1 pound firm, tart cooking apples	⅛ teaspoon ginger
	½ teaspoon nutmeg
4 eggs	½ cup white raisins, minced
3 tablespoons brown sugar	6 tablespoons butter
2 teaspoons rose water	1 lemon

Quarter, core, peel, and mince or grate coarse the apples. Beat together the eggs, sugar, rose water, ginger, and nutmeg. Add the apples and raisins and stir until blended.

Melt the butter in a large skillet and, when it begins to bubble, drop spoonfuls of the apple mixture into the skillet spaced about two inches apart. Cook over medium-high heat until lightly browned on both sides, turning carefully with a broad steel spatula.

As the puffs finish browning, remove them to a warmed serving dish and keep warm over hot water. Squeeze the juice of the lemon over the finished puffs and serve immediately.

The Pomewater was one of England's finest apples, juicy and crisp. "Ripe as a pomewater, who now hangeth like a jewel in the ear of . . . the sky," Holofernes says in *Love's Labour's Lost* (Act IV, Scene 2).

Apple pies and tarts, baked apples, apple fritters, and apple sauce were staple items of English meals. Hot roasted apples were sold by street vendors and must have wafted forth fine odors in the city streets.

Despite the advice of the dietaries, apples were eaten raw more often than cooked. But they were most easily digested, according to Andrewe Boorde, roasted or baked. They were good to eat "after a frost have taken them, or when they be olde, specyally red apples, and they the whiche be of good odor & melow; they should be eaten with sugar or comfettes, or with fenell-sede, or anys-sede [anise seeds] because of theyr ventosyte [flatulency]."

FRICACEE OF CHICKEN

Cut chickens, which must be flead off their skin, into thin slices, and beat them; or the like with Veal. Put about half a pint of water or flesh-broth to them in a frying-pan, and some Thyme, and Sweet-marjoram, and an Onion or two quartered, and boil them till they be tender, having seasoned them with Salt, and about twenty Corns of whole white Pepper, and four or five Cloves. When they are enough, take half a pint of White wine, four yolks of Eggs, a quarter of a pound of butter (or more), a good spoonful of Thyme, Sweet-Marjoram and Parsley (more parsley then of the others) all minced small: a Porrenger full of gravy. When all these are well incorporated together over the fire, and well beaten, pour it into the pan to the rest, and turn it continually up and down over the fire, till all be well incorpo-

rated. Then throw away the Onion and first sprigs of Herbs, squeeze Orange to it, and serve it up hot.

Sir Kenelme Digbie, *The Closet of the Eminently Learned Sir Kenelme Digbie, Kt., Opened*

THE WORKING VERSION:

One 3½-pound frying chicken	5 white peppercorns
½ cup fresh chicken broth	2 cloves
1 small onion, peeled and quartered	½ cup white wine
	¼ cup minced parsley
¼ teaspoon marjoram	3 tablespoons butter
¼ teaspoon thyme	2 egg yolks
1 teaspoon salt	2 tablespoons orange juice

Rinse the chicken under cool water and pull off the skin—this will be easier if you cut the skin loose from the bones at the base of the legs and the second wing joint. With a sharp knife, slice the meat from the frame in thin slices. Starting with the breast, slice downward toward the thighs; then slice the meat from the thighs, legs, and wings parallel with the bones.

Make the chicken broth from the frame of the bird, the giblets, and four cups of water. (In a pressure cooker at ten pounds pressure, this will take forty-five minutes; simmered in a tightly covered saucepan, two to three hours.)

Put ½ cup of broth, the onion, marjoram, thyme, salt, peppercorns, and cloves in a 1½-quart saucepan and bring to a boil. Add the sliced chicken, lower the heat to simmer, and cook only until the meat no longer looks raw. Cover the pan, and continue simmering until the chicken is tender—twenty-five to thirty minutes—stirring the slices gently every ten minutes.

Remove the cloves, peppercorns, and onion. Put the wine, parsley, and butter into a small saucepan and simmer until the butter melts, stirring constantly. Remove the pan from the heat and beat in the egg yolks. Add the sauce to the chicken and cook, stirring constantly, until it begins to thicken. Arrange the chicken in a warmed serving dish and pour the sauce over it. Just before serving add the orange juice.

This dish is almost as good cold as hot. To serve cold, spoon the chicken and sauce into a bowl just large enough to contain

FINE ORANGES AND LEMONS.

Street seller of oranges and lemons (16th-century woodcut)

them and refrigerate for twenty-four hours. Loosen the jelled fricassee from the sides of the bowl with a knife dipped in hot water, and turn it out on a bed of leaf lettuce.

The juice of oranges and lemons was commonly squeezed as a sauce over meat by the diner at the table. *A Proper newe Booke of Cokerye* notes that "sauce orengers" is the correct sauce for veal, lamb, and kid. The oranges used were probably sour oranges, since many recipes say that either oranges or lemons may be used.

Oranges and lemons were imported mainly from Spain. "Fine Seville oranges, fine lemons" the orange sellers called their wares. Such an orange seller appears in *Coriolanus* (Act II, Scene 1), as Menenius chides Brutus and Sicinius: "You wear out a good wholesome forenoon in hearing a cause between an orange-wife and a fosset-seller." (A fosset was a kind of tap for drawing liquor from a barrel.) Beatrice, in *Much Ado About Nothing* (Act II, Scene 1), describes the count as "neither sad, nor sick, nor merry, nor well; but . . . civil as an orange, and something of that jealous complexion." "Civil as an orange" (the sour Seville orange) is not one of Beatrice's wittiest sallies, but it is typical of Shakespeare's punning.

TO BOIL FRENCH BEANS OR LUPINS

First take away the tops of the cods and the strings, then have a pan or skillet of fair water boiling on the fire, when it boils put them in with salt, and boil them up quick; being boild serve them with beaten butter in a fair scowred dish, and salt about it.

Robert May, *The Accomplisht Cook*

THE WORKING VERSION:

1 pound fresh, crisp string beans	4 tablespoons butter
9 cups water	White button thread or cord
½ teaspoon salt	

Buy beans that are clear green in color and that snap when bent. Snip off the ends and pull the strings—really young beans are stringless—and rinse in cold water. Cut six twelve-inch lengths of string or cord. Divide the beans into six bundles and tie each bundle together at the center with a string—be careful not to cut into the beans.

Bring the water to a boil in a large saucepan or deep skillet, add the salt, and place the bundles of beans in the water with kitchen tongs. Cook uncovered, over medium-high heat, until the beans are tender but still crisp.

While the beans are cooking, put the butter and one tablespoon of the water from the pot in which the beans are cooking into a small saucepan and cook over low heat, stirring vigorously with a small wire whisk until the butter begins to thicken. Remove from the heat but keep warm.

Carefully remove the bundles of beans from the water with tongs, let them drain for a moment, and arrange them on a warmed serving dish in the form of either a cross or the spokes of a wheel. Cut the strings from the bean bundles and remove them. Then pour the beaten butter over the beans and serve.

The cross design is suggested by Robert May for serving string beans in another of his recipes.

Many harsh things have been said about contemporary English cooking, and overcooking vegetables is one of the charges. Vegetables are often overcooked in England, just as they are in many other nations. Good cooks are rare in any time and in every clime. Good English cooks in Shakespeare's day appreciated the delicacy of quickly cooked string beans, served simply with butter and salt, as this and other recipes in sixteenth- and seventeenth-century cookbooks show. *The English Hus-wife,* for example, suggests "bean-cods [string beans], boyled and served up with Oyl, Vinegar and Pepper," as a good simple salad that can be eaten hot or cold.

Kitchen gardens provided vegetables, salad greens, and herbs whenever even a bit of land was available. But it was also becoming easier to buy fresh vegetables because commercial truck gardening was steadily increasing. There were large commercial truck gardens just outside London whose wares were brought into town in carts or on men's backs. Such vegetables could be purchased at market stalls or from vendors who hawked their wares through the London streets.

A SALLET OF STRIKED COLEWORTS
AND HERBS

Take small sallet of all good sallet herbs, then mince some white cabbidge or striked coleworts, mingle them amongst the small sallet, or some lilly flowers slit with a pin; then first lay some minced cabbidge in a clean scowred dish, and the minced sallet round about it: then some well washed and picked capers, currans, olives, or none, then about the rest a round of boiled red beets, oranges, or lemons carved.

Robert May, *The Accomplisht Cook*

THE WORKING VERSION:

3 cups minced red cabbage
¼ cup currants, parboiled
1 tablespoon minced celery leaves
1 tablespoon fresh tarragon or fennel, minced
1 tablespoon fresh mint leaves, minced

5 tablespoons olive oil
6 tablespoons red wine vinegar
2 medium-size beets, boiled tender in their skins
1 large lemon
1 tablespoon capers

Remove the outer leaves and the core of the cabbage before you mince it. Add the currants, celery leaves, tarragon, and mint, and pour the oil and vinegar over all. Toss until the cabbage is well coated with the dressing. Refrigerate for twenty-four hours, stirring the mixture several times during this period.

Peel the beets immediately after they are cooked—it is difficult to remove the skin when the beets are cold—cut them in half lengthways, and slice them crossways an ⅛ inch thick. Put the slices into a bowl and pour some of the dressing from the minced cabbage over them. Peel and slice the lemon thin and remove the seeds.

Pile the minced cabbage in the center of a low salad bowl, alternate the slices of beets and lemon around it, pour any dressing left in the bowl over it, sprinkle with the capers, and serve.

Do not substitute canned beets for freshly cooked ones; the

texture and flavor of fresh beets are important to this salad. If you are unable to obtain fresh herbs, dried ones can be substituted, using a teaspoon of the dried herbs for each tablespoon of fresh ones, but the flavor of the salad is thus impaired.

TO MAKE JANNOCKS (OAT BREAD)

According to these two examples before shewed [manchet and fine cheate], you may bake any bread leavend or unleaven'd whatever, or compound graine as wheat and rie, or wheat, rie and barley, or rie and barley, or anie other mixt white corne [grain].

Gervase Markham, *The English Hus-wife*

THE WORKING VERSION:

2 cakes fresh yeast or 2 tablespoons dried yeast	2½ cups oat flour
2 cups lukewarm water	2½ cups sifted unbleached flour
1 tablespoon salt	

Crumble or sprinkle the yeast into the water in a mixing bowl. When the yeast softens and expands, add the salt and oat flour and beat it in. Then stir in the unbleached flour about a cup at a time. Turn the dough out on a floured work surface and knead for five minutes.

Put the dough into a clean mixing bowl large enough to permit it to expand to nearly twice its size. Cover the bowl and set the dough to rise in a warm place or in an unheated oven until it has nearly doubled in bulk—one to two hours. Turn the dough out onto a floured work surface and knead it into a ball. Divide this into two equal parts and knead each one into a round loaf. Set these four or five inches apart in a cookie pan that has been generously sprinkled with whole-wheat flour and set to rise again until nearly doubled in size—1 to 1½ hours—in a warm place. (The loaves can also be baked in eight- or nine-inch cake pans, but it is sometimes difficult to remove the loaves from the pans.) Bake at 400° for thirty-five to forty-five minutes, or until they are nicely brown. Cool on a wire grille.

These can also be made up as rolls, in which case they will

need to bake only twenty minutes at 400°. The dough makes a rather heavy-textured bread, but it is well flavored. Oat flour can be found at most health food stores.

Oat breads were eaten in areas where oats were grown, mainly in the north. Two kinds of breads were made of oat flour: bannocks, which were flat cakes of oat flour and water baked on a gridiron or set up in front of a clear (not smoky) fire to bake, and jannocks, which were loaves baked in an oven.

At Gawthorpe, the Lancashire home of the Shuttleworth family, jannocks were baked regularly. The 1616 and 1617 household accounts show that six to eight bushels of oats were ground each week into flour for jannocks. As the family itself ate white bread, these were probably for the household servants and other laborers employed by the family. Jannocks was an old name for oat bread in both Lancashire and Cheshire.

In Shakespeare's day the northern counties as well as Scotland were oat growers. Most people from regions in which other grains were grown, especially wheat-growing areas, found oat bread rather poor stuff. But Thomas Muffet, in *Health's Improvement,* was enthusiastic about it. "Had Galen seen the Oaten Cakes of the North, the Janocks of Lancashire, and the Grues of Chesire, he would have confessed that Oats and Oatmeal are not only meat for Beasts, but also for tall, fair and strong Men and Women."

The recipe for manchet appears on page 38.

TO MAKE AN ALMOND CUSTARD

Take two pounds of almonds, blanch and beat them very fine with rose-water, then strain [mix] them with some two quarts of creame, twenty whites of eggs, and a pound of double refined sugar; make the paste as beforesaid, and bake it in a milde oven fine and white, strow on them biskets red and white, stick muskedines red and white, and scrape thereon double refined sugar.

Robert May, *The Accomplisht Cook*

THE WORKING VERSION:

½ cup blanched almonds
¼ cup sugar
2 tablespoons rose water
5 egg whites
2 cups light cream
6 candied cherries, minced

THE PASTRY

¼ cup sugar
½ cup butter, at room temperature
1 egg, separated
1 tablespoon cold water
1¼ cups sifted unbleached flour

Grate or grind the almonds very fine. Add the sugar and rose water and mix them into a paste. Beat in the egg whites, one at a time, until well blended.

Add the cream, a few spoonfuls at a time, and blend into the paste. Cover and set aside while you make the pastry shell.

Cream the sugar and butter together until fluffy. Add the egg yolk and the water and beat until well blended. Stir in the flour only until you can form a ball of the dough. Flour your work surface and roll out the dough to fit an eight-inch pie plate with an extra ½ inch for fluting the edge of the shell.

Fit the pastry sheet in the dish—if it breaks, mend it with bits of the dough—and brush it with egg white. Flute the rim by pinching the dough between your fingers every ½ inch. Pour the reserved custard slowly into the pastry shell and bake at 350° for fifteen minutes, then lower the heat to 325° and continue to bake until a knife inserted into the center of the custard comes out clean. This may take from forty minutes to an hour; check after forty minutes, as oven thermostats vary a great deal. Sprinkle the minced cherries over the pie just before serving.

I have substituted a cookie-dough pastry for the shell, and the minced cherries for the biskets and muscadines, to approximate the contrasts in color and flavor that May wanted. The muscadines seemed to me to detract from the flavor and to confuse the texture of the dessert, but if you wish to garnish the pie with them, the recipe appears on page 390.

Custards were probably boiled more often than baked and were frequently served hot. All the recipes for custards that I have seen called for cream rather than milk as the liquid.

The menu quotation for this dish was not a figment of Shakespeare's imagination. It was still considered amusing at great public feasts, such as a London sheriff's dinner or the lord mayor's election feast, to have a jester, fully dressed, take a flying leap over the heads of some of the guests into a huge dish of custard on the table, splattering the guests.

In *The Devil Is an Ass,* Ben Jonson also shows that this form of entertainment was still current. Satan, talking to Pug, says,

> He may perhaps, in tail of a Sheriff's dinner
> Skip with a Rhime o' the table, from New Nothing
> And take his Almaine leap into a custard
> Shall make my lady mayoress and her sisters
> Laugh all their hoods over their shoulders.

In *The Staple of the News,* Jonson calls this kind of prank "the custard politic."

Custards did not disappear from public feast tables until over a century later. As late as 1766, in a letter to a friend, Bishop Warburton lamented their departure: "The Lord Mayor told me 'the Common Council were much obliged to me for that this was the first time he had ever heard them prayed for.' I said, I considered them as a body who much needed the prayers of the Church. But . . . I also told him . . . I was greatly disappointed to see no custard at table. He said, 'that they had been so ridiculed for their custard that none had ventured to make its appearance for many years.' I told him I supposed that Religion and custard went out of fashion together."

TO MAKE A WARDEN OR A
PEAR TART QUARTERED

Take twenty good wardens, pare them, and cut them in a tart, and put to them two pound of refined sugar, twenty whole cloves, a quarter of an ounce of cinamon broke into little bits, and three races [roots] of ginger pared and slic't thin; then close up the tart and bake it, it will ask five hours baking, then ice it with a quarter of a pound of double refined sugar, rosewater, and butter.

Robert May, *The Accomplisht Cook*

THE WORKING VERSION:

2½ pounds cooking pears
½ cup sugar
¼ cup brown sugar
¼ teaspoon cinnamon
⅛ teaspoon cloves
1 tablespoon grated fresh
   (green) ginger

THE PASTRY
2 cups sifted flour

1 teaspoon salt
¾ cup cold butter
½ cup cold water (approximately)
1 egg, separated

THE ICING
2 tablespoons sugar
1 tablespoon rose water
1 teaspoon melted butter

Quarter, core, and peel the pears, then cut the quarters in two. Mix the sugars and seasonings together and stir them into the fruit. Cover and set aside while you make the pastry according to directions given on page 31.

Divide the dough into two pieces, the one for the bottom crust a little larger than the other. On a floured work surface roll out the larger piece to fit an eight-inch pie dish. Fit this into the dish and roll out the piece for the top crust.

Arrange the fruit evenly in the dish. Cover with the top crust and seal the edges with the tines of a wet fork. Slice off any surplus pastry, make fork holes in the top of the pie, and brush with egg white. Bake at 450° for twenty minutes, then lower the heat to 350° and bake for twenty minutes.

Mix together the sugar, rose water, and melted butter. Remove the pie from the oven and brush it with the icing. Return the pie to the oven for five minutes to glaze the frosting. Serve slightly warm.

Wardens are hard winter pears, and some recipes call for stewing them first in a sugar syrup until tender. Wardens were also combined with quinces for pies. Queen Elizabeth received numerous warden-and-quince pies as New Year's gifts from her sergeants of the pastry, perhaps because these were the only fresh fruit other than apples available at that season. The pies she received were elegantly decorated with gold leaf.

PROFESSIONAL COOKS AS
COOKBOOK AUTHORS

There were two kinds of cookbook writers, the compilers and the professional cooks. The compilers collected recipes from individuals or from other cookbooks. For them, such work may have been just another way to help earn a sometimes precarious living, although some of them no doubt had at least an amateur's interest in cooking. Professional cooks who produced cookbooks were men who had spent their working lives in the kitchens of wealthy families and who had perhaps done some private catering. Joseph Cooper had even been cook to royalty.

Several of the cookbooks, such as Robert May's, were written at the end of a long life of professional cooking. Although they were published in the second half of the seventeenth century, their authors' training, professional experience, and style of cooking were of Shakespeare's time.

Women did not write cookbooks, at least not under their own names. The first English cookbook written by a woman—or, at any rate, the first to appear with a woman's name as author—did not appear until 1661, when *The Ladies Directory,* by Hannah Woolley (or Wolley) was published.

Shakespeare was knowledgeable about cooking and appreciative of seasoning and design in the serving of foods. "But his neat cookery!" Guiderius says in *Cymbeline* (Act IV, Scene 2), of the food Imogen (disguised as a boy) has prepared, "he cut our roots [vegetables] In characters, And sauc'd our broths as Juno had been sick And he her dieter."

In *Troilus and Cressida* (Act I, Scene 1), Shakespeare describes the steps involved in bread-making. Troilus has just told Pandarus that he is tired of Troy's war against the Greeks and is preparing to take off his fighting gear. Pandarus, trying to dissuade him, counsels patience: "He that will have a cake out of the wheat must tarry the grinding." To Troilus's rejoinder, "Have I not tarried?" he replies, "Ay, the grinding; but you must tarry the bolting." Troilus again asks, "Have I not tarried?" and Pandarus answers, "Ay the bolting; but you must tarry the leavening." "Still have I tarried," Troilus insists, to which Pandarus responds, "Ay, to the leavening; but here's yet in the word 'hereafter' the kneading, the making of the cake, the heating of the oven, and the baking; nay, you must stay the cooling too, or you may chance to burn your lips."

Most of what we know about the professional cooks of this period who left their cookbooks as a legacy to us is what they themselves tell us in their introductions and prefaces, and what we can glean from a critical reading of the commendatory poems and biographies that were added to the authors' introductions to sell the books.

What Robert May looked like, at least in his old age, we know from an engraved portrait of him on the frontispiece of his book. The engraving is dated 1660, when May was seventy-two years old and when the first edition of *The Accomplisht Cook, or the Art and Mystery of Cookery* appeared. The book was reprinted a number of times.

Eight of the twenty sixteenth- and seventeenth-century cookbooks I worked from were written by professional cooks. Four of these books were by John Murrell. The others in this category were by Thomas Dawson, Joseph Cooper, Robert May, and William Rabisha.

Thomas Dawson, the earliest of the four, published *The good huswifes Jewell* in two separate parts, in 1587. These books were also reprinted several times. The last known reprint was in 1620 when Edward Allde reprinted the first part as *A Booke of Cookerie* without crediting Dawson as the author.

The title page of the book says that the "rare devises for Conceites in Cookery" were "out of the Practice of Thomas Dawson." His book was addressed to housewives and included medicinal recipes and farming information, as was usual in cookbooks of the period. These last make up about one-third of the book. Part II was a reprint of Part I, with some new recipes added, among them nine "sallets for fish dayes" and instructions on how to "bray golde," that is, how to prepare gold leaf for decorating dessert dishes and confections.

The next professional cook to write a cookbook was John Murrell, who, in 1617, published *A New Booke of Cookerie* and *A Daily Exercise for Ladies and Gentlewomen* and again, in 1621, *A Delightfull daily exercise for Ladies and Gentlewomen,* together with *A Booke of Cookerie.* His second *Booke of Cookerie* does not repeat any of the recipes in the earlier book, and

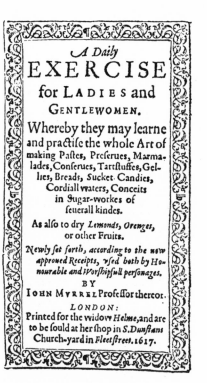

A Delightfull daily exercise has enough new recipes in it, as well as a series of sample banquet menus, to have made it worth purchasing even if one owned the 1617 edition.

As with the other professional cookbook writers, what we know of Murrell comes almost entirely from the lengthy dedications and introductions in his books. He was born in London and probably served his apprenticeship as a cook there, but with whom we do not know. He had traveled, he said, in France, Italy, the Low Countries, and "divers other places."

He must also have had some knowledge of music, as his dedication of *A Daily Exercise for Ladies and Gentlewomen* to "My Much Honored The Truly Vertuous Mris [Mistress] Elizabeth Bingham, wife of Nicholas Bingham, Esquire" shows: "As there is nothing new under heaven; so nothing old . . . yet on olde *Grounds* are new *Descants* [variations] daily, as full of rarietie, as varietie; that doth please." Music often goes with philosophical leanings; so with Murrell, who sees "the pleasure of *Man* consisting in nothing more, than in every thing; that is, in change: *varietie* standing more aloofe from *Sacietie* than *uniformitie,* in whatsoever sensible [experienced through the senses]."

"We alter our *Fashions* and outward *Habits* daily," he continues. "So our Cookery, Pastry, *Distillations, Conserves,* and *Preserves,* are farre otherwise now, than not long since they were." His recipes, Murrell adds, "are all (or at the least most) of the newest Strain, approved and beloved of those that try them." And with a refreshing air of modesty he says, "What else they are I leave to your judgment, and myself to your good favor. . . . So hoping that whosoever shall peruse the same Art and Mystery [craft or trade], by Reading thereof will be more desirous to practice the same without weariness." He ends with "I have thought to reveale it in a small volume, hoping as I have Laboured in travell to attaine to the same, that you will be pleased to thinke well of these my labors. So shall I be encouraged to wade through many more of the like practices."

A Daily Exercise . . . was written for housewives; a *New Booke of Cookerie* was written for professional cooks. In the latter he begins by offering four sample menus—"Bills of Service" he calls them. The first is a three-course dinner with twenty dishes in the first course, twenty in the second, and ten in the third. But, he says, "for the board's end [the lower end of the table, where lower-ranking guests and high-ranking servants sat], "the cook could "leave out some of the costliest dishes . . . if you have ten or twelve for the board's end it is sufficient." As was customary, he lists the dishes on the menu in the order in which they should be set out in the kitchen for the serving men to take into the dining room.

And for the benefit of beginning cooks, Murrell points out that as all meats are not in season all the time, the cook must be prepared to substitute others that are in season, "so that it be not grosse meate, for grosse meat disgraceth a feast." By gross meat, Murrell means what was then called butchers' meat, which was anything but the finest cuts of beef and veal, although lamb, young pork, and kid were also acceptable.

Joseph Cooper, the author of *The Art of Cookery Refin'd and Augmented,* was a former master cook to Charles I (who had succeeded to the throne in 1625). In 1654, when Cooper published his cookbook, the days of glory for all the old-style English cooks had passed, except in a few homes of the old nobility. For Cooper to identify himself with the king who had been executed only five years earlier took courage. He calls himself Mr., a term carrying a distinction that no longer exists.

Cooper might have been the younger son in a gentry family, who was therefore without the right to be addressed as "Sir" but entitled to be addressed as "Mr.," and who, since he would not inherit his father's title or most of his property, chose to follow a natural interest in cooking and learn the trade of professional cook. Apprenticeship, although usually to one of the prestigious trades, was common for younger sons of gentry and even noble families. Or, the right to the "Mr." might have been conferred on him because of his important office in the king's "below-the-stairs" household of cooks, bakers, and food and other purchasing officers. As master cook to the king, he alone would have been permitted to prepare his food.

Cooper is openly scornful of other cookbooks and boastful of his own. The title page of *The Art of Cookery Refin'd and Augmented* assures us that the recipes offered are "rare and rich unpublished Receipts of COOKERY . . . with an addition of Preserves, Conserves, &c., offering an infallible delight to all Judicious Readers." His preface neatly disposes of competing books: "Though the *Cheats* of some preceding *pieces* that treated on this subject (whose *Title-pages,* like the contents of a weekly Pamphlet, promised much more than the Books performed) may have provided this [book] but a cold intertainment at its first coming abroad; yet I know it will not stay long in the world, before every *rationall Reader* will cleare it of all alliance to those false pretenders. Ladies," he continues, "forgive my confidence if I tell you that I know this piece will prove your favorite."

Perhaps his anger at the cold reception that his book received "at its first coming abroad" was directed against other professional cooks who had failed to show proper appreciation of it. But the recipes in Cooper's rather short book are, despite his protestations, much like those in books whose authors had held less exalted posts. He does not object to the use of garlic, which he thinks good with strong-flavored meats such as wild duck, but he uses it with discretion, rubbing it over the serving dish rather than cooking it with the meat. And, like his professional colleagues, he sometimes adds such a conglomeration of seasonings and ingredients that the flavor of the dish is reduced to a blur and the main ingredient sunk almost without a trace. His recipe for frying garden beans, for example, calls for boiling them tender, peeling them, and beating them into a paste with almonds, boiled apples, grated cheese, sugar, ginger, horseradish, cooked spinach, grated bread, eggs, beef marrow, cream, and salt. This mixture was then to be made up into any shape the cook chose, stuck with pine nuts, fried in butter, and served with a sauce of verjuice, spinach juice, orange juice, muscadine (a sweet wine), sugar, butter, and egg yolks, and sprinkled with sugar before serving.

Robert May and William Rabisha, like Joseph Cooper, were cooks of the old school. Although their books were published after the middle of the seventeenth century, they might equally well have been dated half a century or more earlier. Both had been cooks in the time of Shakespeare; both had cooked for members of the nobility as well as for gentry families and wealthy families of lesser social status; both were nostalgic for the old days of expansive—and expensive—hospitality.

Their cookbooks were addressed to professional cooks, but they must have come under strong criticism from other members of the Cook's Mystery (as the guild was known in Shakespeare's day) for giving away the secrets of the trade. Both justified themselves by saying that their books were meant to assist young men who had just finished their apprenticeships and were starting out as journeymen on their way to the goal of master cook.

Robert May addresses his preface to "The master Cooks, and to such young Practitioners of the Art of Cookery, to whom this Book may be usefull. . . . To you first, most worthy Artists, I acknowledge [that] one of the chief Motives that made me to adventure this Volume to your Censures [judgments], hath been to testify my gratitude to your experienced Society; nor could I omit to direct it to you, as it hath been my ambition, that you should be sensible of my Proficiency of Endeavors in this Art. To all honest well intending Men of our Profession, or others, this Book cannot but be acceptable, as it plainly and profitably discovers the *Mystery* of the *whole Art;* for which, though I may be *envied by some that only value their private Interests above Posterity, and publick good,* yet God and my Conscience would not permit me to *bury these my Experiences with my silver Hairs in the Grave.*" At the time he wrote this, according to his biographer, Robert May was still employed, "silver hairs" and all, by Lady Englefield.

Like other professional cooks of his day, he resented the vogue for French cooks, who, he says, "have bewitched some of the *Gallants of our Nation* with Epigram Dishes, smoakt rather than drest." But, he says, those dishes and ideas about cooking that he had found of value during his stay in France he has included in his book.

May dedicated *The Accomplisht Cook* to four of his former employers: Lord Montague, Lord Lumley, Lord Dormer, and Sir Kenelme Digbie, "so well known to this Nation for their admired Hospitalities." His days in their employ he called "Golden Days of Peace and Hospitality." May paid tribute not only to the splendor of the tables of his former employers but also to their generosity. "Nor can I but confess to the world . . . that the onely structure of this my Art and Knowledge, I owed to your costs, generous and inimitable Expenses." Like Rabisha, he alludes to the civil war and the temporary overthrow of the monarchy: "Hospitality, which was once a Relique of the Gentry, and a known Cognizance to all ancient Houses, hath lost her Title through the unhappy and cruel Disturbances of these Times."

Dedications such as these were, at least in part, the self-serving expressions of hopes for increased sales that such patronage might well bring. But they were also expressions of gratitude for the days when these authors were able to fulfill themselves in their professions as artists in cookery.

Robert May lived through fifteen years of the reign of Queen Elizabeth I, through all of the reigns of James I and Charles I, and through the Commonwealth. He published his book the year that Charles II came to the throne.

His father, who, May's biographer says, was considered one of the ablest cooks of his day, was master cook in the household of Sir William Dormer, at Wynge, in Buckinghamshire. Here it was that Robert was born in 1588. And here as a child, under his father's tutelage, he proved such an apt pupil that Lady Dormer sent him, when he was ten years old, to Paris to live for five years in the household of a French nobleman and learn the arts of French cookery. The lad apparently also learned enough French to get around Paris and to read French cookbooks. Robert did return to Lady Dormer's household to serve as one of five cooks under his own father, but not until he had served his seven-year apprenticeship in London to Arthur Hollinsworth (or Hollingsworth), who was then cook to both the Grocers' Company and the Court of the Star Chamber.

The contemporary biographer of Robert May was, perhaps,

What wouldst thou view but in one face
all hospitalitie, the race
of those that for the Gusto stand,
whose tables a whole Ark comand
of Natures plentie wouldst thou see
this fight, peruse Mays booke, 'tis hee,
For Nathaniell Brooke att the Angell in Cornegill

Frontispiece portrait of Robert May, author of The Accomplisht Cook

another nostalgic cook, for he says, after telling of May's return to Wynge, "Such Noble Houses were then kept, the glory of that, and shame of this present age; then were those Golden Days wherein were practised *the Triumphs and Trophies of Cookery;* then was hospitality esteemed, Neighborhood [neighborliness] preserved, the Poor cherished, and God honoured."

Robert May remained in the service of old Lady Dormer, as he called her, until her death, when he returned to London, where he worked first for Lord Castlehaven and then for Lord Lumley. The latter must have been a joy to cook for; May's biographer describes him as "that great lover and knower of Art, who wanted [lacked] no knowledge in the discerning of this mystery."

From Lord Lumley's kitchen May moved to Cowdray in Sussex to serve in the kitchen of Lord Montague (or Mountague as May's biographer spelled the name). Afterwards he served a long series of masters of various high social ranks, some of whom took him with them when they went to Italy and Spain. May's is the only cookbook that gives recipes for Italian pastas, and he includes quite a number of these. But none of these pastas appears in the thirteen "Bills of Fare" he offers, such as were "used before Hospitality left this Nation."

William Rabisha, author of *The whole Body of Cookery Dissected,* first published in 1661, dedicated his book to two duchesses and three ladies of lesser social rank whose "boundless . . . vertues have been daily manifest (even in those late covetous destructive times [the civil war and the Cromwellian rule of England had just been ended by the accession of Charles II a year earlier])." They had been, he says, "upholders and nourishers of all ingenuous Arts and Sciences, and in particular that of the said Mysterie of Cookery."

As qualification for his authorship of a cookery book, he says that he has served as "Master Cook to many honourable Families . . . both in this my native countrey, and with Ambassadors and other Nobles in certain forraign parts." His book, however, has surprisingly few foreign recipes. There are less than a dozen Continental recipes in all, most of these French, along with one or two Spanish, Italian, and Portuguese.

His book, Rabisha says, will teach young practitioners not only how to prepare the many dishes they will need to know, but also how to arrange and garnish them for serving. And he reminds his colleagues how difficult it is to teach apprentices and young journeymen how to dress dishes properly for serving, "for experience shall tell all my Brethren, that it is an hard thing to teach a young Practitioner to dress many hundred . . . dishes, after the composition is made." Even when the younger cooks are supervised and given proper directions, he says, "yet will they spoyl it in the doing." His book offers to help experienced cooks with this problem of training the young.

For young practitioners, he explains in simple terms how to use the book. As a final bit of advice, he tells his readers that if the recipes are too large for their needs, they can cut to the required amount "by taking an equal proportion of each ingredient, according to the quantity as you intend to dress, and if you would augment . . . take a bigger quantity of each simple in your compounds. If the salt has been left out of the recipe, as is possible, correct that fault; also take out your faggot of sweet herbs, onions, Garlick, or whole Spices from your meats, when you go to dish your meats, for I have omitted to mention this in every Receipt." If his ample bills of fare are too large, he points out, it is easy to cut down the number of dishes, but "what an advantage it is to have a choice of so many." And he reminds his readers that all of the recipes cannot be used at all times since some ingredients may be available only during certain seasons of the year. Recipes should therefore be chosen according to the foods that are in season.

Rabisha's defense of his book is vigorous and reasonable. In his preface he says, "Divers Brethren of my own Fraternity may open their mouths against me, for publishing this Treatise, pretending that thereby it may teach every Kitchen-wench, and such as never served their times [apprenticeships], and so be prejudicial to the Fraternity of Cooks." But that, he answers, "may as truly be said of all other Arts and Sciences . . . and what Artists amongst them, make not themselves perfect, as well by studying their Volumes [books written by others], as by practice? It is wrong to refuse to share one's knowledge: There is an evil amongst most men, when they have learned themselves by other mens light, that none might follow them; and so men monopolize all knowledge therein to themselves, and condemn all those that are a guide and light to the ignorant; there is none other but such will condemn me in what I have done."

Robert May's and William Rabisha's books are the only cookbooks of substantial length; the other cookbooks of the period are very short. Rabisha's book is 239 pages long, and May's nearly twice as long. Its length, and the quality of its recipes, explain why so many of the recipes in my book come from *The Accomplisht Cook*.

A Menu in Honor of Portia

Let them be joyful too,
For they shall taste our comfort.
Cymbeline, Act V, Scene 5 (*Cymbeline*)

SACK

*The young lion repents; marry, not in ashes and sackcloth,
but in new silk and old sack.*
Henry IV, Part II, Act I, Scene 2 (*Falstaff*)

SCALLION APPETIZERS

Indeed the tears live in an onion that should water this sorrow.
Antony and Cleopatra, Act I, Scene 2 (*Enobarbus*)

OYSTER POTTAGE

*I will not be sworn but love may transform me to an
oyster; but I'll take my oath on it, till he have made an
oyster of me, he shall never make me such a fool.*
Much Ado About Nothing, Act II, Scene 3 (*Benedick*)

BROILED FRESH HERRINGS

*Fools are as like husbands as pilchards are to herrings
—the husband's the bigger.*
Twelfth Night, Act III, Scene 1 (*Clown*)

A FLORENTINE OF LAMB

*I will some other be; some Florentine,
Some Neapolitan.*
The Taming of the Shrew, Act I, Scene 1 (*Lucentio*)

A ROAST CHINE OF BEEF

*Methinks sometimes I have no more wit than a
Christian or an ordinary man has; but I am a great
eater of beef, and I believe that does harm to my wit.*
Twelfth Night, Act I, Scene 3 (*Sir Andrew*)

A POACHED CHICKEN WITH ASPARAGUS

*And then the justice,
In fair round belly with good capon lin'd.*
As You Like It, Act II, Scene 7 (*Jaques*)

A SALAD OF WATERCRESS AND VIOLETS

I think this word 'sallet' was born to do me good.
Henry VI, Part II, Act IV, Scene 10 (*Jack Cade*)

SOURDOUGH BARLEY BREAD
AND MANCHET

I will knead him; I will make him supple.
Troilus and Cressida, Act II, Scene 3 (*Ajax*)

ALE AND WINES

*He that drinks all night, and is hang'd betimes in
the morning, may sleep the sounder all the next day.*
Measure for Measure, Act IV, Scene 3 (*Pompey*)

ROBERT MAY'S CHEESE CAKE

Why then, can one desire too much of a good thing?
As You Like It, Act IV, Scene 1 (*Rosalind*)

PEARS POACHED IN CLARET

My news shall be the fruit to that great feast.
Hamlet, Act II, Scene 2 (*Polonius*)

*I count myself in nothing else so happy
As in a soul remembering my good friends.*
Richard II, Act II, Scene 3 (*Bolingbroke*)

TO PREPARE CHIBOLS, OR SCALLIONS

Chibols pilled [peeled], washt clean, and half the green topps cut clean away, so served on a fruit dish; or . . . Scallions . . . which such like serve up simply.

Gervase Markham, *The English Hus-wife*

THE WORKING VERSION:

> 2 bunches crisp young scallions
> Ice water

Cut off all but an inch or two of the green part of the scallions. Pull off the outer layer and slice off the roots. Chill them in ice water for half an hour before serving. Shake off the water and arrange them in a sunburst design on a flat dish.

My apologies to Markham for rewriting what was already so clear and simple.

Green onions served raw, said Markham, make a good simple salad with which to begin a meal. And the dietaries agreed that onions could "stirre up appetite to meate" as well as "quicken sight"; eaten "in great abundance with meate," they could help one sleep soundly. But they also warned that onions were thinning [caused loss of weight]. In this respect, said Thomas Elyot, in *The Castle of Health*, long onions sinned more than round ones, red ones more than white, and dry onions more than green ones. Dietary writers did not share our current belief that slimness was a good thing for people.

John Gerard, the herbalist, who disliked onions as food, found another use for them: "The juice anointed upon a pild or bald head in the Sun, bringeth the haire againe very speedily."

TO MAKE OYSTER POTTAGE

Take some boild pease, strain them and put them in a pipkin with some capers, some sweet herbs finely chopped, some salt, and butter; then have some great oysters fryed with sweet herbs and grosly chopped, put them to the strained pease, stew them together, serve them on a clean scowred dish on fine carved sippets, and garnish the dish with grated bread.

Robert May, *The Accomplisht Cook*

THE WORKING VERSION:

½ pound shelled green peas
3 cups water
1 teaspoon capers
2 tablespoons minced parsley
2 tablespoons minced chives
4 tablespoons butter

4 large or 8 medium fresh oysters, chopped coarse
1 scant teaspoon salt
2 slices buttered toast, cut into triangles
1 teaspoon grated bread crumbs

Rinse the peas. Bring the water to a boil, add the peas, and bring to a boil again. Cook, uncovered, until tender—ten to fifteen minutes. Press the peas with the water through a fine sieve or purée them in a blender.

Add the capers, parsley, chives, and two tablespoons of the butter, return the soup to the saucepan, and simmer for five minutes. Melt the rest of the butter in a small skillet, add the oysters, and sauté for one minute, turning them as they cook. Add the oysters and the butter from the saucepan to the pea soup and simmer for two minutes. Then add ½ teaspoon of salt and taste. Add the rest of the salt if needed.

Put the triangles of toast into individual soup bowls and pour the soup over them, dividing the oysters as equally as you can. Sprinkle with the bread crumbs and serve.

If fresh peas are not available, half a ten-ounce package of frozen peas can be substituted.

Given the enormous popularity of oysters, it is surprising that the dietaries had so little to say about them. Sir Thomas Elyot says only that shellfish "engender melancholy"; Vaughan warns that they "must not be eaten in those moneths which in pronouncing want [lack] the letter R." In a more affirmative vein, he adds that "Oysters rosted on the imbers [embers], and then taken with oyle, pepper and the juyce of Orenges provoke appetite and lust."

Wall-fleet oysters, which were highly esteemed, found their way into *Pammelia,* a collection of rounds and catches published in London sometime between 1600 and 1618. One six-part round makes use of the oyster women's cries:

> New Oysters, new Oysters, new Oysters, new,
> New Oysters, new Wall-fleet Oysters—
> At a groat a peck—each Oyster worth twopence.
> Fetch us bread and wine, that we may eate,
> Let us lose no time with such good meate [food]—
> A Banquet for a Prince—New Oysters,
> New Oysters, new Oysters, new Oysters new,
> New Oysters, new Wall-fleet Oysters.

TO BROIL HERRINGS, PILCHARDS, OR SPRATS

Gill them, wash and dry them, salt and baste them with butter, broil them on a soft fire, and being broild serve them with beaten butter, mustard, and pepper, or beaten butter and lemon.

Robert May, *The Accomplisht Cook*

THE WORKING VERSION:

2 pounds fresh herrings	1 tablespoon prepared
5 tablespoons butter, melted	mustard
1 teaspoon salt	¼ teaspoon pepper
	1 lemon

Remove the entrails, cut off the heads and fins, and wash the herrings under cold running water. Dry them in paper towels and brush them with some of the melted butter, sprinkle them with salt, and broil for five minutes on each side.

Add the mustard and pepper to the remaining butter and keep warm over hot water. Slice the lemon and remove the seeds. Arrange the broiled herrings on a warmed serving dish and spoon the sauce over them. Garnish the dish with the slices of lemon and serve immediately.

If you prefer to serve a lemon-and-butter sauce instead of mustard with the herrings, cut out ½-inch-wide strips from the peel of the lemon and set them aside. Squeeze the juice from the lemon, add it to the remaining melted butter, and cook over medium heat, beating constantly until the sauce starts to thicken. Spoon the sauce over the herrings and garnish the plate with the lemon strips.

Salt herrings were used for broiling as well as fresh ones, but these had to be soaked in cold water first, and they lacked the delicate flavor of fresh herrings.

Red herrings were herrings that had been smoked after salting; the smoking gave them the reddish-brown color to which they owed their name. White herrings were unsmoked salt herrings. Tavern keepers sometimes offered red herrings free to their customers to increase their thirst and thus the take in the host's till.

Herrings were often eaten as snacks, sometimes with wine. Nicholas Breton, however, warned that mixing wine and herrings was not a good idea: "A red herring and a cup of Sacke, make warre in a weake stomacke."

Bloats or bloaters, the specialty of Yarmouth—the most important herring-fishing and curing center in England—were cured with saltpeter. Thomas Nashe, in "Lenten Stuff, or the Praise of Red Herring" (1567), lauded Yarmouth's herrings. "A red herring," he wrote, "is wholesome in a frosty morning, it is a most precious fish merchandise, because it can be carried through all Europe [England exported large amounts of salted, smoked, and dried herrings to Catholic countries]. The poorer sort make it three parts [three-fourths] of their sustenance. It is every man's money [income] from the king to the peasant. . . . A red herring drawn on the ground," he added, "will lead hounds to a false scent. [Perhaps this is the source of our current use of the phrase.] A broiled herring is good for rheumatism. The fishery is a great nursery for seamen, and brings more ships to Yarmouth than assembled at Troy to fetch back Helen."

The herring also served Shakespeare as a source for comedy in seven plays. "A plague o' these pickle herring," says Sir Toby in *Twelfth Night* (Act I, Scene 5), coming home "in the third degree of drink." In *Romeo and Juliet* (Act II, Scene 4), Mercutio describes his lovesick friend Romeo "without his roe, like a dried herring." Falstaff, in *Henry IV, Part I* (Act II, Scene 4), blaming the times for his own show of cowardice, says, "If manhood, good manhood, be not forgot upon the face of the earth, then am I a shotten herring." A shotten herring was one with its roe removed.

TO MAKE A FLORENTINE

Take a leg of mutton or veal, shave it into thin slices, and mingle it with some sweet herbs, as sweet marjoram, tyme, savory, parsley, and rosemary, being minced very small, a clove of garlick, some beaten nutmeg, pepper, a minced onion, some grated manchet, and three or four yolks of raw eggs, mix all together with a little salt, some thin slices of interlarded bacon, and some oyster-liquor, lay the meat round the dish on a sheet of paste, or in the dish without paste, bake it, and being baked, stick bay-leaves around the dish.

Robert May, *The Accomplisht Cook*

THE WORKING VERSION:

1½ pounds lamb steak
 2 slices lean bacon, minced
 ¼ cup minced onion
 1 small garlic clove, puréed
 2 tablespoons minced parsley
 ¾ teaspoon salt
 ⅛ teaspoon pepper
 ½ teaspoon thyme
 ⅛ teaspoon marjoram
 ⅛ teaspoon savory
 ⅛ teaspoon ground rosemary
 ¼ teaspoon nutmeg

 1 tablespoon grated bread crumbs
 1 egg yolk
 1 teaspoon oyster liquor or clam juice
    Bay leaves, to garnish

FOR THE PASTRY
 2 cups sifted unbleached flour
 1 teaspoon salt
 ¾ cup cold butter
 ½ cup cold water (approximately)
 1 egg, separated

Ask your butcher to slice the lamb steak almost as thin as chipped beef; or put the meat in the freezer just long enough to stiffen it; then, with a sharp knife, slice the meat across the grain as thin as you can.

Mix together all the rest of the ingredients except the bay leaves and stir the slices of meat into them until they are coated with the seasonings. Cover and set aside while you make the pastry, following directions given on page 31.

Divide the dough into two pieces, the one for the lower crust a little larger than the one for the top crust. On a floured work surface roll out the larger piece to fit an eight-inch pie plate. Then roll out the other piece.

Arrange the slices of meat evenly in the pie, cover with the top crust, and seal the edges with the tines of a wet fork. Slice off the surplus pastry, punch fork holes in the top of the pie, and brush with egg white.

Roll out the surplus pastry and cut out small lambs from it with a cookie cutter or freehand. Arrange these over the top of the pie and brush them with egg white. Bake at 450° for twenty minutes, then lower the heat to 350° and bake twenty-five minutes longer. Garnish the pie by sticking the bay leaves into it and serve hot or cold, but do not refrigerate it—unless you like soggy crusts.

Crusts for florentines were supposed to be delicate. Most recipes call for rolling the pastry very thin, "so thin," *The Good Hous-wives Treasurie* says, "that ye may blowe it up from the table." Cooper uses puff paste for his pastry.

Florentines, or florendines, were usually made with minced meat and dried fruits and were sweet. They were also made with sweetened puréed vegetables. A savory florentine such as this one was unusual. Rice florentines were generally rice puddings baked in a rich pastry.

TO ROAST A CHINE OF BEEF

Draw [*it*] *with parsley, rosemary, tyme, sweet marjoram, sage, winter savory or lemon, or plain without any of them, fresh or salt, as you please; broach it, or spit it, roast it, and baste it with butter; a good chine of beef will ask six hours roasting.*

For the sauce take strait tops of rosemary, sage-leaves, picked parsley, tyme, and sweet marjoram; and stew them in wine vinegar, and the beef gravy; or otherways with gravy and juyce of oranges and lemons. Sometimes for a change in saucers of vinegar and pepper.

Robert May, *The Accomplisht Cook*

THE WORKING VERSION:

3 tablespoons butter	THE BASTING
¼ teaspoon rosemary	SAUCE
¼ teaspoon sage	¼ cup red wine vinegar
¼ teaspoon winter savory	¾ cup clear beef broth
¼ teaspoon marjoram	½ teaspoon salt
¼ teaspoon thyme	½ cup minced parsley
1 teaspoon salt	¼ teaspoon thyme
One 2-pound boned and rolled beef rib roast	

Blend the butter, rosemary, sage, savory, marjoram, thyme, and salt, and rub the mixture into the roast. Bring all the ingredients for the sauce to a boil in a small saucepan. Lower the heat to simmer and cook for five minutes. Baste the roast with this sauce every ten minutes.

If you have a rotisserie, spit the roast so that it is evenly balanced and broil it for forty minutes; to oven-roast it, preheat your oven to 375° and roast the meat for thirty minutes—forty minutes if you prefer less rare meat.

Slice the roast, remove the strings, and arrange the slices in a warmed serving dish. Pour the remaining basting sauce from the pan over the meat and serve.

Even the wealthiest families had little, if any, fresh beef during the winter months, so May's suggestion that the roast can be made of either fresh or salt beef is not surprising. But even so well seasoned a roast as this one, if made from beef that had been soaking for twenty-four hours in water to remove the salt from it, could not have been a mouth-watering dish or a source of pride to a self-respecting cook.

The usual sauce for beef was mustard, and often very hot mustard indeed, as Shakespeare and other writers tell us. In *The*

Taming of the Shrew (Act IV, Scene 3), Grumio taunts the famished Katharina: "What say you to a piece of beef and mustard?" And to her reply, "A dish that I do love to feed upon," he answers, "Ay, but the mustard is too hot a little." Tewksbury mustard was especially noted for its strength and thickness. Falstaff, in *Henry IV, Part II* (Act II, Scene 4), says of Poins that his wit is "as thick as Tewksbury mustard." John Taylor also describes Tewksbury mustard: "Then comes *Jack-Sauce,* with a spoon creeping out of a mustard pot, armed in a pewter saucer, a desperate fellow . . . and many times (with the spirit of Tewksbury) will make a man weep being most merry."

Mustard was commonly prepared by cleaning and grinding the seed into powder and mixing it with vinegar. But other liquids were also used, including aged beer, ale, white and red wines, buttermilk, and cherry juice. If a mustard quern (grinder) was not available, Robert May suggested that the seeds could equally well be powdered in a bowl "with a cannon bullet."

Potluck dinners were not unusual in Shakespeare's day. But when the members of the potluck party included the king, who brought along a large rib roast as his contribution, it was grist for the mills of all the gossip hunters in London. In November, 1618, James I was in Newmarket for a stay of several weeks. John Chamberlain wrote a friend about the event: "We hear nothing from Newmarket, but that they devise all the means they can to make themselves merry, as of late there was a feast appointed at a farmhouse . . . whither each man should bring his dish. The King brought a great chine of beef, the Marquis of Hamilton four pigs incircled with sausages, the Earl of Southampton two turkies, another six partridges, and one a whole tray full of buttered eggs; and so all passed off very pleasantly."

TO BOYLE CHICKENS WITH SPARAGUS

Boyle your Chickens in faire water, with a little whole mace, put into their bellies a little parsley, and a little sweet butter, dish them upon sippets and pour a little of the same broath upon it, and take a handful of sparagus being boyled, and put them into a Ladle full of thicke butter, and stir it together in a dish, and pour it upon your Chickens or pullets, strew on salt, and serve it to the Table hot.

HOW TO DRAW YOUR BUTTER THICKE

Put to every pound of butter, sixe spoonefulls of vinegar, a branch of Rosemary, a little whole mace, & a few cloves, and when the butter begins to melt, take a ladle and powre it up a high till it be all melted, and then it will be as thick as creame.

John Murrell, *A Booke of Cookerie*

THE WORKING VERSION:

One 3-pound frying chicken
2 pounds chicken backs and necks
4 cups water
6 sprigs parsley
1 tablespoon butter
3 large pieces whole mace
2 to 3 teaspoons salt

1½ pounds fresh asparagus
2 cups water
1 teaspoon salt

THE DRAWN BUTTER
½ cup butter
2 tablespoons white wine vinegar
3 cloves
3 large pieces whole mace
1 small sprig fresh rosemary or ½ teaspoon dried rosemary

3 slices buttered toast, quartered

Remove the wing tips, neck, and giblets from the whole chicken. Wash them and add them, with the chicken backs and necks, to four cups of water; cook in a pressure cooker at ten pounds pressure for forty-five minutes, or simmer in a tightly covered pot for three hours. If you use a pressure cooker, remove the pot from the heat and let the pressure go down before opening the cooker.

Strain the broth into the pot in which the chicken is to be poached. Rinse the chicken in cold water and wipe it dry inside and out with a clean cloth. Put three sprigs of the parsley and the tablespoon of butter inside the chicken and tie the legs and wings loosely to the body with white string.

Put three sprigs of parsley, the three pieces of mace, and two teaspoons of the salt in the poaching broth. Taste the broth and add the rest of the salt if needed. Lower the chicken, breast side down, into the broth. Bring the broth to a boil, cover the pot, turn the heat down as low as it will go, and simmer the chicken until it is tender—from 50 minutes to 1¼ hours—turning the chicken over after ½ hour. Turn off the heat but leave the chicken in the broth until needed.

Snap off the tough lower parts of the asparagus stalks and slip off the side scales with a paring knife. Wash the stalks in cold water and cut them into two-inch pieces. In a skillet with a lid, bring the two cups of water to a boil. Add the salt and the asparagus and bring to a boil again. Cover the skillet, lower the heat to medium, and cook until the asparagus is tender but still crisp—from ten to fifteen minutes.

While the asparagus is cooking, prepare the drawn butter. Put the butter, vinegar, cloves, mace, and rosemary into a small saucepan and cook over low heat until the butter is partly melted. Then whip or beat it with a small wire whisk or a spoon until the sauce thickens to the texture of whipping cream. Remove the rosemary, mace, and cloves from the sauce. Drain the asparagus and pour the sauce over it.

Remove the chicken from the poaching broth, snip off the string, and cut the bird into serving-size pieces. Put these into a warmed serving dish, spoon the asparagus and its sauce over the chicken, garnish the dish with the pieces of toast, and serve.

More often than not the instructions in cookbooks called for cooking the chickens in broth, which, of course, improves their flavor as well as that of the broth. With this as a precedent, I used chicken broth as the poaching liquid here. Also, since adding broth to the chicken for serving dilutes the sauce, I suggest that you save the broth for other uses.

Asparagus, which was variously spelled sperage, sparage, sparagras, sparagus, and asparagras, was fairly well known and considered a delicacy in Shakespeare's day. John Gerard grew it in his experimental gardens. He described it as tasting like green beans and suggested that the first sprouts which came up in April could be eaten raw, seasoned with oil, vinegar, salt, and pepper. But, he said, they were more delicate "being so speedily boil'd as not to lose the verdure and agreeable tenderness . . .

letting the water boil before putting them in." He also suggested that asparagus could be boiled in broth and that it made a good salad cooked as well as raw. Gerard, it seems, was something of an amateur cook himself.

A SALAD OF WATERCRESS AND VIOLETS

Watercress being finely picked, washed, and laid in the dish with violets . . . serve it with good oyl and vinegar and scrape on sugar.

Robert May, *The Accomplisht Cook*

THE WORKING VERSION:

½ cup fragrant (*viola odorata*) violets

2 large bunches of crisp watercress

3 tablespoons red wine vinegar

4 tablespoons salad oil

¼ teaspoon salt

1 teaspoon brown sugar

Rinse the flowers in a bowl of cold water and remove the stems. Shake the water from the violets, put them in a clean small jar, cover, and refrigerate until needed. Wash the watercress in cool water and remove the coarse stems. Wrap in a towel and refrigerate.

In a shallow bowl beat the vinegar, oil, salt, and sugar until blended. Toss the watercress and the violets lightly in the dressing and serve.

Shakespeare and his contemporaries ate many flowers and greens that have disappeared from our tables. Strawberry and violet leaves, for example, were often used in pottages and salads, egg dishes, and fritter mixtures. Flowers were made into tarts. One recipe for a tart of "Marigoldes, prymroses, or cowslips" calls for parboiling the flowers and mixing them with egg yolks, butter, and sweet curds (freshly made cottage cheese) or stewed apples that are flavored with mace.

Gervase Markham distinguished between watercress and land

cress. "The first," he said, "growes in moyst places, the latter in Gardens, or by the high-wayes." Some housewives grew land cress in window boxes. (They grow easily in window boxes, but as they go to flower very quickly, the leaves must be picked regularly and often.) Housewives with neither gardens nor window boxes could buy cress from street peddlers, whose cry was "Here's water-cresses and scurvy-grass [horseradish leaves]," or gather land cress along the "high-wayes."

SOURDOUGH BARLEY BREAD

Of a Pecke of Wheate & lieke quantitie of Barley mingled together is made . . . household bread.

The Household Books of the Earles of Derby

THE WORKING VERSION:

1 cup soured cheate dough	2½ cups barley flour
1½ cups warm water	1 cup whole-wheat flour
2 cakes of fresh yeast or	1½ cups sifted unbleached
2 tablespoons dry yeast	flour
1 tablespoon salt	

Make the cheate sourdough two days ahead of time according to directions and ingredients given on page 78.

Pour the water into a large mixing bowl and crumble or sprinkle the yeast into it. When the yeast softens and expands, stir in the salt, then the barley flour about a cup at a time, then stir in the whole-wheat flour and the soured dough. Mix until blended; then add the unbleached flour ½ cup at a time.

Turn the dough out on a floured work surface and knead for five minutes. Put the dough into a warmed mixing bowl large enough to allow it to nearly double in size. Cover the bowl and set to rise in a warm place or in an unheated oven. When the dough has nearly doubled in size—in 1 to 1½ hours—turn it out on a floured work surface and knead into a ball. Divide the ball in two and knead each piece into a round loaf.

Flatten the loaves to about two inches in height and set them,

four to five inches apart, on a cookie sheet that has been floured
with whole-wheat flour. Set to rise again until nearly doubled in
size—1 to 1½ hours. Bake at 400° for thirty to forty minutes, or
until browned. Turn out to cool on a wire cooling grille; if the
bread sticks to the pan, slide a narrow steel spatula under the
loaves to loosen them.

This is a heavy-textured bread, but it has an interesting flavor.
Barley flour does not have the capacity to trap and hold gases and
therefore cannot produce a light loaf. Barley bread was also
baked as flat, unleavened cakes about twelve inches in diameter
and about an inch thick. Usually, however, it was leavened and
made into large loaves weighing about twelve pounds.

The earls of Derby set a good table, and their hospitality was
well known. The earl, his immediate family, and his valued guests
ate manchet made of "fyne wheate." Manchet, however, was only
a small part of the bread eaten in the household. In 1586, according to household accounts, the proportion of household bread to
manchet was 42 to 1. The Derby household books specified that a
peck of wheat and a peck of barley should make sixty loaves of
bread and a bushel of wheat was to make one hundred manchets.

The recipe for manchet appears on page 38.

TO MAKE CHEESECAKES

*Take a good morning milk cheese, or better, of some eight pound
weight, stamp it in a mortar, and beat a pound of butter amongst
it, and a pound of sugar, then mix with it beaten mace, two pound
of currans well picked and washed, a penny manchet grated, or a
pound of almonds blanched and beaten fine with rose-water, and
some salt, then boil some cream, and thicken it with six or eight
yolks of eggs, mixed with the other things, work them well together, and fill the cheesecakes, make the curd not too soft, and
make the paste of cold butter and water according to these forms.*

Robert May, *The Accomplisht Cook*

THE WORKING VERSION:

2 cups cottage cheese

4 tablespoons almond paste

4 tablespoons butter, at
room temperature

4 tablespoons sugar

1 teaspoon rose water

1 teaspoon mace

⅛ teaspoon salt

¼ cup light cream

2 egg yolks

½ cup currants, parboiled

THE PASTRY

2 cups sifted unbleached
flour

½ teaspoon salt

1 tablespoon sugar

¾ cup cold butter

1 egg, separated

½ cup cold water
(approximately)

Drain the liquid from the cottage cheese and press it through a sieve. Rub the almond paste through the medium holes of a grater into the sieved cheese. Add the butter, sugar, rose water, mace, and salt and mix into a smooth paste.

Heat the cream to lukewarm in a small saucepan. Beat in the egg yolks and cook over low heat, stirring constantly, until the custard coats a spoon. Remove from the heat and set aside to cool. When the custard is cold, stir it into the cheese mixture and add the currants. Refrigerate the filling while you make the pastry.

Sift the flour, salt, and sugar together into a large mixing bowl. Add ½ cup of the butter and rub into the flour until the mixture has the consistency of fine meal. Dice the rest of the butter and stir the pieces into the flour.

Beat the egg yolk with the water until blended and pour it into the dry ingredients. Stir with a fork until you can form the dough into a ball—if more liquid is needed, add an additional tablespoonful of water at a time. Sprinkle your work surface with flour and turn the dough out onto it. Pat the dough into a ball and divide it into two pieces, one a little larger than the other. Roll out the smaller piece to a round nine inches in diameter, or an eight-inch square, or any shape you like of approximately this size.

Loosen the sheet of pastry carefully, fold it over and transfer it to a lightly floured cookie sheet. Then open out the pastry on the sheet. Roll out the larger piece of dough an inch larger than the bottom crust, and with a stylus or the point of a paring knife trace a design in the pastry.

Spread the cheese mixture over the pastry on the cookie sheet to within an inch of the edge. Brush the edges of the pastry with egg white and fit the top crust over the filling. Seal the edges by pressing down with the tines of a wet fork. Brush the top with egg white and bake at 450° for fifteen minutes, then lower the heat to 350° and bake ten minutes longer. Cool the cheese cake on the baking sheet.

This is enough filling for an eight-inch pie, if you prefer to bake it as a pie. It is best eaten within an hour or two of baking.

Cheese cakes were very popular. Ordinarily, they were made with fresh curds (cottage cheese), but occasionally a hard, cured cheese was mixed with the curds or hard cheese alone was used. Rabisha offers an elaborate recipe for a tart of Parmesan cheese. The simplest recipe for a cheese tart appears in *The good Huswifes Handmaide for the Kitchin*. This calls for paring and dicing Banbury cheese, putting it between two sheets of pastry, sealing it and baking it. The tart is sprinkled with sugar after being taken from the oven.

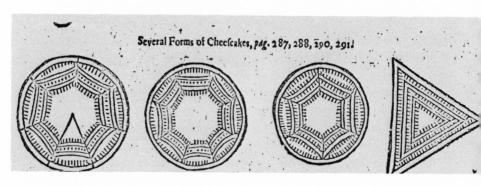

Pastry designs for cheese cakes from Robert May's The Accomplisht Cook

TO STEW WARDENS OR PEARS

Pare them, put them into a Pipkin, with so much Red or Claret Wine and water . . . as will near reach to the top of the Pears. Stew or boil gently, till they grow tender, which may be in two

hours. After a while, put in some sticks of Cinnamon bruised and a few Cloves. When they are almost done, put in Sugar enough to season them well and their Syrup, which you pour out upon them in a deep plate.

> Sir Kenelme Digbie, *The Closet of the Eminently Learned*
> *Sir Kenelme Digbie, Kt., Opened*

THE WORKING VERSION:

4 large firm but ripe pears, with their stems	1 three-inch stick cinnamon
12 cloves	¼ cup brown sugar
1½ cups claret	¼ cup sugar
1½ cups water	

Peel the pears, cutting out the flower ends but leaving the stems on. Stick three cloves into each of the pears and stand them, stem side up, in a deep saucepan that will hold them rather snugly. Add the claret, water, and cinnamon, and bring to a boil. Lower the heat and simmer for ½ hour, uncovered, basting the pears every five minutes with the poaching liquid.

Mix the two sugars, sprinkle them over the pears, and continue cooking and basting until the pears can be easily pierced with a toothpick. Carefully remove the pears to a deep serving bowl, standing them stem side up. Cook the poaching syrup over high heat until it boils down to 1½ cups, pour the syrup over the pears, and serve either hot or cold.

Pears poached in red wine were not new in English cookery. There is at least one recipe dating back to the middle of the fifteenth century that cooks pears in red wine. The medieval recipe called for "Powder of canel," so it is probably of French origin; *cannelle* is the French word for cinnamon.

LITERARY MEN WHO WROTE COOKBOOKS

Gervase Markham, John Partridge, and Sir Hugh Plat were compilers of cookbooks whose major writing ambitions were

Portrait of Sir Kenelme Digbie, whose collection of recipes was printed after his death as The Closet of the Eminently Learned Sir Kenelme Digbie, Kt. Opened

literary. Perhaps they turned to cookbook writing when their other literary endeavors failed to provide sufficient income. They may also have been amateur cooks—certainly Hugh Plat was—for they all wrote with a certain amount of knowledge and enthusiasm for the subject. Some of the recipes in their books were gathered from friends, some from other cookbooks. Occasionally, a personal recipe collection came into the hands of an author who organized and edited it, and sometimes expanded it as Gervase Markham did with *The English Hus-wife*.

The Closet of the Eminently Learned Sir Kenelme Digbie, Kt., Opened is his collection of recipes, published after his death by someone else. Its title page says only that the book was printed with the permission of Sir Kenelme's son, "by E. C. for H. Brome at the Star in Little Britain." E. C. may have been a friend of Sir Kenelme's, a publisher, a printer, or a bookseller.

Sir Kenelme, one of Robert May's numerous employers, was not only an aficionado of cookery and a collector of recipes, he was also a diplomat, a scientist, a patron of the arts, an astrologist, and very popular at court with the ladies, with whom he no doubt often exchanged recipes.

Of the life of John Partridge, author of *The Treasurie of commodious Conceits, and hidden Secrets* and *The good Huswifes Handmaide for the Kitchin,* little is known. His earlier writings were all literary. In 1566 he published three narrative historical poems, two of them based on classical subjects. Though far from great literature, these works show Partridge to be an educated and cultured person. The introductions and dedications in his cookbooks give only vague suggestions about him as a personality. He had friends, one of whom was Thomas Curteyse, Gentleman, whose poem in praise of the author is included in the first (1573) edition of the *Treasurie*. But Partridge also had enemies, or thought he had, although they may only have been critics of his literary works. At the beginning of the first edition of the *Treasurie,* he writes:

> Go foorthe my little Booke,
> That all on thee may looke:
> Feare not the cattynge hook
> of Zoylles spightfull rage.

(Zoilus, a fourth-century B.C. rhetorician and critic, was notable for his severe criticism of Homer's poems. His name became a synonym for harsh or envious criticism.) Defiantly, Partridge goes on:

> More connyng [cunning] workes erst don,
> In any former age
> Thou knowest went never free,
> But that the Cur Dog hee
> Takes his delight and glee
> For to deface the same.

The *Treasurie* may have had a better reception from the critics than Partridge's earlier and more purely literary works, for the defensive poem is missing from the 1586 edition. In its stead he sends the book to the lady who persuaded him (he says) to publish it:

> Go little booke of profit and pleasance,
> Unto thy good mistres without delay;
> And tell her I send thee for the performance
>   of her ernest sute: sith she would have no nay.

Partridge probably also furnished the verses that the printer addresses to the purchaser. They give the table of contents, as well as, in conclusion, the price of the book.

> Therefore good huswives once again, I say to you repayre,
> Unto this Closet when you neede, & mark what ye find there
> Which is a mean to make most things to huswife use pertain
> As all conserves and Sirops sweet, to comfort hart and braine
> For bankets [desserts and sweetmeats] to here may you find,
>   your dishes how to frame:
> As succad, marmilad, Marchpane to, & ech thing els by name.
> . . . .
> Thus to conclude I wish you mark the benefits of this book,
> Both gentles state, the Farmers wife, & crafts mans huswyfe
>   cooke.
> And if we reape commodity by this my freends devise,
> Then give him thankes, and thinke not much of foure pence
>   for the price.

Thanks to this printer, we know the price of least one cookbook published during the sixteenth and seventeenth centuries. For his or her fourpence, the purchaser got a handsome 93-page book.

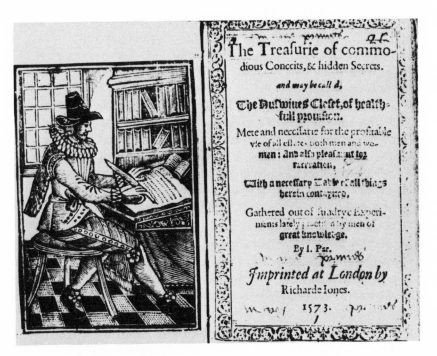

Frontispiece and title page of John Partridge's The Treasurie of
commodious Conceits, & hidden Secrets (*1615 edition*)

To the "Worshipfull, Mayster Richard Wistow, Gentleman:
one of the Assistants of the Company of the Barbours & Sur-
gions," to whom Partridge dedicated the book, he promises that
if the book "be wel accepted at your hands I shall shortly exhibite
unto your worshyp, a thynge of greater valew and estymation."
The "thynge of greater valew and estymation" may have been
The good Huswifes Handmaide for the Kitchin, which did not
see publication until 1594. It was reprinted in 1595 as *The good
Huswives Handmaid for Cookerie in her Kitchen.* The title page
notes that this book contained "Manie principall points of
Cookerie, as well how to dresse meates, after sundrie the best
fashions used in England and other countries, with their apt and
proper sawces, both for flesh and fish, as also the orderly serving
of the same to the Table."

For this book Partridge borrowed from *A Proper newe Booke
of Cokerye* the bills of fare and the seasonal lists of meats,
poultry, game, and game birds. From *The good huswifes Jewell*
he borrowed the list of banqueting necessaries, but he gives few
banquet [dessert] recipes. He offers only two medicinal recipes,
one for cooking mutton "for a sicke bodie," the other a "purga-
tion." These two volumes were reprinted as *The Treasurie of*

. . . *Hidden Secrets,* as late as 1656, but Partridge published no other cookbooks.

About Sir Hugh Plat we know a bit more. He was born in 1552, into the family of a wealthy London brewer, and baptized, fittingly for an infant who was later to write a cookbook as well as farming books, in Garlicke Hythe. He became Sir Hugh in 1605, when he was knighted by James I for some of his scientific experiments—in areas other than cooking.

His father had provided for him financially so amply that, although Hugh, as the third son, did not inherit his estate, he never had to worry about money. This was especially fortunate for a man of his tastes and the size of his families: he had three sons by his first wife and two sons and three daughters by his second wife. We know of no pictures or diaries that might give us a picture of Sir Hugh's childhood, but a man rich enough to possess both a London town house and a country seat in Hertfordshire, as his father did, would probably have had him tutored at home.

When he was sixteen years old, Hugh went to St. John's College, Cambridge. He graduated a bachelor of arts in 1571 or 1572, and shortly thereafter became a member of Lincoln's Inn, one of the London Inns of Court, where the sons of noblemen, gentlemen, and wealthy commoners studied law.

Hugh Plat's serious interests did not, however, include the law, and he tried first for a literary career. But the reading public showed a noticeable lack of interest in his first two literary efforts, and he then turned to a long-standing interest in farming problems—going back perhaps to his summers spent on the family estate in Hertfordshire.

Apparently he also found the housewife's problems interesting and the housewife in need of help, for the preservation of food —a very serious problem—took much of his attention, and other aspects of housewifery interested him too. His *Delightes for Ladies* includes sections on "The Arte of preserving, conserving, &c.," "Secrets in Distillation," "Cookerie and Huswiferie," and "Sweete Powders, oyntments, beauties &c."

Much of this book had already appeared in 1594 in his *Jewel House of Art and Nature containing divers rare and profitable Inventions, together with sundry new Experiments in the Art of Husbandry, Distillation and Moulding* (of sweetmeats). The earlier book was a confused jumble of all sorts of things. *De-*

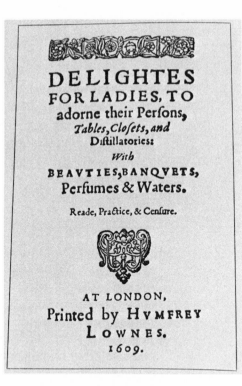

lightes for Ladies, however, was an orderly selection of recipes from the *Jewel House,* plus the new recipes and household hints he had since collected. It was a very successful book, which ran through thirteen editions by 1683, and which has been reprinted at least twice in the twentieth century. Sir Hugh's last book, *Floraes Paradise beautified . . . with sundry sorts of delicate fruites and flowers &c.,* was on horticulture and proved to be as popular with gardeners as *Delightes for Ladies* was with housewives.

He was a great collector of household hints, to which he added a few ideas of his own in *Delightes for Ladies.* The section on "cookerie and huswiferie" is largely a series of such hints, ranging from "How to keep Lobsters, Crafishes, &c., sweet and good for some fewe daies"—by wrapping them separately in cloths and burying them in "Callis" sand—to how to avoid smoking up the kitchen when "broiling of Bacon, Carbonadoes, etc." His suggestion for beating egg whites is ingenious: "breake them up with a stubbed rod" or "wring them often through a sponge." His hint on how to bring egg whites into "an oyle speedily" is to shred several figs and beat them with the egg whites. He does not explain how to get the shreds of figs *out* of the beaten egg whites.

Sir Hugh himself was not always sure that his efforts to improve husbandry were appreciated. In his "Epistle" to *Delightes for Ladies,* he hopes that his efforts in the service of housewifery will find greater appreciation:

> Sometimes I write of lasting Beverage,
> Great *Neptune* and his pilgrims to content:
> Sometimes of food, sweet, fresh, and durable,
> To maintaine life, when all thing els were spent:
> Somtimes I write of sundrie sorts of soile,
> Which neither *Ceres* nor her handmaides knew.
> I write to all, but scarsly one beleaves,
>
> . . . .
>
> But now my pen and paper are perfum'd
> I scorne to write with coppresse [green vitriol] or with gall,
> Barbarian [sugar] canes are now become my quils,
> Rosewater is the inke I write withal.
>
> . . . .
>
> To teach and fine [perfect] each secret I doe strive,
> Accept them well, and let my wearied Muse
> Repose her self in Ladies laps awhile.
> So when she wakes, she happely may record,
> Her sweetest dreames in some more pleasing stile.

Like Hugh Plat, Gervase Markham's interests ranged widely. One of the minor poets of Shakespeare's period, he was a member of the literary group that gathered around the earl of Essex. Markham moved easily from poetry to horsemanship to cookery to husbandry, and he said of himself: "A piece of my life was schollar, a piece Soldiour, and all Horseman." By all accounts he was a magnificent horseman.

His literary writings included a novel, *The English Arcadia,* biographical studies of the earls of Essex, Oxford, Southampton, and Lindsay, which he titled *Honour in His Perfection,* and two unsuccessful plays written in collaboration with others.

Markham's Masterpeece, which he published in 1610, was a very popular manual on the diseases of horses and how to treat them. And in 1615 he published *Countrey Contentments,* the first part of which was devoted mainly to various country sports, such as archery, angling, and riding, with a section on husbandry. Part II of this book was *The English Hus-wife.*

Markham was born, probably in 1568, in Cotham, Nottinghamshire, the third son of Robert Markham. It is possible that he was brought up as a page in the earl of Rutland's household and that he was educated at Cambridge University, but the evidence is uncertain. He seems to have had the right to use "Mr." as part of his name, so he may have been of a gentry family, although going to Cambridge University would also have given him that right.

Somewhere around 1595 he married and proceeded to raise a large family. The need to support them may help to explain why he wrote on so many popular subjects.

As a soldier, he served in the Low Countries against Spain and in the Irish campaign of 1599. He may have held a captain's commission, but his biographers disagree on this. His military experience, however, surely supplied the material for *The Soldier's Exercise,* which discussed the skills a soldier needed.

Markham was a true man of the late Renaissance in England in his love for language, his exuberant use of it, and his literary and philosophical approach to even so simple an activity as fishing. In *The whole Art of Angling,* he tells us that an angler "should be a general scholar . . . in all the liberal sciences; as a grammarian to know how to write, or discourse of his art, in true and fitting terms. He should have sweetness in speech to entice others to delight in an exercise so much laudable. He should have the strength of argument to defend and maintain his profession against envy and slander." Although he expects much from his English housewife, he does not ask these qualities of her.

In his preface to *The English Huswife,* Markham explains his excursion into cookery. "Thou mayst say (Gentle Reader) what hath this man to doe with Hus-wifery, he is out of his element; and to be so generall for all qualities, is to expresse more in one Booke than can be found expresst in two women. I shall desire thee therefore to understand, that this is no collection of his whose name is prefixed to this worke, but an approved Manuscript which he happily [did] light on, belonging sometime to an

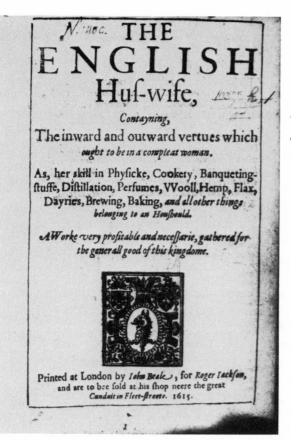

Title page of Gervase Markham's The English Hus-wife (*1615 edition*)

honorable Personage of this Kingdome, who was singular among those of her ranke for many of the qualities here set forth. [Could he have meant the countess of Rutland?] This only hath he done, digested the things of this booke in good method, placing every thing of the same kind together, and so made it common for thy delight and profit."

The fifth edition of *The English Hus-wife*, published in 1637, was dedicated to Lady Francis, the countess dowager of Exeter, no doubt with the expectation that her patronage would help sell the book. "Howsoever, Right Honorable and most vertuous Lady this booke may come to your Noble Goodnesse clothed in an old Name or Garment, yet doubtless . . . it is full of many new vertues which will ever admire and serve you . . . though it can adde nothing to your owne rare and unparalleled knowledge. . . . I do not assume to myselfe (though I am not altogether ignorant in ability to judge of these things) the full intention and scope of this whole worke: for it is true (Great

Lady) that much of it was a Manuscript which many yeeres ago belonged to an Honorable Countesse, one of the greatest Glories of our Kingdome. . . . Yet your Noble vertue will support it and make it so strong in the world, that I doubt not but it shall doe service to all those which will serve you, whilst my selfe and my poor prayers shall to the last gaspe labour to attend you."

But Markham did not live to enjoy any benefits that the countess's name might have brought him. He died in great poverty in his sixty-ninth year. His name appears on the burial register of St. Giles, Cripplegate, in London, on February 3, 1637.

Many of the sixteenth-century cookbooks are anonymous. The earliest edition of *A Proper newe Booke of Cokerye* does not name publisher, author, printer, or bookseller, although later editions do give the printers' names. *A Closet for Ladies and Gentlewomen or The Art of Preserving, Conserving, and Candying . . . and all kinds of Banqueting Stuffe,* published in 1608, is also anonymous. Its title page offers only the information that it was "Printed for Arthur Johnson, dwelling neere the great North dore of Pauls [St. Paul's cathedral in London]."

A Midsummer Night's Banquet

Come, come, Thersites, help to trim my tent;
This night in banqueting must all be spent.
Troilus and Cressida, Act V, Scene 1 (*Achilles*)

A MARCHPANE

Good thou, save me a piece of marchpane.
Romeo and Juliet, Act I, Scene 5 (*First Servingman*)

MUSCADINES (KISSING COMFITS)

Let the sky . . . hail kissing-comfits and snow eringoes.
The Merry Wives of Windsor, Act V, Scene 5 (*Falstaff*)

QUINCE PASTE

It may well be called Jove's tree, when it drops forth such fruit.
As You Like It, Act III, Scene 2 (*Rosalind*)

JOHN MURRELL'S SHELLBREAD

This lapwing runs away with the shell on his head.
Hamlet, Act V, Scene 2 (*Horatio*)

SUCKETS OF LEMON PEELS

Hast thou not learn'd me how
To make perfumes? distil? preserve? yea, so

That our great king himself doth woo me oft
For my confections?
Cymbeline, Act I, Scene 5 (*The Queen*)

CANDIED VIOLETS

The forward violet thus did I chide:
Sweet thief, whence didst thou steal thy sweet that smells,
If not from my love's breath?
Sonnet 99

SPICED BREAD

I must go buy spices for our sheep-shearing.
The Winter's Tale, Act IV, Scene 2 (*Clown*)

FRESH STRAWBERRIES AND CREAM

My Lord of Ely, when I was last in Holborn,
I saw good strawberries in your garden there;
I do beseech you send for some of them.
Richard III, Act III, Scene 4
(*Gloucester*, later *Richard III*)

CALLISHONES

Fresh as a bridegroom . . . perfumed like a milliner.
Henry IV, Part I, Act I, Scene 3 (*Hotspur*)

SWEET POTATO PASTE

How the devil Luxury, with his fat rump and potato
finger, tickles these together!
Troilus and Cressida, Act V, Scene 2 (*Thersites*)

RED MARMALADE OF QUINCES

Will't please your honour taste of these conserves?
The Taming of the Shrew,
Induction, Scene 2 (*Second Servant*)

WHITE GINGERBREAD

An I had but one penny in the world, thou shouldst
have it to buy gingerbread.
Love's Labour's Lost, Act V, Scene 1 (*Costard*)

FRESH SWEET CHERRIES

When he was by, the birds such pleasure took,
That some would sing, some other in their bills
Would bring him mulberries and ripe-red cherries.
                   Venus and Adonis, Lines 1101–3 (*Venus*)

IPOCRAS—RED, AND WHITE

I'll swear upon that bottle, to be thy true subject; for
the liquor is not earthly.
                   The Tempest, Act II, Scene 3 (*Caliban*)

Good-night, good-night! parting is such sweet sorrow.
                   Romeo and Juliet, Act II, Scene 2 (*Juliet*)

TO MAKE A MARCHPANE

*Take two pound of almonds blanched and beaten in a stone
mortar, till they begin to come to a fine paste, then take a pound
of sifted sugar, put it in the mortar with the almonds, and make
it into a perfect paste, putting to it now and then in the beating
of it a spoonful of rose-water to keep it from oyling; when you
have beaten it to a puff-paste, drive it out as big as a charger
[serving platter], and set an edge about it as you do a quodling
[apple] tart, and the bottom of wafers under it, thus bake it in
an oven or baking-pan; when you see it white, and hard, and dry,
take it out, and ice it with rosewater and sugar, being made as
thick as butter for fritters, so spread it on with a wing feather,
and put it into the oven again; when you see it rise high, then take
it out and garnish it with some pretty conceits made of the same
stuff, stick long comfets upright in it, and so serve it forth.*

                Robert May, *The Accomplisht Cook*

THE WORKING VERSION:

THE ALMOND PASTE
½ pound blanched almonds
2¼ cups confectioners' sugar, sifted
2 tablespoons rose water
Two 12-inch sheets of wax paper

THE BASE
½ cup butter
⅓ cup sugar
1 egg, separated
1¼ cups sifted unbleached flour

THE ICING
1 tablespoon rose water
3 tablespoons sugar

CONCEITS TO DECORATE THE MARCHPANE
Reserved almond paste
Green food coloring
Whole cloves, with stems on
12 candied violets
1 ounce candied ginger, cut into narrow strips

To make the paste, grate the almonds (the small "mouli" grater is adequate for this amount of nuts) and remove any coarse bits of nuts. Add two cups of the confectioners' sugar and mix until blended. With your fingertips, work the nuts and sugar into a paste, adding a teaspoonful of rose water at a time—stop working the paste as soon as it is blended; overworking results in an oily, tough paste. Some almonds are drier than others, and you may need a little more rose water; if you do, add it a teaspoonful at a time. Cover the paste and set it aside until needed.

To make the base, cream the butter and sugar together until light. Beat in the egg yolk, stir in the flour, one-third at a time, then refrigerate the dough for fifteen minutes.

Sprinkle a cookie sheet with flour and roll the dough out on it to a round approximately nine inches in diameter. Place a round eight-inch cake tin, open side down, on the pastry and cut around the tin with the tip of a pointed knife. Remove the excess pastry before lifting the tin. Brush the round with egg white.

Set aside two tablespoons of the almond paste for the conceits (decorations). Sprinkle one of the sheets of wax paper with two tablespoons of the remaining confectioners' sugar, place the remaining almond paste on it, sprinkle the paste with the rest of the confectioners' sugar, cover with the second sheet of wax paper, and roll out the paste to a round seven inches in diameter.

Slowly pull off the top sheet of paper and carefully turn the round of almond paste over onto the cookie base, then carefully pull off the other sheet of paper, leaving approximately an inch-wide border of the base free. Turn this up and flute it with your fingers to make a raised border. Punch fork holes in the almond paste and bake at 375° for five minutes, then lower the heat to 325° and bake fifteen minutes longer, or until the pastry is delicately browned—check after ten minutes.

While the marchpane is baking, mix one drop of the green coloring with the reserved almond paste until blended. Divide the paste into ½-inch balls and form tiny apples or pears, or both, using the cloves to make the stems and the bases of the fruits. Brush them with egg white and set aside to dry.

Remove the marchpane from the oven, and brush the top with the icing made by stirring the rose water and granulated sugar together. Return the marchpane to the oven for five more minutes to glaze the icing. Then remove the marchpane from the oven and arrange the decorations over it in any pattern that pleases you. Cool the marchpane on the cookie sheet.

To remove it to your serving dish, slide a long, narrow steel spatula carefully under the base and ease it onto the plate.

If you are pressed for time, use ¾ pound of commercial almond paste, omit the sugar, and work in the rose water. (Avoid buying almond paste with synthetic "improvers" in it.)

Nut graters can be found in the housewares sections of most department stores and in stores that specialize in cooking utensils.

A baking pan, in Shakespeare's day, was an iron box with a tight lid that was placed among the coals in the fireplace.

Marchpane was an essential part of any banquet, as Shakespeare knew and noted in his description of the preparations for Juliet's wedding banquet. It was made in all sizes and shapes. "My Lord of Denbigh's Almond Marchpane" recipe, given in Sir Kenelme Digbie's cookbook, is to be formed in "round cakes about the bigness of your hand, or a little larger, and about a finger thick." In 1562 Queen Elizabeth's "Surveiour of the Workes" gave her, as a New Year's gift, a marchpane with a model of St Paul's cathedral on it. From her yeoman of the chamber, Richard Hickes, came a "very faire marchpane made like a tower, with men and artillery in it." And her master cook, George Webster, presented her with a "faire marchpane being a chessboarde."

Marchpanes were sometimes offered to visiting dignitaries as a sign of appreciation. Lord Burleigh, who was chancellor of Cambridge University, an honorary office, was presented with a marchpane on one of his visits to the university.

Marchpanes were part of funeral feasts as well as of wedding feasts. Henry Machyn noted in his diary that twenty marchpanes were served at one of the numerous funerals he attended. Machyn was a member of the Merchant Taylors' Company of London, but he has so many entries about funerals in his diary that John Nichols, who edited the diary for publication, suspected that Machyn practiced undertaking on the side, or else had a morbid interest in funerals.

TO MAKE MUSCADINES, COMMONLY CALLED KISSING COMFITS

Take halfe a pound of double refined Sugar beaten and cearsed [sieved], put into the beating thereof, two graines of Muske, 3 grains of ambergreese, & a dram of orris powder: beat all these together with gum Dragagon steeped in damaske-rose-water, in an aliblaster [marble] mortar to a perfect paste, then slicke a sheete of white paper, slicked with a slick-stone very smooth, and rowle your sugar paste upon it, then cut it like lozenges with a rowel, & so dry them upon a stone, and when they bee dry they will serve to garnish a marchpaine, or other dishes, tarts, custards, or whatsoever else, if you will have any red you must mingle it with Rosa Paris, if blew, with blew bottles growing in the corne.

John Murrell, *A Delightfull daily exercise for Ladies and Gentlewomen*

THE WORKING VERSION:

3 tablespoons rose water
1 teaspoon gum arabic powder
3 eyedropper drops essence of ambergris
2 eyedropper drops essence of musk
4 cups confectioners' sugar, sifted
1 teaspoon powdered orrisroot
2 drops yellow food coloring (optional)
2 drops blue food coloring (optional)

Pour the rose water into a saucer, add the gum arabic, and stir until the gum is dissolved. Add the ambergris and musk and set aside until needed. Sift two cups of the sugar and the orrisroot powder into a bowl. Add the gum-arabic mixture, a tablespoonful at a time, and work it into the sugar until the paste is smooth.

For white pastilles, sprinkle the third cup of sugar on a large plate and, with your fingers, work the paste into the sugar until it is smooth. For colored pastilles, divide the white paste into two equal parts. Add a drop of one of the coloring liquids to one part and a drop of the other to the second part of the paste. Blend in each of the colors and set one aside, covered —this dries out very quickly—while you work with the other.

To make white pastilles, sprinkle ½ cup of the remaining sugar on a clean plate and work in the paste until it is smooth. Pat the paste into a square and cover it with a piece of wax paper. Roll it out gently to a sheet about ⅜ inch thick. Mark and cut off small squares, triangles, and rectangles with a knife. Sprinkle a cookie sheet with the remaining sugar and place the pastilles on it about an inch apart. Follow the same procedure for colored pastilles but work only ¼ cup of sugar into the paste of each color.

When the pastilles have hardened, loosen them gently with a flexible steel spatula—they break easily—and store them in an airtight container.

You should be able to get about four dozen pastilles from this recipe; of course the number depends on the size of the pastilles you make. They will keep for six to eight weeks. To savor the pastilles at their best, allow them to melt on the tongue.

Orrisroot powder can be obtained at any pharmacy. It is made from the root of a fragrant European variety of iris and is sometimes used in tooth powders as a perfuming agent. Note the warning on the package that the powder may cause allergic reactions to "sensitized individuals." However, neither we nor any of the friends who have tasted the muscadines in our home (after this warning) have yet shown a bad reaction as a result of eating them.

In Shakespeare's day, musk and ambergris came in lumps or as a dry powder. I could purchase them only in liquid form.

For the ambergris, musk, and orrisroot powder, John Murrell used apothecary measurements. Translating these into kitchen measures was something of an adventure. Gervase Markham offered the information that "the least of all weights is a grain, which is the weight either of a barleycorn or of a peppercorn." There are sixty grains in a dram, so I put sixty peppercorns on one dish of my balance scales and poured orrisroot powder into the other dish until they balanced. Markham offered no information on translating dry into liquid measures, so I asked our pharmacist, who told me that fifteen grains dry measure equals one cubic centimeter liquid measure, or twenty drops. So I had only to divide twenty by five for the ambergris and approximate the smaller amount of musk.

Muscadines were expensive; they sold in 1617 for three shillings a half pound in a London confectioner's shop. Clearly, only the well-to-do could afford to fill their comfit bags with them.

Queen Elizabeth's fondness for sweets, which caused her many a toothache and blackened her teeth, was well known and was catered to. She regularly received comfits of various kinds among her New Year's Day gifts. Included among these were "rynds of Lemon," "manus christi," and candied nuts like the box of "Pyne comfetts [pine nuts] musked" that one of the court apothecaries gave her in 1562. Manus christi (the hand of Christ) was a cooked fondant flecked with bits of gold leaf. Some recipes for manus christi used musk or ambergris as a flavoring but most were simple unflavored fondant.

The queen was also frequently given gifts of comfit bags and boxes to hold the sweets she was so fond of. Lady Anne Clifford noted in her diary that she had given the queen a "handsome bag to keep comfits in." In 1589 a Mrs. Huggens gave the queen, as a New Year's Day gift, twenty-four "small sweete bags of sarsenette [silk] of sundry cullors and a large sweete bagg of white satten, ymbrodered all over with Venis gold, silver, & silk of sundry cullors." Some of the comfit boxes the queen received were of gold and often they were richly jeweled.

"Sugar works" of fondant or fondantlike pastes were used as table centerpieces, and often they were ingenious as well as elaborate. Robert May suggested one that fitted in well with that exuberant age—a ship with cannons from which real gunpowder was exploded at the table.

Various gums were used to make sugar pastes pliable, and the gum was always "tempered" (softened) in rose water. Colorings were usually obtained from vegetables, flowers, roots, or barks, and most cooks knew how to prepare these. Coloring could also be purchased commercially. Occasionally, a cookbook would give information on where to buy coloring and other materials for making confectionery. At "Talbutt in Newgate Market," one cookbook advised, "gumme dragon" could be had for fourpence an ounce, "sap green" for twopence an ounce, and "Red Rosset" for only a penny an ounce. Gold leaf could be purchased at the "Gold-beaters" in small booklets. In 1639, according to *The Ladies Cabinet Opened*, published that year, a booklet of "fine gold" could be bought in London for sixteen pence.

Refined sugar, "hard and white," was considered the best sugar for making all kinds of sugar works; however, such sugar was expensive and often difficult to find. For most kitchen purposes a soft brownish sugar was used. English refiners (sùgar "boilers" or "bakers") were frequently criticized for the poor quality of sugar they produced, but the refineries of other countries were often no better.

PASTE OF QUINCES MY LADY OF BATH'S WAY

Take six pounds of flesh of Quince, and two pound of Sugar moistened well with juyce of Quinces. Boil these together in a fit kettle; first gently till the Liquor be sweated out from the quince, and have dissolved all the Sugar; Then very quick and fast, proceeding as in my way (bruising the Quinces with a spoon, &c.) till it be [thick] enough. This will be very fine and quick [tart] in taste; but will not keep well beyond Easter. . . . Then drop it on glasses, or spread it on plates, and set it to dry before a gentle fire.

Sir Kenelme Digbie, *The Closet of the Eminently Learned*
Sir Kenelme Digbie, Kt., Opened

THE WORKING VERSION:

2½ pounds ripe (fragrant) quinces
⅔ cup sugar
¼ cup water

Peel the quinces with a potato peeler. Then, with a sharp knife, cut into the fruit and break off pieces only as deep as the meat is smooth—do not use the grainy part—and dice the meat.

Put the sugar and water into a two-quart saucepan, and stir over low heat until the sugar dissolves. Add the fruit and cook over medium heat, stirring, until the mixture begins to bubble. Lower the heat to simmer, cover the pot, and cook, stirring frequently, until the fruit is almost a sauce.

Press the fruit through a sieve or food mill and return it to the saucepan. Cook over medium-high heat, stirring constantly, until the fruit is so thick that a spoon drawn across the bottom of the pan will leave—for a moment—an open space in its wake. Remove the pot from the heat and cool, uncovered, for ½ hour, stirring every five minutes.

Drop spoonfuls of the fruit onto an unbuttered cookie sheet, in small mounds about an inch apart. Heat your oven to warm—between 150° to 200°—and place the sheet in the oven for twenty-four hours. Then remove from the oven, loosen the pastes with a flexible steel spatula, and turn them over. Turn off the oven heat and return the sheet to the oven for another twelve to twenty-four hours until the pastes are firm. Store them in single layers on sheets of parchment paper in an airtight container.

You can get a fair amount of quince sauce from the meat left on the cores by covering them with water and cooking them at low heat, covered, until the fruit can be scraped easily from the core. Purée the meat and add sugar to suit your taste. This makes a slightly grainy sauce, but the flavor is good.

The usual proportions for fruit pastes were equal parts of puréed fruit and sugar. Cooking with the lesser amount of sugar, as Kenelme Digbie noted, not only preserves more of the fresh fruit flavor but takes less watching during the cooking.

John Murrell and Robert May both used rose water as the liquid and flavored the paste with musk. Both also used equal parts of fruit and sugar.

Fruit pastes were made from whatever fruits and berries were in season. Berries make a less interesting confection, however; the long cooking necessary to get the proper consistency destroys most of the fresh fruit flavor. These fruit confections, which were so popular in Shakespeare's day and long after, deserved their popularity. Recipes for them were much sought after and exchanged.

In 1608 John Chamberlain ended a letter to a friend with "I have nothing else but to pray you to remember my service to your goode Lady, and to tell her that her rasp cakes [raspberry pastes] were so well liked . . . that my Lady Fanshaw hath intreated me to get her receit or the manner of making them: which in requitall of so much sweet I have dayly from her I cannot denie, yf I may obtaine that you wold bring yt with you."

TO MAKE SHELLBREAD

Beate a quarter of a pound of double refined Sugar, cearse it with two or three spoonefuls of the finest, the youlkes of three new laid eggs, and the white of one, beate all this together in with two or three spoonefulls of sweete cream, a grain of muske, a thimble full of the powder of a dried Lemond, and a little Annise-seede beaten and cearsed, and a little Rose-water, then baste Muskle-shells with sweete butter, as thinne as you can lay it on with a feather, fill your shells with the batter and lay them on the gridiron or a lattise of wickers into the oven, and bake them, and take them out of the shells, and ise them with Rose-water & Sugar. It is a delicate bread, some call it the Italian Mushle, if you keepe them any long time, then alwaies in wet weather put them in your oven.

John Murrell, *A Daily Exercise for Ladies and Gentlewomen*

THE WORKING VERSION:

½ cup sifted unbleached flour
¼ cup sugar
¼ teaspoon ground anise
  seed
3 egg yolks
1 egg white
2 tablespoons whipping
  cream
2 teaspoons rose water

1 tablespoon grated fresh
  lemon rind
1 drop essence of musk
2 tablespoons unsalted
  butter

THE ICING
3 tablespoons confectioners'
  sugar
1½ tablespoons rose water

Sift together the flour, sugar, and anise seed. Beat the eggs, cream, rose water, lemon rind, and musk together until blended. Fold in the flour mixture, a tablespoonful at a time.

Butter a madeleine tin with the unsalted butter and dust lightly with flour. Fill each depression half full with the batter and bake in a 350° oven from twelve to fifteen minutes, or until the cakes are lightly browned around the edges. Gently loosen the edges of the cakes with the tip of a paring knife and turn them out, ridged side up, on a wire cooling grille.

An hour before serving them, mix the sugar and rose water together for the icing and brush the ridged sides of the cakes with it. Return the cakes to a 350° oven just long enough to glaze.

Madeleine tins are like cupcake tins, but the depressions are ridged like a cockleshell. These are available in shops that specialize in equipment for gourmet cooking and occasionally in the housewares departments of hardware or department stores.

Shellbread is one of the sweetmeats Murrell included in his banquet menus. These are best eaten fresh, for they dry out rather quickly.

It is possible to bake the cakes in real mussel shells; I did so the first time I tried the recipe, but it is a long, tedious task to clean them. The shells must be scraped free of the mussel flesh adhering to them, soaked in cold salt water for a day or so to rid them of the fish odor, and scraped again. Worse, many of the shells cracked in the baking.

If you noticed that the flour was missing from the original

recipe, it was Murrell's oversight or his printer's. (Without flour these ingredients produce a kind of sweet omelet.)

"Cake" and "bread" were terms used interchangeably at times. In this recipe the word "bread" means cake. But when Gremio tells Lucentio, in *The Taming of the Shrew* (Act I, Scene 1), "Our cake's dough on both sides," the metaphor runs the other way; the "cake" is bread.

TO MAKE SUCADE OF PEELES OF LEMMONS

First take off your peeles by quarters and seeth them in faire water, from three quartes to three pintes, then take them out, and put to as much more water, and seeth them likewise, and doo againe, till the water wherein they are sodden have no bitterness at all of the peeles, then you are ready, now prepare a Sirop as ye do for Quinces condict [preserved] in a Sirop. . . . Take of the same liquor . . . and put in . . . one pint of rosewater, and for every quart of liquor one half pound of sugar; seethe them againe togither on a soft fire of coles till the Sugar bee incorporated with the liquor, then put in your peeles, let them seeth softly till you perceive that your sirop is as thicke as lite hony [honey]. . . . Put them in a pot of stone [pottery].

John Partridge, *The Treasurie of commodious Conceits, and hidden Secrets*

THE WORKING VERSION:

3 large firm lemons	2 cups sugar
water	1 tablespoon rose water

Cut the lemons in half, squeeze out the juice (to use for whatever other purpose you wish), and spoon out the remaining membranes. Rinse the rinds and cut each half into quarters. Put the peels into a saucepan with one pint of cold water and bring to a boil. Boil them for ten minutes, drain off the water, and add a pint of fresh water. Repeat this process twice more.

Drain the peels, add a quart of water, and cook until the peels can be easily pierced with a fork. Drain them again, saving two cups of the water for the candying syrup. Add the sugar and rose water to this water and cook over medium heat until the syrup is clear. Add the lemon peels, lower the heat, and simmer until the peel is translucent and the syrup has thickened to the texture of honey—keep an eye on the pot as sugar burns easily.

Remove the pot from the heat, cover, and set aside until the syrup has cooled. Put the candied peel into a small jar and add enough of the syrup to cover. Cover the jar with a piece of plastic before tightening the lid. Before serving drain off the syrup and let the peels stand awhile uncovered to dry out a bit.

These are what were called wet suckets. They should not, Murrell advised, be put into the same dish with dry suckets on the banquet table. Sometimes the peels were drained and rolled in sugar after candying; then they became dry suckets.

All cookbooks called for cooking the peels in numerous waters to remove the bitter taste. As candied fruit peels were also eaten as "comforting" when one was suffering from an upset stomach or other minor ailment, Nicholas Culpeper's advice on their preparation is relevant. "I like not this way [of preparing them]," he says in his *Complete Herbal,* "and my reason is this, because I doubt [fear] when their bitterness is gone so is their virtue also; I shall then prescribe one common way . . . first boil them till they be soft, then make a syrup with sugar and the liquor you boil them in, and keep them in the syrup . . . in glasses or glazed pots." Whether Culpeper's method makes them a more effective medicament I cannot judge, but we enjoyed the bitterness left in the peel candied according to his instructions.

TO CANDY VIOLET FLOWERS
IN THEIR NATURALL COLOURS

Take of your Violet flowers which are good and new, and wel coloured. . . . Take the flowers with the stalkes, and wash them over with a little Rose water, wherein Gum-arabecke is dissolved, then take fine searced suger, and dust over them, and set them a drying on the bottom of a sive in an oven, and they will glister as if it were Sugar-candy.

Anonymous, *A Closet for Ladies and Gentlewomen or the Art of preserving, Conserving and Candying*

THE WORKING VERSION:

½ cup freshly picked, fragrant violets
1 teaspoon powdered gum arabic
1 tablespoon rose water
¾ cup sugar

Buy or pick fragrant violets. Remove the stems to within ½ inch of the flowers. Rinse them in a bowl of cold water, spread them on a clean cloth, and pat dry.

Add the gum arabic to the rose water and stir until the gum dissolves. Sprinkle half the sugar over a large cake tin. Drop a few violets at a time into the gummed rose water and turn each one in the liquid so it is completely coated. Pick them up carefully, one by one, on a fork and drop them into the sugar in the cake tin. When all the violets have been dipped, sprinkle the rest of the sugar over them.

Heat the oven to warm—150° to 200°—turn off the heat, and place the pan of violets in the oven for three hours, or until the sugar has hardened on them. When they are completely dry, loosen each violet carefully and put them in a small jar or tin with an airtight lid. Put the remaining sugar from the pan through a sieve and sprinkle it over the violets in the jar before sealing it.

You must have fragrant violets for candying, for it is the fragrance that makes them a delightful confection. Not all violets are fragrant, but the dark blue ones, called *viola odorata,* are. and fortunately these are very common. I picked the violets in our garden, just as they were fully opened, early one morning in February; winters are usually mild in the Willamette Valley of Oregon. If you get your violets from the woods, take along a large clean jar that has been rinsed with cold water in which to keep the flowers until you get home.

This was the simplest and best of the recipes I found for candying violets. The flowers kept their natural color and tasted of violets for several months.

Shakespeare must have loved the unassuming violet. In *The Winter's Tale* (Act IV, Scene 3), Perdita has been offering nosegays to the guests who have come to her foster father's

9 How to candy Rosemary flowers, Rose leaues, Roses, Marigoldes, &c. with preseruation of colour.

DIssolue refined, or double refined sugar, or sugar candy it selfe in a little Rosewater, boile it to a reasonable height, put in your rootes or flowers whe your sirup is either fully colde, or almost colde, let them rest therein till the sirup haue pearced them sufficiently, then take out your flowers with a skimmer, suffering the loose sirup to run from them so long as it will, boile that sirup a little more and put in more flowers as before, diuide them also, then boyle all the sirup which remaineth and is not drunke vp in the flowers, to the height of *manus Christi*, putting in more sugar if you see cause, but no more Rosewater, put your flowers therein when your sirup is cold or almost cold, and let them stand till they candie.

B 3   A

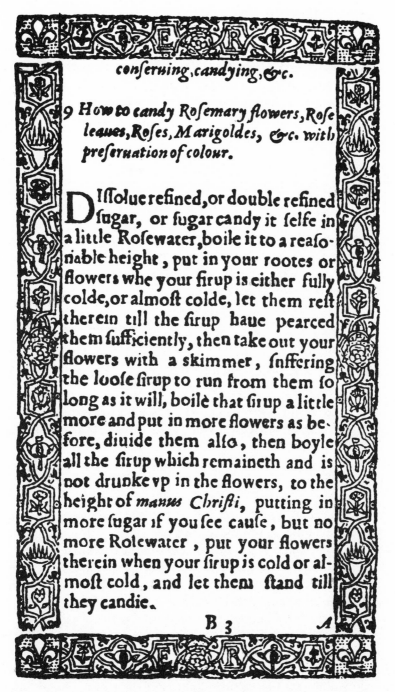

Recipe for candying flowers from Hugh Plat's Delightes for Ladies

sheep-shearing feast. She apologizes to the younger guests because the flowers of spring suitable to their ages are gone:

> I would I had some flowers o' the spring that might
> Become your time of day . . . violets dim,
> But sweeter than the lids of Juno's eyes
> Or Cytherea's breath.

TO MAKE SPICED BREAD

Take two pound of Manchet Paste, sweet butter halfe a pound, Currants halfe a pound, Sugar a quarter, and a little Mace (if you will put in any) and make it into a loafe; bake it in an oven no hotter than for Manchet.

Anonymous, *The Ladies Cabinet Opened*

THE WORKING VERSION:

1 cup lukewarm water	½ cup butter, melted
1 cake fresh yeast or	1 ½ teaspoons mace
1 tablespoon dried yeast	3 ¼ cups sifted unbleached
1 teaspoon salt	flour
½ cup sugar	½ cup currants, parboiled

Pour the water into a mixing bowl and crumble or sprinkle the yeast over it. When the yeast has softened and expanded, add the salt, sugar, butter, and mace, and beat until well blended. Stir in the flour one-third at a time, then stir in the currants. Spoon knead the bread for five minutes—*i.e.,* raise large spoonfuls of the dough up against the side of the bowl and let it fall back into the center, giving the bowl a quarter turn after each spoonful is raised.

Cover the bowl and set the dough to rise in a warm place, or in an unheated oven. When it has doubled in size—forty-five minutes to one hour—turn it out on a well-floured work surface and lightly knead it into a ball. Butter an eight-inch cake pan generously and dust it lightly with flour. Put the ball of dough into the pan, flatten it slightly with your hand, then cut two gashes in the top, crossing them at the center.

Set the loaf to rise again, uncovered. When it has doubled in size—forty-five minutes to one hour—bake at 375° for ten minutes, then lower the heat to 350° and bake twenty-five minutes longer. If the dough seems to be browning too fast, cover the loaf with a piece of clean brown wrapping paper or kitchen parchment. Turn the loaf out onto a wire grille to cool.

This is a simpler and less rich version of Gervase Markham's Banbury cake. It may well have been the kind of cake that Stephen Perlin, in his *Description of the Kingdoms of England and Scotland* (1558), described as "a very soft cake with raisins in it," which, he said, the English ate with their beer, and which made the beer "taste doubly good."

At Christmas, bread bakers sometimes added sugar and currants to bread dough and made little roly-poly figures, with currants for eyes, for the children of their customers. They were not supposed to do this sort of thing, for, according to the statutes governing the various baking crafts, anything made with sugar and fruit was the preserve of the pastry cooks. There were numerous complaints against bread bakers who made the little "Yulebabies" by pastry cooks, who, like all craftsmen, jealously defended their own jurisdictional rights.

TO MAKE CALLISHONES

Take halfe a pound of Marchpane paste, a thimble-full of coriander seeds beaten to a powder, with a graine of Muske, beat all to a perfect paste, print it and drie it.

John Murrell, *A Daily Exercise for Ladies and Gentlewomen*

THE WORKING VERSION:

½ pound almond paste
1½ teaspoons ground coriander
2 drops essence of musk

4 teaspoons rose water
½ cup confectioners' sugar, sifted

Press the almond paste through the medium-fine holes of a grater into a bowl and sprinkle ½ teaspoon of the coriander over it. Add the musk to the rose water and work this into the almond paste by spoonfuls, stopping as soon as the liquid has been blended in.

Mix the remaining coriander with ¼ cup of the sugar and set aside. Sprinkle a piece of wax paper or kitchen parchment with two tablespoons more of the sugar, lay the paste on the sugar, and sprinkle with the remaining sugar. Cover with another sheet of wax paper and roll out the paste to ½ inch in thickness.

Carefully pull off the top sheet of paper. Cut the paste, with a knife dipped in the reserved coriander-sugar, into diamonds, squares, triangles, or rectangles, or mold small spoonfuls of the paste into any forms that suit your fancy. (I make them into rings, pretzels, miniature French loaves, and round loaves, with a wheel pattern etched in the top.) Place the callishones about an inch apart on a cookie sheet that has been lightly sprinkled with the coriander-sugar. Sprinkle the remaining coriander-sugar over the confections and set the sheet in an unheated oven for five or six hours to harden.

Callishones are best eaten within a week after they are made as they tend to become grainy after that. This is one of the many recipes of the time for variously flavored almond paste sweetmeats. When you buy the almond paste, if you don't make it yourself, make sure you get pure, not adulterated, almond paste.

TO MAKE A PASTE OF POTATOES

Boyle your Potatoes very tender, pare them and pricke out all the blackes of them, put to every pound of them a graine of Muske, and beat them in a stone morter very fine, then take as much refined Sugar as the Pulp doth weigh, and boyle it to a candy height with as much Rose-water as will dissolve it, then put in the pulpe into the boiling Sugar, let it boyle alwayes stirring it until it comes from the bottom of the posnet, then lay it on a sheet of glass in round cakes or in what fashion you please, and set it in a warme oven or Stove [a heated box with wire shelves that confectioners used to dry confections], and when it is candied on the top, then turne it on the other side, and let

it candy, and in ten or twelve daies it will be dry, then boxe it for
your use.

John Murrell, *A Delightfull daily exercise for*
Ladies and Gentlewomen

THE WORKING VERSION:

1 pound sweet potatoes	2 tablespoons rose water
½ pound yams	2 drops essence of musk
½ cup sugar	

Scrub the potatoes and yams clean and bake them at 400° until
very soft—about fifty minutes. Split open the potatoes, spoon out
the pulp, removing any black areas or spots, and press the pulp
through a food mill or sieve.

Melt the sugar in the rose water in a two-quart saucepan over
low heat, stirring until it melts. Increase the heat and boil until
the syrup will spin a thread when dropped from the side of the
spoon—this should take about five minutes. Add the puréed
potatoes and the musk and cook over medium heat, stirring constantly, until the mixture comes away from the bottom of the pan
in a mass when stirred.

Remove the pot from the heat and cool the paste for five
minutes, stirring occasionally. Drop by spoonfuls, an inch apart,
onto an unbuttered cookie sheet. Heat the oven to warm—150°
to 200°—and set the sheet in the oven. Let the pastes dry overnight, or all day. Then slide a flexible steel spatula under them
and turn them over. Return the sheets to the oven, and dry the
pastes for another twenty-four hours. Store them in single layers,
on sheets of aluminum foil or kitchen parchment, in an airtight
container; use them within a month, as after that they get
rubbery.

Sweet potatoes, like eringo roots, bone marrow, and numerous
other foods, were considered aphrodisiacs. Although they had
been known in England for many years, they were still very expensive. In 1615 sweet potatoes cost the then large sum of three
shillings a pound. William Harrison, criticizing the lavishness of
the nobility, gentry, and richer merchants, spoke reprovingly of

"the potato and such venerous roots as are brought out of Spain, Portingale, and the Indies to furnish up our banquets." But they were not yet well enough known to be included in many of the dietaries. In 1595 Dr. Thomas Muffet, in *Health's Improvement*, said of them, "They nourish mightily . . . engendering much flesh, blood, and seed, but withal encreasing wind and lust."

Sweet potatoes were usually imported sliced and candied. But in the fall and winter, they arrived raw and were hawked through the streets by peddlers who called "Potatoes, ripe potatoes." They were also sold in dried form.

John Gerard, who grew them in his gardens, described them as "no lesse toothsome, wholesome, and dainty, than the flesh of Quinces." The roots, he said, could serve "as a ground or foundation whereon the cunning Confectioner or Sugar-Baker may worke and frame many comfortable delicate Conserves and restorative sweet-meats."

TO MAKE ROUGH RED MARMALADE OF QUINCES, COMMONLY CALLED LUMP-MARMALADE, THAT SHALL LOOK RED AS ANY RUBY

Pare ripe well couloured Peare-quinces, and cut them in pieces like dice, parboile them very tender; or rather reasonably tender in faire water, then powre them into a Colender, and let the water runne from them into a cleane Bason, then straine that water through a strainer into a Posnet, for if there be any gravell [gritty elements] in the Quinces, it will be in that water: Then take the weight of the Quinces in double refined Sugar very fine, put halfe thereof into the Posnet, into the water with a graine of Muske, a slice or two of Ginger tied in a thrid, and so let boile covered close, when you see your Sugar come to the colour of Claret wine, then uncover it, and take out your Ginger, and so let it boile untill your sirupe begin to consume away, then take it off the fire, and pomice [mash] it with a ladle, and so stirre and coole it, and it will looke thicke like tart-stuffe, then put in your other halfe of your Sugar, and so let it boile, always stirring it untill it come from the bottome of the Posnet, then box it, and it will look red like a Rubie, the putting of the last Sugar brings it to an orient [sparkling] colour.

John Murrell, *A Daily Exercise for Ladies and Gentlewomen*

THE WORKING VERSION:

2 ½ pounds fragrant ripe quinces	2 drops essence of musk
Water	One 2-inch slice fresh ginger
1 cup sugar	

Pare the quinces with a potato peeler. Quarter and core them, removing the grainy-looking meat around the seeds. Rinse the quarters and dice them into ½-inch pieces. Put the fruit into a two-quart saucepan with a lid, and add just enough water to cover. Cook, covered, over medium heat for about fifteen minutes, or until the quinces are soft, stirring them every five minutes.

Place a colander over a bowl and drain the fruit. Then strain the quince water through a clean white cloth into another bowl. Rinse the saucepan and return the cooked quinces to it. Add one cup of the strained quince water, ½ cup of the sugar, the musk, and ginger and cook over medium heat, stirring frequently, until most of the liquid has boiled away—approximately forty-five minutes.

Add the remaining sugar and continue cooking, stirring continuously, until the mixture is very thick. Turn off the heat and stir the marmalade until it cools. Pour it into jelly glasses or jars, cover, and store in a cool place.

Unable to obtain the ruby color of which Murrell spoke so proudly, I settled for a lovely clear carnelian.

Thomas Dawson's recipe for quince marmalade omits the musk. His recipe for quince jelly, which he calls a "Codomacke of Quinces," calls for one quart of "French wine" to five quarts of water, and for ten pounds of peeled, cored, and diced quinces. He warns against using "stony" quinces, and he strains the cooked fruit through a piece of canvas to make sure all gritty elements are eliminated. And to the strained fruit juice he adds "only as much fine sugar as will make it sweet."

Quinces are not difficult to work with when properly handled. It is especially useful to remember that they are more easily peeled with a potato peeler than with a paring knife. They may have fallen from popularity not only because they seemed difficult to handle but also because cooks failed to remove the gritty center meat and therefore produced gritty-textured dishes.

As for their place in diet, all the dietaries offered more or less the same cautionary advice. Quinces belonged in the cold and dry elements, said Sir Thomas Elyot, and should not be eaten before meals for "they bind and restraint the stomacke." Unless "they were either boiled or roasted, the cores removed, and sweetened with clarified honey or sugar"; then they not only caused good appetite but preserved "the head from drunkennesse." Eaten after meals, he said, they relieved indigestion.

TO MAKE WHITE GINGERBREAD

Take halfe a pound of marchpaine past, a quarter of a pound of white Ginger beaten and cerst, halfe a pound of the powder of refined sugar, beate this to a very fine paste with dragagant steept in rose-water, then roule it in round cakes and print it with your moulds: dry them in an oven when the breade is drawne foorth, upon white papers, & when they be very dry, box them, and keepe them all the yeare.

John Murrell, *A Delightfull daily exercise for Ladies and Gentlewomen*

THE WORKING VERSION:

½ pound almond paste   ½ cup confectioners' sugar
 2 tablespoons rose water   1 tablespoon ground ginger
 1 teaspoon gum arabic

Rub the almond paste through the medium holes of a grater into a mixing bowl. Put the rose water into a saucer, add the gum arabic, and stir until the gum dissolves. Sift the sugar with the ginger, stir in the dissolved gum arabic, and mix until well blended. Add this to the almond paste and work it in quickly but thoroughly.

Divide the paste into twenty-four pieces. Roll each piece into a ball, flatten it to ¼ inch thick, and print a design on the top with one of the small ceramic or wood molds used for printing individual servings of butter, or make crisscross patterns with a fork.

Cover a cookie sheet with a piece of rice paper or kitchen parchment and place the cakes on it. Bake at 200° for twenty minutes, then turn off the heat and let the cakes cool in the oven for fifteen minutes. Remove the cakes from the paper and finish cooling on a wire grille. Store in single layers in an airtight container.

These are best eaten fresh because, like most of the almond paste sweetmeats, they tend to dry out after a week.

Ordinary gingerbread was still made as it was in medieval days, with grated bread crumbs sweetened and seasoned with spices, including pepper, and held together with wine or clarified honey. This mixture was made into a very thick paste firm enough to slice or roll out, and cut into various shapes, after which it was dried in the oven. Some of the cookbooks called this "coarse gingerbread" and coarse indeed it is.

This coarse gingerbread was the kind sold at fairs and other places of amusement. "Sit farther with your gingerbread-progeny there, and hinder not the prospect of my shop," Leatherhood tells Trash, a gingerbread seller, in Ben Jonson's *Bartholomew Fair* (Act II, Scene 2).

Gingerbread figures were denounced by some Puritans as "popery," and Jonson refers to this also in *Bartholomew Fair*. In Act II, Scene 6, Busy, a righteous-sounding hypocrite, tells the much-abused Trash, "Hence with thy basket of popery, thy nest of images, and whole legend of gingerwork."

Strawberries were eaten with cream and sugar or honey, or with wine and sugar, or unadorned, as cherries were. They were also made into tarts, pies, creams, conserves, and soothing syrups. Strawberry tarts were usually made of cooked berries, thickened in some recipes with grated bread crumbs, but the berries were also served uncooked in baked tart shells sprinkled with sugar and spices.

STRAWBERRIES RIPE, AND CHERRIES IN THE RISE.

Street seller of strawberries and cherries (15th–16th-century woodcut)

In May, wrote Nicholas Breton in *Fantastickes,* "the strawberry and the peascod want no price [command very high prices]
in the market." Street peddlers, their baskets of fruit balanced
on their heads or hung over their arms, sometimes both, hawked
the delectable fruits. In strawberry season the cries "Fine strawburyes, ripe strawburyes" and "Strawberries Ripe, and Cherries
in the rise" were heard. Fresh cherries were also sold strung on
small sticks, and the calls of "Here's cherries round, and very
sound" and "Cherrie ripe, cherrie ripe" enlivened the air.

Fresh berries and fruit were well known as favorites of James
I. One of the tales told about the king was of the frustration of
an officer of the royal spicery who every year brought the king
the first of the new strawberries and cherries. Each time poor
Mr. French tried to make a small presentation speech and each

time without success, for "the King never had the patience to hear him one word, but his hand was in the basket."

In a letter of June, 1608, John Chamberlain wrote that he and Lady Fanshawe had gone to visit the home of a mutual friend where they "had the honor to see all, but touch nothing so much as a cherry, which are charilie [carefully] preserved for the Quene's comming." In another bit of gossip, he reported that the king, attending the christening of Sir Arthur Ingram's son, afterwards came into the garden to eat cherries and part of the banquet."

Dietaries found both fruits good appetizers as well as beneficial treatment for various ailments, but recommended that they be eaten at the beginning of a meal rather than at the end. Even Vaughan, who had not yet rid himself of some medieval notions about the dangers of eating raw fruit, conceded that "strawberries doe well refresh as coole the fiery fainting stomacke, being used before meales sugred with Creame or Wine; and for want of sugar they may be eaten with honey." Strawberries, said Andrewe Boorde, "be praysed above all buryes, for they do qualifye the heate of the lyver, & dothe ingender good blode, eaten with sugar."

TO MAKE WHITE IPOCRAS

Take a gallon of wine, an ounce of Synamon, two ounces of Ginger, one pound of Sugar, twentie Cloves bruised, and twentie cornes of pepper big beaten, let all these soake together one night, and then let it run through a bag, and it will be good Ipocras.

John Partridge, *The good Huswifes Handmaide
for the Kitchin*

THE WORKING VERSION:

½ cup sugar
1 bottle (⅘ quart) white wine
4 cloves

4 peppercorns
One 2-inch stick cinnamon
One 2-inch piece fresh (green) ginger

Stir the sugar into the wine until it dissolves. Bruise the cloves and peppercorns and add, with the cinnamon and ginger, to the wine. Cover and refrigerate for at least twenty-four hours. Strain the ipocras through a jelly bag or a clean white cloth before serving.

The recipe for red ipocras appears on page 47.

BANQUETS AND BANQUETING

"Banquet" was the term used to describe the dessert served after the main courses of the meal. It was also an informal or formal collation of sweetmeats. This might be as simple as wine and spiced bread or manchet offered to a few friends or to visiting dignitaries by the town councillors. A banquet could be no more than a bowl of strawberries, cherries, or other fruit served in a garden summerhouse on a pleasant afternoon. But for special occasions in wealthy homes or at court functions, a banquet could be a splendid and glittering display of desserts and sweetmeats.

One of the most lavish banquets in English history was given by Cardinal Wolsey for Henry VIII. The occasion was described by Wolsey's biographer: "Then in came . . . a banquet before the King's majesty, and to all the rest of the tables, wherein, I suppose, were served 200 dishes or above of wonderous meats [sweetmeats] and devices, subtilly devised." Queen Elizabeth was apparently not always pleased with the banquets her lord steward, William Knollys, provided, for when, in 1601, she entertained the ambassador from Czar Boris Godunov, she ordered Knollys to see that "the banquet be of better stuff, fit for men to eat, and not of paper shows."

Weddings, christenings, the entertainment of important officials, and the reception of diplomatic visitors or noble guests were occasions for extravagant displays of the arts of cooks, pastry makers, and confectioners. "Come, let us to the banquet," Don John says to Borachio in *Much Ado About Nothing* (Act II, Scene 1), after the supper and masked revels that their host had provided as the first part of the entertainment of his guests.

Funeral banquets could be lavish too. Henry Machyn's diary records a funeral banquet he attended at which, he said, there was "a great table of bankett," on which were sugar-coated spices (whole mace, cloves, and nutmegs were spices often served candied), fruit, gingerbread, jellies, marmalades, sugar plate (fondant), comfits, and "dyvers odurs [several others]."

Families with a garden usually had a small banqueting spot in it where, when the weather was fine, they went after dinner to enjoy the dessert course and where they would entertain friends with a collation of sweetmeats.

The banqueting house at Theobalds, Lord Burghley's home in Hertfordshire, was a magnificent affair set in a beautiful garden, fit for the queen for whose enjoyment it was built. Elizabeth enjoyed her visits to Theobalds and visited there more often than any other of her subjects' homes.

The relatively modest banqueting house at Ingatestone was a two-story building that stood in one corner of the orchard. The second story contained a small study and another room that may have been used as a classroom.

For special occasions, for which more space was required, temporary banqueting structures were sometimes set up. In 1581 an elaborate banqueting house was erected on the south side of Whitehall Palace for the entertainment of the Duc d'Alençon's ambassadors. (François d'Alençon, the youngest brother of the French king, was one of Queen Elizabeth's suitors.) Its walls were of canvas, painted on the outside to look like stone, and 290 windows had been ingeniously fitted into them. The building was 332 feet in circumference and was supported by thirty poles, each 40 feet high. Around the walls were ten tiers of seats for spectators, festooned with holly, ivy, and strange flowers with spangles of gold. The ceiling was painted with suns, clouds, and stars, and adorned with "wicker pendants decorated with exotic fruits, spangled with gold, from which hung strips of rich fabrics." Lupold von Wedel, the German traveler, was told that birds sang in the ceiling hangings during entertainments. This temporary banqueting house was strong enough to hold up until 1606, when James I replaced it with one of brick and stone.

Savory dishes such as cheese and caviar were on occasion mingled among the sweetmeats on the banquet tables. Murrell, the only cookbook author to give examples of banquet menus, includes anchovies, caviar, and Parmesan cheese in one of the menus and notes that these were in "the dutch manner." He offers seven modest menus of only nine different sweetmeats each and

The dining and banqueting hall and minstrel's gallery of Haddon Hall. On the left is a low, round carving table. At the opposite end of the hall (not shown) is a dais built into the room on which the family and their important guests were seated at the "high table." The roof timbering and the chandelier are modern.

illustrates the proper arrangement of dishes of sweetmeats on the table. A typical menu is: "A Marchpaine, Shrewsbury cakes, Sucket lemons, Paste of rasberries, Preserved Damsons, Dry pear plums, Preserved pippins, Candied citron and Almond jumbales [cookies]."

In each menu the marchpane is given the central place on the table. Banqueting stuff, says Murrell, should be served in "Silver or guilt [gold-plated] Boules, or Glass Plates." "Put in every Boule," he says, "two or three severall fruits, but not wet and dry together."

In his "Epistle" to *Delightes for Ladies,* Hugh Plat describes the book's contents, which could as well serve as a menu for a banquet:

. . . Marchpane wals,
Are strong enough and best befits our age;
Let pearcing bullets turne to sugar bals,
The Spanish feare is husht and all their rage [with the de-
    feat of the Spanish Armada in 1588].
Of marmelade and paste of Genua [quince paste],
Of musked sugar I intend to wright,
Of leach of Sucket, and Quidinea [quince jelly],
. . . .
I teach both fruites and flowers to preserve,
And candie them, so Nutmegs, Cloves, and Mace;
To make both marchpane paste, and sugared plate
    [fondant],
And caste the same in formes of sweetest grace,
Each bird and foule, so moulded from the life,
And after cast in sweet compounds of Arte,
As if the flesh and forme which Nature gave,
Did still remaine in every lim and part.

Thomas Dawson, in *The good huswifes Jewell,* gives a list of "necessaries for a banquet" that includes: sugar, pepper, saffron, anise seeds, cinnamon, nutmeg, saunders (for red coloring), coleander (coriander), seeds (probably caraway seeds, a very popular comfit), Licoras (licorice), "all kinds of comfets," oranges, pomegranates, turnsole (for blue coloring), prunes, currants, preserved barberries, lemons, rose water, raisins, ginger, cloves, mace, damask-rose water, dates, preserved cherries, sweet oranges, wafers for marchpanes, "seasoned and unseasoned spinnedges" (puréed spinach), and brown and white paper on which small cakes were baked and confections placed for drying. This is a list that later sixteenth-century books repeat.

Every English housewife, said Gervase Markham, needs to know how to make "Banquetting stuff, and conceited dishes. . . . For albeit they are not of general use, yet in their due times, they are so needful of adornation, that whosoever is ignorant therein, is lame, and but the half part of an housewife."

Having provided the housewife with a supply of banqueting recipes, he goes on to teach her how to "order them in her closet" before taking or sending them out to the banquet table. "Observe," he says, "that March-panes have the first place, the middle place, and last place. . . . Thus you shall order them in the closet, but when they go to the Table, you shall first send forth a dish made for shew only [a centerpiece], as Beast, Bird, Fish, Fowl according to invention [as you are able to devise]; then your March-pane, then Preserved Fruit, then a paste, then a wet Sucket, then a dry sucket, Marmalade, comfets, Apples, Pears, Wardens, Oranges and Lemons sliced, and so consequently all the rest . . . no two dishes of one kind going or standing together, and this will not only appear delicate to the eye, but invite the appetite with the much variety thereof."

All cookbooks contained some recipes for tarts, pies, custards, creams, and sweet puddings, which were served as part of the main courses as a rule. But cookbooks with "Ladies" or "Gentlewomen" in the title devoted all or most of their pages to sweetmeat recipes and to the distilling of "sweet waters [herbs and flowers]." A few medicinal recipes were also usually included, but many of these could have fitted equally well into the sweetmeat sections of the book, for the English thought that sweet syrups and preserves of fruits, herbs, plant barks, and roots were helpful in relieving stomach and intestinal discomforts. By the end of the seventeenth century, most of the general cookery books also included substantial sections of banqueting recipes.

The beverages usually served at banquets were sweet wines like muscadine, spiced wines like ipocras, metheglin (a spiced and herbed mead), or all of these. The quantities of spices called for in many of the spiced wines were considerable. Since spices were expensive and often hard to come by, individual cooks doubtless adjusted the recipes to the spices available to them.

The cost of spices for a banquet could easily exceed the cost for labor. In 1559 the City of London put on a military display at Greenwich for the new queen's benefit, and the expenditures for the banquet that followed were conscientiously itemized. "The cooke and his man for thayre labors" were paid a total of five shillings. For a pound of cinnamon, the city paid four shillings; for ¾ pound of pepper, one shilling tenpence; for an ounce of whole mace, one shilling twopence; and for a pound of ginger, two shillings.

Spices give a vivid description of a fine horse in *Henry V* (Act III, Scene 7): "He's of the colour of the nutmeg," says Orleans. And the Dauphin responds, "And of the heat of the ginger."

Sixteenth- and seventeenth-century English had many similarities with Dutch, as does present-day English. Although "banquet" is no longer used with the old meaning in English, it still retains its earlier meaning in Dutch. In Holland today, *banket* before *bakker* signifies that the baker is a pastry and confectionery maker; a *banket bakkerij* is a shop that makes and sells cakes, pastries, and other sweetmeats.

With banquets and banqueting I bid you farewell. And like Puck, as the curtain goes down on *A Midsummer-night's Dream*, ask, "Give me your hands, if we be friends."

Bibliography

"Shakespeare's time": Shakespeare lived from 1564 to 1616. Many cookbooks, dietaries, books of manners, and books of household and farm management written before 1564 were reprinted, some many times, during and after his lifetime. I have also included in the works of his time some cookbooks first published after 1616, because their authors had been trained and had worked as professional cooks during Shakespeare's lifetime, and their recipes were those they had used in Shakespeare's day.

Most of the titles of books of Shakespeare's time that I give are short titles. Not to lengthen the listing, I have resisted the temptation to give the whole of a number of picturesque long titles. For the same reason this is only a partial bibliography of the works I have used. The listing of the cookbooks and dietaries that I used, however, is complete. For books that appeared in more than one edition, I have put down the edition that I used.

Each work is listed in one place only, although many books deal with a number of subjects. For example, I have listed the two books of *Progresses* by John Nichols under household accounts, because they contain so many of the accounts, although they deal with other matters too. Anonymous works are listed by title within the alphabetical order. The place of publication is London unless otherwise stated.

I have listed publications under the following categories:

A. Works of the Period
   1. Cookbooks
   2. Dietaries
   3. Herbals, Wine Books, Farming Manuals
   4. Household Accounts and Inventories, Books of Household Management
   5. Books of Manners
   6. Letters, Diaries, Pamphlets, Travelers' Accounts, Chronicles, Contemporary Histories and Descriptions of England
   7. Laws and Regulations
   8. Works of Shakespeare and Other Dramatists and Poets of His Day
B. Cookbooks of Other Periods, Histories of Cooking
C. History and Biography Written after Shakespeare's Time
D. Reference Works and Miscellaneous

A.1. *Cookbooks of the Period*

Booke of Cookerie, A. By A. W. Printed by Edw. Allde, dwelling neere Christ-Church, 1620.

Closet for Ladies and Gentlewomen or The Art of preserving, Conserving and Candying, A. Printed for Arthur Johnson, dwelling neere the great North dore of Pauls, 1608.

Cooper, Joseph. *The Art of Cookery Refin'd and Augmented.* By F. G. for R. Lowndes, at the White-lyon in St. Paul's Church-yard, near the end, 1654.

Dawson, Thomas. *The good huswifes Jewell.* Two parts. Imprinted by John Wolfe for Edward White, dwelling . . . North doore of Paules at the sign of the gunne, 1587.

Digbie, Sir Kenelme. *The Closet of the Eminently Learned Sir Kenelme Digbie, Kt., Opened.* Printed by E. C. for H. Brome, at the Star in Little Britain, 1669. Posthumous. (Also often spelled "Digby" in his own time.)

Good Hous-wives Treasurie, The. Printed by Edward Allde, 1588.

Ladies Cabinet Opened, The. Printed by M. P. for Richard Meighen, next to the Middle Temple in Fleet Street, 1639.

Markham, Gervase. *The English Hus-wife.* Printed by J. B., for R. Jackson, 1615. Part 2 of *Countrey Contentments.*

May, Robert. *The Accomplisht Cook, or the Art and Mystery of Cookery.* Printed by N. Brooke for T. Archer, 1660.

Murrell, John. *A Booke of Cookerie, Containing many of the best and choicest workes, that are used at this day, both of the French and Dutch fashions.* Printed for Thomas Dewe, 1621.

———. *A Daily Exercise for Ladies and Gentlewomen.* Printed for the Widow Helme, 1617.

———. *A Delightfull daily exercise for Ladies and Gentlewomen.* Printed for Thos. Dewe, 1621.

———. *A New Booke of Cookerie . . . set forth according to the now, new, English and French fashion.* Printed for John Browne, and are to be sould at his Shop in Dunstanes Church-yard, 1617.

Partridge, John. *The good Huswifes Handmaide for the Kitchin.* Imprinted by Richard Jones, 1594.

———. *The Treasurie of commodious Conceits, and hidden Secrets.* Imprinted by Richard Jones, 1573.

Plat, Sir Hugh. *Delightes for Ladies.* Printed by Humfrey Lownes, 1609.

Proper newe Booke of Cokerye, declaryng what maner of meates be best in season, for al times in the year, and how they ought to be dressed, and served at the table, both for flesshe dayes, and fysshe dayes, A. John Kynge and Thomas March. No date (before 1575). Edited by Catherine Frances Frere. Reprinted Cambridge, 1913.

Queen's Closet Open'd, Incomparable secrets in Physick, Chirurgery, Preserving, Candying and Cookery, The. W. M., 1655.

Queens Delight or The Art of Preserving, Conserving and Candying, A. Printed for Nathaniel Brook at the Angell in Cornhill, 1654.

Rabisha, William. *The whole Body of Cookery Dissected*. Printed by R. W. for Giles Calvert, at the sign of the black Spread Eagle, at the West end of Pauls, 1661.

A.2. *Dietaries*

Boorde, Dr. Andrewe. *A Compendyous Regyment or a Dyetary of healthe*. W. Powell, 1567.

Buttes, Dr. Henry. *Dyets Dry Dinner*. Printed by Thos. Creede for Wm. Wood, 1599.

Cogan, Thomas. *The Haven of Health . . . amplified upon five words of Hippocrates . . . Labor, Meat, Drinke, Sleepe, Venus*. Printed by Melch. Bradwood for John Norton, 1605.

Elyot, Sir Thomas. *The Castle of Health*. Printed for the Company of Stationers, 1610.

Muffet, Dr. Thomas (also called Moffett and Moufet). *Health's Improvement: or, rules comprizing and discovering the nature, method, and manner of preparing all sorts of foods used in this nation*. Tho. Newcomb for Samuel Thomson. 1655 (posthumous).

Vaughan, William. *Directions for Health*. Printed by T. S. for Roger Jackson, 1617.

Venner, Tobias. *Via Recta ad Vitam Longam* (The Right Way to a Long Life). Edward Griffin for Richard More, 1620.

A.3. *Herbals, Wine Books, Farming Manuals*

Culpeper, Nicholas. *Culpeper's Complete Herbal*. First published by Peter Cole, 1652, under title of *The English physitian*. Reprinted, 1932.

Gerard, John. *Herball or General Historie of Plants*. 1597.

Turner, Wm. *A new Boke of the natures and properties of all Wines that are commonlye used here in England*. William Seres, 1568.

Tusser, Thomas. *Five Hundred Points of Good Husbandry . . . Together with a Book of Husewifery*. *1557*. Reprinted, edited by William Mavor, 1812.

A.4. *Household Accounts and Inventories, Books of Household Management*

"A Breviate touching the order and government of a Nobleman's

House." About 1605. Edited by Sir Joseph Banks. *Archaeologia* 13. (1800).

Braithwaite, Richard. *Some Rules and Orders for the Government of the House of an Earl.* About 1648. Miscellanea Anglicana, Tract 8, 1821.

Collection of Ordinances and Regulations for the Governing of the Royal Household, 1455–1689. Society of Antiquaries, 1790.

Derby Household Books: . . . the Household Regulations and Expenses of Edward and Henry, Third and Fourth Earls of Derby. . . . Lancashire, 1561, 1568, 1586–1590. Edited by F. R. Raines for the Chetham Society. Manchester, 1853.

Eden, Sir Frederick. *The State of the Poor.* 3 vols. 1797.

Essex Education Committee. *Ingatestone Hall in 1600: an Inventory.* Essex County Record Office, Publication no. 22, 1954.

Fairfax, Sir William. *Household Accounts for the years 1571–1582.* In Historical Manuscripts Commission, *Report on Manuscripts in Various Collections,* vol. 2, 1903.

House and Farm Accounts of the Shuttleworths of Gawthorpe Hall . . . Lancaster . . . 1582–1621. Edited by John Harland for the Chetham Society. 4 vols. 1856–1858.

Household and Farm Inventories in Oxfordshire, 1550–1590. Edited by M. A. Havinden. Historical Manuscripts Commission, Joint Publication no. 10, 1965.

Household Papers of Henry Percy, Ninth Earl of Northumberland, 1564–1632. Edited by G. R. Batho for the Camden Society. Third series. Vol. 93, 1962.

Howard, Lord William. *Selections from the Household Books of Lord William Howard of Naworth Castle, 1612–1640.* Edited by George Ornsby for the Surtees Society. Durham, 1878.

Montague, Anthony, Viscount. *Booke of Orders and Rules.* 1595. Edited by D. S. Scott. Sussex Archaeological Collections, vol. 7, 1854.

Nichols, John B. *The Progresses and Public Processions of Queen Elizabeth.* 3 vols. 1823.

———. *The Progresses, Processions, and Magnificent Festivities of King James the First, His Royal Consort, Family, and Court.* 3 vols. 1828.

North, Lord. "Extracts from the Booke of Howshold Charges and other Paiments laid out by Lord North and his commandement: beginning 1575 . . ." *Archaeologia* 19 (1820).

Northumberland, Earl of. *The Regulations and Establishment of the household of Henry Algernon Percy, the Fifth Earl of Northumberland. Begun 1512.* Edited by Thomas Percy. 1827.

Ramsey, Sir Thomas. *An Inventory of the Household Goods of Sir Thomas Ramsey, Lord Mayor of London, in 1577. Archaeologia* 40, part 2.

Star Chamber Dinner Accounts . . . during the reigns of Queen Elizabeth I and King James I. Edited by André L. Simon. 1959.

A.5. *Books of Manners*

Byrne, M. St. Clare, ed. *The Elizabethan Home Discovered in Two Dialogues.* 1925.

Erondell, Peter. *The French Garden.* 1606. Reprinted in Byrne.

Furnivall, Frederick, ed. *Early English Meals and Manners.* Early English Text Society. Original series, no. 32, 1894.

Hollyband, Claudius. *The French Schoolemaister.* 1573. Reprinted in Byrne.

Rhodes, Hugh. *The Boke of Nurture, or Schoole of Good maners.* 1557.

Russell, John. *Boke of Nurture.* About 1460–1470. Reprinted in Furnivall.

Seager, Francis. *The schoole of vertue, and booke of good nourture for chyldren, and youth to learne theyr dutie by.* 1557. Reprinted in Furnivall.

Weste, Richard. *The Booke of Demeanor . . .* 1619. Reprinted in Furnivall.

Worde, Wynkyn de. *Boke of Kervynge.* The 1513 edition is reprinted in Furnivall.

A.6. *Letters, Diaries, Pamphlets, Travelers' Accounts, Chronicles, Contemporary Histories and Descriptions of England*

Chamberlain, John. *Letters.* Edited by Norman E. McClure. 2 vols. American Philosophical Society, *Memoirs* XII, part 2. Philadelphia, 1939. Vol. 1, 1597–1616.

Clifford, Lady Anne. *Diary, 1613–1619.* Introduction by V. Sackville-West. 1924.

Coryate, Thomas. *Coryates crudities; hastily gobbled up in five moneths travels.* 1611.

Drayton, Michael. *The Poly-Olbion, a Chorographicall Description of Great Britain.* Part 3, 1622. Reprinted for the Spender Society. 1890.

Harington, Sir John. *Nugae Antiquae.* Edited by Henry Harington, 1779. 3 vols. Vol. 2.

———. *The Letters and Epigrams. . . . Together with the Prayse of Private Life.* Edited by Norman E. McClure. Philadelphia, 1930.

Harrison, Molly, and Royston, O. M., eds. *How They Lived.* Vol. 2, 1485–1700. Oxford, 1965.

Harrison, William. *The Description of England.* From editions of 1577 and 1587. Edited by Georges Edelen for the Folger Shakespeare Library. Ithaca, N.Y., 1968.

Hazlitt, William Carew. *Inedited Tracts: Illustrating the Manners, Opinions, and Occupations of Englishmen during the Sixteenth and Seventeenth Centuries* . . . Edited for the Roxburghe Library. 1868.

Hentzner, Paul. *A Journey into England in the year 1598.* In *Fugitive Pieces on Various Subjects,* vol. 2, 3rd ed. 1771.

Klarwill, Victor von. *Queen Elizabeth and Some Foreigners.* 1928.

Lemnius, Levinus. *Notes on England, 1560.* In W. B. Rye, ed., *England as Seen by Foreigners* (see below).

Machyn, Henry. *The Diary of Henry Machyn from 1550 to 1563.* Edited by John G. Nichols for the Camden Society. 1848.

Meteren, Emanuel van. *Account of a visit to England in 1599.* Translated from the Dutch. In W. B. Rye, ed., *England as Seen by Foreigners* (see below).

Morgan, R. B., ed. *Readings in English Social History,* Vol. 3, 1485–1603. Cambridge, 1921.

Moryson, Fynes. *The Itinerary of Fynes Moryson. Vol. 4, 1605–1617.* Reprinted Glasgow, 1908.

Perlin, Stephen. *Description of the Kingdoms of England and Scotland.* 1558. Translated from the French; excerpted in R. B. Morgan, ed. *Readings in English Social History* (see above).

Platter, Thomas. *Travels in England, 1599.* Translated from the German by Clare Williams. 1937.

Rye, W. B., ed. *England as Seen by Foreigners.* 1865.

Stow, John. *The Survey of London, 1598.* Edited by C. L. Kingsford. 2 vols. Oxford, 1908.

Stubbes, Philip. *The Anatomie of Abuses.* 1583. In J. P. Collier, ed., *Reprints of Early English Literature,* 1863–1874. Vol. 14, no. 1.

Wedel, Lupold von. "A Knight Errant." (Account of a visit to England in 1585.) Translated from the German by T. H. Nash. In Klarwill, *Queen Elizabeth and Some Foreigners* (see above).

Wilson, Sir Thomas. *The State of England Anno Dom. 1600.* Edited by F. J. Fisher. Camden Miscellany, vol. 16, 1939.

A.7. *Laws and Regulations*

Bland, A. E.; Brown, P. A.; and Tawney, R. H., eds. *English Economic History: Select Documents.* 1914.

Hughes, Paul L., and Larkin, James F., eds. *Stuart Royal Proclamations.* Oxford, vol. 1, 1973.

————. *Tudor Royal Proclamations.* New Haven, Conn., 1964–1969. Vols. 2 and 3.

Tawney, R. H., and Power, Eileen, eds., *Tudor Economic Documents,* 3 vols. 1924.

A.8. *Works of Shakespeare and Other Dramatists and Poets of His Day*

Beaumont, Francis, and Fletcher, Richard. *Philaster; The Honest Man's Fortune; The Maid's Tragedy.*

Breton, Nicholas. *The Toyes of an Idle Head; Wits Trenchmour; A Health to the Gentlemanly Profession of Servingmen: or The Servingman's Comfort; I Pray you be not Angrie; Wits Private Wealth; The Court and Country; Fantastickes; An Olde Man's Lesson: and a Young Man's Love; A Farewell to Town; Pasquil's Madcappe; Pasquil's Passe, and passeth not; The Praise of Vertuous Ladies and Gentlewomen; Poems.*

Dekker, Thomas. *The Shoemakers Holiday; The Honest Whore; Old Fortunatus.*

Herrick, Robert. *Hesperides; Other Poems.*

Heywood, John. *A dialogue conteinyng the nomber in effect of all the proverbes in the English tongue.* Edited by R. E. Habenicht. Reprinted Berkeley, Calif., 1963.

Jonson, Ben. *The Alchemist; Bartholomew Fair; The Devil Is an Ass, The New Inn; The Staple of the News; Complete Poetry,* edited by W. B. Hunter, Jr. New York, 1963.

Markham, Gervase, and Machin, Lewis. *The Dumbe Knight.* In *Dodsley's Old Plays.* Vol. 4, 1825.

Overbury, Sir Thomas. *Characters.* 1614–1616.

Roxburghe Ballads. Edited by W. Chappell. Vol. 1, part 1. Reprinted. New York, 1966.

Saltonstall, Wye. *Picturae Loquentes, or Pictures drawne forth in characters.* "A Gentleman's House in the Country." Reprinted for the Luttrell Society. Oxford, 1946.

Shakespeare. I have used the texts of the tragedies, comedies, histories, and poems in the Oxford edition, edited by W. J. Craig. 3 vols. 1924–1925.

Taylor, John. *Taylor's Travels; The Penniless Pilgrimage; Jack-a-Lent; The Great Eater of Kent; The Old, Old, Very Old Man; An Armada, or Navy of Land Ships.* In *Works of John Taylor, the Water Poet,* edited by Charles Hindley, 1876.

B. *Cookbooks of Other Periods, Histories of Cooking*

Cassell's Dictionary of Cookery. No date. Edition of about 1890.

Glasse, Hannah. *The Compleat Housewife.* Edition of 1774.

Hartley, Dorothy. *Food in England.* 1964.

Napier, Robina (Mrs. Alexander), ed. *A Noble Boke of Cookry ffor a prynce houssolde or any other estately housseholde.* From a late fifteenth-century MS. 1882.

Spicer, Dorothy G. *From an English Oven: Cakes, Buns, and Breads of County Tradition.* New York, 1948.

Two Fifteenth-Century Cookery Books, about 1430–1450. Edited by Thomas Austin for the Early English Text Society. Original series, no. 91, 1888.

C. *History and Biography Written after Shakespeare's Time*

Akrigg, G. P. V. *Jacobean Pageant or the Court of King James I.* 1962.

Batho, G. R. "The Finances of an Elizabethan Nobleman: Henry Percy, Ninth Earl of Northumberland." In *Economic History Review,* 2nd series, vol. 9, 1957.

————. "The Wizard Earl in the Tower of London, 1605–1621." In *History Today,* vol. 6, 1956.

Besant, Sir Walter. *London in the Time of the Tudors.* 1904.

Bloom, J. Harvey. *Folk Lore, Old Customs, and Superstitions in Shakespeare Land.* 1929.

Brett, Gerard. *Dinner Is Served: A History of Dining in England, 1400–1900.* 1968.

Bridenbaugh, Carl. *Vexed and Troubled Englishmen, 1590–1642.* New York, 1968.

Byrne, M. St. Clare. *Elizabethan Life in Town and Country.* Revised edition, 1961.

Campbell, Mildred. *The English Yeoman under Elizabeth and the Early Stuarts.* New Haven, Conn., 1942.

Drummond, Jack C., and Wilbraham, Anne. *The Englishman's Food; Five Centuries of English Diet.* 2nd edition, revised by Dorothy F. Hollingsworth. 1957.

Dunlop, Ian. *Palaces and Progresses of Elizabeth I.* 1962.

Emmison, Frederick G. *Tudor Foods and Pastimes: Life at Ingatestone Hall.* 1964.

————. *Tudor Secretary: Sir William Petre at Court and at Home.* Cambridge, Mass., 1961.

Everitt, Alan M. "Farm Labourers." Chapter 7 in Joan Thirsk, ed., *The Agrarian History of England and Wales,* vol. 4 (see below).

Francis, Alan D. *The Wine Trade.* 1972.

Hindley, Charles. *A History of the Cries of London.* 1884. Reprinted Detroit, 1969.

Hoskins, W. G. *Provincial England.* 1963.

Jones, Paul Van B. *The Household of a Tudor Nobleman.* Urbana, Illinois, 1917.

Lee, Sidney. *Stratford-on-Avon from the Earliest Times to the Death of Shakespeare.* Philadelphia, 1907.

Mathias, Peter. *The Brewing Industry in England, 1700–1830.* Cambridge, 1959.

Nicoll, Allardyce, ed. *Shakespeare in His Own Age.* Cambridge, 1964.

Pearson, Lu Emily. *Elizabethans at Home.* Stanford, Calif., 1957.

Pound, John. *Poverty and Vagrancy in Tudor England.* 1971.

Quennell, Marjorie, and Quennell, C. H. B. *A History of Everyday Things in England.* Part 2, 1500–1799, 1954.

Read, Evelyn. *My Lady Suffolk: A Portrait of Catherine Willoughby, Duchess of Suffolk.* New York, 1963.

Renouard, Yves. "The Wine Trade of Gascony In the Middle Ages." In *Essays in French Economic History.* Edited by Rondo Cameron. Homewood, Illinois, 1970.

Salaman, Redcliffe N. *The History and Social Influence of the Potato.* Cambridge, 1949.

Salzman, L. F. *England in Tudor Times.* 1926.

Shakespeare's England. 2 vols. Oxford, 1916.

Sheppard, Ronald, and Newton, Edward. *The Story of Bread.* Boston, 1957.

Shrewsbury Cakes, The Story of a Famous Delicacy. Pamphlet. Shrewsbury, 1957.

Stevens, Denis, ed. *London Street Cries.* University Park, Penna., 1964.

Stone, Lawrence. *The Crisis of the Aristocracy, 1558–1641.* Oxford, 1965.

Thirsk, Joan, ed. *The Agrarian History of England and Wales.* Vol. 4, 1500–1640, Cambridge, 1967.

Thrupp, Sylvia. *A Short History of the Worshipful Company of Bakers of London.* 1933.

Warner, Richard. *Antiquitates Culinariae, or Curious Tracts Relating to the Culinary Affairs of the Old English.* 1791.

Wildeblood, Joan, and Brinson, Peter. *The Polite World: a Guide to English Manners and Deportment from the Thirteenth to the Nineteenth Century.* 1965.

Woodworth, Allegra. "Purveyance for the Royal Household under Elizabeth." *Transactions of the American Philosophical Society,* new series, vol. 35, part 1, 1945.

D. *Reference Works and Miscellaneous*

Bartlett, John. *A Complete Concordance of Shakespeare.* 1894. Reprinted New York, 1967.

Dictionary of National Biography. 22 vols. 1908–1909.

Granger, J. *A Biographical History of England.* 4 vols. 1779.

Hazlitt, William Carew. *Old Cookery Books and Ancient Cuisine.* 1886.

Oxford, Arnold W. *English Cookery Books to the Year 1850.* 1913.

Oxford English Dictionary . . . on Historical Principles. 13 vols. Reprinted. Oxford, 1961.

Short-title Catalogue of Books Printed in England . . . 1475–1640. 1926.

RECIPE INDEX

PAGE NUMBERS are those of the original recipes, which precede the working versions. (The cross-references within the text of the book refer to the pages of the working versions of the recipes.) The recipe titles are meant to be as informative as possible; hence some do not correspond exactly to the original sixteenth-and-seventeenth-century recipe titles, which are sometimes confusing.

SUBJECT INDEX